SÖREN KIERKEGAARD AND HIS CRITICS

SÖREN
KIERKEGAARD
AND HIS CRITICS

AN INTERNATIONAL BIBLIOGRAPHY OF CRITICISM

COMPILED BY
FRANÇOIS H. LAPOINTE

GREENWOOD PRESS
WESTPORT, CONNECTICUT • LONDON, ENGLAND

Library of Congress Cataloging in Publication Data

Lapointe, François.
  Sören Kierkegaard and his critics.

  Includes index.
  1.   Kierkegaard, Sören Aabye, 1813-1855—
Bibliography.   I.   Title.
Z8464.25.L36   [B4377]   016.198'9   80-783
ISBN 0-313-22333-5 (lib. bdg.)

Library of Congress Catalog Card Number: 80-783
ISBN: 0-313-22333-5

First published in 1980

Greenwood Press
A division of Congressional Information Service, Inc.
88 Post Road West, Westport, Connecticut 06881

Printed in the United States of America

10 9 8 7 6 5 4 3 2 1

Contents

80-6175

Introduction

Sören Kierkegaard has finally joined the pantheon of great philosophers, but it did take him many years to reach such an eminent status. When he died 125 years ago, on November 4, 1855, his philosophy was unnoticed beyond the boundaries of Denmark and was misunderstood within those boundaries. His ideas did not explode upon the Western intellectual world until the twentieth century, but since then they have profoundly affected the contemporary philosophical and theological scenes. This increasing interest both in the United States and abroad in the works of Kierkegaard make it seem only natural to compile a comprehensive and up-to-date survey of the critical response to his work.

There can be little doubt that Sören Kierkegaard is receiving the sort of attention given only to great writers. Arduous as the task of compiling this bibliography has been, it was worthwhile, and we can only hope that others will come to share our view when they see the sheer bulk of the data available, and becoming available, on the works of Kierkegaard. The works listed here show that Kierkegaard's ideas are constantly being examined in new ways, in new contexts, and using new resources uncovered by investigations in a variety of fields. This bibliography provides continuing proof that Kierkegaard's work is still found fresh and exciting by a new generation of scholars.

Kierkegaard bibliographies have appeared in great number, and the reader can find a comprehensive list of them in the Appendix. There is Jans Himmelstrup, *Sören Kierkegaard International Bibliografi*, published in 1962. We owe a great debt to Dr. Himmelstrup's pioneering work. Why then published another bibliography? The Himmelstrup bibliography is hard to find, for one thing, and its organization, being alphabetical, makes it somewhat difficult and inconvenient to locate material. The other bibliographies are frequently published in journals not easily found in the average college library, or are restricted to the literature of one language, or cover a very limited span of years. For these reasons, we have felt that a new comprehensive, up-to-date, and well-organized bibliography was justified.

A bibliography always serves a utilitarian purpose. Some order has to be imposed. To compile as complete a collection of entries as possible is one thing. To provide a useful arrangement of this collection is another thing. The decisions a bibliographer makes regarding the organization and character of his work can never satisfy the demands of all users. Nevertheless, flexibility, accuracy, and comprehensiveness are basic requirements.

This bibliography is divided into two parts. The first part lists by language the works of Kierkegaard translated into the other major European languages. The works are listed in their order of composition, and Collected Works, when available, are to be found at the beginning of each section. The second part is divided into six chapters. Chapter 1 contains books devoted to Kierkegaard (or almost exclusively so), including all available reviews, and the books are classified by language. Chapter 2 lists doctoral dissertations and theses, also indicating the entries, when available, in *Dissertation Abstracts International.* In Chapter 3, books and articles presenting a general discussion of Kierkegaard's works and life are listed. Chapter 4 includes entries devoted to a single work by Kierkegaard. Chapter 5 lists other entries by proper names, including material in which Kierkegaard is compared or contrasted with major figures in literature, philosophy, or theology. Chapter 6 lists entries arranged by subject. An Appendix includes the many bibliographies devoted to Kierkegaard. Finally, an Addendum contains entries that arrived too late to be included in the body of the manuscript.

The bibliography is intended to be as complete as is technically feasible. Our purpose is to provide an accurate, reasonably complete and useful arrangement of materials for students and others interested in Kierkegaard. Although no bibliography can claim to be exhaustive, every attempt at completeness and accuracy has been made. All of the standard reference works known to me were consulted, and many periodicals and books were searched individually. Items through December 1979 are included, although no claim for completeness is made for publications that appeared in 1979.

Still, I am fully aware of the provisional nature of this work. As is well known to bibliographers, publication constitutes a stage in the movement toward completeness, a more or less "complete" starting point for further work. My hope is that eventually I can come closer to the ideal of completeness in a second edition which will continue this one beyond 1979, and which will include earlier important items I was regrettably unable to include, as well as corrections of possible errors.

François H. Lapointe

PART 1:

Bibliography
of Sören Kierkegaard

A detailed bibliography of Kierkegaard's Works, beginning in 1834, and including all works of Kierkegaard up to 1855, as well as later editions, is to be found in Jens Himmelstrup, *Sören Kierkegaard International Bibliografi* (1962). We will only provide here the following information as to Kierkegaard's Works in Danish.

DANISH

Samlede Vaerker. Bind I-XX, XXI (3. udgave), udgivet af A. B. Drachmann, J. L. Heiberg og H. O. Lange. *Terminologisk Ordbog* ved. Jens Himmelstrup. Sammenlignende Register til första, anden og naervaerende udgave af *Samlede Vaerker.* Köbenhavn: Gyldendal, 1962-64.

Bind I: *Af en endu Levendes Papirer*, ved J. L. Heiberg og H. O. Lange. *Om begrebet Ironi*, ved J. L. Heiberg og A. B. Drachmann. Köbenhavn: Gyldendal, 1962. 374p.

Bind II: *Enten-Eller.* Första Halvbind, ved J. L. Heiberg. Köbenhavn: Gyldendal, 1962. 438p.

Bind III: *Enten-Eller.* Andet Halvbind, ved J. L. Heiberg. Köbenhavn: Gyldendal, 1962. 339p.

Bind IV: *Atten opbyggelige Taler*, ved H. O. Lange. Köbenhavn: Gyldendal, 1962. 367p.

Bind V: *Frygt og Boeven*, ved A. B. Drachmann. *Gjentagelsen*, ved A. B. Drachmann. *Forord*, ved J. L. Heiberg. Köbenhavn: Gyldendal, 1963. 290p.

Bind VI: *Philosophiske Smuler*, ved A. B. Drachmann.
Begrebet Angest, ved A. B. Drachmann. *Tre Taler ved
toenkte Leilgheder*, ved H. O. Lange. Köbenhavn:
Gyldendal, 1963. 366p.

Bind VII: *Stadier paa Livets Vei*. Förste Halvbind,
ved J. L. Heiberg. Köbenhavn: Gyldendal, 1963. 182p.

Bind VIII: *Stadier paa Livets Vei*. Andet Halvbind,
ved J. L. Heiberg. Köbenhavn: Gyldendal, 1963. 299p.

Bind IX: *Afsluttende uvidenskabelig Efterskrift*.
Förste Halvbind, ved A. B. Drachmann. Köbenhavn:
Gyldendal, 1963. 271p.

Bind X: *Afsluttende uvidenskabelig Efterskrift*.
Andet Halvbind, ved A. B. Drachmann. Köbenhavn:
Gyldendal, 1963. 306p.

Bind XI: *Opbyggelige Taler i forskjellig Aand*, ved
H. O. Lange. Köbenhavn: Gyldendal, 1963. 321p.

Bind XII: *Kjerlighedens Gjerninger*, ved H. O. Lange.
Köbenhavn: Gyldendal, 1963. 376p.

Bind XIII: *Christlegie Taler*, ved H. O. Lange. Köbenhavn: Gyldendal, 1963. 291p.

Bind XIV: *En literair Anmeldelse*, ved J. L. Heiberg.
Krisen og en Krise i en Skuespillerindes Liv, ved
J. L. Heiberg. *Lilien paa Marken og Fuglen under
Himlen*, ved H. O. Lange. *"Ypperstepraesten"--
"Tolderen"--"Synderinden"*, ved H. O. Lange. Köben-
havn: Gyldendal, 1963. 214p.

Bind XV: *Tvende ethisk-religieuse Smaa-Afhandlinger*,
ved A. B. Drachmann. *Sygdommen til Döden*, ved
A. B. Drachmann. Köbenhavn: Gyldendal, 1963. 192p.

Bind XVI: *Indovelse i Christendom*, ved A. B. Drachmann.
Köbenhavn: Gyldendal, 1963. 252p.

Bind XVII: *En opbyggelig Tale. To Taler ved Altergangen
om Fredagen. Til Selvprövelse, Samtider anbefalet
Dommer selv!* ved H. O. Lange. Köbenhavn: Gyldendal,
1964. 238p.

Bind XVIII: *Bladartikler der staar i Forhold til
"Forfatterskabet"*, ved J. L. Heiberg og H. O. Lange.
Om min Forfatter-Virksomhed, ved A. B. Drachmann.
Synspunktet for min Forfatter-Virksomhed, ved
A. B. Drachmann. Köbenhavn: Gyldendal, 1964. 188p.

Bind XIX: *Bladartikler 1854-55*, ved A. B. Drachmann.
Oieblikket 1-10. Hvad Christus dömmer om officiel
Christendom. Guds Uforanderlighed, ved A. B.
Drachmann. Köbenhavn: Gyldendal, 1964. 348p.

Bind XX: *Terminologisk Ordbog*, ved Jens Himmelstrup.
Sammenlignende Register til förste, anden og naer-
vaerende udgave af *Samlede Vaerker*. Köbenhavn:
Gyldendal, 1964. 339p.

Rohde, Peter P. *Sören Kierkegaard. Et Geni i en
Köbstad.* Supplementsbind til Sören Kierkegaard:
Samlede Vaerker I-XX. Köbenhavn: Gyldendal, 1962.
61p.

McKinnon, Alastair. *The Kierkegaard Indices to Kierkegaard's* Samlede Vaerker. Leiden: E. J. Brill. Vol. I:

Vol. I: *Kierkegaard in Translation/en traduction/
in Ubersetzung*, 1970, xxii-133p.

Vol. II: *Kondordans til Kierkegaards* Samlede Vaerker,
1971, xvi-1137p.

Vol. III: *Index Verborum til Kierkegaards* Samlede
Vaerker, 1973, xvi-1322p.

Vol. IV: *Computational Analysis of Kierkegaard's*
Samlede Vaerker, 1975, vii-1088p.

A team directed by Prof. A. McKinnon, Chairman of the
Department of Philosophy, McGill University, Montreal,
has recently completed the construction of a machine-
readable version of Kierkegaard's *Samlede Vaerker*
(3. Udg. 1-19, Gyldendal, Köbenhavn, 1962-64).
This text has now been transferred to tape together with
page and line correlations to the second edition and
to the standard English, French and German translations.
An index-tape has also been constructed giving the
location of every occurrence of every word in the
Danish text in both of the editions and the three
translations. These tapes have now been used to pro-
duce the above series of computer-generated volumes
intended primarily as research tools for the serious
study of Kierkegaard and his works.

Vol. I: *Kierkegaard in Translation*, provides page and
line correlations between all five editions and is
specifically designed to assist the scholar using
any of these three translations to move quickly and
easily to the corresponding section of the text in
either of the Danish originals.

Vol. II: *Kondordans til Kierkegaards* Samlede Vaerker,
lists586 key words and 210 variants. Each of the
approximately 76,000 entries consists of an appropriate
passage of nine to twelve words of the Danish text
together with page and line references to both Danish
editions and to the English, French, and German
translation.

Vol. III: *Index Verborum til Kierkegaards* Samlede
Vaerker, gives page and line locations in terms of the
Danish third edition for every word in the text except
those already listed in the concordance and those
articles, conjunctions, prepositions, etc., of fre-
quency 500 or more. By using this volume in conjunc-
tion with the first, the reader can discover the
location of all occurrences of these words in each of
the other four editions used in this project.

Vol. IV: *Computational Analysis of Kierkegaard's* Samlede
Vaerker, presents the various lexical properties of this
corpus of approximately two million words. It consists
of rank and alphabetical lists together with a number
of summary tables and graphs. It is intended as
empirical data for the science of linguistics, as a
documentation of Kierkegaard's use of the Danish language, and as a record which others may use to attain a
better and more precise understanding of his thought.

ENGLISH

Hong, Howard V., ed. *Kierkegaard's Writings*. Princeton:
Princeton Univ. Press.

Princeton University Press announces the publication in
English of a definitive scholarly edition of the works
of Sören Kierkegaard, consisting of twenty-five volumes
of text and a separate cumulative index. Each volume
of translation will include a historical introduction,
selections from Kierkegaard's journals and provisional
manuscripts, notes, and an index.

Vol. I: *Early Polemical Writings* (1985).
From the Papers of One Still Living; Articles from
Student Days; The Battle between the Old and the
New Soap-Cellars.

Vol. II: *The Concept of Irony; Schelling Lecture Notes*
(1981).

Vol. III: *Either/Or*, I (1983).

Vol. IV: *Either/Or*, II (1983).

Vol. V: *Eighteen Upbuilding Discourses* (1983).

Vol. VI: *Fear and Trembling*; *Repetition* (1980).

Vol. VII: *Philosophical Fragments*; Johannes Climacus,
or De omnibus dubitandum est (1981).

Vol. VIII: *The Concept of Anxiety* (1979).

Vol. IX: *Prefaces*; Articles Related to the Writings
(1986).

Vol. X: *Three Discourses on Imagined Occasions* (1986).

Vol. XI: *Stages on Life's Way* (1984).

Vol. XII: *Concluding Unscientific Postscript* (1982).

Vol. XIII: *The Corsair Affair* (1979).

Vol. XIV: *Two Ages*: The Age of Revolution and the
Present Age, A Literary Review. 1978. 208p.

Vol. XV: *Upbuilding Discourses in Various Spirits* (1986).

Vol. XVI: *Works of Love* (1987).

Vol. XVII: *Christian Discourses*; The Crisis and a
Crisis in the Life of an Actress (1987).

Vol. XVIII: *Without Authority* (1987).
The Lily of the Field and the Bird of the Air; Two
Ethical-Religious Essays; Three Discourses at the
Communion on Fridays; An Upbuilding Discourse;
Two Discourses at the Communion on Fridays.

Vol. XIX: *The Sickness unto Death* (1979).

Vol. XX: *Practice in Christianity* (1984).

Vol. XXI: *For Self-Examination*; Judge for Yourselves!
(1985).

Vol. XXII: *The Point of View* (1985).
The Point of View for My Work as an Author; Armed
Neutrality; On My Work as an Author.

Vol. XXIII: *The Moment and Late Writings* (1987).
Articles from *Faedrelandet*; The Moment; This Must
be Said, So Let It Be Said; Christ's Judgment on
Official Christianity; The Unchangeableness of God.

Vol. XXIV: *The Book on Adler* (1988).

Vol. XXV: *Letters and Documents*. 1978.   584p.

Vol. XXVI: *Cumulative Index* (1988).

Hong, Howard V., and Hong, Edna H., eds. *Sören Kierkegaard's Journals and Papers*. 7 vols. Trans. by H. V. Hong and E. H. Hong. London and Bloomington (Indiana): Indiana Univ. Press. (From *Papirer* I-XI, suppl. vols. XII, XIII, 1969-70, and *Breve og Aktstykker Vedrorende Sören Kierkegaard*, Niels Thulstrup, ed., I-II, 1953-54.)

Vol. I: *A-E*. 1967, xxx-539p.

Vol. II: *F-K*. 1970, xii-616p.

Vol. III: *L-R*. 1973, xii-925p.

Vol. IV: *S-Z*. 1975, xiii-783p.

Vol. V: *Autobiographical, Part One*, 1829-1848. 1978, xiv-559p.

Vol. VI: *Autobiographical, Part Two*, 1848-1855. 1978, xiv-649p.

Vol. VIII: *Index and Composite Collation*. 1978. 131p.

OTHER ENGLISH EDITIONS

The following are listed in order of time of writing, with Danish titles in parenthesis. The various introductions to the English editions are usually very enlightening.

The Concept of Irony. With constant reference to Socrates. Trans. with an introduction by Lee M. Capel. New York: Harper & Row, 1966, 442p.; Bloomington: Indiana Univ. Press, 1968; Vol. 2 in *Kierkegaard's Writings*, Princeton Univ. Press (1981). (*Om Begrebet Ironi*. 1841.)

Either/Or. 2 vols. Vol. I trans. by David F. Swenson and Lilian Marvin Swenson, with revisions and foreword by Howard A. Johnson; Vol. II trans. by Walter Lowrie, with revisions and foreword by Howard A. Johnson (2d ed.). Princeton (New Jersey): Princeton Univ. Press, 1959; Garden City (New York):

Doubleday, 1959; Gloucester (Massachusetts): P. Smith, 1959, 465p. and 372p.; Vols. III and IV in *Kierkegaard's Writings*, Princeton Univ. Press (1983). (*Enten-Eller*. I-II. Victor Eremita, ed. 1843.)

Johannes Climacus or De Omnibus Dubitandum Est, and *A Sermon*. Trans. with an assessment by T. H. Croxall (a Library of Modern Religious Thought. Henry Chadwick, gen. ed.). London: Adam and Charles Black, 1958; Stanford: Stanford Univ. Press, 1958, 196p.; Vol. III in *Kierkegaard's Writings*, Princeton Univ. Press (1981). (*Johannes Climacus eller De Omnibus Dubitandum Est*. Written 1842-43, unpublished. *Papirer* IV B I. *Demis-Praediken*, 1844, unpublished, IV C I.)

Edifying Discourses. 4 vols. Trans. by David F. Swenson and Lillian Marvin Swenson. Minneapolis: Augsburg, 1943-46; Paul L. Holmer, ed., New York: Harper & Bros., 1958, 284p.; Vol. I-II, Minneapolis: Augsburg, 1962, 239p. (*Opbyggelige Taler*. 1843-44.)

Fear and Trembling, and *The Sickness Unto Death*. Trans. with introduction and notes by Walter Lowrie. Princeton (New Jersey): Princeton Univ. Press, 1954; ibid., 1968, 278p.; Garden City (New York): Doubleday, 1954, 287p.; Gloucester (Massachusetts): P. Smith, 1964, 278p.; Vols. VI and XIX in *Kierkegaard's Writings*, Princeton Univ. Press (1980 and 1979). (*Frygt og Baeven*. Johannes de Silentio. 1843.)

Repetition. An essay in experimental psychology. Trans. with introduction and notes by Walter Lowrie. Princeton (New Jersey): Princeton Univ. Press, 1941; New York, London: Harper & Row, 1964, 144p.; Vol. VI in *Kierkegaard's Writings*, Princeton Univ. Press (1980). (*Gjentagelsen*. Constantine Constantius. 1843.)

Philosophical Fragments. Or, A Fragment of Philosophy. Johannes Climacus [pseud.]. Original trans. and introduction by David F. Swenson; new introduction and commentary by Niels Thulstrup. Trans. rev. and commentary trans. by Howard V. Hong, 2d ed. Princeton: Princeton Univ. Press, 1962, xcvii-206p.; ibid., 1967; Vol. VII in *Kierkegaard's Writings*, Princeton Univ. Press (1981). (*Philosophiske Smuler*. Johannes Climacus. S. Kierkegaard, ed. 1844.)

The Concept of Anxiety [Dread].   Trans. with introduction
and notes by Walter Lowrie.   2d ed.   Princeton (New Jersey):
Princeton Univ. Press, 1957, 154p.; Vol. VIII in *Kierke-*
gaard's Writings, Princeton Univ. Press (1979).   (*Begrebet*
Angest. Virgilius Haufniensis. S. Kierkegaard, ed.   1844.)

Thoughts on Crucial Situations In Human Life.   Trans. by
David F. Swenson.   Lilian Marvin Swenson, ed.   Minneapolis:
Augsburg, 1941.   (*Tre Taler ved taenkte Leiligheder.*   1845.)

Stages on Life's Way.   Trans. by Walter Lowrie.   Princeton
(New Jersey): Princeton Univ. Press, 1940; New York: Schocken
Books (introduction by Paul Sponheim), 1967, 472p.; Vol. XI,
in *Kierkegaard's Writings*, Princeton Univ. Press (1984).
(*Stadier paa Livets Vej.* Hilarius Bogbinder, ed.   1845.)

Concluding Unscientific Postscript.   Trans. by David F.
Swenson.   Completed after his death and provided with intro-
duction and notes by Walter Lowrie.   Published for American-
Scandinavian Foundation.   Princeton (New Jersey): Princeton
Univ. Press, 1941; 9th printing, ibid., 1968, xxi-577p.;
Vol. XII in *Kierkegaard's Writings*, Princeton Univ. Press
(1982).   (*Afsluttende uvidenskabelig Efterskrift.* Johannes
Climacus. S. Kierkegaard, ed.   1846.)

The Present Age [part of *Two Ages: The Age of Revolution and*
the Present Age.   A Literary Review] and *Two Minor Ethico-*
Religious Treatises.   Trans. by Alexander Dru and Walter
Lowrie.   London and New York: Oxford Univ. Press, 1940.
The Present Age and Of the Difference Between a Genius and
an Apostle.   Trans. by Alexander Dru, introduction by Walter
Kaufmann (Harper Torchbook).   New York: Harper, 1962, 108p.
Two Ages: The Age of Revolution and the Present Age.   A
Literary Review.   Trans., with introduction and notes by
Howard V. Hong and Edna H. Hong, eds.   Vol. XIV in
Kierkegaard's Writings, Princeton Univ. Press, 1978, 187p.
(*En literair Anmeldelse, To Tidsaldre,* 1846; *Tvende ethisk-*
religieuse Smaa-Afhandlinger. H. H., 1849.)

> After deciding to terminate his authorship with the
> pseudonymous *Concluding Unscientific Postscript*, Kier-
> kegaard composed reviews as a means of writing without
> being an author. *Two Ages* is simultaneously a review
> and a book in its own right. In it Kierkegaard comments
> on the anonymously published Danish novel *Two Ages*, com-
> mends its author's writings, and offers a cultural
> critique of compelling interest for our time.
> *Kierkegaard's Writings*, XIV.

On Authority and Revelation. The Book on Adler. Or:
A Cycle of Ethico-Religious Essays. Trans. with introduc-
tion and notes by Walter Lowrie. Princeton (New Jersey):
Princeton Univ. Press, 1955, xxvii-205p.; New York: Harper
& Row, 1966; Vol. XXIV in *Kierkegaard's Writings*, Princeton
Univ. Press (1988). ("Bogen om Adler," written 1846-47,
unpublished. *Papirer* VII B 235.)

Purity of Heart (Is to Will One Thing). Spiritual prepara-
tion for the office of confession. Trans. by Douglas V.
Steere. New York: Harper & Bros., 1948; ibid., 1956, 220p.
(Opbyggelige Taler i forskjellig Aand. Part 1, *"En Leilig-
heds-Tale."* 1847.)

The Gospel of Suffering and *The Lilies of the Field.* Trans.
by David F. Swenson and Lillian Marvin Swenson. Minneapolis:
Augsburg, 1948. *The Gospel of Our Sufferings. Christian
Discourses.* Part 3 of *Edifying Discourses (in a Different
Vein)*. Trans. by A. S. Aldworth and W. S. Ferrie.
Grand Rapids: Eerdmans, 1964, 150p. *(Opbyggelige Taler i
forskjellig Aand.* Part 3, *"Lidelsernes Evangelium;"*
part 2, *"Hvad vi laere af Lilierne paa Marken og af
Himmelens Fugle."* 1847.)

Works of Love. Some Christian reflections in the form of
discourses. Trans. by Howard V. Hong and Edna H. Hong.
New York: Harper & Row, 1962, 383p.; ibid., preface by
R. Gregor Smith, 1964, 378p. *Works of Love.* Trans. by
David F. Swenson and Lillian Marvin Swenson, with introduc-
tion by Douglas V. Steere [copyright 1946]. Port Washing-
ton (New York): Kennikat Press, 1972, 317p.; Folkestone
(Kent): Bailey Bros. & Swinfen. Vol. XVI in *Kierkegaard's
Writings*, Princeton Univ. Press (1987). *(Kjaerlighedens
Gjerninger.* 1847.)

The Crisis and *The Crisis in the Life of an Actress* (and
other essays on drama). Trans. with introduction and notes
by Stephen Crites. New York: Harper & Row, 1967, 154p.;
New York: Humanities press, 1967; London: William Collins;
Vol. XVII in *Kierkegaard's Writings*, Princeton Univ. Press,
(1987). *(Krisen og en Krise i en Skuespillerindes Liv.
Inter et Inter. Faedrelandet,* Nos. 188-191. 24-27 July
1848.)

Christian Discourses. Including also *The Lilies of the Field and the Birds of the Air* and *Three Discourses at the Communion on Fridays*. Trans. by Walter Lowrie. London and New York: Oxford Univ. Press, 1939; Fair Lawn (New Jersey): Oxford Univ. Press (introduction by Walter Lowrie), 1961, 389p.; Vols. XVII and XVIII in *Kierkegaard's Writings*, Princeton (New Jersey): Princeton Univ. Press (1987). (*Christelige Taler*, 1849; *Lilien paa Marken og Fuglen under Himlen*, 1849; *"Ypperstepraesten"--"Tolderen"--"Synderinden," Tre Taler ved Altergangen om Fredagen*, 1849.)

The Sickness Unto Death (with *Fear and Trembling*).   Trans. with introduction and notes by Walter Lowrie. Princeton (New Jersey): Princeton Univ. Press, 1954; ibid., 1968, 278p.; Gloucester (Massachusetts): P. Smith, 1964, 278p.; Vols. XIX and VI in *Kierkegaard's Writings*, Princeton Univ. Press (1979 and 1980). (*Sygdommen til Döden*. Anti-Climacus. S. Kierkegaard, ed. 1949.)

Training in Christianity. Including also *The Woman Who Was a Sinner*. Trans. by Walter Lowrie. Princeton (New Jersey): Princeton Univ. Press, 1944; Vol. XX in *Kierkegaard's Writings*, Princeton Univ. Press (1984). (*Indovelse i Christendom*, Anti-Climacus. S. Kierkegaard, ed. 1850; *En opbyggelig Tale*, 1850.)

Armed Neutrality and *An Open Letter*. With relevant selections from his journals and papers. Trans. with an introduction by Howard V. Hong and Edna H. Hong, eds. Background essay and commentary by Gregor Malantschuk. Bloomington and London: Indiana Univ. Press, 1968, 179p.; Vol. XXII in *Kierkegaard's Writings*, Princeton (New Jersey): Princeton Univ. Press (1985). (*Den bevaebnede Neutralitet*, written 1848-49, published 1965; *Foranledigt ved en Yttring af Dr. Rudelbach mig betraeffende*, Faedrelandet, No. 26. 31 January 1851.)

The Point of View for My Work as an Author. Including "Two Notes about 'the Individual'," and *On My Work as an Author*. Trans. with Introduction and notes by Walter Lowrie. London and New York: Oxford Univ. Press, 1939; Gloucester (Massachusetts): P. Smith (newly edited with a preface by Benjamin Nelson), 1962, xxiv-170p.; Vol. XXII in *Kierkegaard's Writings*, Princeton (New Jersey): Princeton Univ. Press (1985). (*Synspunktet for min Forfatter-Virksomhed*, written 1848, published 1859; *Om min Forfatter-Virksomhed*, 1951.)

For Self-Examination. Trans. by Howard V. Hong and Edna H.
Hong. Minneapolis: Augsburg, 1940. For Self-Examination
and Judge for Yourselves! and three discourses, 1851.
Trans. by Walter Lowrie. Princeton (New Jersey): Princeton
Univ. Press, 1968, 243p. [first published in Great Britain
in 1941; reprinted by offset in U.S.A. in 1944]; Vol. XXI
in Kierkegaard's Writings, Princeton Univ. Press (1985).
(Til Selvprövelse. 1851.)

Judge for Yourselves! in For Self-Examination and Judge for
Yourselves!. . ., with Two Discourses at the Communion on
Fridays. Trans. by Walter Lowrie. Also includes The
Unchangeableness of God. Trans. by David F. Swenson.
Princeton (New Jersey): Princeton Univ. Press, 1944.
For Self-Examination and Judge for Yourselves! and three
discourses, 1851. Trans. by Walter Lowrie. Princeton
Univ. Press, 1968, 243p. [first published in Great Britain
in 1941; reprinted by offset in U.S.A. in 1944]; Vol. XXI
in Kierkegaard's Writings, Princeton Univ. Press (1985).
(Dömmer Selv! 1852; To Taler ved Altergangen om Fredagen,
1851; Guds Uforanderlighed, 1855.)

Kierkegaard's Attack upon "Christendom," 1854-1855. Trans.
Trans. by Walter Lowrie. Princeton (New Jersey): Princeton
Univ. Press, 1944; with an introduction by Walter Lowrie,
Boston: Beacon Press, 1956, 321p.; Toronto: S. J. R.
Saunders; London, Cumberlege: Oxford Univ. Press; Princeton
Univ. Press, 1968, xxxii-303p.; Vol. XXIII in Kierkegaard's
Writings (1987). (Bladartikler I-XXI, Faedrelandet, 1854-
55; Dette skal siges, saa vaere det da sagt, 1855;
Oieblikket, 1-9, 1855; 10, unpublished, S.V., XIV;
Hvad Christus dömmer om officiel Christendom, 1855.)

The Journals of Sören Kierkegaard. . .a Selection. . . .
Trans. by Alexander Dru. London and New York: Oxford Univ.
Press, 1938; with an introduction by Alexander Dru (Harper
Torchbooks). New York: Harper, 1959, 256p. The Diary
of Sören Kierkegaard. Trans. by Gerda M. Anderson, Peter
P. Rohde, ed. New York: Philosophical Library, 1960, 255p.
The Last Years [Sel. from the] Journals 1853-1855. Trans.
by Ronald Gregor Smith, ed. New York: Harper & Row, 1965,
383p.; London: Collins. Sören Kierkegaard's Journals and
Papers. Vol. I. Trans. by Howard V. Hong and Edna H. Hong,
eds., assisted by Gregor Malantschuk. Bloomington: Indiana
Univ. Press, 1967, xxx-539p.; Vol. II. Ibid., 1970, 616p.;
Vol. III-IV. Ibid., 1976, 925p., 782p.; Vol. V, Autobiographical, part 1: 1829-1848, Vol. VI, Autobiographical,
part 2: 1848-1855, Vol. VII, Index and composite collation.
Ibid., 1978, 557p., 647p., 132p. (From Papirer, published
in 20 vols. 1909-1948.)

Letters and Documents. Trans. by Henrik Rosenmeier with
introduction and notes. Vol. XXV in *Kierkegaard's Writings*,
Princeton (New Jersey): Princeton Univ. Press, 1978. 584p.

  This volume provides the first English translation of
  all the known correspondence to and from Sören Kierkegaard. It includes a number of his letters in draft
  form and papers pertaining to his life and death.
  These fascinating documents offer new access to the
  character and lifework of the gifted philosopher,
  theologian, and psychologist. *Kierkegaard's Writings*,
  XXV.

Meditations. Trans. by T. H. Croxall, ed. Philadelphia:
Westminster Press, 1955, 165p.; London: Nisbet, 1956.

Kierkegaard: The Difficulty of being Chrisitan. Texts
introduced by Jacques Colette, ed. English version by
Ralph M. McInerny and Leo Turcotte. Notre Dame (Indiana),
London: Univ. of Notre Dame Press, 1969, xx-311p.

Diary of a Seducer. Trans. with an introduction by Gerd
Gillhoff. New York: Frederick Ungar, 1969, 181p.; London:
Elek Books, 1969.

Prayers. Perry D. Le Fevre, ed., with a new interpretation
of K's life and thought. Chicago: Univ. of Chicago Press,
1956. 244p.

Parables of Kierkegaard. Thomas C. Oden, ed. Princeton
Univ. Press, 1978, xxv-186p. [With bibliography, appendix]

A *Kierkegaard Anthology*. Robert Bretall, ed. Introduction
and notes. Princeton, 1946; New York: Modern Library (of
the world's best books), 1959, xxv-494p.; Princeton (New
Jersey): Princeton Univ. Press, 1973.

Glimpses and Impressions of Kierkegaard. Selected and
trans. by T. H. Croxall. London: James Nisbet & Co., 1959,
xv-134p.

Selection from His Writings (Kierkegaard). Trans. by Lee M.
Hollander. Garden City: Doubleday, 1960. 259p.

The Living Thoughts of Kierkegaard. Presented by W. H.
Auden (The Living Thoughts Library). New York: David
McKay Co., 1952, 225p.; Bloomington: Indiana Univ. Press,
1963; Toronto: Copp Clark. *Kierkegaard*. Sel. and introduced by W. H. Auden. London: Cassel, 1955. 184p.

FRENCH

OEuvres Complètes. Trad. de Paul-Henri Tisseau et Else-
Marie Jacquet-Tisseau. Introduction de Jean Brun.
Paris: Éditions de l'Orante.

   Les Éditions de l'Orante are in the process of publishing
   in French *OEuvres Complètes* (*The Complete Works of Sören
   Kierkegaard*), which will consist of 20 volumes.

   Vol. II: *Le Concept d'Ironie Constamment Rapporté à
   Socrate; Confession Publique; Johannes Climacus ou
   De Omnibus Dubitandum Est*: 1841-1843. 1975,
   xxii-367p.

   Vol. III: *L'Alternative*. 1re partie: 1843. 1970,
   xxxvii-415p.

   Vol. IV: *L'Alternative*. 2e partie. Trois articles de
   Foedrelandet; Post-scriptum à *L'Alternative*: 1843-44.
   1970, x-335p.

   Vol. V: *La Répétition; Crainte et Tremblement*: 1843
   [Une petite annexe, 1844]. 1972, xxvii-233p.

   Vol. VII: *Miettes Philosophiques; Le Concept d'Angoisse;
   Préfaces*: 1844. 1973, xxix-328p.

   Vol. IX: *Stades sur le Chemin de la Vie*: 1845.
   1978, xxii-456p.

   Vol. X, T. 1: *Post-scriptum Définitif et Non Scientifique aux* Miettes Philosophiques: 1846.
   1977. 279p.

   Vol. XI, T. 2: *Post-scriptum Définitif et Non Scientifique aux* Miettes Philosophiques: 1846.
   1977, x-306p.

   Vol. XIII: *Discours Édifiants à Divers Points de Vue*:
   1847. 1966, xviii-336p.

Vol. XVI: *Point de Vue Explicatif de mon Oeuvre d'Écrivain; Deux Petits Traités Éthico-religieux; La Maladie à la Mort; Six Discours*: 1848-49. 1971, xxxiv-373p.

Vol. XVIII: *Quatre Discours; Pour un Examen de Conscience; Jugez Vous-mêmes*: 1849-52. 1966, xx-264p.

book review:
A. A. Philonenko, *Revue de Métaphysique et de Morale* 83 (1978):422-427.

OTHER FRENCH EDITIONS

OEuvres Complètes. Trad. de Paul-Henri Tisseau et Else-Marie Jacquet-Tisseau. Introduction de Jean Brun. Vol. II: *Le Concept d'Ironie Constamment Rapporté à Socrate. Confession Publique. Johannes Climacus ou De Omnibus Dubitandum Est*: 1841-1843. Paris: Éditions de l'Orante, 1975, xxii-367p.

Ou Bien. . .Ou Bien. . . . Trad. par F. et O. Prior et M. H. Guignot. Introduction de F. Brandt (trad. par Marie-Louise de Jessen. 11e ed.). Paris: Gallimard, 1949, xix-631p.

OEuvres Complètes. Trad. par Paul-Henri Tisseau et Else-Marie Jacquet-Tisseau. Sous la direction de Jean Brun. Vol. III: *L'Alternative*. 1re partie: 1843. Vol. IV: *L'Alternative*. 2e partie. Trois articles de *Foedrelandet*. Post-scriptum à *L'Alternative*: 1843-1844. Paris: Éditions de l'Orante, 1970, xxxvii-415p.; x-335p.

Hâte-toi d'Écouter. Quatre Discours Édifiants. (*Fire Opbyggelige Taler*). 1843. Introduction, trad., notes par Nelly Viallaneix (Bibliothèque Philosophique Bilingue). Paris: Aubier Montaigne, 1970. 270p.

Discours Édifiants. La Pécheresse. De l'Immutabilité de Dieu. Trad. et introduction de Jacques Colette O. P. avec une étude de Gregor Malantschuk (Collection "Carnets DDB"). Bruges: Desclée de Brouwer, 1962, 140p. *OEuvres Complètes*, XIII: *Discours Édifiants à Divers Points de Vue*, 1847. Trad. par Paul-Henri Tisseau, Else-Marie Jacquet-Tisseau,

directeur de publication, Jean Brun (Fondation Jean-Luc
Boudet). Paris: Éditions de l'Orante, 1966, xviii-336p.

Crainte et Tremblement. *Réimpression*. Paris: Aubier,
Éditions Montaigne, 1952. *OEuvres Complètes*. Trad. par
Paul-Henri Tisseau et Else-Marie Jacquet-Tisseau. Sous la
direction de Jean Brun. Vol. V: *La Répétition*. *Crainte
et Tremblement*. 1843 [Une petite annexe, 1844]. Paris:
Éditions de l'Orante, 1972, xxviii-233p.

La Répétition. *Crainte et Tremblement*. Vol. V, 1843
[Une petite annexe, 1844], in *OEuvres Complètes*. Trad.
par Paul-Henri Tisseau et Else-Marie Jacquet-Tisseau. Sous
la direction de Jean Brun. Paris: Éditions de l'Orante,
1972, xxviii-233p.

Les Miettes Philosophiques. Trad. de Paul Petit. Paris:
Éditions du Seuil, 1967, 192p. *Riens Philosophiques*
[*Filosofiske Smuler Eller en Smule Filozofi*]. Trad. par
Knud Ferlov et Jean J. Gateau (Idées, 197). Paris:
Gallimard, 1969, 192p. *OEuvres Complètes*. Trad. de Paul-
Henri Tisseau et Else-Marie Jacquet-Tisseau. Publié sous
la direction de Jean Brun. Vol. X: *Post-scriptum Définitif
et Non Scientifique aux* Miettes Philosophiques. 1846, I.
Paris: Éditions de l'Orante, 1977, 279p.

Le Concept de l'Angoisse. Trad. par Knud Ferlov et Jean-J.
Gateau (Collection Idées, 369. Philosophie). Paris:
Gallimard, 1976. 183p.

Etapes sur le Chemin de la Vie. Trad. par F. Prior et
M. H. Gigniot. Paris: Gallimard, 1948. 424p.

La Crise et Une Crise dans la Vie d'Une Actrice (Trad. par
M. E. Jacquet-Tisseau d' après le texte édité par Drachmann,
Heiberg et Lange, t. X). *Études Philosophiques* 18 (1963):
279-298.

Traité du Désespoir (Collection Les Essais). *Réimpression*
Paris: Gallimard, Hachette, 1954. *Traité de Désespoir*
Collection Idées, 25). Paris: Gallimard, 1963, 256p.

*L'École du Christianisme. Suivi de Point de Vue Explicatif
de Mon Oeuvre.* Trad. par M. Tisseau. Prés. par Jean Brun
(Collection Littérature). Paris: Librairie Académique
Perrin, 1963.

L'Instant. Trad. par Paul-Henri Tisseau. Bazoges-en-Pareds:
Vendée, in-8, 217p.

*L'Attente de la Foi. Discours Édifiant pour le Jour de
l'An.* Préface, Trad. et notes par Nelly Viallaneix.
Genève: Éditions Labor et Fides; Paris: Librairie Protestante,
1967, 93p.

Discours Chrétiens. Trad. et introduction de Paul-Henri
Tisseau. Neuchâtel-Paris: Delachaux & Niestlé, 1952, 276p.
Discours Chrétiens. I: *Les Soucis des Païens*; II: *Dans la
Lutte des Souffrances* (Foi vivante, 63, 84). Neuchâtel,
Paris: Delachaux et Niestlé, 1967, 125p.; 1968, 123p.

Le Journal du Séducteur. Trad. par F. et O. Prior et M.-H.
Giugnot (Idées, 84). Paris: Gallimard, 1965, 256p.
*Le Stade Esthétique: Le Journal du Séducteur. In Vino
Veritas.* Précédé de *Kierkegaard et l'Érotisme,* par
Marguerite Grimault (Le Monde en 10/18, n. 303-304).
Paris: U. G. E., 1966, 320p. *Le Journal d'Un Séducteur.*
Trad. du danois. Préf. de Fernand Cuvelier (Les Maudits
de la Littérature Mondiale, 6). Kalmthout-Anvers: Beckers,
[1969], 231p.

Diapsalmata. Trad. originale de P.-H. Tisseau. Préface de
Jean Brun (La Fenêtre ardente). Lavaur: La Fenêtre ardente,
1963, 55p.; Gravures de Louis Pons (L'Originale). Paris:
R. Morel, 1963.

Journal. Trad. par Knud Ferlov et Jean-J. Gateau (Collection Les Essais). *Extraits*, I: 1840-45. Paris: Gallimard, 1954. *Extraits*, II: 1846-49. Paris: Gallimard, 1954, 408p. *Extraits*, III: 1849-50. Paris: Gallimard, 1955, 424p. *Extraits*, IV: 1850-53. Paris: Gallimard, NRF, 1957. *Extraits*, V: 1854-55. Paris: Gallimard, 1961, 413p.

Lettres des Fiançailles. Trad. et avant-propos de Marguerite Grimault (Les Carnets, 14). Paris: Éditions Falaize, 1956. 115p.

La Difficulté d'Être Chrétien. Présentation et choix de textes par Jacques Colette O. P. (Chrétiens de Tous les Temps, 5). Paris: Éditions du Cerf, 1964. 312p.

L'Existence. Textes trad. par P. H. Tisseau et choisis par Jean Brun (Collection Les Grandes Textes). Paris: Presses Universitaires de France, 1962, 220p. 2e ed. rev. et corr., 1967, 221p. 3e ed., 1972, 223p.

Kierkegaard [Textes choisis] (Philosophes). 4e ed. Paris: Presses Universitaires de France, 1970. 104p.

GERMAN

Gesammelte Werke (Complete Works of Kierkegaard) in German published at Düsseldorf by Diederichs. This publication consists of 35 volumes.

Abt. 1: *Entweder/Oder (Enten-Eller*, dt.). T. I: Uebers. von Emanuel Hirsch. 1956, xiv-509p.

Abt. 2/3: *Entweder/Oder (Enten-Eller*, dt.). T. II: *Zwei erbauliche Reden (To Opbyggelige Taler*, dt.), 1843. Uebers. von Emanuel Hirsch. 1957, 1966, xii-447p.

Abt. 4: *Furcht und Zittern*. Uebers. von Emanuel Hirsch. 1950, xiii-162p.; 1971, 172p.

Abt. 5/6: *Die Wiederholung. Drei erbauliche Reden*, 1843. Uebers. von Emanuel Hirsch. 1955, 1967, x-167p.

Abt. 7-9. *Erbauliche Reden*, 1843-44. Uebers. von Emanuel Hirsch. 1956, ix-218p.

Abt. 10: *Philosophische Brocken. De Omnibus Dubitandum
Est.* Uebers. von Emanuel Hirsch. 1952, 1967, xii-191p.

Abt. 11/12: *Der Begriff Angst.* (Begrebet Angest, dt.).
Eine schlichte psycholog.-andeutende Ueberlegung in
Richtung auf d. dogmat. Problem d. Erbsünde. Vorworte.
Unterhaltungslektüre f. einzelne Stände je nach Zeit
und Gelegenheit. Uebers. von Emanuel Hirsch. 1952,
1958, x-280p.

Abt. 13/14: *Vier erbauliche Reden, 1844. Drei Reden
bei gedachten Gelegenheiten, 1845.* Uebers. von
Emanuel Hirsch. 1952, viii-227p.

Abt. 15: *Stadien auf des Lebens Weg.* Unter Mitarb. von
Rose Hirsch, übers. von Emanuel Hirsch. 1958, xiv-569p.

Abt. 16, T. 1, 2: *Abschliessende unwissenschaftliche
Nachschrift zu den Philosophischen Brocken.* Uebers.
von Hans Martin Jughans. 1957, ix-355p.; 1958, x-418p.

Abt. 17: *Eine literarische Anzeige.* Uebers. von
Emanuel Hirsch. 1954, xxxii-163p.

Abt. 18: *Erbauliche Reden in verschiedem Geist, 1847.*
1964, xi-377p.

Abt. 19: *Der Liebe Tun. Etliche christl. Erwägungen in
Form von Reden.* Uebers. von Hayo Gerdes. 1966, xi-459p.

Abt. 20: *Christliche Reden, 1848.* Unter Mitarb. von
Rose Hirsch, übers. von Emanuel Hirsch. 1959, ix-342p.

Abt. 24/25: *Die Krankheit zum Tode. Der Hohepriester--
der Zöllner--die Sünderin.* Uebers. von Emanuel Hirsch.
1954, xi-185p.

Abt. 26: *Einübung im Christentum.* Uebers. von Emanuel
Hirsch. 1951, xii-298p.; 3. Aufl., 1962, xii-298p.;
4. Aufl., 1971, 311p.

Abt. 27-29: *Erbauliche Reden, 1850-51. Zur Selbstprüfung. Der Gegenwart anbefohlen. Urteilt selbst.*
Uebers. von Emanuel Hirsch. 1953, x-264p.

Abt. 30: *Erstlingsschriften.* Unter Mitarb. von Rose
Hirsch, übers. von Emanuel Hirsch. 1960, xix-195p.

Abt. 31: *Ueber den Begriff der Ironie mit ständiger
Rücksicht auf Sokrates.* Unter Mitarb. von Rose Hirsch,
übers. von Emanuel Hirsch. 1961, xiii-373p.

Abt. 32: *Kleine Aufsätze, 1842-51. Der Corsarenstreit.*
Uebers. von Hayo Gerdes. 1960, xi-237p.

Abt. 33: *Die Schriften über sich selbst*. Uebers. von
Emanuel Hirsch. 1951, xiv-175p.; 2. Aufl., 1964.

Abt. 34: *Ser Augenblick. Aufsätze und Schriften d.
letzten Streits*. Uebers. von Hayo Gerdes. 1959,
xv-364p.

Abt. 35: *Briefe*. Unter Mitarb. von Rose Hirsch, ausgew.,
neugeordnet und übers. von Emanuel Hirsch. 1955,
xv-278p.

Die Tagebücher, I. Ausgew., neugeordn. u. übers. von
Hayo Gerdes. 1962, xv-444p.; 2. Aufl., 1975.

Die Tagebücher, II. Ausgew., neugeordn. u. übers. von
Hayo Gerdes. 1963, ix-296p.

Die Tagebücher, III. Ausgew., neugeordn. u. übers. von
Hayo Gerdes. 1968, ix-357p.

Die Tagebücher, IV. Ausgew., neugeordn. u. übers. von
Hayo Gerdes. 1968, vii-347p.

Die Tagebücher, V. Ausgew., übers. u. erl. von Hayo
Gerdes. 1974, x-422p.

OTHER GERMAN EDITIONS

Der Begriff Angst. Uebers. u. mit Glossar, Bibliographie
sowie e. Essay: *Zum Verständnis des Werkes*, hrsg. von
Liselotte Richter (Rowohlts Klassiker d. Literatur u. d.
Wissenschaft, 71). 2. Aufl., Reinbek b. Hamburg: Rowohlt,
1963, 202p.; 3. Aufl., 1964; 6. Aufl., 1969. (*Gesammelte
Werke*, I.)

*Die Wiederholung. Die Krise und eine Krise im Leben einer
Schauspielerin*. Mit Erinnerungen an Kierkegaard von Hans
Bröchner. Uebers. u. mit e. Glossar, Bibliographie sowie
e. Essay: *Zum Verständnis des Werkes*, hrsg. von Liselotte
Richter (Rowohlts Klassiker der Literatur und der Wissenschaft, 81). Reinbek b. Hamburg: Rowohlt, 1961, 146p.;
3. Aufl., 1969. (*Gesammelte Werke*, II).

Furcht und Zittern. Mit Erinnerungen an Kierkegaard von Hans
Bröchner. Uebers. u. mit Glossar, Bibliographie sowie e.
Essay: *Zum Verständnis des Werkes*, hrsg. von Liselotte
Richter (Rowohlts Klassiker der Literatur u. der Wissenschaft,
89). Reinbek b. Hamburg: Rowohlt, 1961, 149p.; 1964; 3. Aufl.
1967; 4. Aufl. 1969. (*Gesammelte Werke*, III.)

Furcht und Zittern. Dialektische Lyrik. Uebers. von Helmut
de Boor. Nachwort von Friedrich Grossart. Krefeld:
Scherpe-Verlag, 1949. 179p.

Die Krankheit zum Tode. Uebers. u. mit Glossar, Bibliographie sowie e. Essay: *Zum Verständnis des Werkes,* hrsg.
von Liselotte Richter (Rowohlts Klassiker der Literatur und
der Wissenschaft, 113). Reinbek b. Hamburg: Rowohlt, 1962,
151p.; 4. Aufl., 1969. (*Gesammelte Werke,* IV.)

*Die Krankheit zum Tode. Furcht und Zittern. Die Wieder-
holung. Der Begriff der Angst.* Uebers. von Walter Rest,
Günther Jungbluth, Rosemarie Lögstrup (*Gesammelte Werke,*
dt., hrsg. von Hermann Diem und Walter Rest. *Philosophisch-
theologische Schriften,* 2). Köln: Hegner, 1956. 767p.

*Die Krankheit zum Tode. Furcht und Zittern. Die Wieder-
holung. Der Begriff der Angst.* Unter Mitw. von Niels
Thulstrup und d. Kopenhagener Kierkegaard-Ges., hrsg. von
Hermann Diem und Walter Rest (dtv, 6070; dtv-Dünndr.-Ausg.:
dtv-Bibliothek). Ungekürzte Augs. München: Deutscher
Taschenbuch-Verlag, 1976. 767p.

Philosophische Brocken. Uebers. u. mit Glossar, Bibliographie sowie e. Essay: *Zum Verständnis des Werkes,* hrsg.
von Liselotte Richter (Rowohlts Klassiker d. Literatur und
d. Wissenschaft, 147). Reinbek b. Hamburg: Rowohlt, 1964.
157p. (*Gesammelte Werke,* V.)

Philosophische Brocken. De Omnibus Dubitandum Est. Uebers.
von Emanuel Hirsch (Suhrkamp-Taschenbücher Wissenschaft,
147). Frankfurt am Main: Suhrkamp, 1975. 190p. [Lizenz d.
Diederichs-Verlag, Düsseldorf, Koln.]

Existenz im Glauben. [*Werke,* Ausz., dt.] Aus Dokumenten,
Briefen und Tagebüchern. Nach neuen dänischen Quellen
übers., ausgew. und eingel. von Liselotte Richter. Berlin:
Evang. Verlag-Anst., 1956. 271p.

Einübung im Christentum. Deutsch von Hans Winkler.
Zwei ethische-religiöse Abhandlungen. Deutsch von Walter
Rest. *Das Buch Adler oder Der Begriff des Auserwählten.*
Deutsch von Theodor Haecker. Unter Mitwirkung der Kopen-
hagener Kierkegaard-Gesellschaft , hrg. und eingel. von
Walter Rest (*Philosophisch-theologische Schriften,* S. Kier-
kegaard). Köln-Olten: J. Hegner, 1951. 733p.

Philosophisch-theologische Schriften. Bd. III: *Philoso-
phische Brosamen und unwissenschaftliche Nachschrift.*
Deutsch von Börge und Susanne Diderichsen (*Gesammelte Werke,*
dt. Unter. Mitw. von Niels Thulstrup und d. Kopenhagener
Kierkegaard-Gesellschaft hrsg. von Hermann Diem und Walter
Rest. Gruppe I). Köln-Olten: Hegner, 1959. 1031p.

Aesthetisch-Philosophisches. Bd. I: *Entweder-Oder.* Dt. von
Heinrich Fauteck (*Gesammelte Werke,* dt. Unter Mitw. von
Niels Thulstrup und d. Kopenhagener Kierkegaard-Gesellschaft
hrsg. von Hermann Diem und Walter Rest. Gruppe 2).
Köln-Olten: Hegner, 1960. 1038p.

Entweder-Oder [*Enten-Eller,* Ausz., dt.]. Uebers. von
Christoph Schrempf. Zsgefasst hrsg. von Fritz Droop. Mit
Einf. von Max Bense. Mit 3 Abb. (Sammlung Dieterich, 40).
Wiesbaden: Dieterich; Bremen: Schünemann, 1955, lx-508p.

Entweder-Oder. Unter Mitw. von Niels Thulstrup und d.
Kopenhagener Kierkegaard-Ges. hrsg. von Hermann Diem und
Walter Rest. Dt. ubers. von Heinrich Fauteck (dtv, 6043;
dtv-Bibliothek). Ungekürzte Ausg. München: Deutscher
Taschenbuch-Verlag, 1975. 1038p.

Johannes Climacus oder De Omnibus Dubitandum Est. Uebers.
und eingeleitet von Wolfgang Struve. Darmstadt: Claassen
& Roether, 1948. 83p.

Kleine Aufsätze, 1842-51. *Der Corsarenstreit.* Uebers. von
Hayo Gerdes (*Gesammelte Werke,* Abt. 32, dt.). Düsseldorf-
Köln: Diederichs, 1960, xi-237p.

Religiöse Reden. Deutsch von Theodor Haecker (Hegner-
Bücherei). München: Kösel, 1950. 365p.

Die Gültigkeit der Ehe. Dt. von Heinrich Fauteck. Köln-Olten: Hegner, 1963. 204p.

Das Tagebuch des Verführers. Teilausg. Dt. von Heinrich Fauteck (Hegner-Bücherei). Köln: Hegner, 1967. 248p.

Philosophische Brosamen und unwissenschaftliche Nachschrift. Unter Mitw. von Niels Thulstrup und d. Kopenhagener Kierkegaard-Ges. hrsg. von Hermann Diem und Walter Rest (dtv, 6064; dtv-Bibliothek). München: Deutscher Taschenbuch-Verlag, 1976. 1031p.

Christliche Reden. Uebers. und mit e. Nachw. hrsg. von Wilhelm Kütemeyer (Kleine Vandenhoeck-Reihe, 16). Göttingen: Vandenhoeck & Ruprecht, 1955. 101p.

Der Einzelne und sein Gott. Ausgew. und eingel. von Walter Rest (Herder-Bücherei, 105). Freiburg i. Br., Basel, Wien: Herder, 1961. 181p.

Der Pfahl im Fleisch sowie Wider Feigheit und Vom Gebet [*Teilsamml.*, dt.]. Neu übers. und erl. von Anna Paulsen (Stundenbücher, 12). Hamburg: Furche-Verlag, 1962. 113p.

Gebete. Hrsg. und eingel. von Walter Rest. Köln-Olten: Hegner, 1952. 107p.

Religion der Tat. Uebers. und hrsg. von Eduard Geismar. 5. Aufl. (Kröners Taschenausgabe, Bd. 63). Stuttgart: Kröner, 1952; Furche-Verlag, 1952, 45p.

Die Liebe deckt auch der Sünden Menge [*Teilsamml.*, dt.]. Nach d. dän. Originalausg. übers. und hrsg. von Robert Dollinger. Neuendettelsau: Freimund-Verlag, 1955. 71p.

Die Lilien auf dem Felde. Wien: Thomas Morus Verlag, 1948. 130p.

Was wir lernen von den Lilien auf dem Felde und den Vögeln unter dem Himmel. Nach d. Dän. frei übers. von Robert Dollinger (Furche-Bücherei, 6). 21.-25. Tsd. Hamburg: Furche-Verlag, 1956. 45p.

Reden beim Altargang am Freitag. Aus d. Dän. übers. und eingel. von Daniel Hoffmann. Berlin: Evang. Verlag-Anst., 1962. 126p.

Christ aus Leidenschaft. Eine Ausw. aus d. Gesamtwerk. Hrsg., übers. und eingel. von Daniel Hoffmann. Witten und Berlin: Eckart-Verlag, 1963. 394p.

Freude in der Anfechtung. Gedanken aus den Werken Kierkegaards. Herausgegeben von E. Schick. 2. Aufl., Basel: Verlag der Basler Missionsbuchhandlung, [1948]. 64p.

Kierkegaard. [Werke, Ausz., dt.] Ausgew. und eingel. von Hermann Diem (Fischer Bücherei, 109). Frankfurt am Main: Fischer, 1956. 208p.

Briefe. Ausgew., uebers. und mit einem Nachw. versehen von Walter Boehlich. Köln-Olten: Hegner, 1955. 163p.

So spricht Kierkegaard. [Werke, Ausz., dt.]. Bearb. von Fritz Kraus (Lebendige Quellen zum Wissen um die Ganzheit des Menschen). München-Planegg: O. W. Barth, 1954. 128p.

Kierkegaard-Brevier. [Werke, Ausz., dt.]. Hrsg. von Peter Schäfer und Max Bense. (Insel-Bücherei, 519). 26.-35. Tsd. Wiesbaden: Insel-Verlag, 1955. 78p.

Tagebücher. Eine Auswahl. Ausg. und übers. von Elisabeth Feuersenger. 6.-9. Tsd. Wiesbaden: Metopen-Verlag, 1949. 207p.

Die Tagebücher, 1834-55. Ausg. und übers. van Theodor Haecker. 3. Aufl. (Hegner-Bücherei). München: Kösel, 1949, 607p.; 4. Aufl., 1953, 663p.

Auswahl aus dem Gesamtwerk. Unter Mitarb. von Rose Hirsch
besorgt von Emanuel Hirsch (Diederichs Taschenausgaben, 25).
Düsseldorf: Diederichs, 1961. 448p.

*Auswahl aus dem Gesamtwerk des Dichters, Denkers und
religiösen Redners.* Unter Mitarb. von Rose Hirsch besorgt
von Emanuel Hirsch (Siebensterntaschenbuch, 141/143).
München: Siebenstern-Taschenbuch-Verlag, 1969. 448p.
[Lizenz d. Diederichs-Verlag, Düsseldorf.]

Christentum und Christenheit. Aus Kierkegaards *Tagebüchern*
ausgewählt und ubers. von Eva Schlechta. München: Kösel,
1957. 438p.

Sören Kierkegaard. Ausgew. *Aufsätze.* K. Olesen Larsen.
Aus d. Dän. übers. von Eva Schlechta-Nordentoft. Gütersloh:
Gütersloher Verlagshaus Mohn, 1973. 164p.

Die Leidenschaft des Religiösen. Eine Auswahl aus *Schriften*
und *Tagebüchern.* Von Heinz Küpper aus d. Dän. und mit einer
Einl. von Liselotte Richter (Reclams Universal-Bibliothek,
7783/84). Stuttgart: Reclam, 1953,184p.; 1968, 182p.

Die nackte Wahrheit. Aphorismen und andere kurze Notizen.
Eine Ausw. Zusammengest. und übers. von Sixtus Scholtens und
Paulus Ter Doest. Kamp-Lintfort: Verlag der Karmel-Stimmen,
1978. 106p.

SPANISH

Temor y Temblor. Trad. de Jaime Grinberg (Biblioteca
Filosófica). Buenos Aires: Editorial Losada, 1947. 143p.

Temor y Temblor. Diario di un Seductor. Trad. Demetrio
Gutiérrez Rivero (Col. Bolsillo Enlace, 439). Madrid:
Guadarrama, 1975. 400p.

La Repetición. Trad. Demetrio Gutiérrez Rivero (Col. Bolsillo Enlace, 428). Madrid: Guadarrama, 1975. 288p.

Diapsalmata. Trad. del danés de Javier Armada. Prólogo de Carlos Martín Ramírez (Biblioteca de Iniciación Filosófica, 72). Buenos Aires: Aguilar, 1961. 63p.

Estudios Estéticos, I: *Diapsalmata* [y] *El Erotismo Musical*. II: *De la Tragedia y Otros Ensayos*. Trad. del danés, prólogo y notas de Demetrio Gutiérrez Rivero (Obras y papeles de S. Kierkegaard, 8-9). Madrid: Guadarama, 1969, 251p., 260p.

Diario de un Seductor. Trad. de Aristides Gregori. Buenos Aires: Santiago Rueda, 1951. 185p.; Barcelona: Edics. 29, 1973. 148p.

Diario di un Seductor. *Temor y Temblor*. Trad. Demetrio Gutiérrez Rivero (Col. Bolsillo Enlace, 439). Madrid: Guadarrama, 1975. 400p.

In Vino Veritas. *La Repetición*. Trad. Demetrio Gutiérrez Rivero (Col. Bolsillo Enlace, 428). Madrid: Guadarrama, 1975. 288p.

El Concepto de la Angustia. Trad. de Demetrio G. Rivero (*Obras y Papeles* de Soeren Kierkegaard). Madrid: Edics. Guadarrama, 1965. 291p.

El Concepto de la Angustia. *Una Sencilla Investigación Psicológica Orientada Hacia el Problema Dogmático del Pecado Original* (Austral, 158). 7a ed. Madrid: Espasa-Calpe, 1967. 159p.

Estética y Ética en la Formación de la Personalidad. Buenos Aires: Nova, 1955. 237p.

Las Obras del Amor. *Meditaciones Cristianas en Forma de Discursos* [Primera y secunda parte]. Trad. directa del danés y prólogo por Demetrio G. Rivero (*Obras y Papeles* de Soeren Kierkegaard, IV y V). Madrid: Edics. Guadarrama, 1965, 341p., 286p.

*Los Lirios del Campo y las Aves del Cielo. Trece Discursos
Religiosos.* Trad. directa del danés y prólogo por Demetrio
G. Rivero (*Obras y Papeles* de Soeren Kierkegaard, 3).
Madrid: Edic. Guadarrama, 1963. 286p.

La Enfermedad Mortal o De la Desesperación y el Pecado.
Trad. directa del danés y prólogo por Demetrio G. Rivero.
Madrid: Guadarrama, 1969. 246p.

Mi Punto de Vista. Trad. por José María Velloso. Pról.
de José Antonio Míguez (Biblioteca de Iniciación Filosófica,
59). Buenos Aires: Aguilar, 1959. 210p.

Dos Diálogos Sobre el Primer Amor y el Matrimonio. Trad.
directa del danés y prólogo por Demetrio G. Rivero (*Obras
y Papeles* de S. Kierkegaard, 2). Madrid: Edic. Guadarrama,
1961. 378p.

Ejercitación del Cristianismo. Trad. directa del danés y
pról. por Demetrio G. Rivero (*Obras y Papeles* de Soeren
Kierkegaard, 1). Madrid: Ediciones Guadarrama, 1961. 356p.

ITALIAN

Opere. A cura di Cornelio Fabro (Le voci del mondo).
Firenze: Sansoni, 1972, lxxvi-1026p.

Enten-Eller. Un Frammento di Vita, I-II. A cura di
Alessandro Cortese (Piccola Biblioteca Adelphi, 42, 53).
Milano: Adelphi Edizioni, 1976, 223p.; 1977, 217p.

*Aut-Aut. Estetica ed Etica Nella Formazione della Person-
alità.* Trad. di Kirsten Montanari Guldbrandsen e Remo
Cantoni (Gli Oscar, L. 178). Milano: A. Mondadori, 1975.
213p.

Diario del Seduttore. Introduzione di Remo Cantoni. Trad.
di Attilio Veraldi (Biblioteca Universale Rizzoli). 2a ed.
Milano: Rizzoli, 1973. 149p.

Timore e Tremore. (Lirica dialettica di Johannes de Silent Silentio). Prefazione di Jean Wahl. Trad. F. Fortini, K. Montanari Gulbrandsen (Humana Civiltas, 14). Milano: Edizioni di Comunità, 1948, xxxii-150p.; 3a ed., 1962, 182p.

La Ripresa. Tentativo di Psicologia Sperimentale di Costantin Constantius. Trad. di A. Zucconi (Humana Civiltas, 17). Milano: Edizioni di Comunità, 1954, xvi-131p.; 2a ed., 1963, 153p.

Bricole di Filosofia, e Postilla Non Scientifica. A cura di Cornelio Fabro. Vol. I-II (Crntro di Studi Filosofici di Gallarate. Collana di Filosofi Moderni, 1-2). Bologna: Zanichelli, 1962, 381p., 455p.

Il Concetto dell' Angoscia. Trad. e scelta di M. F. Sciacca. 3a ed. Milano: Fratelli Bocca, 1951. 90p.

Il Concetto dell' Angoscia. A cura di E. Paci. Torino: Paravia, 1954. 148p.

Il Concetto dell' Angoscia. La Malattia Mortale. Trad. avvertenza e note a cura di Cornelio Fabro (Classici della Filosofia). Firenze: G. C. Sansoni, 1953, xxx-370p.

Discorsi Cristiani. Trad. e introd. di Dino T. Donadoni. Torino: Borla, 1963. 254p.

La Malattia Mortale. Svolgimento Psicologico Cristiano di Anti-Climacus. (*Sygdommen til Döden*). Trad. dal danese a cura di Meta Corssen, prefazione di Paolo Brezzi. Milano: Edizioni di Comunità, 1947, xxiii-173p.; 2a ed., 1952, xxviii-169p.; 1965, 198p.; Introduz. di Remo Cantoni (Paperbacks saggi, 101). Roma: Newton Compton, 1976, xx-134p.

La Malattia Mortale. Il Concetto dell' Angoscia. Trad., avvertenza e note a cura di Cornelio Fabro (Classici della Filosofia). Firenze: G. C. Sansoni, 1953, xxx-370p.

Diario. Trad. a cura di Cornelio Fabro. Vol. I, Brescia:
Morcelliana, 1948; Vol. II, 1950, 652p.; Vol. III (1852-55),
1951, xix-567p.; 2a ed. [in 2 vol.] riveduta, 1962-63,
1040p., 975p.

Diario. Ed. ridotta. A cura di Cornelio Fabro (I tascabili
della BUR. L. 34). Milano: Biblioteca Universale Rizzoli,
1975. 368p.

Preghiere. A cura di Cornelio Fabro (Fuochi). Brescia:
Morcelliana, 1951, vii-58p.; 4a ed., 1963, 91p.

Esercizio del Cristianesimo. Introduzione, trad. e note a
cura di Cornelio Fabro (Cultura, 41). Roma: Ed. Studium,
1971. 408p.

La Neutralita Armatà e il Piccolo Intervento. A cura di
Mariano Cristaldi e Gregor Malantschuk. Trad. Italiane di
Nicola De Domenico e Pina Zaccarin-Lauritzen (Filosofia e
Tempo Presente, 2). Messina: A. M. Sortino Editore, 1972.
210p.

L'ora: Atti di Accusa Contro il Cristianesimo di Danimarca.
Trad. di A. Banfi, introd. di M. Dal Pra (Nuova Biblioteca
Filosofica, serie prima, III). Milano: Bocca, 1951. 200p.

Dell'autorità e della Rivelazione (Libro su Adler). Introduzione, trad. e note a cura di C. Fabro. Padova: Gregoriana
Editrice, 1976. 469p.

Suola di Cristianesimo. Trad. A Miggiano, K. Montanari
Gulbrandsen (Humana Civiltas, 8). Milano: Edizioni di
Comunità, 1950, 305p.; 1960, 292p.

Lo Specchio della Parola (Collezione Socrate). Firenze:
Fussi, 144p.

La Lotta Tra il Vecchio e il Nuovo Negozio del Sapone.
Trad., intr., commento di Alessandro Cortese (Studium
Sapientiae, 8). Padova: Liviana, 1967, xi-164p.

Peccato, Perdono, Misericordia. Trad. a cura di L. Vaglia-
sindi (Una Ragione per Vivere). Torino: P. Gibraudi, 1973.
108p.

Don Giovanni. La Musica di Mozart e l'Eros. Trad. di
Remo Cantoni e Kirsten Montanari Guldbrandsen. Saggio
introduttivo di Remo Cantoni (Gli Oscar, 646). Milano:
A. Mondadori, 1976. 145p.

La Comunicazione della Singolarità. A cura di Mauro La
Spisa (Collana Pedagogica, 1). Napoli: Istituto Editoriale
del Mezzogiorno, 1969. 91p.

È Magnifico Essere Uomini. Libera traduzione di Luigi
Rosadoni (Una Ragione per Vivere). Torino: P. Gribaudi
[1971?]. 125p.

La Dialettica della Comunicazione Etica ed Etico-Religiosa.
A cura di Cornelio Fabro, in *Studi Kierkegaardiani.*
Brescia: Morcelliana, 1957, 359-413.

Fabro, Cornelio. *Antologia Kierkegaardiana.* Torino: Soc.
ed. Internazionale, 1952. 275p.

La Difficoltà di Essere Cristiani. Presentazione e scelta
dei testi di Jacques Colette (Dimensioni dello Spirito. S.
II. 65). Alba: Edizioni Paoline, 1967. 324p.

L'inquietudine della Fede [Antologia da scritti vari]. A
cura di Massimo Tosco (Biblioteca della Gioventù, 20).
Torino: P. Gribaudi, 1968. 112p.

Breviario. Antologia a cura di P. Schäfer e M. Bense, introd. di M. Bense, trad. di Domenico Tarizzo e Pucci Panzieri (Biblioteca delle Silerchie, 26). Milano: Il Saggiatore, 1959. 83p.

PORTUGUESE

Tratado de Desespêro. Trad. e introd. de José Xavier de Melo Carneiro. Brasília: Coordenadora Ed., 1969. 170p.

Antologia, Seleção. Trad. e notas de Ernani Reichmann. Curitiba: Editora JR, 1972. 403p.

DUTCH

Climacus, Johannes [S. Kierkegaard]. *Wijsgerige Kruimels of een Kruimeltje Filosofie. Meditaties over Humaniteit en Christendom* [Vert. door J. Sperna Weiland]. Utrecht: J. Bijleveld, 1955. 151p.

Fragmenten Uitgekozen en Ingeleid door W.Leendertz. Uit het Deens vert. met medew. van N. Boelen-Ranneft. Haarlem: De Erven F. Bohn, 1955. 276p.

Johannes Climacus. De Omnibus Dubitandum Est. Vertaald, ingeleid en toegelicht door Johan Grooten [Met *In Memoriam J. Grooten* door E. de Bruyne]. (Klassieke Galerij, 110). Amsterdam: Wereldbibliotheek, 1957. 88p.

Een Keuze uit Zijn Dagboeken. Vert. en ingeleid door H. A. van Munster (Prisma-boeken, 283). Utrecht: Het Spectrum, 1957. 197p.

Het Begrip Angst. Een Eenvoudige Psychologische Meditatie, die Heenwijst naar het Dogmatisch Probleem van de Erfzonde door Vigilius Haufniensis [Begrebet Angest]. Uit het Deens vert., ingel., en van aantek. voorzien door J. Sperna Wieland. Utrecht: Erven J. Bijleveld, 1958. 200p.

Over het Verschil Tussen een Genie en een Apostel. Vert.
ingeleid en van Aantek. voorzien door S. van Lienden. Ten
geleide van K. A. Deurloo [Vert. van een van de: *Twee Kleine
Ethisch-Religieuze Verhandelingen*] (Eltheto brochure reeks.
Uitgeg. door de Ned. Christenstudenten Vereniging, 1).
Zeist: N.C.S.V. (Woudschoten), 1959, ix-29p.

De Herhaling [*Gjentagelsen*]. *Een Proeve in de Experimen-
terende Psychologie door Constantin Constantius.* Uit het
deens vert. door Johan Vanderveken. Ingeleid door L. Flam.
Amsterdam: Wereldbibliotheek, 1960. 144p.

Over de Vertwijfeling. De Ziekte tot de Dood. Ingeleid,
uit het Deens vertaald en van noten voorzien door H. A.
van Munster en A. P. Klaver (Prisma-boeken, 893). Utrecht,
Antwerpen: Het Spectrum, 1963. 154p.

Kierkegaard Dagboeknotities. Een keuze samengesteld,
vertaald en van biografische inleidingen voorzien door
W. R. Scholtens. Met een woord vooraf van B. Delfgaauw.
Baarn: Ten Have [1971], 280p. *Wilde Ganzen. Dagboeknotities*
1846-55. Baarn: Ten Have, 1978, 300p.

De Naakte Waarheid. Aforismen en Andere Korte Notities.
Een keuze samengesteld en vert. uit het Deens door W. R.
Scholtens. Baarn: Ten Have, 1974. 103p.

Tot Zelfonderzoek. Mijn Tijdgenoten Aanbevolen. Ingeleid
en vert. uit het Deens door W. R. Scholtens. Baarn: Ten
Have, 1974. 91p.

PART 2:
Bibliography
on Sören Kierkegaard

CHAPTER 1:
Books and Reviews

ENGLISH

1. Allen, E. L. *Kierkegaard: His Life and Thought*.
London: Stanley Nott, 1935; New York: Harper, 1936, x-210p.

book reviews:
Anonymous, *Expository Times* 47 (1936):196-197, 214;
G. d R. [Pseud.], *Critica* 34 (1936):358-364;
T. S. Gregory, *Criterion* 15 (1936):305-307;
Herbert Read, *The Spectator* 135 (1935):471; *Living Age.
The World in Review* 349 (1936):536-538;
Edward Sackville-West, *New Statesman and Nation* 10 (1935):
884, 886;
W. B. Selbie, *Congregational Quarterly* 14 (1936):114-115.

2. Anderson, Barbara Carol. *Kierkegaard*. Syracuse (N.Y.):
Syracuse Univ. Press, 1974. 155p. [A novel]

3. Four articles on Kierkegaard. *Anglican Theological
Review* 38 (1956):1-41.

CONTENTS:
Pittinger, W. Norman. "Editorial: S. Kierkegaard." 1-3;
Minear, Paul S. "Thanksgiving as a synthesis of the
temporal and the eternal." 4-14;
Wild, John. "Kierkegaard and contemporary existentialist
philosophy." 15-31;
Johnson, Howard A. "Kierkegaard and politics." 32-41.

4. Arbaugh, George E., and Arbaugh, G. B. *Kierkegaard's
Authorship. A guide to the Writings of Kierkegaard*.
Rock Island (Ill.): Augustana College Library, 1967, 431p.;
London: George Allen & Unwin, 1968, 50p.

book reviews:
A. Bharadi, *Philosophischer Literaturanzeiger* 23 (1970):
  364-366;
J. Brun, *Etudes Philosophiques* (1968):218;
S. Decloux, *Nouvelle Revue Théologique* 91 (1969):213;
M. Hanna, *The Personalist* 50 (1969):412;
L. P. Pohman, *Kierkegaardiana* 8 (1971):216-218;
J. H. Walgrave, *Tijdschrift voor filosofie* 30 (1968):795.

5. Bain, John A. *Sören Kierkegaard, his Life and Religious
Teaching.* London: Student Christian Movement Press, 1935;
New York: Kraus reprint, 1971. 160p.

book reviews:
Anonymous, *Expository Times* 47 (1936):196-197, 215-216;
G. H. [Pseud.], *Church Quarterly Review* 122 (1936):147-149;
W. B. Selbie, *Congregational Quarterly* 14 (1936):114-115.

6. Becker, Ernest. *The Denial of Death* [Kierkegaard].
New York: The Free Press, 1973, 314p.; London: Collier-
Macmillan.

7. .Bedell, George C. *Kierkegaard and Faulkner. Modalities
of Existence.* Baton Rouge (La.): Louisiana State Univ.
Press, 1972. 261p.

8. Bell, Richard H., and Hustwit, Ronald E., eds. *Essays
on Kierkegaard and Wittgenstein: On Understanding the Self.*
College of Wooster, 1978.

9. Bonifazi, Conrad. *Christendom Attacked. A Comparison
of Kierkegaard and Nietzsche.* London: Rockliffe, 1953. 190p.

book reviews:
E. L. Allen, *Expository Times* 65 (1953-54):73;
A. Levi, *Dublin Review* 119 (1955):364-366;
R. G. Lunt, *Hibbert Journal* 52 (1953-54):207-208;
Carl Michalson, *Religion in Life* 24 (1954):152-153.

10. Brandt, Frithiof. *Sören Kierkegaard, 1813-1855. His
Life, his Works.* Trans. by Ann R. Born (Danes of the present
and past). Copenhagen: Det Danske Selskab, 1963. 110p.

11. Bykhovskii, Bernard Emmanuilovich. *Kierkegaard.* Trans.
by Henry F. Mins (Philosophical currents, 16). Atlantic
Highlands (N.J.): Humanities Press, 1977, 122p.; Amsterdam:
B. R. Grüner B.V., 1976, ix-122p.

book review:
Howard L. Parsons, *Philosophy and Phenomenological Research* 39 (1978):139-140.

12. Carnell, Edward J. *The Burden of Sören Kierkegaard.*
Grand Rapids: Eerdmans, 1965, 174p.; Exeter (Devon.):
The Paternoster Press, 1966, 174p.

13. Chaning-Pearce, M. *The Terrible Crystal. Studies in
Kierkegaard and Modern Christianity.* London: Kegan Paul,
Trench, Trubner, 1940, xvii-232p.

    book review:
    G. C. S. [Pseud.], *Journal of Philosophy* 39 (1942):306-307.

14. Chaning-Pearce, M. *Sören Kierkegaard. A Study.*
New York: Devin-Adair, 1947; London: Clarke, 1948, 104p.
(Modern Christian revolutionaries, Donald Attwater, ed., 6)

    book review:
    George Seaver, *The Nineteenth Century* 139 (1946):287-291.

--   Chestov (see Shestov)

15. Cole, J. Preston. *The Problematic Self in Kierkegaard
and Freud.* New Haven (Conn.), London: Yale Univ. Press,
1971. 244p.

    book reviews:
    A. Belforte, *Filosofia* 23 (1972):322-324;
    H. Hofstee, *Bijdragen* 35 (1974):217-219;
    A. Koutsouvilis, *The Heythrop Journal* 14 (1973):233-236;
    B. S. Llamzon, *Thought* 47 (1972):472-475;
    G. L. Steugren, *Journal of the History of Philosophy*
     13 (1975):117-119;
    S. Sugerman, *Theological Studies* 23 (1972):364-366;
    J. H. Thomas, *Journal of the British Society for
     Phenomenology* 4 (1973):174-175.

16. Collins, James. *The Mind of Kierkegaard.* Chicago:
Henry Regnery, 1953; London: Secker & Warburg, 1954, xiv-
304p.; Chicago: Regnery, 1965, xii-308p.

    book reviews:
    M. T. Antonelli, *Giornale di Metafisica* 12 (1957):255-256;
    H. S. Broudy, *Philosophy and Phenomenological Research*
     15 (1954-55):443-445;
    A. P. Dobsevage, *Journal of Philosophy* 53 (1956):336-340;
    A. Duhrssen, *Ethics* 66 (1956):230-231;

R. Harper, *New Scholasticism* 28 (1954):349-351;
M. Harrington, *Commonweal* 59 (1953):289-290;
P. L. Holmer, *Meddelelser fra S.K. Selskabet.* 5 (1954):
1-18;
W. Kaufmann, *Kenyon Review* 16 (1954):486-490;
A. D. Kelley, *Anglican Theological Review* 36 (1954):
302-304;
H. Kuhn, *Philosophische Rundschau* 9 (1961):76-77;
J. V. Mullaney, *The Thomist* 17 (1954):261-264;
D. H. Rhoades, *The Personalist* 35 (1954):400;
J. H. Thomas, *Hibbert Journal* 54 (1955-56):207-208;
J. Wild, *Modern Schoolman* 32 (1955):186-190.

17.   Crites, Stephen Decatur. *In the Twilight of Christendom.*
Hegel vs. Kierkegaard on Faith and History (AAR studies in
religion, 2). Chambersburg (Pa.): American Academy of
Religion, Wilson College, 1972. 109p.

18.   Croxall, T. H. *Kierkegaard Studies. With Special*
Reference to (a) The Bible, (b) Our Own Age. Foreword by
Lord Lindsay of Birker. London: Lutterworth, 1948; New York:
Roy, 1956, 227p.

     book reviews:
     J. Drever, *Philosophical Quarterly* 1 (1950):90-91;
     A. M. Fairweather, *Philosophical Quarterly* 1 (1950-51):90.

19.   Croxall, T. H. *Kierkegaard Commentary.* New York:
Harper; London: Nisbet, 1956, 263p.

     book reviews:
     P. Le Fevre, *Journal of Philosophy* 37 (1957):56-57;
     J. V. Mullaney, *The Thomist* 20 (1957):379;
     P. Ramsey, *Review of Religion* 21 (1956-57):202-205;
     J. H. Thomas, *Hibbert Journal* 55 (1956-57):206-208.

20.   Dahl, Arthur, ed. *Sören Kierkegaard's Pilgrimage to*
Jutland. Prepared by Arthur Dahl. Drawings by Ebbe Sadolin.
Trans. from Danish by T. H. Croxall. Ringkjobing (Danish
Tourist Association), 1948. 56p.

21.   Dewey, Bradley R. *The New Obedience. Kierkegaard on*
Imitating Christ. Foreword by Paul L. Homer (Corpus Book).
Washington-Cleveland: Corpus Books, 1968, xxv-247p.

22.   Diem, Hermann. *Kierkegaard: an Introduction.* Trans.
by David Green. Richmond (Va.): John Knox Press, 1966. 124p.

23.   Diem, H.   *Kierkegaard's Dialectic of Existence.*   Trans.
from German by H. Knight.   London: Oliver & Boyd, 1959,
viii-218p.

24.   Duncan, Elmer H.   *Sören Kierkegaard.*   With an additional
chapter by Danny Floyd Walker (*Makers of the Modern Theological Mind*).   Waco (Texas): Word Books, 1976.   155p.

   book review:
   E. G. Lawry, *Southwestern Journal of Philosophy* (1977):
   197-198.

25.   Dupré, Louis K.   *Kierkegaard as Theologian. The Dialectic of Christian Existence.*   New York: Sheed & Ward, 1963,
xx-229p.

   book reviews:
   J. M. Demske, *Thought* 39 (1964):303-306;
   M. R. Holloway, *Modern Schoolman* 42 (1964-65):121-122;
   P. Holmer, *Journal of Religion* 43 (1963):255-256;
   Q. Lauer, *Theological Studies* 24 (1963):510-512;
   R. E. Santoni, *Philosophy and Phenomenological Research*
   25 (1964-65):301-302.

26.   Eller, Vernard M.   *Kierkegaard and Radical Discipleship.
A New Perspective.*   Princeton (N.J.): Princeton Univ. Press,
1968, xii-445p.

   book reviews:
   J. Collins, *Modern Schoolman* 46 (1968-69):63-64;
   S. Decloux, *Nouvelle Revue Théologique* 91 (1969):213.

27.   Elrod, John W.   *Being and Existence in Kierkegaard's
Pseudonymous Works.*   Princeton (N.J.): Princeton Univ. Press,
1975.   271p.

28.   Friedmann, Rudolph.   *Kierkegaard. The Analysis of the
Psychological Personality.*   London: Peter Nevill, 1949;
New York: New Directions, 1950, 68p.

   book review:
   V. Massuh, *Notas y Estudios de Filosofía* 4 (1953):255-259.

29.   Fullford, Francis W.   *Sören Aabye Kierkegaard. A Study.*
Cambridge: Wallis, 1913.   75p.

30.   Garelick, Herbert M.   *The Anti-Christianity of Kierkegaard. A Study of* Concluding Unscientific Postscript.
's Gravenhage: Martinus Nijhoff, 1965, vii-73p.; New York:

Humanities Press, 1966, 73p.

book reviews:
P. Fuss, *Journal of the History of Philosophy* 5 (1967):
180-183;
A. Wildermuth, *Studia Philosophica* 28 (1968):210-213.

31. Gates, John A. *The Life and Thought of Kierkegaard for Everyman*. Philadelphia: The Westminster Press, 1960, 172p.; London: Hodder, 1961.

book review:
W. L., *The Personalist* 42 (1961):439-440.

32. Gates, John A. *Christendom Revisited. A Kierkegaardian View of the Church Today*. Philadelphia: Westminster Press, 1963. 176p.

33. Geismar, Eduard. *Lectures on the Religious Thought of Sören Kierkegaard*. With an introduction by David F. Swenson. Minneapolis (Minn.): Augsburg, xlix-97p.

book reviews:
C. H. Moehlmann, *Church History* 8 (1938):208-209;
D. V. Steere, *American-Scandinavian Review* (1938):277-278.

34. George, Arapura Ghevarghese. *The First Sphere. A Study in Kierkegaardian Aesthetics*. Bombay: Asia Publishing House, 1966. 80p.

35. Gill, Jerry H., ed. *Essays on Kierkegaard*. Minneapolis: (Minn.): Burgess, 1969. 197p.

CONTENTS:
Part One: The Philosophical Context, 1;
Rohde, Peter P. "Sören Kierkegaard: The father of
  existentialism." 6;
Mackey, Louis. "Kierkegaard and the problem of existen-
  tial philosophy." 31;
Gill, Jerry H. "Kant, Kierkegaard and religious know-
  ledge." 58;
Campbell, Richard. "Lessing's problem and Kierkegaard's
  answer." 74;
Part Two: Reason and Faith, 91;
Murphy, Arthur E. "On Kierkegaard's claim that 'Truth
  is Subjectivity.'" 94;
McKinnon, Alastair. "Kierkegaard: Paradox and irrational-
  ism." 102;
Blanshard, Brand. "Kierkegaard on faith." 113;
Allison, Henry. "Christianity and nonsense." 127;

Part Three: The Ethico-Religious, 151;
Sontag, Frederick. "Kierkegaard and the Search for a
  Self." 154;
Hamilton, Kenneth. "Man: Anxious or Guilty? A Second
  Look at Kierkegaard's Concept of Dread." 167;
Thomas, J. Haywood. "The relevance of Kierkegaard to
  the demythologizing controversy." 175;
Holmer, Paul. "Theology and belief." 186-197.

36. Grimsley, Ronald. *Sören Kierkegaard and French Litera-
ture: Eight Comparative Studies*. Cardiff: Univ. of Wales
Press. [K and Moliere, Laclos, Chateaubriand, Montaigne,
Pascal, Rousseau, Scribe, and Vigny.]

37. Grimsley, Ronald. *Sören Kierkegaard. A Biographical
Introduction*. London: Studio Vista, 1973. 127p.

book reviews:
A. Koutsouvilis, *The Heythrop Journal* 15 (1974):345-347;
W. E. May, *Review of Metaphysics* 27 (1973-74):794-795;
P. M. Simons, *Journal of the British Society for
  Phenomenology* 5 (1974):93-95;
J. H. Thomas, *Religious Studies* 10 (1974):510-511.

38. Haecker, Theodor. *Sören Kierkegaard*. Trans. with a
biographical note by Alexander Dru. London, New York and
Toronto: Oxford Univ. Press, 1937. 67p.

book reviews:
D. C. Butler, *The Downside Review* 55 (1937):363-369;
R. Cant, *Church Quarterly Review* 127 (1938-39):268-294;
H. H. Farmer, *Journal of Theological Studies* 39 (1938):
  209-212;
H. Read, *The Spectator* 158 (1937):671;
D. V. Steere, *American-Scandinavian Review* 26 (1938):85;
D. V. Steere, *Christendom* 3 (1938):146-151;
D. F. Swenson, *Church History* 6 (1937):397-398;
C. C. J. Webb, *Philosophy* (London) 12 (1937):483-485.

39. Haecker, Theodore. *Kierkegaard the Cripple*. Trans.
by C. Van O'Bruyn with an introduction by A. Dru. London:
Harvill Press, 1948, 53p.; New York: Philosophical Library,
1950, xi-54p.

book reviews:
Anonymous, *Christian Century* 67 (1950):1137;
R. Bierstedt, *Saturday Review of Literature* 37 (1951):
  29-39;
T. H. Croxall, *Meddelelser fra S.K. Selskabet*. 2 (1950):
  58-60;
E. Dahlberg, *New York Herald Tribune Books* 55 (1950):26;

Ralph Harper, *Renascence* 4 (1951):79-81;
P. L. Holmer, *Philosophy and Phenomenological Research*
12 (1951-52):307-311;
D. H. Rhoades, *The Personalist* 32 (1951):412-413.

40.   Hamilton, Kenneth. *The Promise of Kierkegaard*.
Philadelphia: J. B. Lippincott, 1969.   116p.

book review:
J. J. Ansbro, *Philosophical Studies* (Maynooth) 18 (1969):
326-327.

41.   Harper, Ralph. *The Seventh Solitude. Metaphysical
Homelessness in Kierkegaard, Dostoevsky, and Nietzsche*.
Baltimore: Johns Hopkins Press, 1967.   153p.

41a.   Heinecken, Martin V. *The Moment before God*.   Philadelphia: Muhlenberg Press, 1956.   368p.

42.   Heiss, R. *Hegel, Kierkegaard, Marx. Three Great
Philosophers Whose Ideas Changed the Course of Civilization*.
New York: Dell, 1975.   438p.

43.   Henriksen, Aage. *Methods and Results of Kierkegaard.
Studies in Scandinavia. A Historical and Critical Survey*
(Publications of the Kierkegaard Society, Copenhagen, I).
Copenhagen: Einar Munksgaard, 1951.   160p.

book reviews:
C. Fabro, *Rassegna di Scienze Filosofiche* 2 (1953):289-
290;
A. L. Olson, *Journal of Philosophy* 49 (1952):427-428;
H. J. Paton, *Philosophy* (London) 27 (1952):84.

44.   Hult, Adolf. *Sören Kierkegaard in his Life and Literature*.   Chicago (privately printed), 1905.   21p.   (Lecture
in commemoration of the 50th anniversary of the death of
Kierkegaard in Haskell Hall, Univ. of Chicago.)

45.   Hohlenberg, Johannes. *Sören Kierkegaard*.   Trans. by
T. H. Croxall.   New York: Pantheon, 1954; London: Routledge,
1954, x-321p.

book reviews:
A. Fowler, *University of Kansas Review* 22 (1955):89-92;
W. E. Garrison, *Christian Century* 71 (1954):851-852;
R. A. Hunter, *American-Scandinavian Review* 42 (1954):
380-381;

H. D. Lewis, *Philosophy* (London) 30 (1955):367-369;
J. W. Mullaney, *Commonweal* 60 (1954):323-324;
R. Phelps, *Yale Review* 44 (1954):138-139;
J. H. Thomas, *Hibbert Journal* 53 (1954):97-98.

46. Johnson, Howard A., and Thulstrup, Niels, eds.
*A Kierkegaard Critique: An International Selection of Essays
Interpreting Kierkegaard by F. J. Billeskov Janson* [and
others]. New York: Harper, 1962. 311p.

CONTENTS:
Foreword. 1;
Billeskov Jansen, F. J.   "The literary art of Kierke-
gaard." 11;
Wild, John. "Kierkegaard and contemporary existential-
ist philosophy." 22;
Holmer, Paul L. "On understanding Kierkegaard." 40;
Richter, Liselotte. "Kierkegaard's position in his
religio-sociological situation." 54;
Johnson, Howard A. "Kierkegaard and politics." 74;
Slök, Johannes. "Kierkegaard and Luther." 85;
Mesnard, Pierre. "Is the category of the tragic absent
from the life and thought of Kierkegaard?" 102;
Malantschuk, Gregor. "Kierkegaard and Nietzsche." 116;
Prenter, Regin. "Sartre's concept of freedom considered
in the light of Kierkegaard's thought." 130;
Collins, James. "Faith and reflection in Kierkegaard."
141;
Fabro, Cornelio. "Faith and reason in Kierkegaard's
dialectic." 156;
Söe, N. H. "Kierkegaard's doctrine of the paradox." 207;
Lindström, Valter. "The problem of objectivity and
subjectivity in Kierkegaard." 228;
Diem, Hermann. "Kierkegaard's bequest to theology." 244;
Thulstrup, Marie Mikulová. "Kierkegaard's dialectic of
imitation." 266;
Thulstrup, Niels. "The complex of problems called
'Kierkegaard'." 286;
Minear, Paul S. "Thanksgiving as a synthesis of the
temporal and the eternal." 297-312.

book reviews:
F. J. Billeskov Jansen, *Symposion Kierkegaardianum* (1955):
18-28;
J. Collins, *The Journal of Religion* 37 (1957):10-19;
H. Diem, *Antwort Festschrift zum 70 Geburtstag von Karl
Barth* (1956):472-489;
C. Fabro, *Dall'Essere All'Esistente* Brescia: Morcelliana,
1957, 127-185;
P. L. Holmer, *Symposion Kierkegaardianum* (1955):93-106;
H. A. Johnson, *American-Scandinavian Review* (1955):246-
254; *Anglican Theological Review* (1956):32-41;
V. Lindström, *Nordisk Teologi, Festskrift till Ragnar
Bring* (1955):85-102;

G. Malantschuk, *Det danske Magasin* (1955):381-396;
P. Mesnard, *Symposion Kierkegaardianum* (1955):178-191;
P. S. Minear, *Anglican Theological Review* (1956):4-14;
R. Prenter, *Ordet og Aanden* (1952):177-189;
J. Slök, *Kierkegaardiana II* (1957):7-24;
N. H. Söe, *Nordisk Teologi, Festskrift till Ragnar Bring* (1955):102-122;
M. M. Thulstrup, *Dansk teologisk Tidsskrift* (1958):193-209;
N. Thulstrup, *Det danske Magasin* (1955):369-381;
J. Wild, *Anglican Theological Review* (1956):15-32.

47.   Johnson, Ralph Henry. *The Concept of Existence in the Concluding Unscientific Postscript.* The Hague: Martinus Nijhoff, 1972, xvii-226p.

48.   Jolivet, Regis. *Introduction to Kierkegaard.* Trans. by W. H. Barber. London: Frederick Muller, 1950, xv-233p.

   book reviews:
   Anonymous, *Times Literary Supplement* 49 (1950):361;
   J. Collins, *Thought* 22 (1952):106.

49.   Kern, Edith G. *Existential Thought and Fictional Technique: Kierkegaard, Sartre, Beckett.* New Haven: Yale Univ. Press, 1972.

   book review:
   R. Grimsley, *Journal of the British Society for Phenomenology* 2 (1971):90-91.

50.   Klemke, E. D. *Studies in the Philosophy of Kierkegaard.* The Hague: Nikhoff, 1976. 79p.

   book review:
   T. R. Flynn, *Review of Metaphysics* 30 (1976-77):767-768.

51.   Lawson, Lewis A., ed. *Kierkegaard's Presence in Contemporary American Life: Essays from Various Sources.* Metuchen (New Jersey): Scarecrow Press, 1971, xx-299p.

   CONTENTS:
   Introduction, vii;
   Essays:
   Swenson, David F.   "The anti-intellectualism of Kierkegaard." 23;
   Wilshire, Bruce W.   "Kierkegaard's theory of knowledge and new directions in psychology and psychoanalysis." 43;
   Holmer, Paul L. "Kierkegaard and logic." 60;

52. Lowrie, Walter. *Kierkegaard*. London, New York and Toronto: Oxford Univ. Press, 1938, 636p.; New York: Harper Torchbooks (2 vol.), 1962; Magnolia (Mass.): Peter Smith, 1970, 290p.

book reviews:
E. E. Aubrey, *Journal of Religion* 19 (1939):256-260;
R. Cant, *Church Quarterly Review* 127 (1939):268-294;
D. E. Emmet, *Philosophy* (London) 13 (1938):499-500;
T. M. Greene, *Journal of Philosophy* 35 (1938):663-665;
V. Hansen, *Theoria* 6 (1940):83-87;
J. C. Mantripp, *Hibbert Journal* 37 (1938-39):661-665;
J. C. Mantripp, *London Quarterly Review* 164 (1939):237-243;
W. G. Moore, *Journal of Theological Studies* 40 (1939): 225-231;
H. Read, *The Spectator* 160 (1938):25-26;
D. V. Steere, *American-Scandinavian Review* 27 (1939):84-85;
D. F. Swenson, *Christian Century* 55 (1938):847;
R. A. Tsanoff, *Ethics* 49 (1938-39):237-238;
E. Underhill, *London Mercury and Bookman* 38 (1938):168-169;
A. de Waelhens, *Tijdschrift voor Filosofie* 2 (1940):669-671.

53. Lowrie, Walter. A *Short Life of Kierkegaard*. Princeton: Princeton Univ. Press, 1942, xi-271p., and 1958, 284p.; Garden City (N.Y.): Doubleday, 1961, xii-226p.

book reviews:
W. B. Blakemore, Jr., *Christian Century* 60 (1943):139;
B. S. Easton, *Churchman* 157 (1943):19;
H. A. Reinhold, *Commonweal* 37 (1943):475.

54. Mackey, Louis Henry. *Kierkegaard: A Kind of Poet*.
Philadelphia: Univ. of Pennsylvania Press, 1972. 327p.

   book reviews:
   R. C. Solomon, *Philosophical Review* 83 (1974):244-247;
   G. J. Stack, *Journal of Value Inquiry* 12 (1978):157-159;
   G. L. Stengren, *Journal of the History of Philosophy*
   11 (1973):421-424.

55. Malantschuk, Gregor. *Kierkegaard's Way to the Truth.
An Introduction to the Authorship of Sören Kierkegaard*.
Trans. from Danish by Mary Michelsen. Minneapolis: Augsburg
Publishing House, 1963. 126p.

56. Malantschuk, Gregor. *Kierkegaard's Thought*. Trans.
by Howard V. and Edna H. Hong. Princeton: Princeton Univ.
Press, 1971. 388p. [Originally pub. in Danish, *Dialektik
og Eksistens hos Sören Kierkegaard*, 1968.]

   book reviews:
   H. Kassim, *Philosophy and Phenomenological Research*
   33 (1972-73):286-288;
   D. Z. Phillip, *Mind* 83 (1974):299-300;
   G. J. Stack, *Journal of the History of Philosophy* 12
   (1974):278-280; 538-539.

57. Manheimer, Ronald J. *Kierkegaard as Educator*. Berkeley:
Univ. of California Press, 1977. 218p.

   book review:
   J. E. Christenson, *Educational Studies* 9 (1978):326-327.

58. Martin, H. V. *Sören Kierkegaard. The Prophet of the
Absolute. An Interpretative Study*. Madras & Co., 1942. 71p.

   book review:
   N. Goodall, *International Review of Missions* 32 (1943):
   456-458.

59. Martin, Harold Victor. *Kierkegaard, the Melancholy Dane*.
New York: Philosophical Library, 1950; London: Epworth
(Philosophers' Library, 3), 1950, 119p.

   book reviews:
   Anonymous, *Expository Times* 62 (1950-51):267-268;
   J. Collins, *Theological Studies* (New York) 12 (1951):
   448-450;
   R. Harper, *Renascence* 4 (1951):79-81;
   L. Marcuse, *The Personalist* 32 (1951):411-412.

60. Martin, H. V. *The Wings of Faith. A Consideration of the Nature and Meaning of Christian Faith in the Light of the Work of Sören Kierkegaard.* New York: Philosophical Library, 1951. 132p.

61. McCarthy, Vincent A. *The Phenomenology of Moods in Kierkegaard.* The Hague: Nijhoff, 1978, ix-169p.

62. McKinnon, Alastair. *The Kierkegaard Indices, I: Kierkegaard in translation. En traduction. In Übersetzung; The Kierkegaard Indices, II: Konkordans til Kierkegaards samlede vaerker. Fundamental polyglot; The Kierkegaard Indices, III: Index verborum til Kierkegaards samlede vaerker; The Kierkegaard Indices, IV: Computational Analysis of Kierkegaard's samlede vaerker.* Leiden: E. J. Brill, 1970 [1971], xxii-133p.; 1971, xx-1137p.; 1973, xvi-1322p.; 1975, vi-ix-1050p.

    book reviews:
    Indices I-II:
     J. Collins, *Dialogue* 11 (1972):450-452;
    Indices I-II (1973):
     V. Cauchy, *Cir* (?) 1 (1973):60-62;
    Indices II-III:
     N. H. Söe, *Erasmus* 26 (1974):464-467.
    H. Deuser, *Neue Zeitschrift für systematische Theologie und Religionsphilosophie* 17 (1975):195-198.

63. Miller, Libuse Lukas. *In Search of the Self. The Individual in the Thought of Kierkegaard.* Philadelphia: Muhlenberg Press, 1962. 317p.

64. Minear, Paul S., and Morimoto, Paul S., eds. *Kierkegaard and the Bible. An Index.* Princeton (New Jersey): Book Agency Theological Seminar, 1953, 34p. (Princeton Pamphlets, 9.)

65. Nordentoft, Kresten. *Kierkegaard's Psychology.* Trans. by Bruce H. Kirmmse (Psychological series, 7). Pittsburgh (Pennsylvania): Duquesne Univ. Press, 1978, xxii-408p.

66. Paley, Alan L. *Sören Kierkegaard: Philosopher and Existentialist.* Charlottesville: SamHar Press, 1972. 32p.

67. Patrick, Denzil G. M. *Pascal and Kierkegaard. A Study in the Strategy of Evangelism.* Vol. 1-2. London: Lutterworth, 1947, xvi-234p.; xvii-413p.

book reviews:
A. de L., *Irenikon* 23 (1950):110-111;
R. Ulrich, *Isis* 38 (1948):266-267;
V. [Pseud.], *Synthese* (Bussum) 6 (1947-48):260-262;
J. H. Walgrave, *Tijdschrift voor Philosophie* 11 (1949):
302-303;
P. S. Watson, *London Quarterly Review* (1948):264-265.

68. Perkins, Robert L. *Sören Kierkegaard*. Richmond: John
Knox Press, 1969.

69. Price, George. *The Narrow Pass. A Study of Kierkegaard's Concept of Man*. London: Hutchinson & Co., 1963. 224p.

book reviews:
M. Grene, *Philosophical Review* 74 (1965):113-115;
A. L. Leroy, *Journal of the History of Philosophy*
3 (1965):136-138;
R. E. Santoni, *Philosophy and Phenomenological Research*
25 (1964-65):302.

70. Riviere, William T. *A Pastor Looks at Kierkegaard.
The Man and his Philosophy*. Grand Rapids (Michigan):
Zondervan, 1941. 231p.

71. Rohde, Peter P. *Sören Kierkegaard. The Danish
Philosopher*. Published by the press department of the
ministry for foreign affairs. Copenhagen: Udenrigsministeriets Pressebureau, 1955. 23p.

72. Rohde, Peter P. *Sören Kierkegaard. An Introduction to
his Life and Philosophy*. Trans. from Danish with a foreword
by Allan Moray Williams. London: George Allen & Unwin,
1963. 165p.

book review:
J. Brun, *Etudes Philosophiques* 20 (1965):554;
R. M. McInerny, *Modern Schoolman* 43 (1965-66):193-194;
R. P. Scharlemann, *The Personalist* 46 (1965):573.

73. Roos, H. *Sören Kierkegaard and Catholicism*. Trans.
from Danish with author's sanction by Richard M. Brackett.
Westminster (Maryland): Newman, 1954, xx-62p.

book reviews:
Anonymous, *Thought* 29 (1955):620-621; 30 (1956):158-159;
R. F. C. [Pseud.], *Dominicana* 40 (1956):61-67;
C. Fabro, *Divus Thomas* (Piacenza) 59 (1956):67-70;

D. O'Donoghue, *Irish Theological Quarterly* 23 (1956):
423-242;
P. P. Ottonello, *Gironale di Metafisica* 21 (1966):130-131.

74. Shestov, Lev. *Kierkegaard and the Existential Philosophy*. Trans. by Elinor Hewitt. Athens (Ohio): Ohio Univ.
Press, 1970. 314p.

   book reviews:
   G. J. Stack, *Journal of the History of Philosophy* 9
     (1971):392-393;
   J. H. Thomas, *Journal of the British Society for Philo-
     sophy* 4 (1973):81-83.

75. Sikes, Walter W. *On Becoming the Truth. An Introduction to the Life and Thought of Sören Kierkegaard*.
St. Louis (Missouri): The Bethany Press, 1968. 190p.

76. Shmuëli, Adi. *Kierkegaard and Consciousness*. Trans.
by Naomi Handelman. Princeton (New Jersey): Princeton Univ.
Press, 1971. 202p.

77. Sperna Weiland, J. *Philosophy of Existence and
Christianity. Kierkegaard's and Jaspers Thoughts on
Christianity*. (Philosophia religionis, III). Assen:
Van Gorcum and Co., 1951. 144p.

78. Sponheim, Paul Ronald. *Kierkegaard on Christ and
Christian Coherence*. New York: Harper & Row, 1968, 332p.;
London: Student Christian Movement Press; Westport
(Connecticut): Greenwood Press, 1975, 332p.

79. Stack, George Joseph. *On Kierkegaard: Philosophical
Fragments*. Atlantic Highlands (New Jersey): Humanities
Press, 1976, 127p.; Nyborg (Denmark): F. Lökkes Forlag.

80. Stack, George Joseph. *Kierkegaard's Existential Ethics*.
(Studies in humanities, 16). Univ. of Alabama Press, 1977.
237p.

   book review:
   W. E. Steinkrauss, *Philosophy and Phenomenological
   Research* 39 (1978):145-146.

81. Stark, W. *Kierkegaard on Capitalism*. Ledbury: Le Play
House Press, 1950.

82. Stendahl, Brita K. *Sören Kierkegaard*. Boston (Massachusetts): G. K. Hall & Co., 1976. 235p.

book review:
E. Sprinchorn, *Scandinavian Studies* 51 (1979):86-88.

83. Swenson, David F. *Sören Kierkegaard*. Reprinted from *Scandinavian Studies and Notes*, Vol. 6, No. 1. Menasha (Wisconsin): (Privately printed), 1923. 41p.

84. Swenson, David F. *Something About Kierkegaard*. Ed. by Lillian Marvin Swenson. Minneapolis: Augsburg, 1941, 173p.; revised and enlarged ed., Augsburg, 1945 & 1948, x-259p.

book reviews:
W. B. Blakemore, *Christian Century* 59 (1942):282;
K. Löwith, *Journal of Religion* 26 (1946):155-156;
H. L. Searles, *The Personalist* 31 (1950):191-192.

85. Swenson, David F. *Kierkegaardian Philosophy in the Faith of a Scholar*. Ed. by Lillian M. Swenson. Philadelphia: Westminster Press, 1949. 159p.

book reviews:
W. Hamilton, *American-Scandinavian Review* 37 (1949):
   290-291;
S. Nilson, *Philosophical Review* 60 (1951):390-394.

86. Taylor, Mark C. *Kierkegaard's Pseudonymous Authorship: A Study of Time and The Self*. Princeton (New Jersey): Princeton Univ. Press, 1975, xiv-391p.

book reviews:
P. Palmer, *Philosophical Quarterly* 27 (1977):177-180;
R. L. Perkins, *Journal of the History of Philosophy* 15
   (1977):116-118;
R. H. Popkin, *International Journal for the Philosophy
   of Religion* 8 (1977):207-209;
C. Raschke, *Kierkegaardiana* (1977):328-332.

87. Thomas, John Heywood. *Subjectivity and Paradox*.
[A study of Kierkegaard.] New York: Macmillan Co.; Oxford: B. Blackwell, 1957, 174p.

88. Thompson, Josiah. *The Lonely Labyrinth. Kierkegaard's Pseudonymous Works*. Foreword by George Kimball Plochmann. Carbondale: Southern Illinois Press, 1967, xx-242p.

book reviews:
J. Brun, *Études Philosophiques* (1968):247-248;

J. T. King, *Philosophical Forum* 10 (1971):382-384;
L. Mackey, *Review of Metaphysics* 23 (1969-70):316-332.

89. Thompson, Josiah, ed. *Kierkegaard: A Collection of Critical Essays*. (Modern Studies in Philosophy.) Garden City: Doubleday & Co./Anchor Books, 1972. 464p. [Rptd. essays plus Josiah Thompson, "The Master of Irony," 103-163; Stephen Crites, "Pseudonymous Authorship as Art and as Act," 183-229; Louis Mackey, "The View from Pisgah: A Reading of *Fear and Trembling*," 394-428; "A Bibliography of Books and Articles About Sören Kierkegaard in English for the Years 1956-70."]

90. Thompson, Josiah. *Kierkegaard*. New York: Alfred A. Knopf, 1973, 286p.; London: Victor Gollancz, 1974, 286p.

   book reviews:
   1973:
   B. C. Anderson, *Man and World* 7 (1974):300-306;
   S. Crites, *Journal of Religion* 55 (1975):235-246;
   J. Rudoff, *Dialogue* (PST) 18 (1975):26-28;
   R. J. Westley, *Modern Schoolman* 53 (1975):96-97;
   1974:
   T. R. Flynn, *The Thomist* 38 (1974):182-184;
   R. P. McArthur, *Review of Metaphysics* 27 (1973-74):
    816-817;
   J. H. Thomas, *Religious Studies* 13 (1977):101-104.

91. Thomte, Reidar. *Kierkegaard's Philosophy of Religion*. Princeton (New Jersey): Princeton Univ. Press, 1948, viii-228p.

   book reviews:
   H. S. Broudy, *Philosophy and Phenomenological Research*
    10 (1949-50), 293-295;
   J. Collins, *The Thomist* 12 (1949):380-382;
   G. P. Conger, *Review of Religion* 14 (1950):429-430;
   F. C. Copleston, *Philosophy* 25 (1950):86-87;
   L. J. Eslick, *Modern Schoolman* 28 (1951):305-305;
   P. L. Holmer, *Philosophical Review* 59 (1950):408-410;
   G. E. Hughes, *Mind* 59 (1950):413-415;
   V. E. Smith, *Thought* 24 (1949):549-550.

92. Walker, Jeremy Desmond Bromhead. *To Will One Thing. Reflections on Kierkegaard's Purity of Heart*. Montreal: McGill-Queen's Univ. Press, 1972. 167p.

93. Wyschogrod, Michael. *Kierkegaard and Heidegger. The Ontology of Existence*. New York: Humanities Press, 1954; London: Routledge & Kegan Paul, 1954, 156p.

book reviews:
W. Cerf, *Philosophical Review* 64 (1955):669-670;
J. G. Gray, *Journal of Philosophy* 53 (1956):21-22;
H. D. Lewis, *Philosophy* (London) 30 (1955):367-369;
M. Natanson, *Philosophy and Phenomenological Research*
16 (1955):56, 269-270;
G. C. Stewart, *Christian Century* 71 (1954):1336-1337;
J. H. Thomas, *Hibbert Journal* 53 (1954-55):97-98.

94. Zuidema, Sytse Ulbe. *Kierkegaard*. Trans. by David H.
Freeman (Int. Lib. of Philosophy and Theology; Modern
Thinkers Series). Philadelphia: Presbyterian & Reformed,
1960. 50p.

FRENCH

95. Agacinski, Sylviane. *Aparté, conceptions et morts de
Sören Kierkegaard* (La philosophie en effet). Paris:
Aubier-Flammarion, 1977. 254p. [essai-roman][Dé-cryptage
d'une "énigme" à partir d'une méthode inaugurée par la
psychanalyse lacannienne et J. Derrida.]

96. Bellessort, André. *Le crépuscule d'Elseneur*. In his
A travers les pays et les livres. Huit articles. Paris:
Perrin, 1926, 11-299p.

97. Bohlin, Torsten. *Sören Kierkegaard, l'homme et l'oeuvre*.
Trad. par P-H Tisseau. Bazoges-en-Pareds: 1941, viii-268p.
Appendice: Pascal et Kierkegaard, 265-266.

98. Chaplain, Denise. *Etudes sur* In vino veritas *de
Kierkegaard*. Préface de Pierre Aubenque (Annales de
l'Université de Besançon, 69). Paris: Les Belles Lettres,
1965. 102p.

99. Chestov, Leon (Sjestov, Lev). *Kierkegaard et la
philosophie existentielle*. (Vox clamantis in deserto).
Trad. du russe par T Rageot et B de Schloezer. Paris:
Vries, 1936, 384p. (Les amis de Leon Chestov). 2d ed.,
1948, 384p. 3d ed., Paris: Vrin, 1972, 385p.

book reviews:
E. Brehier, *Revue Philosophique* 63 (1938):123-124;
D. M. Emmet, *Philosophy* (London) 12 (1937):359;
B. Fondane, *Revue de Philosophie* 37 (1937):381-414;
F. Jansen, *Nouvelle revue Théologique* 69 (1937):687-688;
D. Van Steere, *Christendom* 3 (1938):145-151.

100.   Clair, André. *Pseudonyme et paradoxe. La pensée dialectique de Kierkegaard* (Bibliotheque d'Histoire de la Philosophie). Paris: Librairie Philosophique, J. Vrin, 1976.   375p.

101.   Colette, Jacques. *Kierkegaard, chrétien incognito. La neutralité armée.* Paris: Éd. du Cerf, 1968.   76p.

102.   Colette, Jacques. *Histoire et absolu. Essai sur Kierkegaard* (L'athéisme interroge). Paris: Tournai, Desclée et Cie, 1972.   284p.

103.   Condette, J. P. *Sören Kierkegaard, penseur de l'existence* (Contribution à la connaissance des auteurs). Bordeau: Kronos Édition, 1977.   166p.

104.   Cornu, Michel. *Kierkegaard et la communication de l'existence* (Dialectica). Lausanne: L'Age d'Homme, 1973.   306p.

     book reviews:
     J. Brun, *Etudes Philosophiques* (1973):233-235;
     J. Villard, *Revue de Théologie et de Philosophie* (1973):
       250-254;
     A.-J. Voelke, *Studia Philosophica* 33 (1973):224-228.

105.   Deleuran, Victor. *Esquisse d'une étude sur Sören Kierkegaard.* Paris: Ch. Noblet, 1897, iv-98p.

106.   Drolet, Bruno. *Le démoniaque chez S. A. Kierkegaard.* Joliette (Québec): Centre de Diffusion Lanaudière, 1971.   98p.

107.   Exposition Kierkegaard 1963. *Bibliothèque nationale et universitaire de Strasbourg. Sören Kierkegaard (1813-1855), exposition organisée à l'occasion du 150ᵉ anniversaire de la naissance, 18 mai au 1ᵉʳ juin 1963.* (Catalogue de Théodore et Madeleine Lang.) Strasbourg: Bibliothèque nationale et universitaire, 1963, iv-61p.

108.   Grimault, Marguerite. *Kierkegaard par lui-même* (Collections Microcosme. Ecrivains de toujours, 59). Paris: Edit. due Seuil, 1962, 192p.; 1978, 179p.

     book reviews:
     J. Brun, *Revue d'Histoire et de Philosophie Religieuses* 47 (1967):389-390;
     J. Colette, *Revue Nouvelle* 37 (1963):181-182;
     H. de Lavalette, *Etudes* 316 (1963):415.

109. Grimault, Marguerite. *La mélancolie de Kierkegaard* (Coll. "Présence et pensée"). Paris: Aubier, 1965. 310p.

    book reviews:
J. F. Catalan, *Archives de Philosophie* 28 (1965):476-477;
J. Ecole, *Etudes Philosophiques* 20 (1965):352;
P. P. Ottonello, *Giornale di Metafisica* 22 (1967):330-332.

110. Grimault, Marguerite. *Kierkegaard et l'érotisme*. Suivi de "Le Stade esthétique:Le journal du séducteur," par Sören Kierkegaard. Paris: U.G.E., 1966.

111. Gusdorf, Georges. *Kierkegaard* (Coll. "Philosophes de tous les temps"). Paris: Seghers, 1963.

112. Haecker, Theodor. *La notion de la verité chez Sören Kierkegaard*. Trad. de l'allemand par Jean Chuzeville. Anon ed.: Essais sur Kierkegaard, Petrarque, Goethe. Religion et philosophie, musique et poésie. Paris: 1934, 9-83. (Collections des Iles, 4).

113. Henein, Georges, et Wahba, Magdi, eds. *Vues sur Kierkegaard*. La Part du Sable, le Caire, mai 1955 (Soc. Orient. de Publicité), 108p. [French and English texts]

114. Hohlenberg, Johannes. *Sören Kierkegaard*. Trad. du danois par P.-H. Tisseau. Paris: Albin Michel, 1956. 384p.

    book reviews:
F. Ricci, *Pensée* (1957):139-140;
X. Tilliette, *Etudes* 289 (1956):293.

115. Hohlenberg, Johannes. *L'oeuvre de Sören Kierkegaard. Le chemin du solitaire*. Trad. du danois par P.-H. Tisseau. Paris: Albin Michel, 1960. 320p.

    book reviews:
J. Boisset, *Revue de Synthèse* 83 (1962):280-281;
J. Colette, *Revue Nouvelle* 32 (1960):467-468;
T. Quoniam, *Etudes Philosophiques* 5 (1960):543-544;
M. Vanhoutte, *Revue Philosophique de Louvain* 59 (1961): 136-138.

116. Jolivet, Régis. *Introduction à Kierkegaard*. Paris: Abbaye S. Wandrille, 1946, xvii-253p.; *Aux sources de l'existentialisme chrétien: Kierkegaard* ("Les idées et la vie). *Nouvelle* édition. Paris: Arthème Fayard, 1958, 288p.

book reviews:
J. W. Alexander, *The Philosophical Quarterly* 1 (1950):
  79-80;
P. Ayraud, *Témoignages* 11 (1946):536-537;
L. Boyer, *Dieu Vivant* 10 (1948):148-150;
Ch. Deuivaise, *Études Philosophiques* (1946):250-252;
G. Fessard, *Études* 252 (1947):134;
J.-Ph. G., *L' Année Théologique* 8 (1947):103-105;
C. Terzi, *Filosofia* 17 (1966):546-551;
S. Vanni-Rovighi, *Rivisti di Filosofia Neo-scolastica*
  40 (1948):364-365;
A. de Waelhens, *Revue Philosophique de Louvain* 44 (1946):
  448-449.

117. *Kierkegaard et la Philosophie contemporaine*. Institut
International de Philosophie. Entretiens de Copenhague,
8-15 septembre 1966. *Kierkegaard and Contemporary Philosophy*.
Colloquies in Copenhagen, 8-15 September 1966. Ed. by
Johs. Witt-Hansen, *Danish Yearbook of Philosophy* 8 (1971).
Copenhagen: Munksgaard, 1972. 204p.

CONTENTS:
Séance inaugurale (Allocutions de Johs. Pedersen,
  A. Guzzo, J. Witt-Hansen, G. Calogero, A. Mercier).
  9-15;
Billeskov Jansen, F. J. "Le climat philosophique du
  Danemark au temps de Kierkegaard." 16-21 (Discussions,
  21-36);
Huber, G. "Comment les philosophies de l'existence se
  sont-elles approprié la pensée kierkegaardienne?" 37-42
  (Discussions 42-64);
Naess, Arne. "Kierkegaard and educational crisis."
  65-70 (Discussions, 70-93);
Gibson, A. Boyce. "Existential religion and existential
  philosophy (Kierkegaard)." 94-98 (Discussions, 99-114);
Mátrai, L. "Three antagonists of Hegel: Feuerbach,
  Kierkegaard, Marx." 115-119 (Discussions, 119-134);
Lombardi, F. "Kierkegaard aujourd'hui." 135-140
  (Discussions, 140-158);
Lögstrup, K. E. "Le néant et l'action (Kierkegaard)."
  159-167 (Discussions, 167-180);
Séance de clôture (Allocutions de G. Calogero, A. Guzzo,
  M.-L. Iltis, Ch. Perelman, J. Ebbinghaus, A. J. Ayer,
  J. Jörgensen). 183-193;
Jolivet, R. "Kierkegaard, penseur existentiel." 194-200.

book reviews:
B. Delfgaauw, *Algemeen Nederlands tijdschrift voor
  Wijsbegeerte en Psychologie* 48 (1955-56):98-106;
A. Guzzo, *Filosofia* 18 (1967):180-194;
A. Guzzo, *Filosofia* (1967?):15p;
P. Mesnard, *Studi Kierkegaardiani* 267-282;
N. Thulstrup, *Table Ronde* (Paris) (1955):86-87.

118. *Kierkegaard vivant*. Colloque organisé par l'Unesco à
Paris du 23 avril 1964. Paris: Gallimard, 1966.

CONTENTS:
Maheu, René. "Allocution." 9-19;
Sartre, Jean-Paul. "L'Universel singulier." 20-63;
Marcel, Gabriel. "Kierkegaard en ma pensée." 64-80;
Jaspers, Karl, 81-93;
Hersch, Jeanne. "L'Instant." 94-110;
Paci, Enzo. "Kierkegaard vivant et la véritable
 signification de l'histoire." 111-124;
Goldmann, Lucien, 125-164;
Heidegger, Martin. "La fin de la philosophie et la
 tâche de la pensée." 167-204;
Wahl, Jean, 205-212;
Thulstrup, Niels, 314-317.

book review:
R. C. Poole, *Table Ronde* 230 (1967):139-144.

119. *Kierkegaard*. Special issue, *Etudes Philosophiques* 18
(1963). Paris: Presses universitaires de France, 1963, 279-392.

CONTENTS:
Kierkegaard, S. "La crise et une crise dans la vie
 d'une actrice (inéd. en France)." Tr. par E.-M.
 Jacquet-Tisseau, 279-298;
Mesnard, Pierre. "Le 'journal' de Kierkegaard a-t-il
 une valeur philosophique?" 299-314;
Tisseau, Pierre-Henri. "Kierkegaard et la souffrance."
 315-322;
Brun, Jean. "Kierkegaard penseur tragique." 323-332;
Lapassade, Georges. "Le deuil de la philosophie:
 Kierkegaard et Marx." 333-341.

120. *Kierkegaard and Christianity*. In *Foi et Vie* 69 (1970):
2-60.

CONTENTS:
Brun, J. "Actualité de Kierkegaard."
Viallaneix, N. "Kierkegaard ou l'anti-théologie."
Clet, J. "Une histoire presque comme les autres."

121. Koch, Carl. *Soeren Kierkegaard*. Paris: Ed. "Je sers,"
1934; Geneve: Ed. "Labor," 1934, 219p.

book reviews:
M. J. Congar, *Revue des Sciences Philosophiques et
 Theologiques* 23 (1934):512-513;
Th. Preiss, *Revue d'Histoire et de Philosophie Religieuses*
 17 (1936):46-64.

122.   Lefebvre, Henri. *Le maître en la servante*. Pièce en
trois actes representée au Théatre des Mathurins à Paris en
septembre 1954.

123.   Lilienfeld, André de. *A la rencontre de Kierkegaard*.
Liége: La sixaine, 1946. 52p.

124.   Malaquais, Jean. *Sören Kierkegaard, foi et paradoxe*.
Paris: Union générale d'éditions, 1971. 320p.

125.   Mesnard, Pierre. *Le vrai visage de Kierkegaard*.
Paris: Beauchesne, 1948. 494p. (Bibliotèque des archives
de philosophie.)

     book reviews:
     A. de L., *Irenikon* 23 (1950):110-111;
     Anonymous, *Revue de Métaphysique et de Morale* 54 (1949):
       205-207;
     P. Burgelin, *Revue d'Histoire et de Philosophie Reli-
       gieuses* 28-29 (1948-49):354-356;
     R. Ceñal, *Pensamiento* 5 (1949):504-505;
     A. Forest, *Revue Philosophique de la France et de
       l'Étranger* 75 (1950):226-227;
     M. de Gandillac, *Dieu Vivant* 14 (1949):149-151;
     L. Gardet, *Revue Thomiste* 49 (1949):589-601;
     L. B. Geiger, *Revue des Sciences Philosophiques et
       Théologiques* 35 (1951):78-79;
     A. Hayen, *Nouvelle Revue Théologique* 72 (1950):884-885;
     J. Havet, *Philosophy and Phenomenological Research*
       11 (1950-51):234;
     F. Heidsieck, *Revue des Sciences Humaines* (1949):119-123;
     H. Kuhn, *Journal of Philosophy* 46 (1949):729-731;
     L. Lavelle, *La Table Ronde* (1955):73-75;
     S. Nilson, *Philosophical Review* 58 (1949):510-514;
     H. J. Paton, *Mind* 57 (1948):522-524;
     M. E. Sciacca, *Giornale Metafisica* 4 (1949):418-419;
     L. M. Simon, *Revue de l'Université d'Ottawa* 20 (1950):
       129-130;
     V. E. Smith, *Thought* 24 (1949):170-171.

126.   Mesnard, Pierre. *Kierkegaard. Sa vie, son oeuvre,
avec un exposé de sa philosophie*. Paris: Presses Universitaires de France, 1954. 100p. (Coll. "Philosophes.")
3d ed., 1963.

     book reviews:
     Anonymous, *Revue de Métaphysique et de Morale* 59 (1954):
       340;
     L. Martinez Gomez, *Pensamiento* 10 (1954):501-502;
     L. Vigone, *Rivista di Filosofia Neo-Scolastica* 48 (1956):
       397-398.

127. Müller, Philippe. *Kierkegaard lecteur de Hegel.*
Basel: Verlag für Recht und Gesellschaft, 1973.

128. Nguyên Van Tuyên, J. *Foi et existence selon S. Kierkegaard.* (Présence et pensée 23.) Paris: Aubier-Montaigne,
1971. 251p.

129. Rohde, Peter P. *Sören Kierkegaard. Le philosophe
danois.* Publié par le service de presse du ministère des
affaires étrangères. Copenhagen: Udenrigsministeriets
Pressebureau, 1955. 23p.

130. Romain, Willy-Paul. *Soeren Kierkegaard ou l'esprit
d'Elseneur.* Paris-Lyon: Vitte, 1955. 180p.

> book reviews:
> R. Kemp, *Les Nouvelles Littéraires* 5 (1956).
> L. Vigone, *Rivista di Filosofia Neo-Scolastica* 49 (1957):
>   286-287.

131. Roos, H. *Kierkegaard et le catholicisme.* Traduit du
danois par André Renard (Philosophes contemporains. Textes
et Etudes, 7). Louvain: E. Nauwelaerts, 1955. 92p.

> book reviews:
> Anonymous, *Civiltà Cattolica* 107, II (1956):299-300;
> J. D. Bastable, *Philosophical Studies* (Maynooth) 6
>   (1956):241;
> B. Baudoux, *Antonianum* 31 (1956):132;
> S. Calnort-Bodet, *Etudes Philosophiques* 11 (1956):362-363;
> F. C. Copleston, *Month* 16 (1956):55-57;
> B. Delfgaauw, *Tijdschrift voor Philosophie* 18 (1956):135;
> H. Diederich, *Franziskanssche Studien* 38 (1956):436-437;
> L. Dupre, *Streven* 8, II (1955):278;
> E. F., *Etudes Franciscaines* 9 (1959):247-248;
> P. Fransen, *Bijdragen* 17 (1956):331;
> J. Giblet, *Collectanea Mechliniensia* 41 (1956):657-658;
> N. Gonzalez Caminero, *Pensamiento* 14 (1958):513;
> J. Herrero, *Revista de Filosofía* 15 (1956):347-348;
> R. Kemp, *Les Nouvelles Littéraires* 5 (1956);
> P. Mc. Kevitt, *Irish Theological Quarterly* (Maynooth)
>   23 (1956):82-83;
> C. Lopes, *Theologica* (Braga) 2 (1958):197-200;
> J. Terme, *Etudes Théologiques et Religieuses* 31 (1956):68;
> A. Thiry, *Nouvelle Revue Théologique* 79 (1957):323;
> H. Van Lier, *La Revue Nouvelle* 23 (1956):566;
> G. Widmer, *Revue de Théologie et de Philosophie* (1957):
>   140;
> B. Willaert, *Collationes Brugenses et Gandavenses* 2
>   (1956):414-415;
> J. L. Witte, *Gregorianum* 37 (1956):673-674.

132. *Soeren Kierkegaard 1813-1963* (*Revue de Théologie et de Philosophie* (1963)). Lausanne, 29 rue des Terreaux, 1963, 273-350.

133. Sur, Françoise. *Kierkegaard. Le devenir chrétien* (Coll. "Humanisme et religion"). Paris: Éditions du Centurion, 1967. 176p.

　　book review:
　　J. Colette, *Revue Philosophique de Louvain* 65 (1967): 558-559.

134. Stucki, P.-A. *Le christianisme et l'histoire d'après Kierkegaard* (Coll. *Studia Philosophica*, Suppl. II). Bâle: Verlag Recht und Gesellschaft; Paris: Interdoc, 1964, xvi-277p.

　　book reviews:
　　A. Contesse, *Revue de Théologie et de Philosophie* 98 (1965):58-59;
　　L.-J. Delpech, *Revue de Synthèse* 87 (1966):102-103.

135. Viallaneix, Nelly. *Kierkegaard, l'unique devant Dieu* (Collection Horizon philosophique). Paris: Editions du Cerf, 1974. 190p.

　　book review:
　　H. B. Vergote, *Kierkegaardiana* (1977):353-355.

136. Viallaneix, Nelly. *Ecoute Kierkegaard: Essai sur la communication de la parole.* Paris: Le Cerf, 1979.

137. Wahl, Jean. *Études Kierkegaardiennes.* Paris: F. Aubier, Édition Montaigne, 1938, vi-744p (Philosophie de l'esprit); réédition, Paris: Vrin, 1951.

　　book reviews:
　　R. Bespaloff, *Revue de Philosophie* 64 (1939):301-324;
　　B. Fondane, *Cahiers du Sud* 26 (1938-39):169-171;
　　H.-D. Gardeil, *Revue des Sciences Philosophiques et Théologiques* 29 (1940):126-127;
　　B. Groethuysen, *La Nouvelle Revue Française* 26 (1938): 845-848;
　　V. Hansen, *Theoria* 6 (1940):83-87;
　　R. Jolivet, *Revue Thomiste* 44 (1937-38):822-826;
　　W. Lowrie, *Religio* (Roma) 15 (1938-39):277-279;
　　J. Mercier, *Culture* (Paris-Neuilly) 2 (1938):12-23;
　　E. Morot-Sir, *Études Philosophiques* (1940):33-37;
　　D. Parodi, *The Philosophical Review* (New York) (1939):22;
　　A. de Waelhens, *La Cité Chrétienne* 12 (1938):501-504;
　　A. de Waelhens, *Revue Neoscolastique de Philosophie* 41 (1938):302-308;

T. Wiesengrund-Adorno, *The Journal of Philosophy* (New York
and Lancaster, Pa.) 36 (1939):18-19.

138. Wahl, Jean. *La pensée de l'existence* (Kierkegaard-
Jaspers) (Bibliothèque de philosophie scientifique). Paris:
Flammarion, 1951. 292p.

GERMAN

139. Adorno, Theodor Wiesengrund. *Kierkegaard. Konstruktiin
des Ästhetischen.* Tübingen: Mohr, 1933, viii-165p. (Beiträge
zur Philos. u. ihrer Gesch., 2). - Phil. Diss. Frankfurt, 1931;
Mit e. Beil. (Neue, um d. Beil. erw. Ausg.), Frankfurt am
Main: Suhrkamp, 1962, 294p.; 3, um e. 2. Beil. erw. Ausg.,
Frankfurt am Main: Suhrkamp, 1966, 323p.; Mit e. Beil.
(Suhrkamp-Taschenbucher Wissenschaft, 74), Frankfurt am Main:
Suhrkamp, 1974, 294p.

> book reviews:
> F. J. Brecht, *Kant-Studien* 40 (1935):327;
> J. Colette, *Revue des Sciences Philosophiques et
> Theologiques* 54 (1970):657-664;
> H. Fels, *Philosophisches Jahrbuch der Görres-Gesellschaft*
> 48 (1935):396-397;
> H. Kuhn, *Zeitschfrft für Aesthetik* 28 (1934):102-109;
> K. Löwith, *Deutsche Literaturzeitung* 55 (1934):156-177;
> W. Marseille, *Imago* 20 (1934):502-504;
> W. Ruttenbeck, *Zeitschrift für Kirchengeschichte* 53
> (1934):695-701;
> H. Stephan, *Zeitschrift für Theologie und Kirche*, N.F.
> 14 (1933):186-188.

140. Anz, Wilhelm. *Kierkegaard und der deutsche Idealismus*
(Sammlung gemeinverständlicher Vorträge und Schriften aus
dem Gebiet der Theologie und Religionsgeschichte, 210, 211).
Tübingen: J. C. B. Mohr (Paul Siebeck), 1956. 78p.

> book reviews:
> A. Alvarez Bolado, *Convivium* (1963):208-209;
> R. Boehm, *Etudes Philosophiques* 12 (1957):74;
> L. Dupre, *Bijdragen* 18 (1957):293-295;
> H. Fahrenbach, *Philosophische Rundschau* 3 (1962):57-63;
> L. Monteneri, *Sophia* 27 (1959):399;
> K. Oedinger, *Revue Internationale de Philosophie* 10
> (1956):515-517.

141. Baerthold, A. *Aus und über Sören Kierkegaard. Früchte
und Blätter.* Balberstadt: 1874, viii-132p.

142.   Baerthold, A. *Noten zu Sören Kierkegaards* Lebens-
geschichte. Halle: Jul Fricke, 1876, iv-141p.

143.   Baerthold, A. *Lessing und die objective Wahrheit, aus*
Sören Kierkegaards Schriften zusammengestellt. Halle:
1877, vii-99p.

144.   Baerthold, A. *Die Bedeutung der ästhetischen Schriften*
Sören Kierkegaards mit Bezug auf G. Brandes: Sören Kierkegaard, ein literatisches Characterbild. Halle: J. Fricke,
1879. 47p.

145.   Bärthold, A. *Zur theologischen Bedeutung Sören Kier-*
kegaards. Halle: J. Fricke, 1880. 80p.

   book review:
   H. Lindenberg, *Theologische Literaturzeitung* 5 (1880):
     594-595.

145a. Bärthold, A. *S. Kierkegaards Persönlichkeit in ihrer*
Verwirklichung der Ideale. Gütersloh: Bertelsmann, 1886,
viii-141p.

   book reviews:
   A. Werner, *Theologischer Jahresbericht* 6 (1887):240;
   P. F. Wetzel, *Theologische Literaturzeitung* 12 (1887):9-10.

146.   Becker, Ernest. *Dynamik des Todes: d. Überwindung d.*
Todesfurcht. Ursprung d. Kultur (The denial of death)
[Kierkegaard]. Die Übers. aus d. Amerikan. besorgte
Eva Bornemann. Olten, Freiburg i. Br.: Walter, 1976. 435p.

147.   Bense, Max. *Hegel und Kierkegaard. Eine prinzipielle*
Untersuchung. Köln: Staufen-Verlag, 1948. 83p.

   book reviews:
   H. Dempe, *Philosophischer Literaturanzeiger* 3 (1951):36-39;
   F. Grossart, *Philosophische Studien* 2 (1950):217-221;
   W. Joest, *Theologische Literaturzeitung* 75 (1950):533-538;
   F. Voltaggio, *Rassegna di Filosofia* 7 (1957):280-289.

148.   Besch, Johannes, ed. *Welt über der Welt. Worte Sören*
Kierkegaards, die nicht vergessen werden durfen. Berlin:
Christl. Zeitschriftenverlag, 1952. 88p.

149.   Billeter, Fritz. *Das Dichterische bei Kafka und Kier-*
kegaard. Ein typolog. Vergleich. Winterthur: Keller, 1965.
206p.

150. Blass, Josef Leonhard. *Die Krise der Freiheit im Denken Sörens Kierkegaards. Untersuchungen z. Konstitution d. Subjektivität.* Ratingen b. Düsseldorf: Henn, 1968. 246p.

151. Bohlin, Torsten. *Sören Kierkegaard und das religiöse Denken der Gegenwart. Eine Studie.* Aus dem Schwedischen von Ilse Meyer-Lüne. München & Berlin: 1923. 179p. (Philos. Reihe, hersg. von Alfred Werner, bd. 78.)

152. Bohlin, Torsten. *Sören Kierkegaards Leben und Werden. Kurze Darstellung auf Grund der ersten Quellen.* Im Einvernehmen mit der Verfasser übers. von Peter Katz. Gütersloh: Bertelsmann, 1925. 242p.

   book reviews:
   H. Faber, *Deutsche Literaturzeitung* 48 (1927):1297-1300;
   E. W. Mayer, *Theologische Literaturzeitung* 51 (1926):
   356-357;
   G. Stocks, *Theologischer Literaturbericht* 49 (1926):43-44;
   K. Warmuth, *Theologisches Literaturblatt* 47 (1926):201-202.

153. Bohlin, Torsten. *Kierkegaards dogmatische Anschauung in ihren geschichtlichen Zusammenhange.* Aus dem Schwedischen von Ilse Meyer-Lüne. Gütersloh: Bertelsmann, 1927, xii-592p.

   book reviews:
   W. Rodmann, *Kirchliche Zeitschrift* (Chicago) 52 (1928):
   273-276;
   R. W. Stewart, *Expository Times* 38 (1926-27):520-521.

154. Brandes, Georg. *Sören Kierkegaard: Ein literarisches Charakterbild.* Autorisierte deutsche Ausgabe, ubers. v. Adolf Strodtmann. Lpz: Barth, 1879, iv-240p; Hildesheim/New York: Georg Olms, 1975, 240p.

   book reviews:
   R. Garnett, *The Saturday Review* (London) 47 (1879):219-220;
   H. Herrig, *Magazin für die Literatur des Auslandes* 48
   (1879):105-108;
   P. Keppler, *Literarische Rundschau* 5 (1879):184-186.

155. Brandt, Frithiof. *Sören Kierkegaard 1813-1855. Sein Leben, seine Werke.* Uebers. R. Drinkuth. Hersg. in Verb. mit d. Presse- u. Informationsdienst d. Aussenministeriums (Gestalten dänischen Geistesleben). Kopenhagen: Det Danske Selskab, 1963. 122p.

156. Brechtken, Josef. *Kierkegaard, Newman. Wahrheit u. Existenzmitteilung* (Monographien zur philosophischen Forschung, 66). Meisenheim a. Glan: Hain, 1970. 234p.

book review:
E. Bischofberger, *Tijdschrift voor Philosophie* 46 (1971):
470-471.

157. Bremi, Willy. *Was sagt uns Kierkegaard? Kurze
Darstellung seines Lebens und seines Werks.* Von des Christen
Freude und Freiheit: 1956. 46p.

158. Brinkschmidt, Egon. *Sören Kierkegaard und Karl Barth.*
Neukirchen-Vluyn: Neukirchener Verlag, 1971. 171p.

159. Buss, Hinrich. *Kierkegaards Angriff auf die bestehende
Christenheit* (Theologische Forschung. Veröffentlichung 49).
Hamburg-Bergstedt: Reich, 1970. 214p.

160. Chestov (Sjestov), Leo. *Kierkegaard und die Existenzphilosophie. Die Stimme eines Rufenden in der Wüste.*
Graz: Schmidt-Dengler, 1949. 283p.

    book reviews:
    R. M. Müller, *Philosophischer Literaturanzeiger* 2
      (1950-51):28-33.

161. Dallago, Carl. *Ueber eine Schrift*: Sören Kierkegaard
und die Philosophie der Innerlichkeit (von Theodor Haecker).
(Zuerst erschienen in der Innsbrucker Halbmonatsschrift
Der Brenner.) Innsbruck: Brenner-Verlag, 1914. 48pp.
[See no. 189]

162. Dallago, Carl. *Der Christ Kierkegaards.* Innsbruck:
Brenner-Verlag, 1922. 80p. ("Geschrieben. . .1914.")

163. Deuser, Hermann. *Sören Kierkegaard, die paradoxe
Dialektik des politischen Christen: einer Voraussetzungen bei
Hegel: die Reden von 1947-48 im Verhältnis von Politik und
Ästhetik.* München: Mathias Grünewald Verlag, 1974. 254p.

    book review:
    A. Pieper, *Philosophische Rundschau* 24 (1977):140-143.

164. Dempf, Alois. *Kierkegaards Folgen.* Leipzig: Hegner,
1935. 232p.

    book reviews:
    Anonymous, *Catholica* 4 (1935):1-14;
    B. Lakebrink, *Hochland* 33 (1935):567-569;
    J. Lenz, *Zeitschrift fur Kirchl. Wissenschaft u. Praxis*
      (Trier) 47 (1936):361-363.

165. Diem, Hermann. *Philosophie und Christentum bei Sören Kierkegaard*. München: Kaiser, 1929, viii-368p. (Forschungen zur Gesch. u. Lehre des Protestantismus. Rh. 2, Bd. 1.)

book reviews:
H. Barth, *Zwischen den Zeiten* 8 (1930):446-447;
T. Bohlin, *Zeitschrift für Kirchengeschichte* 49 N.F. 12 (1930):247-255;
G. Lehmann, *Blätter für deutsche Philosophie* 3 (1930): 448-449;
E. Przywara, *Stimmen der Zeit* 117 (1929):476-477;
K. Warmuth, *Theologisches Literaturblatt* 52 (1931):108-109.

166. Diem, Hermann. *Die Existenzdialektik von Sören Kierkegaard*. Zürich: Zollikon, 1950, xi-207p.

book reviews:
W. Anz, *Theologische Rundschau* 20 (1952):26-72;
H. Fahrenback, *Philosophische Rundschau* 3 (1962):28-32;
W. Lowrie, *Theology Today* 8 (1951-52):275-276.

167. Diem, Hermann. *Sören Kierkegaard. Spion im Dienste Gottes*. Frankfurt am Main: S. Fischer, 1957. 116p.

book reviews:
H. Fahrenbach, *Philosophische Rundschau* 3 (1962):28-32;
L. Tichter, *Theologische Literaturzeitung* 83 (1958): 101-102.

168. Diem, Hermann. *Sören Kierkegaard. Eine Einführung* (Vorlesungen. Durchges. u. erw. Ausg.)(Kleine Vandenhoeck-Reihe, 185/186). Göttingen: Vandenhoeck & Ruprecht, 1964. 107p.

book review:
S. Holm, *Theologische Literaturzeitung* 91 (1966):291-292.

169. Fahrenbach, Helmut. *Die gegenwartige Kierkegaard--Auslegung in der deutschsprachigen Literatur von 1948 bis 1962 (Philosophische Rundschau 3)*. Tübingen: J. C. B. Mohr, 1962. 82p.

170. Fahrenbach, Helmut. *Kierkegaards existenz-dialektische Ethik* (Philosophische Abhandlungen, 29). Frankfurt am Main: Klostermann, 1968. 194p.

book reviews:
J. Colette, *Revue des Sciences Philosophiques et Theologiques* 54 (1970):669-671;
A. Pieper, *Philosophischer Literaturanzeiger* 22 (1969) 193-196;

W. Ries, *Philosophische Rundschau* 18 (1972):262-264.

171. Fischer, Friedrich Carl. *Die Nullpunkt-Existenz dargestellt an der Lebensform Sören Kierkegaards*. München: C. H. Beck, 1933, viii-224p.

book reviews:
T. Bohlin, *Theologisches Literaturblatt* 55 (1934):373-376;
K. Dingelstedt, *Deutsches Volkstum* (Halbmonatsschr. f. das deutsche Geistesleben, Hamburg) 16 (1934):1003-1004;
K. Leese, *Christliche Welt* 48 (1934):540-543;
K. Löwith, *Deutsche Literaturzeitung* 55 (1934):156-157;
E. Przywara, *Stimmen der Zeit* 64 (1934):423-424;
E. Reisner, *Theologische Blätter* 14 (1935):10-16;
J. Ritter, *Blatter für deutsche Philosophie* 8 (1934-35): 431-437;
W. Ruttenbeck, *Zeitschrift für Kirchengeschichte* 53 (1934):695-701.

172. Fischer, Friedrich Carl. *Existenz und Innerlichkeit. Eine Einf. in d. Gedankenwelt Soren Kierkegaards*. München: Beck, 1969, ix-350p.

173. Fischer, Hermann. *Subjektivität und Sünde. Kierkegaards Begriff d. Sunde mit ständiger Rucks. auf Schleiermachers Lehre von d. Sünde*. Itzehoe: Verlag Die Spur, 1963. 155p.

174. Fischer, Hermann. *Die Christologie des Paradoxes: Zur Herkunft und Bedeutung des Christusverständnisses Sören Kierkegaards*. Göttingen: Vandenhoeck & Ruprecht, 1970. 134p.

175. Friemond, Hans. *Existenz in Liebe nach Sören Kierkegaard* (Salzburger Studien zur Philosophie, 6). Salzburg, München: Anton Puslet, 1965. 152p.

book review:
D. Hoffmann, *Theologische Literaturzeitung* 92 (1967): 537-539.

176. Fritzsche, Helmut. *Kierkegaards Kritik an der Christenheit* (Arbeiten zur Theologie, Reihe 1, H. 27). Stuttgart: Calwer Verlag, 1966. 84p. (Lizenz d. Evang. Verl.-Anst., Berlin.)

177. Geismar, Eduard. *Sören Kierkegaard*. Gütersloh: Bertelsmann, 1925. 51p. (Ogs. m. tit.:) Studien des apologetischen Seminars, hersg. von Carl Stange, n. 13, ibid. eod. 51p.

178. Geismar, Eduard. *Sören Kierkegaard. Seine Lebens-
entwicklung und seine Wirksamkeit als Schriftsteller.* Unter
Mitwirkung des Verfassers aus dem Dänischen übersetzt von
E. Krüger und L. Geismar. 6 Teile. Göttingen: Vandenhoek
& Ruprecht, 1927-1929, vi-672p.

> book reviews:
> T. Bohlin, *Zeitschrift für Kirchengeschicht* 49 (N.F. 12)
>   (1930):247-255;
> M. Gierens, *Scholastik* 5 (1930):404-406;
> E. Hirsch, *Theologische Literaturzeitung* 54 (1929):224-230;
> G. Kochheim, *Eckart* 4 (1928):228; 524-526;
> A. Liebert, *Kantstudien* 38 (1933):452-454.

179. Gemmer, Anders, und Messer, August. *Sören Kierkegaard und
Karl Barth.* Stuttgart: Strecker & Schroder, 1925, xii-307p.
(I. *Sören Kierkegaard. Sein Leben und sein Werk.* Von Anders
Gemmer, 1-133; II. *Karl Barth.* Von August Messer, 135-302.)

> book reviews:
> H. Getzeny, *Una Sancta* 3 (1927):216-220;
> A. Kuberle, *Deutsche Literaturzeitung* 47 (N.F. 3)(1926):
>   1830-1834.

180. Gerdes, Hayo. *Das Christus bild. Sören Kierkegaards
Verglichen mit d. Christologie Hegels und Schleiermachers.*
Düsseldorf: Diedericks, 1960. 216p.

> book reviews:
> H. Fahrenbach, *Philosophische Rundschau* 3 (1962):74-75;
> P. Henrici, *Gregorianum* 48 (1967):729-731;
> P. Henrici, *Archives de Philosophie* 31 (1968):57-58;
> C. G. Schweitzer, *Hegel-Studien* 2 (1963):334-336.

181. Gerdes, Hayo. *Das Christusverständnis des jungen
Kierkegaard. Ein Beitr. z. Erläuterung d. Paradox-Gedankens.*
Itzehoe: Verlag Die Spur, 1962. 89p.

182. Gerdes, Hayo. *Sören Kierkegaard. Leben und Werk*
(Sammlung Göschen, 1221). Berlin: de Gruyter, 1966. 134p.

183. Gerdes, Hayo. *Der geschichtliche biblische Jesus oder
der Christus der Philosophen. Erwägungen z. Christologie
Kierkegaards, Hegels und Schleiermachers* (Radicale Mitte, 5).
2 Aufl. Berlin: Verlag Die Spur, 1974. 230p.

184. Giess, Ludwig. *Liebe als Freiheit. Eine Kierkegaard-
Aneignung.* Temeschburg: Anwenden & Sohn, 1939. 54p.

185.   Gilg, Arnold. *Sören Kierkegaard*. München: C. Kaiser,
1926, viii-231p.

   book reviews:
W. Rodemann, *Kirchliche Zeitschrift* (Chicago) 50 (1926):
  299-305;
F. Sawicky, *Zeitschrift für Religionspsychologie* 1 (1928):
  94-95;
H. Schlier, *Christliche Welt* 40 (1926):1073-1074.

186.   Goetz, Diego Hanns. *Über Sören Kierkegaard: "In vino
veritas" und "Unterschiedliche Gedanken über die Ehe gegen
Einwendungen."* In his *Das Vaterunser der Liebenden*. Wien:
Herald, 1952, 59-160.

187.   Grau, Gert-Günther. *Die Selbstauflösung des christlichen
Glaubens. Eine religionsphilosophische Studie über Kierkegaard*. Frankfurt am Main: Schulte-Bulmke, 1963. 344p.

188.   Guarda, Victor. *Kierkegaardstudien: Mit besonderer
Berücksichtigung des Verhältnisses Kierkegaards zu Hegel*.
(Beihefte zur Zeitschrift für philosophische Forschung 34).
Meisenheim: Hain, 1975, viii-98p.

189.   Haecker, Theodor. *Sören Kierkegaard und die Philosophie
der Innerlichkeit*. München: J. F. Schreiber, 1913; Innsbruck:
Brenner-Verlag, 71p.

   book reviews:
F. Blei, *Die weissen Blätter* 1 (1914):92-94;
C. Dallago, *Ueber eine Schrift*: Sören Kierkegaard und
  die Philosophie der Innerlichkeit (von Theodor Haecker).
  Innsbruck: 1914, 48p.

190.   Haecker, Theodor. *Der Begriff der Wahrheit bei Sören
Kierkegaard*. Innsbruck: Brenner-Verlag, 1932. 76p.

191.   Haecker, Theodor. *Der Buckel Kierkegaards*. Geleit-
wort von Richard Seewald. Zürich: Thomas Verlag, 1947. 102p.

   book reviews:
J. Collins, *Theological Studies* 9 (1948):479-481;
C. Fabro, *Humanitas* 2 (1947):1053-1054;
F. Hansen-Löve, *Wort und Wahrheit* 2 (1947):492-496;
P. L. Holmes, *Philosophy and Phenomenological Research*
  12 (1951-52):307-311;
D. H. Rhoades, *The Personalist* 32 (1951):412-413;
F. J. Schöningh, *Hochland* 40 (1947-48):384-386.

192. Hagen, Edward von. *Abstraktion und Konkretion bei Hegel und Heidegger.* Bonn: Bouvier, 1969. 108p.

193. Heiss, Robert. *Die grossen Dialektiker des 19. Jahrhunderts. Hegel, Kierkegaard, Marx.* Koln: Kiepenheuer und Wilsch, 1963. 437p.

194. Henningsen, Bernd. *Poul Martin Möller oder die dänische Erziehung des Sören Kierkegaard. Eine krit. Monographie mit e. ersten Übers. seiner Abhandlung über d. "Affectation"* (Studien zur Politikwissenschaft)(Studienreihe Humanitas). Frankfurt am Main: Akademische Verlagsgesellschaft, 1973. 134p.

195. Himmelstrup, J. *Sören Kierkegaards Sokratesauffassung.* Mit einem Vorwort von Gerh. v. Mutius. Neumünster i. Holst: K. Wachholz, 1927. 274p.

   book review:
   R. Schottlaender, *Philosophischer Anzeiger* 4 (1929-30): 27-41.

196. Hirsch, Emanuel. *Kierkegaard-Studien.* 1 Bd.: 1. Zur inneren Geschichte 1835-41; 2. Der Dichter (Studien des apologetischen Seminars. Hrsg. von Carl Stange, 29 & 31 Heft), Gutersloh: C. Bertelsmann, 1930-33, xii-128-318p. 2 Bd.: Der Denker (Studien. . .32 & 36 Heft), ibid. eod., ix-156-359p.

   book reviews:
   K. Beth, *Zeitschrift für Religionspsychologie* 6 (1933): 91-92;
   T. Bohlin, *Theologisches Literaturblatt* 52 (1931):305-311;
   M. J. Congar, *Revue des Sciences Philosophiques et Theologiques* 23 (1934):512-513;
   E. Geismar, *Zeitschrift für Kirchengeschicht* 55 (1936): 424-429;
   K. E. J. Jorgensen, *The Lutheran Church Quarterly* 7 (1934):430-431;
   H. Preuss, *Theologie der Gegenwart* 25 (1931):54-55, 61-63;
   W. Rodemann, *Kirchliche Zeitschrift* (Chicago) 55 (1931): 359; 57 (1933):107-110, 619; 58 (1934):625-627.

197. Hirsch, Emanuel. *Wege zu Kierkegaard.* Berlin: Die Spur, 1968. 135p.

   CONTENTS:
   "Die Stellung von Kierkegaards *Entweder-Oder* in der Literatur- und Geistesgeschichte." 9-19;
   "Kierkegaard als Erzähler." 20-33 (orig. pub. 1956);
   "Kierkegaards Antigone und Ibsens Frau Alving." 34-53 (orig. pub. 1967);

"Kierkegaards Sprache und Stil." 54-59 (orig. pub. 1955);
"Anhang: Kierkegaards gelegentliche Reflexionen über die
Sprache." 60-64;
"Die Umbildung des überlieferten Vorsehungsglaubens
durch Sören Kierkegaard." 65-112;
"Kierkegaards letzter Streit." 113-124 (orig. pub. 1953);
"Dank an Sören Kierkegaard." 125-131 (orig. pub. 1963).

198. Hoehne, Edmund. *Deutsche, Dänen und Kierkegaard.
Roman*. Hamburg: Ag. d. Rauhen Hauses, 1948. 279p.

199. Hofe, Gerhard vom. *Die Romantikkritik Sören Kierkegaards*. (Goethezeit 6.) Frankfurt am Main: Athenäum, 1972.
194p.

200. Hoffding, Harald. *Sören Kierkegaard als Philosoph.*
Übers. von A. Dorner u. Chr. Schrempf. Mit einem Vorwort
von Christoph Schrempf. Stuttgart: F. Frommann, 1896, x-170p.
(Frommanns Klassiker der Philosophie, III.) 2. durchges.
Aufl. ibid. 1902, 167p.; 3. deutsche, nach der letzten
 1919 dänische Ausg., geänderte Aufl., ibid. 1922, 167p. M.
protr.; 4. Aufl. ibid. eod., 167p.

   book reviews:
   E. Adickes, *Philosophical Review* 8 (1899):282-283;
   J. G. Appledorn, *Theologisch Tijdschrift* 34 (1900):227-260;
   W. Dilthey, *Archiv für Geschicht der Philosophie* 12
    (1899):358-360;
   A. Heubaum, *Archiv für Geschicht der Philosophie* (Abth.
    1 von: *Archiv für Philosophie*) 12 (N.F. 5) (1899):
    358-360;
   A. Heubaum, *Preussische Jahrbücher* 90 (1897):50-86;
   T. J. McCormack, *The Monist* 7 (1897):136-139;
   F. Paulsen, *Deutsche Literaturzeitung* 17 (1896):1286-1287,
   F. Paulsen, *Preussische Jahrbücher* 86 (1896):609-611;
   K. Vorländer, *Zeitschrift für Philosopie und philosoph-
    ische Kritik* N.F. 111 (1897):213-222.

201. Hoffman, Karl. *Kierkegaard als Denker*. In his *Zur
Litteratur und Ideengeschichte. 12 Studien*. Charlottenburg:
1908 (viii-165p.), 26-49.

202. Hoffmann, Raoul. *Kierkegaard und die religiöse Gewiss-
heit. Biographisch-kritische Skizze*. Aus dem Französischen
übers. von G. Deggau, vorwort von H. Gottsched. Göttingen:
Vandenhoeck & Ruprecht, 1910, ix-210p.

   book reviews:
   P. Jaeger, *Theologische Rundschau* 14 (1911):163-187;
   Fr. Niebergall, *Theologische Literaturzeitung* 37 (1912):
    116-120;

Ch. Schrempf, *Deutsche Literaturzeitung* 32 (1911):
1426-1427.

203. Hohlenberg, Johannes. *Sören Kierkegaard*. Hrsg. von
Th. W. Bätscher. Deutsche Uebersetzung von Maria Bachmann-
Izler. Basel: Benno Schwabe, 1949. 455p.

    book reviews:
    W. Anz, *Theologische Rundschau* 26 (1960):166-188;
    L. Richter, *Theologische Literaturzeitung* 77 (1952):142-143;
    H. Schlötermann, *Philosophischer Literaturanzeiger* 1
    (1950):244-249.

204. Holl, Jann. *Kierkegaards Konzeption des Selbst. Eine
Untersuchung über d. Voraussetzungen u. Formen seines Denkens*
(Monographien zur philosophischen Forschung, 81). Meisenheim
am Glan: Hain, 1972. 280p.

205. Holm, Sören. *Grundtvig und Kierkegaard. Parallelen und
Kontraste.* Übers. aus dem dänischen Manuskript von Günther
Jungbluth. Kbh: Nyt Nord. Forl., 1956; Tübingen: Katzmann,
1956, 101p.

206. Holm, Sören. *Sören Kierkegaards Geschichtsphilosophie*
[*Sören Kierkegaards historiefilosofi*, dt.] Einzig berecht.
Uebers. aus d. Dän. von Günther Jungbluth (Forschungen zur
Kirchen- u. Geistesgeschichte, N.F. Bd. 4). Stuttgart:
Kohlhammer, 1956. 120p.

    book reviews:
    H. Fahrenbach, *Philosophische Rundschau* 3 (1962):11-17;
    J. Rodrigues, *Augustinus* 4 (1959):449-450.

207. Holm, Sören. *Kierkegaard. Vortrag. gehalten am 25 Jan.
1955* (Institut fur Europäische Geschichte, Mainz. Vorträge.
N. 11). Wiesbaden: Steiner, 1956. 27p.

208. Hügli, Anton. *Die Erkenntnis der Subjektivität und die
Objektivität des Erkennens bei Sören Kierkegaard* (Basler
Beiträge zur Philosophie und ihrer Geschichte, 7). Zürich:
Theologischer Verlag, Editio Academica, 1973. 354p.

209. Jolivet, Régis. *Kierkegaard*. Übers. von Olof Gigon.
Bern: A. Francke, 1948. 33p. (Bibliographische Einführungen
in das Studium der Philosophie, hrsg. von I. M. Bochenski.)

    book review:
    P. Wyser, *Divus Thomas* 27 (1949):469-472.

210. Jörgensen, Alfred Th. *Sören Kierkegaard und das biblische Christentum*. Berlin: E. Runge, 1914. 31p. 283-310 (Biblische Zeit- und Streitfragen zur Aufklärung der Gebildeten, 9 Ser., Heft 9).

211. Kampmann, Theoderich. *Kierkegaard als religiöser Erzieher*. Paderborn: Schöningh, 1949. 64p.

  book review:
  A. Hayen, *Nouvelle Revue Théologique* 75 (1953):203-204.

212. Kawamura, Eiko. *Das Problem des Weltbezugs bei Kierkegaard. Dargestellt am Begriff d. Angst* (Schriften der Stiftung Europa-Kolleg Hamburg, 24). Hamburg: Stiftung Europa-Kolleg; Hamburg: Fundament-Verlag Sasse, 1973, iii-139p.

213. Koktanek, Anton Mirko. *Schellings Seinslehre und Kierkegaard*. Mit Erstausgabe der Nachschriften zweier Schellingvorlesungen von G. M. Mittermair und Sören Kierkegaard. Vorwort von Alois Dempf. München: Oldenbourg, 1962. 179p.

  book reviews:
  A. Edmaier, *Theologische Revue* 60 (1964):382-383;
  H. Fahrenbach, *Philosophische Rundschau* 3 (1962):63-68;
  M. Theunissen, *Philosophisches Jahrbuch* 71 (1963):176-177.

214. Kühnhold, Christa. *Der Begriff des Sprunges und der Weg des Sprachdenkens. Eine Einf. in Kierkegaard*. Berlin, New York: de Gruyter, 1975, xi-183p.

215. Künneth, Walter. *Die Lehre von der Sünde dargestellt an dem Verhältnis der Lehre Sören Kierkegaards zur neuesten Theologie* (Ein Auszug des Buches erschien als Inaug.-Diss.). Gütersloh: Bertelsmann, 1927, viii-274p.

  book review:
  C. W. Hodge, *Princeton Theological Review* 26 (1928):459-459-461.

216. Künzli, Arnold. *Die Angst als abendländische Krankheit. Dargestellt am Leben und Denken Soeren Kierkegaards*. Zürich: Rascher, 1948, iv-290p.

  book review:
  H. Kunz, *Sutdia Philosophica* 8 (1948):205-206.

217. Leisegang, Hans. *Hegel, Marx, Kierkegaard. Zum dialektischen Materialismus und zur dialektischen Theologie*. Berlin: Wissensch. Editionsgesellsch., 1948. 41p.

218. Lögstrup, K. E. *Kierkejaards und Heideggers Existenz-analyse und ihr Verhältnis zur Verkündigung.* Berlin: Blaschker, 1951. 127p.

book reviews:
Anonymous, *Expository Times* 63 (1950-51):90-91;
G. Deleuze, *Revue Philosophique de la France et de l'Étranger* 78 (1953):108-109.

219. Lögstrup, K. E. *Auseinandersetzung mit Kierkegaard* (Kontroverse um Kierkegaard und Grundtvig). Ed. K. E. Lögstrup and G. Harbsmeier, 2. Munich: Chr. Kaiser, 1968. ["Mit Erweiterungen für die deutsche Ausgabe aus dem Dänischen übersetzt von Rosemarie Lögstrup." Cf. Bibliog. for 1968, Item 19680.]

220. Lorentz, E. *Ueber die sogenannten ästhetischen Werke Sören Kierkegaards. Versuch einer Deutung.* Leipzig: F. Richter, 1892. 105p.

221. Löwith, Karl. *Kierkegaard und Nietzsche, oder philosophische und theologische Überwindung des Nihilismus.* Frankfurt am Main: Klostermann, 1933. 32p.

book reviews:
Anonymous, *Philosophische Hefte* 5 (1936):104-105;
K. Friedemann, *Philosophisches Jahrbuch der Görres-Gesellschaft* 47 (1934):519-521;
K. Leese, *Zeitschrift für Theologie und Kirche* N.F. 16 (1935):94-95.

222. Lowrie, Walter. *Das Leben Sören Kierkegaards A Short Life of Kierkegaard* . Uebers. von Günther Sawatzki. Düsseldorf-Köln: Kiederichs, 1955. 237p.

book review:
H. Fahrenbach, *Philosophische Rundschau* 3 (1962):7-11.

223. Lowtzky, F. *Sören Kierkegaard. Das subjektive Erlebnis und die religiöse Offenbarung. Eine psychoanalytische Studie einer Fast-Selbstanalyse.* Wien: Internat. Psychoanalyt. Verlag, 1935, ii-124p.

book reviews:
G. Gero, *Imago* (Zeitschrift für Psychoanalyt. Psychologie 22 (1936):242-244;
A. Romer, *Archiv für die Gesamte Psychologie* 95 (1936): 571-572.

224. Lund, Henriette. *S. Kierkegaards Familie und Privat-
leben.* Originalauszüge aus einer nur als Mskpt. gedr. und
daher wenig bekannten dän. Schrift von Sören Kierkegaard's
Nichte, Fräulein K. Lund. Übers. von Julie von Reincke.
In Kierkegaard's *Ausgewählte christliche Reden.* Giessen:
J. Ricker, 1901 (xv-158p.), 121-158; 2. Aufl. Giessen:
A. Töpelmann, 1909, 140 p.; 3. Aufl. ibid., 1923, 128p.

225. Malantschuk, Gregor. *Sören Kierkegaard und seine
Bedeutung als Denker* (Eröffnungsansprache z. Buchausstellung
"Aus Kultur u. Geschichte Dänemarks," am. 14 Mai 1963 anlässl.
d. Auslandskulturtage Deutschland-Dänemark in Dortmund)
(Dortmunder Vorträge. H. 64). Dortmunt Schönhauser Str. 15:
Kulturamt d. Stadt, 1963. 15p.   Nicht im Buchhandel

    book review:
    J. Colette, *Revue des Sciences Philosophiques et Théo-
    logiques* 54 (1970):671-673.

226. Matura, Ottokar. *Die Aesthetik in der Existential-
philosophie Kierkegaards.* Wien: Verf. Verlag, 1933. 55p.

227. Meerpohl, Bernhard. *Die Verzweiflung als metaphysisches
Phänomen in der Philosophie Sören Kierkegaards.* Würzburg:
C. I. Becker, 1934, xi-131p. (Abhandlungen zur Philos. u.
Psychol. der Religion, n. 30.) Phil. Diss. Münster, 1934.

    book review:
    F. J. Brecht, *Deutsche Literaturzeitung* 56 (1935):448-451.

228. Metzger, Hartmut. *Kriterien christlicher Predigt nach
Sören Kierkegaard* (Arbeiten z. Pastoraltheologie, 3).
Göttingen: Vandenhoeck & Ruprecht, 1964. 196p.

229. Mörhing, Werner. *Ibsen und Kierkegaard.* Leipzig:
Mayer & Müller, 1928, viii-187p. (Palaestra, n. 160.)

230. Monrad, O. P. *Sören Kierkegaard. Sein Leben und seine
Werke.* Jena: Diederichs, 1909, iv-152p.

    book reviews:
    R. Bell, *Review of Theology and Philosophy* 6 (1910):
    304-308;
    K. Hoffmann, *Die Tat* 5 (1913):910-912.

231. Münch, Ph. *Relative Absoluta?* (Persönlichkeit Gottes?
Individuelle Unsterblichkeit?). Eine Auseinandersetzung
Sören Kierkegaards mit dem Geiste der Gegenwart. 2. Aufl.
Leipzig & Gotha: R. Wöpke, 1903, ii-92p.

232. Münch, Philipp. *Die Haupt- und Grundgedanken der Philosophie Sören Kierkegaards in kritischer Beleuchtung.* Dresden & Leipzig: F. Richter, 1901, iv-79p.

233. Niedermeyer, Gerhard. *Sören Kierkegaards philosophischer Werdegang.* Leipzig: Quelle & Meyer, 1909. 73p.

234. Niedermeyer, Gerhard. *Sören Kierkegaard und die Romantik.* Leipzig: Quelle & Meyer, 1909, ii-83p. (Abhandl. zur Philos. u. ihrer Geschichte, hrsg. v. R. Falckenberg, n. 11.)

235. Niedermeyer, Gerhard. *Das Dogma von der Person Jesu Christi in seinem Verhältnis zum persönlichen Heilsglauben.* Zum Andenken Sören Kierkegaards 100. Geburtstag (5 Mai 1813). In His *Die Furche.* Berlin: 1913, Hefte zur Furche, n. 1, 25p.

236. Nielsen, Christian. *Der Standpunkt Kierkegaards innerhalb der Religionspsychologie.* Borna-Leipzig: R. Noske, 1911, vi-72p.

237. Niessen, Elisabeth. *Der anthropologische Geistbegriff bei Sören Kierkegaard.* Fulda: Parzeller, 1939. 51p.

238. Nigg, Walter. *Sören Kierkegaard 1813-1855.* In his *Religiöse Denker.* Bern & Leipzig: P. Haupt, 1942, 1-105. 2. Aufl. ibid. 1946, 1-105.

239. Paulsen, Anna. *Religiosität oder Glaube. Eine Einführung in Sören Kierkegaard.* (Schule und Evangelium I.) Stuttgart: 1926 (Vortrag, 1926). Sonderdr. ibid., 1927, 19p.

240. Paulsen, Anna. *Sören Kierkegaard. Deuter unserer Existenz.* Hamburg: F. Wittig, 1955. 463p.

book reviews:
W. Anz, *Theologische Rundschau* 26 (1960):188-205;
L. Dupré, *Bijdragen* 18 (1957):297-298;
H. Fahrenbach, *Philosophische Rundschau* 3 (1962):25-28.

241. Paulsen, Anna. *Menschsein heute: Analysen aus Reden Sören Kierkegaards.* Hamburg: Friedrich Wittig Verlag, 1973. 204p.

book review:
H. Deuser, *Evangelische Theologie* 34 (1974):511-514.

242. Perpeet, Willi. *Kierkegaard und die Frage nach einer Aesthetik der Gegenwart*. Halle: M. Niemeyer, 1940. 284p.

book reviews:
O. F. Kraushaar, *Journal of Philosophy* 39 (1942):583-586;
J. B. Lotz, *Scholastik* 17 (1942):112-114.

243. Pieper, Annemarie. *Geschichte und Ewigkeit in den pseudonymen Schriften Sören Kierkegaards*. Meisenheim: Anton Hain, 1968, viii-240p. "Monographien zur Philosophischen Forschung, begr. v. G. Schischkoff, Bd. 55."

244. Pivcevic, Edo. *Ironie als Daseinsform bei Sören Kierkegaard*. Gütersloh: Gütersloher Verl.-Haus G. Mohn, 1960. 140p.

book reviews:
H. Fahrenbach, *Philosophische Rundschau* 3 (1962):69-71;
M. Theunissen, *Philosophisches Jahrbuch* 71 (1963):177-180.

245. Przywara, Erich. *Das Geheimnis Kierkegaards*. München & Berlin: R. Oldenburg, 1929, xv-176p.

book reviews:
A. Brunner, *Scholastik* 5 (1930):409-410;
E. Griesebach, *Deutsche Literaturzeitung* 51 (1930):1345-
  1353;
R. Jelke, *Theologisches Literaturblatt* 51 (1930):252-253;
A. Mager, *Benediktinische Monatsschrift* 13 (1931):91-92;
G. Mueller, *Books Abroad* (Norman, Oklahoma) 5 (1931):390;
E. Przywara, *Stimmen der Zeit* 117 (1929):477-478.

246. Rest, Walter. *Indirekte Mitteilung als bildendes Verfahren dargestellt am Leben und Werk Sören Kierkegaards*. Emsdetten i. Westfalen: H & J Lechte, 1937, xv-194p.

247. Rehm, Walther. *Kierkegaard und der Verführer*. München: Rinn, 1949. 620p.

book reviews:
M. Beck, *Review of Religion* 15 (1951):193-195;
J. Ernst, *Zeitschrift für Religions- und Geistesgeschicht* 3 (1951):89-91;
F. Grossart, *Philosophische Studien* 2 (1950):217-221;
P. L. Holmer, *Philosophy and Phenomenological Research* 12 (1951-52):307-311;
P. L. Holmer, *Philosophical Review* 61 (1952):270-273;
K. A. Horst, *Merkur* 4 (1950):229-233;
H. Jaeger, *Scholastik* 25 (1950):408-411;
W. Lowrie, *Theology Today* (1950):261-264;
K. W. Rankin, *Philosophical Quarterly* 2 (1952):375-377;
D. V. Steere, *Journal of Religion* 31 (1951):73-74.

248.   Reuter, Hans. *S. Kierkegaards religionsphilosophische Gedanken im Verhältnis zu Hegels religionsphilosophischen System.* Erfurt: G. Richter, 1913, vi-68p.

249.   Reuter, Hans. *S. Kierkegaards religionsphilosophische Gedanken im Verhältnis zu Hegels religionsphilosophischen System.* Leipzig: Quelle & Meyer, 1914, vi-131p. (Abhandlungen zur Philosophie und ihrer Geschichte, hrsg. von R. Falckenberg, Nr. 23.)

> book reviews:
> H. Dorner, *Theologische Literaturzeitung* 41 (1916):81-83;
> W. Elert, *Theologisches Literaturblatt* 35 (1914):474-475;
> H. Gottsched, *Zeitschrift für Philosophie und Philosophische Kritik* 158 (1915):117-126.

250.   Richter, Liselotte. *Der Begriff der Subjektivität bei Kierkegaard. Ein Beitrag zur christlichen Existenzdarstellung.* Würzburg: K. Triltsch, 1934, iv-110p. Phil. Diss. Marburg, 1934.

> book reviews:
> R. Fritze, *Deutsche Literaturzeitung* 58 (1937):1442-1443;
> W. Ruttenbeck, *Theologische Literaturzeitung* 63 (1938): 71-72.

251.   Rodemann, Wilhelm. *Hamann und Kierkegaard.* Gütersloh: C. Bertelsmann, 1922, vi-152p. Phil. Diss. Erlangen, 1922.

252.   Rohde, Peter P. *Sören Kierkegaard. Der dänische Philosoph.* Kopenhagen: Pressebureau des Kgl. Dän. Ministeriums des Aeusseren, 1955. 22p.

253.   Rohde, Peter P. *Sören Kierkegaard in Selbstzeugnissen und Bilddokumenten.* Aus d. Dän. übertr. von Thyra Dohrenburg. Den dokumentar. u. bibliogr. Anh. bearb. Paul Raabe (Rowohlts Monographien, 28). Hamburg: Rowohlt, 1959, 172p.; 7. Aufl. Reinbek b. Hamburg: Rowohlt, 1969, 174p.

254.   Roos, Heinrich. *Sören Kierkegaard auf der Suche nach dem wahren Christentum* (Institut f. Europäische Geschichte, Mainz. Vorträge. Nr. 30). Wiesbaden: Steiner, 1961. 32p.

255.   Ruttenbeck, Walter. *Sören Kierkegaard. Der christliche Denker und sein Werk.* Berlin & Frankfurt a. d. Oder: Trowitzsch & Sohn, 1929, xii-379p. Neue Studien zur Gesch. der Theologie u. der Kirche, hrsg. von N. Bonwetsch u. R. Seeberg, St. 25, 361-371.

book reviews:
T. Bohlin, *Zeitschrift für Kirchengeschicht* 49 (N.F. 12)
(1930):247-255;
T. Bohlin, *Theologische Blätter* 9 (1930):182-184;
A. Brunner, *Scholastik* 5 (1930):410-411.

256. Sawatzki, Günther. *Das Problem des Dichters als Motiv
in der Entwicklung Sören Kierkegaards bis 1841.* Borna-Leipzig:
Noske, 1935, vi-94p. Phil. Diss. Danzig, 1933.

257. Schaal, Helmut. *Erziehung bei Kierkegaard. Das "Aufmerksammachen auf das Religiöse" als pädagog. Kategorie*
(Pädagogische Forschungen, 8). Heidelberg: Quelle & Meyer,
1958. 128p.

   book reviews:
   H. Fahrenbach, *Philosophische Rundschau* 3 (1962):17-20;
   M. von Tiling, *Theologische Literaturzeitung* 86 (1961):
   856-858.

258. Schäfer, Klaus. *Hermeneutische Ontologie in den
Climacus-Schriften Sören Kierkegaards.* München: Kösel, 1968.
333p.

259. Schestow, Leo. *Kierkegaard und die Existenzphilosophie.
Die Stimme eines Rufenden in der Wüste.* Graz: Verlag Schmidt,
1949. 288p.

260. Schilder, Klaas. *Zur Begriffsgeschichte des "Paradoxon"
mit besonderer Berücksichtigung Calwins und das nach-Kierkegaardschen "Paradoxon."* Kampen: J. J. Kok, 1933. 472p.
Phil. Diss. Erlangen, 1933.

261. Schmid, Heini. *Kritik der Existenz. Analysen zum
Existenzdenken Sören Kierkegaards.* Zürich: EVZ-Verlag, 1966.
235p.

   book reviews:
   J. Colette, *Revue des Sciences Philosophiques et Theo-
   logiques* 54 (1970):673;
   S. Holm, *Theologische Literaturzeitung* 93 (1968):370-372;
   R. G. Smith, *Journal of Theological Studies* 18 (1967):
   539-542.

262. Schrempf, Christoph. *Sören Kierkegaard und sein neuester
Beurteiler in der Theologischen Litteraturzeitung* (Herr Wetzel
in Dornreichenbach). Ein Pamphelt. Leipzig: Fr. Richter,
1887. 32p.

263. Schrempf, Christoph. *Sören Kierkegaard. Ein unfreier Pionier der Freiheit*. Mit einem Vorwort von Harald Hoffding. Frankfurt am Main: Neuer Frankfurter Verlag, 1907. 100p. (Bibliothek der Aufklärung.)

264. Schrempf, Christoph. *Sören Kierkegaard. Eine Biographie*. 1. Bd. Jena: Diederichs, 1927, xvi-364p.; 2. Bd. ibid., 1928, iv-344p.

    book reviews:
    Anonymous, *Zeitschrift für Menschenkunde* (1929):337-338;
    M. Gierens, *Scholastik* 5 (1930):406-407;
    J. Herzog, *Christliche Welt* 43 (1929):438-448;
    H. Jancke, *Archiv für die gesamte Psychologie* 65 (1928):
      541-542;
    H. Leisegang, *Blätter für deutsche Philosophie* 2
      (1927-28):80-81;
    H. Raschke, *Protestantenblatt* 62 (1929):45-47;
    M. Stallmann, *Christliche Welt* 42 (1928):928-929;
    K. Warmuth, *Theologisches Literaturblatt* 50 (1929):182-183.

265. Schröer, Henning. *Die Denkform der Paradoxalität als theologisches Problem. Eine Untersuchung zu Kierkegaard u. d. neueren Theologie als Beitrag zur theolog. Logik* (Forschungen zur systematischen Theologie u. Religionsphilosophie, 5). Göttingen: Vandenhoeck & Ruprecht, 1960. 207p.

266. Schüepp, Guido. *Das Paradox des Glaubens. Kierkegaards Anstösse f. d. christl. Verkündigung*. München: Kösel, 1964. 292p.

267. Schulz, Walter. *Sören Kierkegaard. Existenz und System* (Opuscula aus Wissenschaft und Dichtung, 34). Pfullingen: Neske, 1967. 36p.

    book review:
    J. Colette, *Revue des Sciences Philosophiques et Theologiques* 54 (1970):668-669.

268. Schulz, Walter. *John Gottlieb Fichte. Sören Kierkegaard*. Pfullingen: Neske, 1977. 70p.

269. Schultzky, Gerolf. *Die Wahrnehmung des Menschen bei Sören Kierkegaard. Zur Wahrheitsproblematik d. theolog. Anthropologie* (Studien zur Theologie und Geistesgeschichte des neunzehnten Jahrhunderts, 28). Göttingen: Vandenhoeck & Ruprecht, 1977. 244p.

270.   Schweppenhäuser, Hermann.   *Kierkegaards Angriff auf die Spekulation. Eine Verteidigung.*   Frankfurt am Main: Suhrkamp, 1967.   247p.

   book reviews:
   J. Colette, *Revue des Sciences Philosophiques et Theologiques* 54 (1970):664-668;
   W. Ries, *Philosophische Rundschau* 18 (1972):259-261;
   K. J. Schmidt, *Hegel-Studien* 7 (1972):378-383.

271.   Seifert, Hans.   *Die Konkretion des Daseins bei Sören Kierkegaard.*   Erlangen: Reinhold & Limmert, 1929.   96p. Phil. Diss. Erlangen, 1929.

272.   Slök, Johannes.   *Die Anthropologie Kierkegaards.* Köbenhavn: Rosenkilde og Bagger, 1954.   144p.

   book review:
   L. Richter, *Deutsche Literaturzeitung* 77 (1956):168-170.

273.   Slotty, Martin.   *Die Erkenntnislehre S. A. Kierkegaards. Eine Würdigung seiner Verfasserwirksamkeit vom zentralen Gesichtspunket aus.*   Cassel: Pillardy & Augustin, 1915.   78p. Phil. Diss. Erlangen, 1915.

274.   Sodeur, Gottlieb.   *Kierkegaard und Nietzsche. Versuch einer vergleichender Würdigung.*   Tübingen: Mohr & Siebeck, 1914.   48p.   (Religionsgeschichliche Volksbücher für die deutsche christliche Gegenwart, 5. Reihe, 14. Heft.)

   book review:
   P. Schwartzkopf, *Theologische Literaturzeitung* 39 (1914): 594-598.

275.   *Sören Kierkegaard. 1855/1955. Zum Kierkegaard-Gedenkjahr vorgelegt vom Eugen Diederichs Vorlag.*   Düsseldorf-Köln: Diederichs, 1955.   30p.

276.   Steilen, Josef.   *Der Begriff "Paradox": Eine Begriffsanalyse im Anschluss am Sören Kierkegaard.*   Trier: Theologische Fakultät, 1974, xix-295p.   (Univ. of Trier diss.)

277.   Theunissen, Michael.   *Der Begriff Ernst bei Sören Kierkegaard* (Symposion, 1).   Freiburg: Alber, 1958, x-186p.

   book review:
   S. Holm, *Theologische Literaturzeitung* 84 (1959):783-785.

279. Thulstrup, Niels. *Kierkegaards Verhältnis zu Hegel,*
Forschungsgeschichte. Stuttgart: W. Kohlhammer, 1970. 204p.

book review:
Kl. J. Schmidt, *Hegel-Studien* 7 (1972):383-389.

280. Thulstrup, Niels. *Kierkegaards Verhältnis zu Hegel und
zum spekulativen Idealismus: 1835-1846. Histor.-analyt.
Untersuchung.* Stuttgart: Kohlhammer, 1972. 320p.

book reviews:
J. Colette, *Revue Philosophique de Louvain* 70 (1972):
   116-123;
A. Pieper, *Philosophische Rundschau* 24 (1977):130-133;
J. Splett, *Tijdschrift voor Philosophie* 48 (1973):470-471.

Thust, Martin. *Sören Kierkegaard. Der Dichter des Religiösen
Grundlagen eines Systems der Subjektivität.* München: C. H.
Beck, 1931, viii-619p.

book reviews:
A. Adam, *Theologisches Literaturblatt* 53 (1932):121-124;
R. Dollinger, *Die Furche* 17 (1931):419-427;
E. Geismar, *Theologische Literaturzeitung* 57 (1932):450-
   453;
F. Grossart, *Kant-Studien* 37 (1932):186-187;
H. Kuhn, *Archiv für Geschichte der Philosophie* N.F. 41
   (1932):604-606;
K. Löwith, *Deutsche Literaturzeitung* 55 (1934):13-19;
E. Przywara, *Stimmen der Zeit* 61 (1931):471-472;
E. Reisner, *Blätter für deutsche Philosophie* 6 (1932-33):
   406-408.

282. Tielsch, Elfriede. *Kierkegaards Glaube. Der Aufbruch
d. frühen 19. Jahrhunderts in d. Zeitalter moderner, realist.
Religionsauffassung.* Göttingen: Vandenhoeck & Ruprecht, 1964.
413p.

book reviews:
J. Colette, *Revue des Sciences Philosophiques et Theo-
   logiques* 51 (1967):139-140;
S. Holm, *Theologische Literaturzeitung* 91 (1966):58-60;
C. Kahl-Fuhlmann, *Philosophische Literaturanzeiger* 18
   (1965):65-70;
X. Tilliette, *Archives de Philosophie* 28 (1965):632-635;
X. Tilliette, *Revue des Sciences Religieuses* 54 (1966):
   168-172.

283. Tzavaras, Johann. *Bewegung bei Kierkegaard* (Europäische
Hochschulschriften. Reihe XX, Philosophie, 32). Frankfurt
am Main: Peter Lang, 1978. 122p.

284.   Vetter, August. *Frömmigkeit als Leidenschaft. Eine Deutung Kierkegaards.* 2. Aufl. (Die 1. Aufl. erschien im Insel-Verlag, Leipzig, 1928). Freiburg i. Br.: Alber, 1963. 275p.

285.   Vogt, Friedrich Adolf. *Kierkegaard in Kampfe mit der Romantik, der Theologie und der Kirche. Zur Selbstprüfung unserer Gegenwart anbefohlen.* Berlin: Furche-Verlag, 1928. 426p.

   book reviews:
   R. Dollinger, *Die Furche* 14 (1928):89-92;
   E. Geismar, *Zeitschrift für Kirchengeschichte* 47 (N.F.
      10)(1928):586-587;
   E. Hirsch, *Theologische Literaturzeitung* 54 (1959):260-
      262;
   H. Lilienfein, *Die Literatur* 31 (1928-29):143-145;
   K. Warmuth, *Theologisches Literaturblatt* 50 (1929):117-118.

286.   Walther, Werner. *Die Angst im menschlichen Dasein. Eine psycholog. Betrachtung über d. Angst, aufgezeigt am Leben und Werk Sören Kierkegaards* (Psychologie und Person, 10). München, Basel: E. Reinhardt, 1967. 147p.

287.   Walz, K. *Sören Kierkegaard, der Klassiker unter den Erbauungsschriftstellern des 19. Jahrhunderts. Ein Vortrag.* Giessen: J. Ricker, 1898, iv-28p.

288.   Weisshaupt, Kurt. *Die Zeitlichkeit der Wahrheit. Eine Untersuchung z. Wahrheitsbegriff Sören Kierkegaards* (Symposion, 41). Freiburg i Br.: Alber, 1973. 160p.

289.   Wilde, Franz-Eberhard. *Kierkegaards Verständnis der Existenz* (Publications of the Kierkegaard Society, III). Copenhagen: Rosenkilde & Bagger, 1969. 170p.

   book reviews:
   A. Paulsen, *Kierkegaardiana* 8: 182-192;
   A. Pieper, *Philosophischer Literaturanzeiger* 25 (1972):
      26-27;
   D. Roubiczek, *Erasmus* 23 (1971):842-843;
   G. J. Stack, *Journal of the History of Philosophy* 11
      (1973):275-277.

290.   Wolf, Herbert C. *Kierkegaard and Bultmann: The Quest of the Historical Jesus.* Minneapolis: Augsburg, 1965. 100p.

ITALIAN

291. Adorno, Theodor Wiesengrund. *Kierkegaard. Costruzione dell'estetico.* Milano: Longanesi, 1962. 404p.

292. Armetta, Francesco. *Storia e idealità in Kierkegaard.* S. I. , Dialogo. Palermo: Fiamma Scrafica, 1972. 180p.

293. Armieri, Salvatore. *Sören Kierkegaard e il Christian-esmo* (Quaderni del Cenobio, 12). Lugano: Cenobio, 1956. 72p.

     book review:
     D. D'Orsi, *Sophia* 27 (1959):265-266.

294. Bochi, Giulia. *Peccato e fede. Motivi pietistici nel pensiero di Kierkegaard.* Faenza: Tip. F. Lega, 1957. 150p.

295. Cantoni, Remo. *La coscienza inquieta. Sören Kierke-gaard.* Milano: Modadori, 1949, 430p.; (La Cultura. Biblio-teca di filosofia e metodo scientifico, 43). 2d. ed. aggior-nata e ampliata. Milano: Il Saggiatore, 1976, 403p.

     book reviews:
     E. Caruso, *Giornale Metafisica* 5 (1950):241-242;
     C. Fabro, *Meddelelser fra S. K. Selskabet* 3 (1952):134-135.

296. Cantoro, Umberto. *Variazoni zull' angoscia di Kierke-gaard.* Padova: Editoria Liviana, 1948. 63p.

297. Castagnino, Franca. *Gli studi italiani su Kierkegaard, 1906-1966* (Collana del Centro di ricerche di storia della storiografia filosofica, 2). Roma: Edizioni dell' Ateneo, 1972. 307p.

298. Castagnino, Franca. *Ricerche non scientifiche su Sören Kierkegaard.* Prefazione di Antimo Negri (Opuscoli filosofici). Roma: Cadmo, 1977. 103p.

299. Castelli, E., ed. *Kierkegaard e Nietzsche. Scritti di E. Paci, C. Fabro, F. Lombardi, G. Masi, V. A. Bellezza, P. Valori, T. Moretti Costanzi, R. Cantoni, A. Santucci.* Milano-Roma: Bocca, 1953. 281p. Ogs. m. titlen: Archivio di Filosofia, Organo dell'istituto di studi filosofici. Ibid. eod., n. 2.

book reviews:
J. Gilbert, *Nouvelle Revue Théologique* 76 (1954):881;
A. Pigliaru, *Rivista internazionale di Filosofia del
  Diritto* 31 (1954):324-329;
V. Sechi, *Meddelelser fra S. K. Selskabet* 5 (1954):10-16
  (English text).

300. Cristaldi, Mariano. *Problemi di storiografia kierkegaardiana* (Istituto di filosofia teoretica). Catania:
N. Giannotta, 1973. 197p.

301. De Feo, Nicola Massimo. *Kierkegaard, Nietzsche,
Heidegger* ("Laocoonte"). Milano: Silva, 1964. 279p.

book reviews:
A. Negri, *Giornale Critico della Filosofia Italiana* 47
  (1968):154-156;
B. Salmona, *Giornale di Metafisica* 22 (1967):112-114.

302. Ducci, Edda. *La maieutica kierkegaardiana* ("Studi
superiori"). Torino: Societa editrice internazionale, 1967.
41p.

book reviews:
P. O. Ottonello, *Giornale di Metafisica* 24 (1969):346-347;
G. Vansteenkiste, *Angelicum* 46 (1969):164-166.

303. Fabro, Cornelio. *Tra Kierkegaard e Marx. Per una
definizione dell'esistenza.* Firenze: Vallecchi, 1952. 242p.
(Pensiero contemporaneo.)

book reviews:
R. Drudis Baldrich, *Revista di Filosofia* 14 (1955):617-
  618;
N. Gonzalez Caminero, *Erasmus* 7 (1954):196-197;
G. Caporali, *Rassegna di scienze filosofiche* 2 (1933):
  284-287;
N. Incardona, *Humanitas* 8 (1953):476-479.

304. Fabro, Cornelio. *Antologia kierkegaardiana.* Torino:
Societa editrice internazionale, 1952. 275p.

book reviews:
L. Bogliolo, *Salesianum* 15 (1953):721;
G. Caporali, *Rassegna di scienze filosofiche* 2 (1953):
  284-287;
E. Prete, *Rivista di Filosofia Neo-Scolastica* 46 (1954):
  306-307.

306. Gigante, Mario. *Religiosità di Kierkegaard.* Napoli: Morano, 1972. 302p.

book reviews:
L. Caldarulo, *Rivista di Filosofia Neo-Scolastica* 65 (1973):864-865;
M. Carbonara Noddel, *Logos* (Italy) 4 (1972):520-522.

307. Häcker, Theodor. *La nozione della verità in Sören Kierkegaard.* Trad. di Lamberto Meini. Milano: Ballo, 1945. 95p. (Testi-Pretesti, 4.)

308. Jolivet, Régis. *Kierkegaard. Alle fonti dell'esistenzialismo cristiano.* Roma: Ed. Paoline, 1960. 307p.

book review:
V. Capánaga, *Augustinus* 7 (1962):260-261.

309. Klein, A. *Antirationalismo di Kierkegaard.* Mursia: Mursia, 1979.

310. Lombardi, Franco. *Kierkegaard.* Con una scelta di passi nuovamente tradotti, una bibliografia e due tavole fuori tests. Firenze: La nuova Italia, 1936,322p. (Pensatori antichi e moderni); 2d ed., accresciuta, Firenze: G. C. Sansoni, 1967, 310p.

book reviews:
A. Brunner, *Scholastik* 12 (1937):430-431;
D. Cantimori, *Studi e materiali di storia delle religioni* 14 (1937-38):136-138;
W. G. Moore, *Journal of Theological Studies* 40 (1939): 225-231;
L. Quattrocchi, *Bollitino Filosofico* 3 (1969):64-66;
D. Van Steere, *Christendom* 3 (1938):145-151;
K. Wein, *Blatter fur deutsche Philosophie* 12 (1938-39): 316-319.

311. Masi, Giuseppe. *La determinazione della possibilità dell'esistenza in Kierkegaard. Studi e ricerche III.* Università degli studi di Bologna. Facoltà di lettere e filosofia. Bologna: Zuffi, 1949. 160p.

book reviews:
A. Franchi, *Humanitas* 5 (1950):371-372;
J. R. Gironella, *Pensamiento* 8 (1952):88-89.

312. Masi, Giuseppe. *Disperazione e speranza. Saggio sulle categorie kierkegaardiane* (Collana di studi filosofici, 19). Padova: Gregoriana, 1971. 208p.

313.   Nardi, Lorenzo. *Kierkegaard e il cristianesimo tragico.*
Roma: Edizioni Cremonese, 1976. 128p.

   book review:
   G. Cagnetti, *Doctor Communis* 29 (1976):376-378.

314.   Navarria, Salvatore. *Sören Kierkegaard e l'irrazionalismo di Karl Barth.* Palermo: Palumbo, 1943. 248p.
(Ricerche filosofiche. Collezione Renda, 3.)

   book reviews:
   R. Allers, *The Thomist* 11 (1948):374-380;
   S. Gomez Nogales, *Pensamiento* 4 (1948):88-91.

315.   Ottonello, Pier Paolo. *Kierkegaard e il problema del
tempo.* Genova: Tilgher, 1972. 126p. (Includes "Studi
Kierkegaardiani in Italia," 93-108.)

316.   Paci, Enzo. *Relazioni e significati, II: Kierkegaard
e Thomas Mann* (Saggi, 2). Milano: Lampugnani Nigri, 1965.
341p.

317.   Pareyson, Luigi. *L'etica di Kierkegaard nella prima
fase del suo pensiero.* Corso di filosofia morale dell'anno
accademico 1964-65 (Corsi universitari). Torino: G. Giappichelli, 1965. 226p.

318.   Pastore, A. *Il messagio di Sören Kierkegaard.* In his
La volontà dell'assurdo. Storia e crisi dell'esistenzialismo.
Milano: Bolla, 1948. 237p.

319.   Perlini, Tito. *Che cosa ha veramenta detto Kierkegaard*
(Che cosa hanno veramente detto, 9). Roma: Ubaldini, 1968.
187p.

320.   Riconda, Giuseppe. *L'eredità di Kierkegaard e la
teologia dialettica nel suo significato speculativo* (Saggi
filosofici, 33). Torino: Edizioni di Filosofia, 1975(?).

321.   Romano, Bruno. *Il senso esistenziale del diritto nella
prospettiva di Kierkegaard* (Pubblicazioni dell'Istituto di
filosofia del diritto dell'Università di Roma. S. III. 9).
Milano: Giuffrè, 1973, xviii-321p.

322.   Sciacca, Giuseppe Maria. *L'esperienza religiosa e
l'io in Hegel e Kierkegaard.* Palermo: Palumbo, 1948. 60p.
(Ricerche filosofiche, 7.)

323. Sciacca, Michele Federico. *L'estetismo. Kierkegaard.
Pirandello.* Milano: Marzorati, 1974. 416p.

324. Velocci, Giovanni. *Filosofia e fede in Kierkegaard*
(Idee, 17). Roma: Città Nuova, 1976. 278p.

SPANISH

325. Bense, Max. *Hegel y Kierkegaard. Una investigación de
principios.* Traducción de Guillermo Floris Margadant
(Colección Cuadernos, 28). México: UNAM, 1969. 81p.

326. Bonifaci, C. F. *Kierkegaard y el amor.* Prólogo de
Joaquín Carreras Artau. Barcelona: Herder, 1963. 293p.

   book reviews:
   S. Alvarez Turienzo, *La Ciudad de Dios* 176 (1963):358-359;
   A. de Arin, *Razon y Fe* 169 (1964):433-435;
   G. Fraile, *Salmanticensis* 11 (164):595;
   D. Herrera R., *Franciscanum* (Bogotà) 6 (1964):66;
   D. Lauria, *Sophia* 33 (1965):178-179;
   P. T. Montull, *La Ciencia Tomista* 92 (1965):345;
   J. Roig Gironella, *Espíritu* 14 (1965):88;
   F. Ruiz, *Augustinus* 8 (1963):429-430.

327. Chestov, Leon. *Kierkegaard y la filosofía existencial*
(Vox clamantis in deserto). Trad. de José Ferrater Mora.
Buenos Aires: Ed. Sudamericana, 1947, 332p.; 2d ed. Ibid.,
1952, 327p.

328. Collins, James. *El pensamiento de Kierkegaard.* Trad:
Elena Lendázun (Breviarios, 140). México, Buenos Aires:
Fondo de Cultura Económica, 1958. 325p.

   book reviews:
   C. Chatte Reme, *Sapientia* 16 (1961):77-79;
   V. Rodríguez Gallán, *Universidad Pontificia Bolivariana*
     23 (1959):420-423;
   L. W. V., *Revista Brasileira de Filosofía* 9 (1959):278-280.

329. Collado, Jésus-Antonio. *Kierkegaard y Unamuno. La
existencia religiosa* (Biblioteca hispanica de filosofía, 34).
Madrid: Gredos, 1962. 571p.

   book reviews:
   S. Alvarez Turienzo, *La Ciudad de Dios* 175 (1962):368-369;
   Sor Maria Candida, *Sapientia* 19 (1964):235-236;

G. Gutierez, *Estudios Filosóficos* 12 (1963):560-561;
G. de Sotiello, *Naturaleza y Gracia* 11 (1964):361-362;
J. Yague, *Augustinus* 8 (1963):137-138.

330. Estelrich y Artigues, Joan. *Sören Kierkegaard*. In his
Entre la vida y els llibres. Barcelona: Llibreria catalonia;
El Ram d'olivera, 1926 (344p.), 63-218.

331. Faîré, Luis. *Unamuno, William James, Kierkegaard
y otros ensayos*. Buenos Aires: Editorial La Aurora, 1967.
270p.

332. *Filosofia. Revista do Centro de Estudos Escolásticos*.
Lisboa, Ano II, No. 8 (Numéro consacré à S. Kierkegaard).
Lisboa: Centro de Estudos Escolásticos, 1956, 209-280.

333. Haecker, Theodor. *La joroba de Soren Kierkegaard*.
Trad. de Valentín Gracía Yebra. Estudio preliminar sobre la
filosofia de K. por Ramón Roquer. Madrid: Ed. Rialp, 1948.
197p. (Biblioteca del pensamiento actual.)

   book reviews:
   B. Trejos Areila, *Ideas y Valores* 2 (1952-53):755-757;
   C. Láscaris-Comneno, *Revista de Filosofia* 8 (1949):327;
   V. Massuh, *Notas y Estudios de Filosofía* 4 (1953):255-259;
   F. Secadas, *Revista de Psicología General y Aplicada*
     7 (1952):371-372.

334. Hoeffding, Harald. *Sören Kierkegaard*. Prólogo y
traducción por F. Vela. 2d ed. Madrid: Rev. de Occidente,
1949. 219p.

335. Jolivet, Régis. *Introducción a Kierkegaard*. Traducción
española de D. Manuel Rovira. Madrid: Editorial Greeos,
1950, 335p.; Buenos Aires: El Ateneo, 1951.

   book reviews:
   R. Conde, *Convivium* 2 (1957):196-197;
   C. Láscaris Comneno, *Arbor* 19 (1951):571-572.

336. Jolivet, Régis. *El existencialismo de Kierkegaard*.
Traducción del francés por María Mercedes Bergadá. Madrid
& Buenos Aires: Espasa-Calpe Argentina, 1952. 118p.
(La filosofia de nuestro tiempo.)

337. Kampmann, Theoderich. *Kierkegaard como educador religioso*. Trad. por José Artigas. Madrid: C.S.I.C. (Instituto

de Pedagogia "San José de Calasane), 1953.   82p.

book reviews:
J. M. Velez Cantarell, *Arbor* 27 (1954):106-107;
S. de Montsonis, *Estudios Franciscanos* 55 (1954):515-516.

338. *Kierkegaard vivo*, [por] *Jean-Paul Sartre y otros.*
Coloquio organizado por la Unesco en París, del 21 al 23 de
abril de 1964. Discurso inaugural de René Maheu. Trad. del
francés por Andrés-Pedro Pascual (Col. El libro de Bolsillo,
131). 2d ed. Madrid: Alianza Ed., 1970. 243p.

339. Petroccione, Alfredo. *La vida estética en el pensamiento*
de Kierkegaard (Symposium sobre existencialismo, 4). Rosario:
Universidad del Litoral - Instituto de Filosofía, 1955.   26p.

340. Rohde, Peter P. *Sören Kierkegaard. El filósofo danés.*
Publicado por la sección de prensa del ministerio de asuntos
extranjeros. Copenhagen: Udenrigsministeriets pressebureau,
1955. 23p.

341. Rivero Astengo, Agustin. *Sören Kierkegaard, el buscactor*
de Dios. Ensayo historico-filosófico. Buenos Aires: Emecé,
1949. 101p. (Selección Emecé de obras contemporáneas.)

342. Roos, H. *Sören Kierkegaard y el catolicismo.* Trad. de
l'all. par J. Oyarzun (Razón y fe, 40). Madrid: Razón y Fe,
1959, 1961. 106p.

book reviews:
A. Alvarez de Linera, *Revista de Filosofía* 19 (1960):
  515-516;
S. Alvarez Turienzo, *La Ciudad de Dios* 173 (1960):742;
A. Camps, *Estudios Franciscanos* 62 (1961):132-133;
V. Capanaga, *Augustinus* 5 (1960):583;
G. Fraile, *Salmanticensis* 8 (1961):526-527;
T. Montull, *Estudios Filosóficos* 9 (1960):369-370;
T. Montull, *La Civiltà Cattolica* 89 (1962):496.

343. Vasseur, A. A. *Sören Kierkegaard.* Madrid: 1918. 259p.

344. Viallaneix, Nelly. *Kierkegaard, el único ante Dios.*
Trad. Joan Llopis (Col. Biblioteca de Filosofia). Barcelona:
Editorial Herder, 1977. 164p.

345. Wahl, Jean. *Kierkegaard.* Tr. Rovira Armengol (Colección
"Filosofos y Sistemas"). Buenos Aires: Edic. Losange, 1956.

OTHER LANGUAGES

346. Andersen, K. Bruun. *Sören Kierkegaards store jordry-stelser* [Sören Kierkegaard's great earthquakes]. Copenhagen: Hagerup, 1953. 142p.

347. Andersen, K. Bruun. *Sören Kierkegaard og kritikeren P. L. Mölner* [S. K. et le critique P. L. Mölner]. Copenhagen: Munksgaard, 1950. 52p.

348. Becker, Ernest. *De ontkenning van de dood. De inge-boren vrees voor leven en dood als drijfveer van het menselijk handelen* [Kierkegaard]. Vert. uit het Amerikaans door P. Nijhoff en Karel Hofland. Baarn: Ambo, 1976. 348p.

349. Bejerholm, Lars. *"Meddelelsens dialektik." Studier i Sören Kierkegaards teorier om sprak, kommunikation och pseudonymitet* ["Meddelelsens dialektik." Studies in Sören Kierkegaards theories about language, communication and pseudonymity]. With a summary in English (Publications of the Kierkegaard Society, Copenhagen, 2). Copenhagen: Munksgaard, 1962. 329p.

350. Börsand, Grete. *Forbilde og utfordring. En Kierkegaard-studie* (Idé og tanke, XIV). Oslo: Tanum.

351. Brandes, Georg. *Sören Kierkegaard: En kritisk Fremstil-ling i Grundrids.* Copenhagen: Gyldendal. (Orig. pub. 1877.)

352. Brandt, Frithiof. *Sören Kierkegaard* (Världsförfattare). Stockholm: Natur och Kultur, 1955. 95p.

353. Brandt, Frithiof. *Syv Kierkegaard studier.* Udg. i anledning af forfatterens 70 aars födelsesdag den 23. maj 1962, ved Selskabet for Filosofi og psykologi. Copenhagen: Munksgaard, 1962.

354. Bredsdorff, Elias. *Corsaren, Goldschmidt og Kierkegaard.* Copenhagen: Corsarenl, 1972, 2d ed. rev.

355. Bröchner, Hans. *Erindringer om Sören Kierkegaard* [Memories of S. Kierkegaard]. With an introduction and informatory notes by Steen Johansen. Copenhagen: Gyldendal, 1953. 96p.

356. Bukdahl, Jörgen. *Sören Kierkegaard: Hans fader og slaegten i Saedding.* Ribe: Dansk Hjemstavns Forlag.

357. Bukdahl, Jörgen. *Sören Kierkegaard og den menige mand.*
2d ed. Copenhagen: Gyldendal. (Orig. pub. 1961.)

358. Bychovskij, B. E. *K'erkegor.* Moscow: Izdatel'stvo
Nauka, 1972. 238p.

359. Christensen, Villads. *Sören Kierkegaard og Friedriks-berg.* Copenhagen: Rosenkilde og Bagger, 1959.

360. Christensen, Villads. *Sören Kierkegaard i Lys af Shakespeares Hamlet.* Copenhagen: Rosenkilde og Bagger, 1960.

361. Christensen, Villads. *Sören Kierkegaard: Det centrale i hand livssyn.* Copenhagen: Gad, 1963.

362. Christensen, Villads. *Kierkegaard-Dramaet.* Copenhagen:
Nyt Nordisk Forlag. 1967.

363. *Den Levende Kierkegaard* [Kierkegaard vivant].   Trans.
by Lars Roar Langslet et al. Oslo: Gyldendal norsk forlag,
1968. 133p.

364. Dokter, T. *De structuur van Kierkegaard's oeuvre.*
Assen: Van Gorcum & Co., 1936. 164p. Bijl. Diss. Groningen.
Teol (Van Gorcums Theolog. Bibl., 5).

365. Dupré, L. *Kierkegaards theologie of de dialectiek van het christen-worden.* Utrecht, Het Spectrum; Antwerpen:
N. V. Standaard-Boekhandel, 1958. 230p.

    book reviews:
    P. Fransen, *Bijdragen* 20 (1959):213-214;
    J. H. Walgrave, *Tijdschrift voor Filosofie* 26 (1964):
      533-536;
    B. Willaert, *Collationes Brugenses et Gandavenses* 5
      (1959):275-276.

366. Esser, P. H. *Kierkegaard.* Baarn: Hollandia-drukkerei,
1941. 194p. (Serie: Uren met K.)

367. *Exil, nordisk tidsskrift for eksistentialistisk debat*
3, 1: Specialnummer om Sören Kierkegaard.

CONTENTS:
Carrasco de la Vega, Rubén. "Eksistentialismens
  oprindelse: Sjaelen i Kierkegaards laere." 1-10;
Naess, Arne. "Kierkegaard og utdannelseskrisen." 11-14;
Horgby, Ingvar. "Kierkegaards svar pa den gnostiska
  utmaningen." 15-23;
Aalbaek-Nielsen, Kaj. "Den levende Kierkegaard." 24-26;
Bukdahl, Jörgen K. "Sören Kierkegaard: Personligheds-
  princippets forkaemper--eller undergraver?" 27-31.

368. Fenger, Henning. *Kierkegaard-Myter og Kierkegaard-
Kilder: 9 kildekritiske studier i de Kierkegaardske papirer,
reve og aktstykker* (Odense Univ. Studies in Scandinavian
Langs. & Lits. 7). Odense: Odense Universitetsforlag. 286p.

  book review:
  T. Brunius, *Lier en Boog* 2 (1976-77):204.

369. Fetter, J. C. A. *Inleiding tot het denken van Kierkegaard* (Hoofdfiguren van het menselijk denken, 11). Assen:
Born, 1953, 48p.; 1960, 51p.

370. Frandsen, Hans E. A. *Historieproblemet hos Kierkegaard
og den unge Marx* (Poetik 26). Roskilde: Universitetsforlag,
1976. 90p.

371. Gajdenko, P. P. *Tragedija èstetizma (Opyt xarakteristiki
mirosozercanija Serena Kirkegora)*. Moscow: Iskusstvo.

372. Gregaard, Michael. *Fortid i Nutid: Et essay om Sören
Kierkegaards Ottevejskrog*. Stockholm: Kerberos, 1967.

373. Grimault, Marguerite. *Kierkegaard. Leven en werk*
[Kierkegaard par luimême]. Vert. door H. Bakker (Prismaboeken,
1258). Utrecht: Het Spectrum, 1967. 190p.

374. Hansen, Knud. *Sören Kierkegaard, ideens digter*
[S. Kierkegaard, the poet of ideas]. Köbenhavn: Gyldendal,
1954. 383p.

375. Heiss, Robert. *Hegel, Kierkegaard, Marx. De grote
dialectische denkers van de negentiende eeuw.* Vertaald door
M. Mok (Aulaboeken, 418). Utrecht, Antwerpen: Het Spectrum,
1969. 408p.

  book review:
  D. Scheltens, *Tijdschrift voor Filosofie* 32 (1970):128-129.

376. Henningsen, Bernd. *Poul Martin Möller oder Die dänische Erziehung des Sören Kierkegaard: Eine kritische Monographie mit einer ersten Übersetzung seiner Abhandlung über die "Affectation."* Frankfurt am Main: Akademische Verlags., 1973. 134p.

377. Henriksen, Aage. *Kierkegaards romaner* [Kierkegaard's novels]. Köbenhavn: Gyldendal, 1954, 196p.; 2d ed., photo. reprint.

    book review:
    L. Richter, *Theologische Literaturzeitung* 83 (1958): 102-103.

378. Hohlenberg, Johannes. *Den ensommes vej: Ein fremstilling af Sören Kierkegaards vaerk.* 2d ed. Copenhagen: Aschehoug, 1968 (Orig. pub. 1948).

379. Hohlenberg, Johannes. *Sören Kierkegaard.* Vert. door Dr. S. Ferwerda. Utrecht: Erven Bijleveld, 1949. 380p.

380. Holm, Kjeld, Jacobsen, Malthe, and Troelsen, Bjarne. *Sören Kierkegaard og romantikerne.* Copenhagen: Berlingske, 1974. 159p.

381. Holm, Sören. *Sören Kierkegaards historiefilosofi* [S. Kierkegaard's philosophy of history]. Copenhagen: Nyt Nordisk Forlag, 1952. 120p.

    book review:
    L. Richter, *Theologische Literaturzeitung* 83 (1958): 100-101.

382. Jacobsen, Ole, og Fischer, Rasmus. *Om mig selv: Sören Kierkegaards breve og optegnelser.* With introduction by N. H. Söe. Köbenhavn: Munksgaard, 1957.

383. Jansen, F. J. Billeskov. *Studier i Sören Kierkegaards litteraere Kunst.* 2d Impr. Copenhagen: Rosenkilde & Bagger, 1972. 83p. (Photo reprint; 1st impr., 1951.)

384. Jonker, G. J. A. *Sören Kierkegaard.* Baarn: Hollandia-drukkerij, 1920, 43p. (Groote Denkers (Nieuwe Reeks), 4 Ser., n. 3.)

385. Jor, Finn. *Sören Kierkegaard. Den eksisterende tenker.* Oslo: Land or Kirke, 1954. 176p.

book review:
B. Delfgaauw, *Revue Philosophique de la France et de l'Etranger* 80 (1955):243-245.

386. Jörgensen, Aage. *Sören Kierkegaard-litteratur 1961-1970. En forelöbig bibliografi.* Aarhus: Akademisk Boghandel, 1971. 99p.

387. Jörgensen, Aage. *Dansk Litteraturhistorisk Bibliografi 1974* [Includes numerous references to literature about Soren Kierkegaard]. Copenhagen: Akademisk Forlag, 1975. 64p.

388. Jörgensen, Aage. *Omkredsninger-Artikler og anmeldelser.* Copenhagen: Akadekisch Forlag, 1974. 136p. (Essay on Kierkegaard.)

389. Jörgensen, Carl. *Sören Kierkegaard: En biografi I-V.* Copenhagen: Nyt Nordisk Forlag, 1964.

390. Jörgensen, Carl. *Sören Kierkegaards skuffelser.* Copenhagen: Nyt Nordisk Forlag, 1967.

391. Jörgensen, Gunnar F. *Sören Kierkegaard som tvivler: Variationer over temaet fader--sön.* Copenhagen: Rosenkilde, 1977. 216p.

392. *Katalog over Sören Kierkegaards Bibliotek.* With introduction by Niels Thulstrup. (Sören Kierkegaard Selskabet.) Köbenhavn: Munksgaard, 1957.

393. *Kierkegaard Herdenking.* Werken uitgeg. door het Rectoraat van de Rijksuniversiteit de Gent, No. 10, 1964.

    CONTENTS:
    Bolckmans, A. "Kierkegaards betekenis voor de literatuur."
        5-14;
    Raes, R. "Het esthetisch levensstadium." 15-20;
    van Eeckhaut, P. "Het ethisch levensstadium." 21-32;
    Vermeersch, E. "Het religieus levensstadium." 33-40;
    Kruithof, J. "Slotbeschouwing." 41-46.

394. *Kierkegaard-Studiet, International Edition* (Osaka, Japan) 2 (1965).

    CONTENTS:
    Abstracts of arts. in the Jap. ed., 1-9;

Holm, Sören. "Sören Kierkegaard og 'Graeciteten'." 10-17;
Thulstrup, Niels. "Student Sören Kierkegaard i Rollen som
Dramatiker." 18-32.

395. *Kierkegaard-Studiet, International Edition* (Osaka,
Japan) 3 (1966).

CONTENTS:
Abstracts of arts. in the Jap. ed., 1-10;
Egon Hessel, R. A. "Kierkegaard und Kafka." 11-16;
Christensen, Villads. "Hvorledes saa Sören Kierkegaard
  ud?" 17-21;
Malantschuk, Gregor. "Begrebet Erindring og dets
  Aspekter i Sören Kierkegaards Forfatterskab." 22-33.

396. *Kierkegaard-Studiet, International Edition* (Osaka,
Japan) 4 (1967).

CONTENTS:
Abstracts of arts. in the Jap. ed., 1-8, 35-37;
Perkins, Robert L. "Two Nineteenth Century interpretations
  of Socrates: Hegel and Kierkegaard." 9-14;
Steffensen, Steffen. "Kierkegaard and Hamann." 15-34.

397. *Kierkegaard-Studiet, International Edition* (Osaka,
Japan) 5 (1968).

CONTENTS:
Abstracts of arts. in the Jap. ed., 1-8;
Bukdahl, Jörgen J. "'Hjertekenderen' Kierkegaard: Om
  Kierkegaards tvetydige forhold til tvetydigheden." 9-14;
Rohde, H. P. "Opklaring af et Kierkegaard-citat med
  auktionsprotokollen over hans bogsamling som vejleder."
  15-22;
Skjoldager, Emanuel. "Sören Kierkegaard om 'at vaelge sig
  selv'." 23-27.

398. *Kierkegaard-Studiet, International Edition* (Osaka,
Japan) 6 (1969).

CONTENTS:
Abstracts of arts. in the Jap. ed., 1-7, 44-48;
Fenger, Henning. "Kierkegaards onsdagskorrespondance:
  Et forsog pa en datering af Kierkegaards breve til
  Regine Olsen." 8-31;
Nielsen, Svend Aage. "Assessor Wilhelms syn pa Kierke-
  gaards forfatterskab: Det etiske stadium er det höjeste."
  32-44.

399. *Kierkegaard. Herdenking* (Voordrachten gehouden op 5 mei 1963, ter gelegenheid van de herdenking aan de Rijks-universiteit te Gent van de honderdvijftigste verjaardag van Kierkegaard's geboorte, 1813) (Werken uitgegeven door het Rectoraat van de Rijksuniversiteit te Gent, 10). Gent: Rijksuniversiteit te Gent, 1964. 46p.

400. Kühle, Sejer. *Sören Kierkegaard. Barndom og Ungdom* (S. K. childhood and youth). Copenhagen: Aschehoug, 1950. 211p.

401. Leemans, Victor. *Sören Kierkegaard*. Met een inleiding van A. De Waelhens (Filosofische Bibliotheek). Antwerpen-Amsterdam: N. V. Standaard-Boekhandel, 1956. 177p.

book reviews:
L. Dupre, *Streven* 10 (1956-57):90;
H. van Munster, *Revue Philosophique de Louvain* 55 (1957):
  287-288;
D.M. D.P., *Tijdschrift voor Philosophie* 18 (1956):701-702.
B. Delfgaauw, *Algemeen Nederlands Tijdschrift voor Wijsbegeerte en Psychologie* 49 (1956-57):315-316;
J. Nota, *Bijdragen* 18 (1957):213.
H. Van den Bulcke, *Collationes Brugenses et Gandavenses* 4 (1958):273;
A. Westerlinck, *Dietsche Warande en Belfort* (1957):55-60.

402. Lindström, Valter. *Efterföljelsens teologi hos Sören Kierkegaard* (La théologie de l'imitation chez Sören Kierke-gaard). Stockholm: Diakonistyrelsens bokförlag, 1956. 310p.

book review:
S. Holm, *Theologische Literaturzeitung* 84 (1959):853-854.

403. Ljungdal, Arnold. *Problemet Kierkegaard*. Stockholm: Norstedt, 1964.

404. Lögstrup, K. E. *Opgör med Kierkegaard*. Copenhagen: Gyldendal.

405. Lönning, P. *"Samtidighedens situation."* En studie i *Sören Kierkegaards kristendomsforstaelse*. Oslo: Land og Kirke, 1954. 328p.

406. Lowrie, Walter. *Het leven van Kierkegaard* (A short life of Kierkegaard). Nederlands van H. C. de Wolf (Prisma-boeken, 443). Utrecht: Het Spectrum, 1959. 191p.

407. Malantschuk, G. *Indförelse i Sören Kierkegaard For-*
fatterskab. Köbenhavn: Einer Munksgaard, 1953. 83p.

408. Malantschuk, G., and Söe, N. H. *Sören Kierkegaards*
kamp mod Kirken [S. Kierkegaard's struggle against the
Church] (Sören Kierkegaards Selskabets populaere Skrifter, 6).
Copenhagen: Munksgaard, 1956. 77p.

409. Malantschuk, G. *In het voetspoor van Kierkegaard.*
Een inleiding op zijn oeuvre. Vert. Sixtus Scholtens.
Inleiding Bernard Delfgaauw. 's Gravenhage: H. P. Leopold,
1960. 95p.

410. Malantschuk, G. *Dialektik og eksistens hos Sören Kier-*
kegaard. Köbenhavn: Hans Reitzels Forlag, 1968. 356p.

411. Malantschuk, G. *Frihedens Problem i Kierkegaards*
Begrebet Angest. Mit einer deutschen Zusammenfassung
(Publications of the Kierkegaard Society, Copenhagen, 4).
Kobenhavn: Rosenkilde og Bagger, 1971. 132p.

412. McKinnon, Alastair. *Fundamental Polyglot: Konkordans*
til Kierkegaards Samlede Vaerker. (Kierkegaard Indices 2.)
Leiden: E. J. Brill, 1971. 1137p.

413. Möller, A. Egelund. *Sören Kierkegaard om Politik.*
Copenhagen: Forlaget "Strand," 1975. 191p.

414. Müller, Paul. *Kristendom, etik og majeutik i Sören*
Kierkegaards "Kjerlighedens Gjerninger." (Skrifter udg. af
Kobenhavns Univ. Inst. for Religionshist. 1.) Copenhagen:
n.p., 1976. [Summary in English]

415. Naesgaard, Sigurd. *En psykoanalyse af Sören Kierkegaard*
[Psychoanalysis of Sören Kierkegaard]. Odense: Psykoanalytisk
Forlag. 150p.

416. Nielsen, Edith. *Sören Kierkegaard.* Kopenhagen: Ejnar
Munksgaard, 1951. 96p.

417. Nordentoft, Kresten. *Kierkegaards psykologi.* Copenhagen: Gad, 1972. 522p. [Summary in English, 493-518]

      book review:
      W. von Kloeden, *Theologische Literaturzeitung* 98 (1973):
      853-859.

418.   Nordentoft, Kresten.   "Hvad siger Brand-Majoren?"
Kierkegaards opgör med sin samtid.   Copenhagen: Gad, 1973.
295p.

419.   Norrby, Tore.   Sören Kierkegaard.   Stockholm: Wahlström
and Widstrand, 1951.   193p.

420.   Ortmann Nielsen, Edith, and Thulstrup, Niels.   Sören
Kierkegaard.   Bidrag til en bibliografi (Contributions towards
a bibliography).   Copenhagen: E. Munksgaard, 1951.   96p.

421.   Ostenfeld, Ib.   Sören Kierkegaards Psykologi: Undersögelse og Indlevelse.   Copenhagen: Rhodos, 1972.   79p.

422.   Petersen, Ernst.   Tre foredrag over emnet begrebet angst
af Sören Kierkegaard [Three lectures on the theme "the concept
of fear" by S. Kierkegaard].   Odense: Landsretssagförer Ernst
Petersen, 1954.   64p.

423.   Petersen, Teddy.   Kierkegaards polemiske debut: Artikler
1834-34 i historisk sammenhaeng (Odense Univ. Studies in
Scan. Langs. and Lits. 9).   Odense: Odense Univ. P., 1977.
181p.

424.   Polysemus, Frater [pseud. of Hans Sörensen].   Forord til
Sören Kierkegaards Billedbog: Alvorlig Laesning i travle
Tider.   Fundet og befordret til trykken af Petrus Solniensis
[pseud. of Per Olsen].   Copenhagen: Munksgaard.   29p.

425.   Poulsen, Morgens.   Kierkegaardske skaebner.   Fire radio-
foredrag.   Emil Boesen, Ilia Fibiger, Mathilde Leiner, Ernesto
Dalgas [Persons influenced by Kierkegaard].   Four broadcast
talks.   Copenhagen: Petit Forlaget, 1955.   45p.

426.   Reichmann, Ernani.   Intermezzo lirico-filosófico -
VII parte, Kierkegaardiana.   Curitiba (Brasil): Ediçâo do
Autor, 1963.   441p.

427.   Rohde, P. P.   Et geni i köbstad.   Et essay om Sören
Kierkegaard [A genius in a commercial town.   An essay on
S. Kierkegaard] (Studentersamfunds skrifter).   Oslo: Det
Norske Studentersamfunds kulturutvalg, 1956.   46p.

428.   Rohde, Peter.   Sören Kierkegaard.   Copenhagen: Thanning
and Appel, 1960.

429. Rohde, H. P. *Gaadefulde stadier paa Kierkegaards vej.*
Copenhagen: Rosenkilde & Bagger, 1974. 126p. (11 essays,
all prev.)

430. Roos, Carl. *Kierkegaard og Goethe.* Copenhagen: Gad,
1955. 231p.

431. Roos, H. *Sören Kierkegaard og Katolicismen* (Foredrag
holdt i Sören Kierkegaard Selskabet den 22. januar 1952).
Köbenhavn: Ejnar Mucksgaard, 1952. 58p.

   book reviews:
   R. M. Brackett, *Thought* 29 (1954):620-621;
   B. Delfgaauw, *Tijdschrift voor Philosophie* 17 (1955):
     529-530;
   H. Ukkola, *Teologinen Aikakauskirja* (1953):224-237.

432. Rubow, Paul V. *Kierkegaard og Hans Samtidige* [K. et ses
contemporains]. Copenhagen: Gyldendal, 1950. 67p.

433. Rubow, Paul V. *Goldschmidt og Kierkegaard. Nye
litteraere studier.* Copenhagen: Gyldendal, 1952. 120p.

434. Scholtens, W. R. *De onbekende Kierkegaard. Zijn
werken--Zijn gebeden.* Baarn: Ten Have, 1972. 188p.

435. Skjodager, Emanuel. *Sören Kierkegaards syn pa samvit-
tigheden.* Copenhagen: Munksgaard, 1967.

436. Slök, Johannes. *Sören Kierkegaard.* Copenhagen: Gad,
1960.

437. Slök, Johannes. *Sören Kierkegaard.* Vert. uit het
Deens van Ga. J. Droogleever Fortuyn. Met een ten geleide
van J. Sperna Weiland (Carillonreeks, 55). Amsterdam: W. ten
Have, 1967. 107p.

438. Slök, Johannes. *Shakespeare og Kierkegaard.* Copenhagen: Berlingske, 1972. 205p.

439. *Sören Kierkegaard International Bibliography.* Ed. by
Jens Himmelstrup and Kjeld Dirket-Smith. Köbenhavn: Nyt
Nordisk Forlag-Arnold Busck, Munksgaard, 1962. 224p.

440.   Thulstrup, Marie Mikulová.   *Kierkegaard og Pietismen*
[Kierkegaard and Pietism].   Copenhagen: Munksgaard, 1967.
66p.

441.   Thulstrup, Maria Mikulová.   *Kierkegaard, Platons skuen
og kristendommen* (Sören Kierkegaard Selskabets populaere
Skrifter 15).   Copenhagen: Munksgaard, 1970.

442.   Thulstrup, Niels.   *Katalog over Sören Kierkegaards
Bibliotek, udgivet af Sören Kierkegaard Selskabet met indledning ved Niels Thulstrup.*   Kopenhagen: Munksgaard, 1957.
111p.

443.   Thulstrup, Niels.   *Kierkegaards forhold til Hegel og
til den spekulative idealisme indtil 1846.*   Copenhagen:
Gyldendal, 1967.

444.   Toeplitz, Karol.   *Kierkegaard.*   Introduction by
B. Suchodolski.   Warszawa: Wiedza Pawszechva, 1975.   323p.
[Biography-critical study and Polish trans. of K.]

445.   Toftdahl, Hellmut.   *Kierkegaard först-og Grundtvig sa.*
Copenhagen: Nyt Nordisk Forlag, 1969.   ("Kierkegaard og
digtningen." *Exil, Nordisk Tidsskrift for Faenomenologisk
Debat* 4:25-44.)

446.   van den Nieuwenhuizen, M.   *Dialectiek van de vrijheid.
Zonde en zondevergeving bij Sören Kierkegaard* (Philosophia
religionis.   Bibliotheek van geschriften over de godsdienst-
wijsbegeerte, 13).   Assen: Van Gorcum, 1968, xiv-146p.

447.   van der Wey, A.   *Met Kierkegaard op zoek.   Zijn er nog
echte Christenen?*   Amsterdam: Lieverlee, 1956.   64p.

448.   van Dijk, A. F. L.   *Perspectieven bij Kierkegaard.*
Woord vooraf W. J. Aalders.   Amsterdam: H. J. Paris, 1940.

449.   van Munster, H. A.   *O. F. M., De filosofische gedachten
van de jonge Kierkegaard, 1831-1841.*   Arnhem: Van Loghum
Slaterus, 1958.   166p.

450.   van Munster, H. A.   *Sören Aabye Kierkegaard* (Denkers
over God en Wereld, 6).   Tielt: Lannoo; 's-Gravenhage:
Anna Paulownastraat 73, 1963.   152p.

451.   van Raalten, F. *Schaamte en existentie. Een onderzoek naar de plaats en de werking van de schaamte in de menselijke existentie in het bijzonder met betrekking tot het werk van Sören Kierkegaard.* Nijkerk: G. F. Callenbach, 1965. 196p.

452.   van Rhijn, M. *Sören Kierkegaard. Een indruck van zijn leven en denken.* Baarn: Bosch & Keuning, 1941. 56p.

453.   van der Waals, Jacqueline E. *Kierkegaard.* Blaricum: De Waelburgh, Waelburgh boekjes, 1925. 82p.

454.   Wagndahl, Per. *Gemenskapsparblemet hos Sören Kierkegaard.* The problem of communion in S. Kierkegaard (Studia Theologica Lundensia, 6). Lund: Gleerup, 1954. 264p.

455.   Weltzer, Carl. *Grundtvig og Sören Kierkegaard* [Grundtvig et S. Kierkegaard](Skrifter udg. af Grundtvig- selskabet, 5). Copenhagen: Gyldendal, 1952. 192p.

CHAPTER 2:
Dissertations

456. Allen, Kenneth Ralph. "Identity and the Individual Personhood in the Thought of Erik Erikson and of Soeren Kierkegaard." Ph.D., Boston Univ., 1967, 294p. *Dissertation Abstracts* 28 (1967):1885A.

457. Angell, John W. "The Theological Methodology of Soeren Kierkegaard." Ph.D., The Southern Baptist Theological Seminary, 1949, 176p.

458. Ansbro, John Joseph. "Kierkegaard's Critique of Hegel-- An Interpretation." Ph.D., Fordham Univ., 1964, 356p. *Dissertation Abstracts* 25 (1964):3615.

459. Anz, Wilhelm. "Die Wiederholung der socratischen Methode durch Sören Kierkegaard." Phil. Diss. Marburg, Marburg a. d. Lahn, 1940, 122p.

460. Baas, Fritz. "Das Asthetische bei Sören Kierkegaard in seinen Grudnbestimmungen." Phil. Diss. Heidelberg, 1923, xiv-125p.

461. Bauer, Wilhelm. "Die Ethik Sören Kierkegaards." Phil. Diss. Jena, Kahla, 1913, iv-63p.

462. Beauchamp, Richard Arthur. "Passion and Prudence: A Study of Kierkegaard's Ethics." Ph.D., Duke Univ., 1970, 290p. *Dissertation Abstracts* 32 (1971):1605A.

463. Bedell, George Chester. "Kierkegaard and Faulkner: Modalities of Existence." Ph.D., Duke Univ., 1969, 344p. *Dissertation Abstracts* 30 (1970):5056A.

464. Berberich, Gerta. "La notion métaphysique de la personne chez Kant et Kierkegaard." Diss. Fribourg (Suisse), Fribourg (Suisse): St. Paul, 1942, 81p.

465.   Bjarnason, Loftur L.   "Categories of Sören Kierkegaard's
Thought in the Life and Writings of August Strindberg."
Abstracts of Dissertations, Stanford Univ. 26 (1950-51):
144-146.

466.   Braun, Günther.   "Der Begriff des Humors in Sören
Kierkegaards Werk und die Bedeutung des Humors für dieses."
Phil. Diss. Univ. Mainz, Bad Neuenahr, 1952, xii-95p.

467.   Burgess, Andrew John.   "The Concept of Passionate
Faith : Kierkegaard and Analytical Philosophy of Mind."
Ph.D., Yale Univ., 1969, 250p.   *Dissertation Abstracts* 31
(1970):1319A.

468.   Cain, David A.   "Reckoning with Kierkegaard's
Christian Faith and Dramatic Literature."   Princeton Univ.,
1976, 325p.   *Dissertation Abstracts* 37 (1976):2240A.

469.   Campbell, Charles Ray.   "The Attack from Behind
Irony and Soeren Kierkegaard's Dialectic of Communication."
Ph.D., Syracuse Univ., 1949, 345p.   *Dissertation Abstracts*
34 (1974):6696A.

470.   Carnell, Edward J.   "The Problem of Verification in
Soeren Kierkegaard."   Ph.D., Boston Univ., 1949, 270p.

471.   Chervin, Ronda de Sola.   "The Process of Conversion in
the Philosophy of Religion of Soeren Kierkegaard."   Ph.D.,
Fordham Univ., 1967, 209p.   *Dissertation Abstracts* 28:4207A.

472.   Christopherson, Myrvin Frederick.   "Soren Kierkegaard's
Dialectic of Communication: An Approach to the Communication
of Existential Knowledge."   Purdue Univ.   *Dissertation
Abstracts* 27:271-272A.

473.   Clive, Geoffrey H.   "The Connection Between Ethics and
Religion in Kant, Kierkegaard, and F. H. Bradley."   Ph.D.,
Harvard Univ., 1953.

474.   Cole, James Preston.   "Kierkegaard's *Concept of Dread*;
with Constant Reference to Sigmund Freud."   Ph.D., Drew
Univ., 1964, 361p.   *Dissertation Abstracts* 25 (1964):3136.

475.   Congleton, Ann.   "Spinoza, Kierkegaard, and the
Eternal Particular."   Ph.D., Yale Univ., 1962.

476.   Copp, John D.   "The Concept of the Soul in Kierkegaard
and Freud."   Ph.D., Boston Univ., 1953.

477.   Crumbine, Nancy Jay.   "The Same River Twice: A Critique
of the Place of Eros in the Philosophy of Kierkegaard."
Ph.D., The Pennsylvania State Univ., 1972, 191p.

478.   Cutting, Patricia M.   "The Possibility of Being-With-
Others for Kierkegaard's Individual One (Der Enkelte)."
Ph.D., Univ. of New Mexico, 1976, 240p.   *Dissertation
Abstracts* 37 (1976):2939A.

479. Daab, Anneliese. "Ironie und Humor bei Kierkegaard."
Phil. Diss., Heidelberg, 1926, vi-79p. [Maschinenschr.]

480. Daane, James. "Kierkegaard's Concept of the Moment.
An Investigation into the Time-Eternity Concept of Sören
Kierkegaard." Princeton Theological Seminary 35 (1974):
2379A.

481. Daise, Benjamin. "Kierkegaard's Pseudonymous Works."
Ph.D., The Univ. of Texas at Austin, 1973, 216p. *Dissertation
Abstracts* 34 (1974):6040A.

482. Davis, Clifford. "The Philosophy of Sören Kierkegaard
and Its Implications for Education." Univ. of Southern
California, 1977. *Dissertation Abstracts* 38 (1978):5984A.

483. Despland, Michel Samuel. "The Idea of Divine Education:
A Study in the Ethical and the Religious as Organizing Themes
for the Interpretation of the Life of the Self in Kant,
Schleiermacher, and Kierkegaard." Ph.D., Harvard Univ., 1966.

484. Dewey, Bradley Rau. "The Imitation of Christ in the
Thought of Soeren Kierkegaard." Ph.D., Yale Univ., 1964,
357p. *Dissertation Abstracts* 30 (1967):380A.

485. DeYoung, Quintin R. "A Study of Contemporary Christian
Existential Theology (Kierkegaard and Tillich) and Modern
Dynamic Psychology (Freud and Sullivan) Concerning Guilt
Feelings." Ph.D., Univ. of Southern California, 1959, 329p.
Dissertation Abstracts 20 (1959):1883.

486. Donnelly, John Joseph Patrick. "Sören Kierkegaard's
Teleological Suspension of the Ethical: A Reinterpretation."
Ph.D., Brown Univ., 1970, 168p. *Dissertation Abstracts* 32
(1971):483A.

487. Donohue, Kevin E. "Reflection and Faith in Sören
Kierkegaard." Ph.D., The Catholic Univ. of America, 1973,
264p. *Dissertation Abstracts* 33 (1973):6963A.

488. Duncan, Elmer Hubert. "Kierkegaard and Value Theory:
A Study of the Three Spheres of Existence." Ph.D., Univ. of
Cincinnati, 1962, 136p. *Dissertation Abstracts* 23 (1962):
2171.

489. Dunne, Mary Rachel. "Kierkegaard and Socratic
Ignorance: A Study of the Task of a Philosopher in Relation
to Christianity." Ph.D., Univ. of Notre Dame, 1970, 356p.
Dissertation Abstracts 31 (1971):4835A.

490. Düwel, Hans. "Der Entwicklungsgedanke in Sören Kier-
kegaards *Entweder-Oder* und in Henrik Ibsens *Komödie der Liebe*."
Phil. Diss. Rostock, 1919. Auszug: Rostock: Winterberg, 1920.
[Vervielfältigt nur im.]

491. Early, Firman Anderson. "The Problem of Religious
Knowledge in the Writings of Kierkegaard." Ph.D., The
Southern Baptist Theological Seminary, 1945, 228p.

492. Eilers, Herbert. "Das geistige Jahr. Untersuchungen
und Interpretationen zu s. relig. Struktur im Vergleich mit
S. Kierkegaard." Phil. Diss. Univ. Münster, 1951, 278p.
[Maskinskr.]

493. Eller, Vernard Marion. "A Protestant's Protestant:
Kierkegaard from a New Perspective." Th.D., Pacific School
of Religion, 1964, 451p. *Dissertation Abstracts* 25 (1964):
3719.

494. Elrod, John W. "An Interpretation of Sören Kierkegaard's Concept of the Self in the Pseudonymous Corpus."
Princeton, 1972, 412p. *Dissertation Abstracts* 37 (1976):404A.

495. Engelbrecht, Barend Jacobus. "Die tijdsstruktuur in
die gedagtekompleks: Hegel--Kierkegaard--Barth." Diss.
theol., Groningen, 1949, 83p. (Groninger schrijfkamer.)

496. Evans, Charles Stephen. "Subjective Justifications of
Religious Belief: A Comparative Study of Kant, Kierkegaard,
and James." Ph.D., Yale Univ., 1974, 285p. *Dissertation
Abstracts* 35 (1975):4611A.

497. Fackre, Gabriel Joseph. "A Comparison and Critique
of the Interpretations of Dehumanization in the Thought of
Sören Kierkegaard and Karl Marx." Ph.D., Univ. of Chicago,
1962.

498. Fallon, Richard J. "Sören Kierkegaard's Concept of
Madness." Ph.D., Boston College, 1979.

499. Fitzpatrick, T. Mallary, Jr. "An Interpretation of
the Thought of Sören Kierkegaard with Special Regard for
the Problem of Method." Ph.D., Univ. of Chicago, 1969.

500. Flottorp, Haakon. "Kierkegaard and Norway: A Study in
'Inwardness' in History with Illustrative Examples from
Religion, Literature, and Philosophy." Ph.D., Columbia Univ.,
1955, 345p. *Dissertation Abstracts* 15 (1954):890.

501. Frieser, Ingeborg. "Beträge zum ästhetischen Phäno-
menen bei Sören Kierkegaard mit besonderer Rücksicht auf
das Theater." Phil. Diss. Freiburg i. Br., 1950, 226p.
[Maschinenschr.]

502. Gerry, Joseph. "Kierkegaard: The Problem of Transcendence: An Interpretation of the Stages." Ph.D., Fordham
Univ., 1959.

503. Giess, Ludwig. "Liebe als Freiheit. Eine Kierke-
gaard-Aneignung. Phil. Diss., Temeschburg: Anwenden & Sohn,
1939, 54p.

504.   Gilmartin, Thomas V.   "Soul Sickness. A Comparison of
William James and Sören Kierkegaard." Graduate Theological
Union, 1974, 321p. *Dissertation Abstracts* 36 (1976):6763A.

505.   Goicoechea, David L.   "The Equivalence of the Existential and the Religious in Kierkegaard." Ph.D., Loyola
Univ. of Chicago, 1972.

506.   Gottlieb, Roger S. "*The Existing Individual and the
Will-to-Power*. A Comparison of Kierkegaard's and Nietzsche's
Answers to the Question: What Is It to Make a Transition
from One Value System to Another." Ph.D., Brandeis Univ.,
1975, 365p. *Dissertation Abstracts* 36 (1975):2894A.

507.   Guiraud, Paul.   "Recontre de Kierkegaard. Thèse
(Dactylogr.), Genève, 1942, 130p.

508.   Gwaltney, Marilyn E.   "The Concept of Alienation in
Kierkegaard." Syracuse Univ. N.Y., Buffalo, 1976, 171p.
Dissertation Abstracts 37 (1977):5181A.

509.   Halevi, Jacob.   "A Critique of Martin Buber's Interpretation of Sören Kierkegaard." Ph.D., Hebrew Union College,
1960.

510.   Hamilton, Wayne Bruce.   "Sören Kierkegaard's Conception of Temporality." Ph.D., McGill Univ. (Canada), 1972.
Dissertation Abstracts 33 (1972):2977A.

511.   Hamrick, William Spencer.   "Sören Kierkegaard's
Category of the Distinct Individual." Ph.D., Union Theological Seminary in Virginia, 1962.

512.   Hanna, Thomas L.   "The Lyrical Existentialists: The
Common Voice of Kierkegaard, Nietzsche, and Camus." Ph.D.,
Univ. of Chicago, 1960.

513.   Hansen, Olaf.   "The Problem of Alienation and Reconciliation: A Comparative Study of Marx and Kierkegaard in
the Light of Hegel's Formulation of the Problem." Ph.D.,
Princeton Theological Seminary, 1956, 449p. *Dissertation
Abstracts* 35 (1975):4680A.

515.   Heinecken, Martin John.   "Absolute Paradox in Sören
Kierkegaard." Ph.D., The Univ. of Nebraska-Lincoln, 1942.

516.   Hitchkock, John.   "A Comparison of 'Complementarity'
in Quantum Physics with Analogous Structures in Kierkegaard's
Philosophical Writings, from a Jungian Point of View."
Graduate Theological Union, 1975, 363p. *Dissertation
Abstracts* 36 (1976):6764A.

517.   Hoffmann, Raoul.   "Kierkegaard et la certitude religieuse. Esquisse biografique et critique." Diss. Theol.,
Genève, 1907, 168p.

518.   Hohbein, Leonard L.   "Kierkegaard's Understanding of
Love, Particularly as presented in the *Works of Love*."
Ph.D., De Paul Univ., 1979.

519.   Holmer, Paul L.   "Kierkegaard and the Truth: An
Analysis of the Presuppositions Integral to his Definition of
the Truth."   Ph.D., Yale Univ., 1946, 312p.   *Dissertation
Abstracts* 26 (1966):4002.

520.   Hudson, Deal W.   "Three Responses to Romanticism:
Baudelaire, Nietzsche and Kierkegaard."   Ph.D., Emory Univ.,
1978, 188p.   *Dissertation Abstracts* 40 (1979):317A.

521.   Hughes, Roderick P., III.   "The Notion of the Ethical
in Kierkegaard."   Ph.D., Univ. of Notre Dame, 1973, 307p.
Dissertation Abstracts 33 (1973):6398A.

522.   Hultgren, Lawrence D.   "The Problem of Religious
Consciousness in Kierkegaard's Thought."   Vanderbilt Univ.,
1976, 494p.   *Dissertation Abstracts* 38 (1977):845A.

523.   Humphries, Hugh Will.   "Soeren Kierkegaard's Concept
of Sanctification."   Ph.D., New York Univ., 1962, 249p.
Dissertation Abstracts 23 (1962):1096.

524.   Hunt, George W.   "John Updike: The Dialectical Vision.
The Influence of Kierkegaard and Barth."   Syracuse Univ.,
1974, 298p.   *Dissertation Abstracts* 36 (1976):6674A.

525.   Ietswaart, Willem L.   "Kierkegaard's Concept of Faith."
Ph.D., Princeton Theological Seminary, 1952, 175p.

526.   Jones, Charles Edwin.   "The Theory of Truth as
Subjectivity in Kierkegaard, Compared with Theories of
Truth in Blanshard and Ayer."   Ph.D., Univ. of Arkansas,
1973, 190p.   *Dissertation Abstracts* 34 (1973):2699A.

527.   Jones, Jere Jene.   "On the Distinction Between
Religiousness 'A' and Religiousness 'B' in the *Concluding
Unscientific Postscript* of Sören Kierkegaard."   Ph.D., The
Univ. of Nebraska-Lincoln, 1971, 256p.   *Dissertation
Abstracts* 32 (1971):1017A.

528.   Jones, Ozro T., Jr.   "The Meaning of the 'Moment' in
Existential Encounter According to Kierkegaard."   S.T.D.,
Temple Univ., 1962, 196p.   *Dissertation Abstracts* 26 (1963):
6197.

529.   Kaltreider, Kurt.   "The Self, Existence and Despair
in Kierkegaard. A Secular Interpretation."   Univ. of Tennessee, 1977, 209p.   *Dissertation Abstracts* 38 (1978):4211A.

530.   Keane, Ellen Marie.   "The Equation of Subjectivity and
Truth in Kierkegaard's *Postscript*."   Ph.D., Univ. of Notre
Dame, 1965, 188p.   *Dissertation Abstracts* 26 (1965):5485.

531. Khan, Abrahim Habibulla. "The Treatment of the Theme of Suffering in Kierkegaard's Works." Ph.D., McGill Univ. (Canada), 1973. *Dissertation Abstracts* 34 (1974):7823A.

532. Khan, Theodore A. R. "A Critique of Kierkegaard's Category of the Individual Based on His Philosophico-Religious View of Man." Ph.D., New York Univ., 1962, 417p. *Dissertation Abstracts* 24 (1963):778.

533. Kirbach, Ernst Hellmuth. "Die ethischen Grundansichten Sören Kierkegaards." Phil. Diss. Giessen: P. Welzel, 1927, 59p.

534. Kirmmse, Bruce H. "Kierkegaard's Politics. The Social Thought of Sören Kierkegaard in Its Historical Context." Univ. of California-Berkeley, 1977, 1030p. *Dissertation Abstracts* 39 (1978):1047A.

535. Kleinman, Jaquline Agnew. "Public/Private--The Education of Sören Kierkegaard." Ph.D., The Ohio State Univ., 1971, 174p. *Dissertation Abstracts* 32 (1972):4064A.

536. Koller, Kerry Joseph. "Christianity and Philosophy According to Kierkegaard's Johannes Climacus." Ph.D., Univ. of Notre Dame, 1975, 196p. *Dissertation Abstracts* 36 (1975):1582A.

537. Kristensen, John-Bagge. "The Relevance of Sören Kierkegaard's Existentialism to a Philosophy of Education." Ph.D., State Univ. of New York at Buffalo, 1971.

538. Künzli, Arnold. "Die Angst des modernen Menschen. Sören Kierkegaards Angstexistenz als Spiegel der geistigen Krise unserer Zeit." Phil. Diss. Zürich: Rascher, 1974, 80p.

539. Laporte, André. "Trois témoins de la liberté: Erasme de Rotterdam, Martin Luther, Soeren Kierkegaard." Genève 1949, 128 + 4p. (dactylogr.) + 1 annexe: Théses et épithèses. (Thèse bach. theol.)

540. Larson, Curtis W. "A Comparison of the Views of Paul and Kierkegaard on Christian Suffering." Ph.D., Yale Univ., 1953.

541. Leendertz, Willem. "Sören Kierkegaard." Diss. Groningen, Theol. Amsterd.: A. H. Kruyt, 1913, viii-315p.

542. Likins, Marjorie Harjes. "The Concept of Selfhood in Freud and Kierkegaard." Ph.D., Columbia Univ., 1963, 210p. *Dissertation Abstracts* 26 (1965):1805.

543. Lin, Tian-Min. "Paradox in the Thought of Soeren Kierkegaard." Ph.D., Boston Univ., 1969, 241p. *Dissertation Abstracts* 30 (1969):2133A.

544. Link, Mae M. "Kierkegaard's Way to America: A Study
in the Dissemination of His Thought." Ph.D., The American
Univ., 1951.

545. Loder, James Edwin. "The Nature of Religious Con-
sciousness in the Writings of Freud and Kierkegaard. A
Theoretical Study in the Correlation of Religious and
Psychiatric Concepts." Ph.D., Harvard Univ., 1962.

546. Mackey, Louis H. "The Nature and the End of the
Ethical Life According to Kierkegaard." Ph.D., Yale Univ.,
1954.

547. Madden, Myron C. "The Contribution of Soeren Kierkegaard to a Christian Psychology." Ph.D., The Southern
Baptist Theological Seminary, 1950, 176p.

548. Magel, Charles R. "An Analysis of Kierkegaard's
Philosophic Categories." Univ. of Minnesota, 1960, 314p.
Dissertation Abstracts 21 (1961):3488.

549. Marsh, James L. "Hegel and Kierkegaard: A Dialectical
and Existential Combat." Ph.D., Northwestern Univ.
Dissertation Abstracts 32 (1971):3371A.

550. Martin, George Arthur. "An Interpretive Principle for
Understanding Kierkegaard." Ph.D., Univ. of Notre Dame,
1969, 244p. *Dissertation Abstracts* 30 (1969):2079A.

551. Massimo, Hermes. "Der Begriff des Wagnisses bei Sören
Kierkegaard." Phil. Diss. Innsbruck, 1948, 153p.
[Maschinenschr.]

552. Matthis, Michael J. "Kierkegaard and the Problem of
Community." Fordham Univ., 1977, 277p. *Dissertation
Abstracts* 38 (1977):322A.

553. McCarthy, Robert E. "The Wonder-Wounded Hearer. The
Problem of Communication in Sören Kierkegaard's Authorship
and Its Application to an Understanding of *Hamlet*."
Syracuse Univ., 1977, 261p. *Dissertation Abstracts* 38
(1977):2814A.

554. McCarthy, Vincent A. "The Meaning and Dialectic of
Moods in Kierkegaard." Stanford Univ., 1974, 339p.
Dissertation Abstracts 35 (1974):3871A.

555. McInerny, Ralph. "The Existential Dialectic of Soeren
Kierkegaard." Ph.D., Universite Laval (Canada), 1954.

556. McLane, Henry Earl, Jr. "Kierkegaard's Use of the
Category of Repetition: An Attempt to Discern the Structure
and Unity of His Thought." Ph.D., Yale Univ., 1961.

557. McLaughlin, Wayman Bernard. "The Relation Between
Hegel and Kierkegaard." Ph.D., Boston Univ., 1958, 346p.
Dissertation Abstracts 19 (1958):1788.

558.   Manheimer, Ronald J.   "Kierkegaard and the Education of Historical Consciousness."   Univ. of California, Santa Cruz.   *Dissertation Abstracts International* 35 (1974):1163A.

559.   Meusers, Karl.   "Der existierende Denker bei Sören Kierkegaard."   Phil. Diss. Köln, 1925.   Koln: E. Pilgram, 1926, viii-39p.

560.   Michalson, Gordon E.   "Baron von Huegel and Soeren Kierkegaard: Similarities and Differences in Their Expositions of the Christian Faith."   Ph.D., Drew Univ., 1947, 365p.

561.   Milne, Gretchen Elizabeth.   "Soeren Kierkegaard: A Philosophy by Indirection."   Ph.D., The Univ. of Texas at Austin, 1964, 247p.   *Dissertation Abstracts* 25 (1964):3034.

562.   Moore, Stanley Raymond.   "The Social Implications of the Category of the Single One in the Thought of Soeren Kierkegaard."   Ph.D., Drew Univ., 1964, 312p.   *Dissertation Abstracts*   25 (1964):4843.

563.   Mouty, Friedrich.   "Zum Rechtsgedanken bei Kierkegaard."   Munich: Dissertationsdruk Schön, 1969, 332p.

564.   Mueller, Robert William.   "A Critical Examination of Martin Buber's Criticisms of Soeren Kierkegaard."   Ph.D., Purdue Univ., 1974, 228p.   *Dissertation Abstracts* 35 (1974): 3816A.

565.   Muska, Rudolph Charles.   "Antithetical Religious Conceptions in Kierkegaard and Spinoza."   Ph.D., Michigan State Univ., 1960, 173p.   *Dissertation Abstracts* 21 (1961): 3489.

566.   Nauman, St. Elmo H., Jr.   "The Social Philosophies of Soeren Kierkegaard and Nikolai Frederik Severin Grundtvig."   Ph.D., Boston Univ., 1969, 224p.   *Dissertation Abstracts* 30 (1969):2081A.

567.   Nielsen, William M.   "Kierkegaard on Change, History, and Faith."   Ph.D., Harvard Univ., 1949, 288p.

568.   Niessen, Elisabeth.   "Der anthropologische Geistbegriff bei Sören Kierkegaard."   Phil. Diss. Bonn, 1939.   Fulda: Parzeller, 1939, 51p.   Ogs. tr. i: *Philosophische Jahrbuch der Görres-Gesellschaft* 52 (1939):59-84; 181-201.

569.   Nussbächer, Konrad.   "Psychologie und Dichtung.   Über ihre Zusammenhänge im allgemeinen und bei Otto Ludwig und Kierkegaard im besonderen (Maschinenschrift)."   Phil. Diss. Heidelberg, 1923, iv-164p.   4to [Lag nicht vor.-Auszug nicht gedruckt.]

570.   Ohara, Shin.   "Kierkegaard's Authorship Considered as an Ethical Argument."   Ph.D., Yale Univ., 1966, 387p. *Dissertation Abstracts* 27 (1967):4301A.

571. Oliver, Richard L. "Schnelling and Kierkegaard.
Experimentations in Moral Autonomy." Univ. of Oklahoma,
1977, 184p. *Dissertation Abstracts* 28 (1977):2175A.

572. O'Neill, Kevin David. "Kierkegaard's Attempt at a
Balanced Philosophy of Religion." Ph.D., Yale Univ., 1967,
271p. *Dissertation Abstracts* 28 (1968):4215A.

573. Oppenheim, Michael. "Sören Kierkegaard and Franz
Rosenzweig: The Movement from Philosophy to Religion."
Univ. of California-Santa Barbara, 1976, 384p. *Dissertation
Abstracts* 37 (1977):5898A.

574. Parrill, Lloyd Ellison. "The Concept of Humor in the
Pseudonymous Works of Soeren Kierkegaard." Ph.D., Drew Univ.,
1975, 296p. *Dissertation Abstracts* 36 (1975):3772A.

575. Patterson, David G. ."The Literary and Philosophical
Expressions of Existential Faith: A Study of Kierkegaard,
Tolstoi and Shestov." Ph.D., Univ. of Oregon, 1978, 274p.
Dissertation Abstracts 39 (1979):4228A. [*Fear and Trembling*]

576. Peck, William Dayton. "On Autonomy: The Primacy of
the Subject in Kant and Kierkegaard." Ph.D., Yale Univ.,
1974, 297p. *Dissertation Abstracts* 35 (1974):3063A.

577. Peiros, Sherri. "Kierkegaardian Parody." Ph.D.,
Univ. of California-Santa Cruz, 1974, 205p. *Dissertation
Abstracts* 35 (1975):7964A.

578. Penn, William Y., Jr. "Kierkegaard: A Study in Faith
and Reason." Univ. of Texas at Austin, 1976, 224p.
Dissertation Abstracts 37 (1976):2948A.

579. Perkins, Robert Lee. "Kierkegaard and Hegel: The
Dialectical Structure of Kierkegaard's Ethical Thought."
Ph.D., Indiana Univ., 1965, 316p. *Dissertation Abstracts*
26 (1965):2809.

580. Plekon, Michael P. "Kierkegaard: Diagnosis and Disease.
An Excavation in Modern Consciousness." State Univ. of
New Jersey, 1977, 414p. *Dissertation Abstracts* 38 (1977):
3098A.

581. Pojman, Louis Paul. "The Dialectic of Freedom in the
Thought of Sören Kierkegaard." Th.D., Union Theological
Seminary, New York City, 1972, 287p. *Dissertation Abstracts*
33 (1972):8200A.

582. Pomerleau, Wayne P. "Perspectives on Faith and Reason.
Studies in the Religious Philosophy of Kant, Hegel and
Kierkegaard." Northwestern Univ., 1977, 266p. *Dissertation
Abstracts* 38 (1978):5531A.

583. Quinn, Wylie S. "Kierkegaard and Wittgenstein: The
'Religious' as a 'Form of Life'." Duke Univ., 1976, 222p.
Dissertation Abstracts 37 (1977):7804A.

584.   Read, Lawrence McKim.   "Hegel and Kierkegaard: A Study
in Antithetical Concepts of the Incarnation." Ph.D., Columbia
Univ., 1967, 212p. *Dissertation Abstracts* 28 (1967):1852A.

585.   Reed, Walter L. "Meditations on the Hero: Narrative
Form in Carlyle, Kierkegaard, and Melville." Yale Univ.,
1970. *Dissertation Abstracts International* 31 (1970):1288A.

586.   Refsell, Lloyd. "Kierkegaard's Understanding of Luther."
Ph.D., Jewish Theological Seminary of America, 1964.

587.   Rose, Mary C. "Three Hierarchies of Value: A Study in
the Philosophies of Value of Henri Bergson, Alfred North
Whitehead, and Soeren Kierkegaard." Ph.D., The Johns Hopkins
Univ., 1949, 310p.

588.   Safier, Fred J. "The Philosophy of Sören Kierkegaard."
Ph.D., Harvard Univ., 1934, 392p. (Cambridge, Mass.).
[Maskinskr.]

589.   Salladay, Susan. "A Study of the Nature and Function
of Religious Language in Relation to Kierkegaard's Theories
of Subjective Truth and Indirect Communication." *Dissertation
Abstracts International* 35 (1974):1166-1167A.

590.   Salomon, Gottfried. "Beitrag zur Problematik von
Mystik und Glauben." Phil. Diss. Strassburg, 1916.
Strassburg & Leipzig: J. Singer, 1916, vi-99p. (om S.K.,
61-70: Von der Sünde und der Nachfolge.)

591.   Sandok, Theresa H. "Kierkegaard on Irony and Humor."
Ph.D., Univ. of Notre Dame, 1975, 251p. *Dissertation Abstracts*
36 (1975):1586A.

592.   Sauer, Ralph-Werner. "Ansätze zu einer Bestimmung der
Geschichtlichkeit im Denken Sören Kierkegaards." Phil.
Diss. Univ. Freiburg i. Br., 1953, 150-xxivp. [Maskinskr.]

593.   Sawatzki, Günther. "Das Problem des Dichters als
Motiv in der Entwicklung Sören Kierkegaards bis 1841."
Phil. Diss. Danzig, 1933. Borna-Leipzig: Noske, 1935, vi-94p.

594.   Schamp, Adele. "Die Ethik Sören Kierkegaards." Phil.
Diss. Wien, 1949, 81p. [Maschinenschrift]

595.   Schlechta, Eva. "Die Systemsproblematik bei Sören
Kierkegaard." Phil. Diss. München, 1955, 104p. [Maskinskr.]

596.   Schmid, G.-R. "Introduction à Kierkegaard." Thèse
Théol. (Duplikeret) Neuchatel, 1949, 77p.

597.   Schrag, Calvin Orville. "The Problem of Existence:
Kierkegaard's Descriptive Analysis of the Self and Heidegger's
Phenomenological Ontology of 'Dasein'." Ph.D., Harvard Univ.,
1975.

598. Schückler, Georg. "Die Existenzkategorie der Wieder-holung dargestellt am Werk Sören Kierkegaards." Phil. Diss. Bonn, 1952, 333p. [Maschinenschr.]

599. Schweickert, Alfred. "Sören Kierkegaards Soziologie." Phil. Diss. Heidelberg, 1924, v-83p. [Maschinenschrift]

600. Scimeca, Ross V. "The Ontological Status of the Irrational in Kierkegaard and Nietzsche: A Study of Its Origins and Importance." Ph.D., Univ. of Southern California, 1978. Dissertation Abstracts 39 (1979):5557A.

601. Seat, Leroy Kay. "The Meaning of 'Paradox': A Study of the Use of the Word 'Paradox' in Contemporary Theological and Philosophical Writings with Special Reference to Sören Kierkegaard." Th.D., The Southern Baptist Theological Seminary, 1967, 351p. Dissertation Abstracts 27 (1967):3927A.

602. Seifert, Hans. "Die Konkretion des Daseins bei Sören Kierkegaard." Phil. Diss. Erlangen, 1929. Erlangen: Reinhold & Limmert, 1929, 96p.

603. Seymour, Betty J. "The Dyer's Hand: Kierkegaardian Perspectives on Person, Word, and Art Re-discovered in W. H. Auden." Duke Univ., 1975, 155p. Dissertation Abstracts 36 (1976):4583A.

604. Shearson, William Arrindell. "The Notion of Encounter in Existentialist Metaphysics: An Inquiry into the Nature and Structure of Existential Knowledge in Kierkegaard, Sartre, and Buber." Ph.D., Univ. of Toronto (Canada), 1970. Dissertation Abstracts 32 (1971):3374A.

605. Sherwood, Vance Robert, Jr. "Kierkegaard's Attack on the Church: Images of Ministry to the Church." D. Div., Vanderbilt Univ. Divinity School, 1972, 182p. Dissertation Abstracts 33 (1972):1828A.

606. Sieber, Fritz. "Der Begriff der Mitteilung bei Sören Kierkegaard." Theol. Diss. Heidelberg, 1938. Wurzburg: Triltsch, 1938, iii-39p.

607. Silvern, Jeffrey H. "Kierkegaard's Psychology of Health and Alienation." Ph.D., Graduate Theological Union, 1978, 147p. Dissertation Abstracts 39 (1978):3650-3651A. [Psychology, health and alienation]

608. Simon, Richard K. "Comedy, Suffering and Human Exis-tence: The Search for a Comic Strategy of Survival from Sören Kierkegaard to Kenneth Burke." Stanford Univ., 1977, 275p. Dissertation Abstracts 38 (1977):3471A.

609. Sivertsen, Eddie. "Faith and Reason in Soeren Kier-kegaard's Philosophy of Religion." Ph.D., Northern Baptist Theological Seminary, 1953.

610. Sjursen, Harold P. "Kierkegaard: The Individual and the Public. A Study in the Problem of Essential Communication." Ph.D., New School for Social Research, 1974, 283p. *Dissertation Abstracts* 35 (1975):6764A.

611. Slotty, Martin. "Die Erkenntnislehre S. A. Kierkegaards. Eine Würdigung seiner Verfasserwirksamkeit von zentralen Gesichtspunkte aus." Phil. Diss. Erlangen, 1915. Cassel: Pillardy & Augustin, 1915, 78p.

612. Smith, Joel R. "The Dialectic of Selfhood in the Works of Sören Kierkegaard." Vanderbilt Univ., 1977, 198p. *Dissertation Abstracts* 38 (1977):1456A.

613. Smith, Kenneth R. "Dialectical Conceptions of the Spirit: Hegel, Kierkegaard and Nietzsche." Ph.D., Yale Univ. *Dissertation Abstracts* 33 (1973):3720A.

614. Soneson, Joseph Melburn. "The Individual: A Comparison of the Philosophical Anthropologies of Sören Kierkegaard and Alfred North Whitehead with Theological Implications." Ph.D., Univ. of Chicago, 1969.

615. Soper, William Wayne. "The Self and Its World in Ralph Barton Perry, Edgar Sheffield Brightman, Jean-Paul Sartre and Soeren Kierkegaard." Ph.D., Boston Univ., 1962, 563p. *Dissertation Abstracts* 23 (1962):1042.

616. Soulès, Alberte Noéli. "La médecine et les médecins dans l'oeuvre de Kierkegaard." Thèse pour de doctorat de médecine, Paris: Foulon, 1949, 50p.

617. Sponheim, Paul Ronald. "The Christological Formulations of Schleiermacher and Kierkegaard in Relation to Fundamental Options Discernible in Divergent Strands in Their Discussion of God and Man." Ph.D., Univ. of Chicago, 1961.

618. Start, Lester J. "Kierkegaard and Hegel." Ph.D., Syracuse Univ., 1953.

619. Stavrides, Maria Margareta. "The Concept of Existence in Kierkegaard and Heidegger." Ph.D., Columbia Univ., 1952, 205p. *Dissertation Abstracts* 12:641.

620. Stevens, Eldon Lloyd. "Kierkegaard's Categories of Existence." Ph.D., Univ. of Colorado, 1964, 283p. *Dissertation Abstracts* 26 (1965):5487.

621. Stines, James William. "Phenomenology of Language in the Thought of Soeren Kierkegaard." Ph.D., Duke Univ., 1970, 279p. *Dissertation Abstracts* 31 (1971):6152A.

622. Suber, Peter Dain. "Kierkegaard's Concept of Irony, Especially in Relation to Personality, Freedom, and Dialectic." Ph.D., Northwestern Univ., 1978.

623. Sugerman, Shirley Greene. "Sin and Madness: A Study of the Self in Sören Kierkegaard and Ronald D. Laing." Ph.D., Drew Univ., 1970, 321p. *Dissertation Abstracts* 31 (1970):3029A.

624. Sullivan, Frank Russell, Jr. "Faith and Reason in Kierkegaard." Ph.D., Boston Univ., 1973, 185p. *Dissertation Abstracts* 34 (1973):1976A.

625. Taylor, Douglas R. "The aesthetic Methodology of Sören Kierkegaard's Pseudonymous Works." Florida State Univ., 1977, 328p. *Dissertation Abstracts* 38 (1977):2854A.

626. Taylor, Lewis Jerome, Jr. "The Becoming of the Self in the Writings of Walker Percy: A Kierkegaardian Analysis." Ph.D., Duke Univ., 1972, 349p. *Dissertation Abstracts* 33 (1972):1224A.

627. Teschner, George A. "The Relation of Man to Transcendence in the Philosophy of Kierkegaard." New School for Social Research, 1975, 251p. *Dissertation Abstracts* 36 (1976):6152A.

628. Thomasson, James William. "Concepts: Their Role, Criteria and Correction in the Thought of Sören A. Kierkegaard." Ph.D., Yale Univ., 1968, 303p. *Dissertation Abstracts* 29 (1969):4098A.

629. Thompson, Hugo W. "Ethics and Religion in the Philosophy of Kierkegaard." Ph.D., Yale Univ., 1935.

630. Thompson, Josiah Donald, Jr. "The Lonely Labyrinth: A Study in the Pseudonymous Works of Soeren Kierkegaard, 1843-1846." Ph.D., Yale Univ., 1964.

631. Timmerman, John H. "Feet of Clay--Concepts of Heroism in the Works of Carlyle, Dickens, Browning, Kierkegaard and Nietzsche." Ph.D., Ohio Univ. *Dissertation Abstracts* 34 (1974):5933A.

632. Tweedie, Donald F., Jr. "The Significance of Dread in the Thought of Kierkegaard and Heidegger." Ph.D., Boston Univ., 1954.

633. Underwood, Byron Edward. "Kierkegaard's Category of the Concrete Individual." Ph.D., Harvard Univ., 1966.

634. Utterbach, Sylvia W. "Kierkegaard's Dialectic of Christian Existence." Emory Univ., 1975, 373p. *Dissertation Abstracts* 36 (1975):2914A.

635. Van Roekel, Joseph G. "Decisive Christianity in the Authorship of Soeren Kierkegaard." Ph.D., The Southern Baptist Theological Seminary, 1954.

636.   Viallaneix, Nelly.   "Kierkegaard et la parole de
Dieu, I-II."   Lille, Atelier de reproduction des thèses,
Université de Lille III; Paris: H. Champion, 1977, 478p.;
502p.

637.   Vogt, Annemarie.   "Das Problem des Selbsteins bei
Heidegger und Kierkegaard."   Phil. Diss. Giessen, 1936.
Giessen: H. & J. Lechte, 1936, 61p.

638.   Wade, Donald Vance.   "The Concept of Individuality in
Soeren Kierkegaard."   Ph.D., Univ. of Toronto (Canada),
1944.

639.   Weiland, Jan Sperna.   "Humanitas Christianitas.   A
Critical Survey of Kierkegaards and Jaspers."   Schrift ter
verkrijging van de graad van doctor in de godgeleerdheit
aan de rijksuniversiteit te Groningen.   Theol. Disp.,
Engelsk & hollandsk tekst, Assen: Van Gorcum, 1951, 144p.

640.   Wells, William Walter, III.   "The Influence of Kierkegaard on the Theology of Karl Barth."   Ph.D., Syracuse
Univ., 1970, 294p.   *Dissertation Abstracts* 32 (1971):531A.

641.   West, Georg K.   "Kierkegaard and Adler.   A Comparison
of the Categories of Life as Seen by Both Authors and the
Consequent Implications for Therapy."   Florida State Univ.,
1975, 274p.   *Dissertation Abstracts* 37 (1976):138A.

642.   White, Carol Jean.   "Time and Temporality in the
Existential Thought of Kierkegaard and Heidegger."   Univ.
of California-Berkeley, 1976, 369p.   *Dissertation Abstracts*
38 (1977):853A.

643.   White, Willie.   "Faith and Existence: A Study in
Aquinas and Kierkegaard."   Ph.D., Univ. of Chicago, 1966.

644.   Wiseman, William J. J.   "Subjectivity in the Existential
Method of Soren Kierkegaard."   Ph.D., Temple Univ., 1948.

645.   Wolf, William.   "Alienation and Reconciliation in the
Writings of Sören Kierkegaard."   Th.D., Union Theological
Seminary, New York, 1945, 333p.   [Maskinskr.]

646.   Wüsten, Ewald.   "Die Bedeutung der Subjektivität für
die christliche Wahrheitsfrage.   Eine Studie über Sören
Kierkegaard."   Theol. Diss. Heidelberg, 1924, 177p.
[Maschinenschr.]

647.   Wünsche, Horst.   "*Der Begriff der Angst* und seine
Stellung im Kierkegaardischen Philosophieren."   Phil. Diss.
Univ. Mainz, 1953, ix-183p.

648.   Wyschgorog, Michael.   "Kierkegaard and Heidegger--The
Ontology of Existence."   Ph.D., Columbia Univ., 1954.

CHAPTER 3:
General Discussion
of Sören Kierkegaard's
Works and Life

ENGLISH

649. Aiken, H. D., ed. "Advent of existentialism: Sören Kierkegaard." In *Age of Ideology*. Boston: Houghton Mifflin, 1956, 225-244.

650. Allen, E. L. "Introduction to Kierkegaard." *Durham University Journal* 36 (1943):9-14.

651. Allen, W. Gore. "The Protestants: Sören Kierkegaard." In *Renaissance in the North*. London and New York: Sheed & Ward, 1946, 60-71.

652. Allison, Henry E. "Christianity and nonsense [Kierkegaard]." *Review of Metaphysics* 20 (1966-67):432-460.

653. Anderson, Barbara C. "Kierkegaard's despair as a religious author." *International Journal for Philosophy of Religion* 4 (1973):241-254.

654. Angoff, Charles. "Letters and the Arts." *Living Age* 357 (1940):89.

655. Anonymous. "The 'offence' of the God-Man: Kierkegaard's way of faith." *Times Literary Supplement* 36 (1937):229-230.

656. Anonymous. "Choose, leap and be free [on Kierkegaard]." *Times Literary Supplement* 45 (1946):109-111.

657. Anonymous. "Kierkegaard, the Dane. A personal Christian protest." *NewsWeek* 43 (1954):66.

658. Anonymous. "Meant for mankind: Kierkegaard and Christianity as the regulating weight." *Times Literary Supplement* 20 (1969):281-283.

659. Anshen, Ruth Nanda. "Accents of humanism in Sören."
Religious Humanism 5 (1971):54-58.

660. Arendt, Hannah. "Tradition and the modern age."
Partisan Review 21 (1954):53-75.

661. Attwater, Donald, ed. *Modern Christian Revolutionaries:
An Introduction to the Lives and Thought of Kierkegaard,
Eric Gill, G. K. Chesterton, C. F. Andrews, Berdyaev.*
New York, 1947 ["Soren Kierkegaard" by Melville Chaning-
Pearce]; Freeport (New York): Books for Libraries, 1971, 390p.

662. Auden, W. H. "A preface to Kierkegaard." *New Republic*
110 (1944):683-684.

663. Auden, W. H. "Knight of doleful countenance."
New Yorker 44 (1968):141-142, 146-148, 151-154, 157-158.

664. Auden, W. H. "Sören Kierkegaard." In his *Forewords
and Afterwards*. New York: Random House, 1973, 168-181.

665. Babbage, S. Barton. "Sören Kierkegaard." *Evangelical
Quarterly* (1943):56-72.

666. Barckett, Richard M., S. J. "Sören Kierkegaard:
'Back to Christianity!'" *Downside Review* 73 (1955):241-255.

667. Barckett, Richard M. "Kierkegaard: A Christian
protest." *America* 92 (1955):380-382.

668. Barrett, Cyril. "Sören Kierkegaard: An exception,
1813-1855." *Studies* 45 (1956):77-83. [Includes evaluation
of Kierkegaard's method of analysis.]
669.
669. Barrett, E. E. "Beyond absurdity." *Asbury Seminarian*
11 (1957):33-45.

670. Barrett, William. "Kierkegaard." In his *Irrational
Man. A Study in Existential Philosophy*. Garden City
(New York): Doubleday, 1958; Anchor Books ed., 1962, 149-176.

671. Barth, Karl. "Thank you and a bow: Kierkegaard's
reveille." Tr. by H. M. Rumscheidt. *Canadian Journal of
Theology* 11 (1965):3-7.

672. Barth, Karl. "Kierkegaard and the theologians."
Tr. by H. M. Rumscheidt. *Canadian Journal of Theology*
13 (1967):64-65.

673. Beach, Waldo, and Niebuhr, H. Richard, eds. "Sören
Kierkegaard." In *Christian Ethics. Sources of the Living
Tradition*. Ed. with introductions. New York: Ronald,
1955, 414-443.

674. Beck, Maximillan. "Existentialism, rationalism, and
Christian faith." *Journal of Religion* 26 (1946):283-295.

675. Beck, Maximillan. "Existentialism versus naturalism and idealism." *South Atlantic Quarterly* 47 (1948):157-163.

676. Belitt, Ben. "A reading in Kierkegaard." *Quarterly Review of Literature* 4 (1947):67-76.

677. Bernstein, Richard J. "Consciousness, existence, and action: Kierkegaard and Sartre." In *Praxis and Action: Contemporary Philosophies of Human Activity*. Philadelphia: Univ. of Pennsylvania Press, 1971.

678. Bertman, Martin A. "Kierkegaard: A sole possibility for individual unity." *Philosophy Today* 16 (1972):306-312.

679. Bertman, Martin A. "The Hebrew encounter with evil." *Apeiron* 9 (1975):43-47.

680. Bethurum, Dorothy. "The retreat of the intellectuals." *Vanderbilt Alumnus* 36 (1950):6-7.

681. Bierstedt, R. "An unripe philosopher." *Saturday Review of Literature* 30 (1947):17.

682. Billeskov Jansen, F. J. "The universality of Kierkegaard." *American-Scandinavian Review* 50 (1963):145-149.

683. Bixler, J. S. "On being absurd." *Massachusetts Review* 10 (1969):407-412.

684. Blackham, H. J. "Sören Kierkegaard (1813-1855)." In his *Six Existentialist Thinkers* (Kierkegaard, Nietzsche, Jaspers, Marcel, Heidegger, Sartre). London: Routledge & Kegan Paul, 1952; New York: Harper Torchbooks, 1953, 1-22.

685. Blanshard, Brand. *Reason and Belief*. London: George Allen, 1974.. 620p.

686. Boas, G. "Kierkegaard." In *Dominant Themes of Modern Philosophy*. New York: Ronald, 1957, 638-640.

687. Bolman, Frederick de W., Jr. "Kierkegaard in limbo." *Journal of Philosophy* 41 (1944):711-721.

688. Bourgeois, Patrick. "Kierkegaard: Ethical marriage or aesthetic pleasure?" *The Personalist* 57 (1976):370-375.

689. Brackett, Richard M. "Sören Kierkegaard: 'Back to Christianity!'" *Downside Review* 73 (1955):241-255.

690. Brackett, Richard M., S. J. "Kierkegaard: A Christian protest." *America* 90 (1955):380-382.

691. Brandes, Georg. *Main Currents in Nineteenth Century Literature*. 1-6. London: 1901; reprint, William Heinemann, 1906; New York: Boni & Liveright, 1923.

692. Bredsdorff, Elias. "Sören Kierkegaard." In his
Danish Literature in English Translation. With a special
Hans Christian Andersen supplement. A bibliography.
Copenhagen: Munksgaard, 1950, 79-87.

693. Bretall, Robert W. "Sören Kierkegaard: A critical
survey." *Examiner* 2 (1939):327-345.

694. Bretall, Robert, ed. *A Kierkegaard Anthology.* Introduction and notes. Princeton: Princeton Univ. Press, 1946.

695. Brock, W. "Nietzsche and Kierkegaard: Their importance
for contemporary German philosophy." In *Introduction to
Contemporary German Philosophy.* Cambridge, 1935, 45-86.

696. Brookfield, Christopher M. "What was Kierkegaard's
task? A frontier to be explored." *Union Seminary Quarterly
Review* 18 (1962):23-35.

697. Brophy, Liam. "Sören Kierkegaard: The Hamlet in
search of holiness." *Social Justice Review* 47 (1955):291-292.

698. Brown, James. *Kierkegaard, Heidegger, Buber and Barth.
Subject and Object in Modern Theology* (Croall lectures,
1953). [Originally appeared with title: *Subject and Object
in Modern Theology.*] New York: P. F. Collier, 1962. 192p.

699. Buch, Jorgen. "A Kierkegaard museum." *American Book
Collector* 12 (1961):5-7.

700. Bugbee, Henry. "Loneliness, solitude, and the twofold
way in which concern seems to be claimed." *Humanitas* 10
(1974):313-327.

701. Butler, Christopher. "Impressions of Kierkegaard."
Downside Review 55 (1937):363-369.

702. Bykhovski, Bernard. "A philosophy of despair."
Philosophy and Phenomenological Research 34 (1973):187-200.

703. Calhoun, Robert L. "Kierkegaard's writings." *Yale
Review* 34 (1945):370-375.

704. Cant, Reginald. "Sören Kierkegaard." *Church Quarterly
Review* 127 (1938-39):268-294.

705. Caponigri, Robert. "Sören Kierkegaard." In his
A History of Western Philosophy 4. Univ. of Notre Dame
Press, 1971, 159-190. (Chap. 6, B)

706. Cavell, Stanley. "Kierkegaard's *On Authority and
Revelation.*" In *Must We Mean What We Say: A Book of Essays.*
Cambridge, 1976. First pub. New York: Scribners, 1969.

707. Chaning-Pearce, Melville. "Kierkegaard's message to
our age." *Journal of the Transactions of the Victoria
Institute* 74 (1945):27-52.

708. Chaning-Pearce, M. "Sören Kierkegaard." In *Modern Christian Revolutionaries: An Introduction to the Lives and Thought of Kierkegaard, Eric Gill, G. K. Chesterton, C. F. Andrews, Berdyaev.* Donald Attwater, ed. New York: Devin-Adair, 1947, 1-85.

709. Chaning-Pearce, M. "Denmark's dead man." In *Terrible Crystal: Studies in Kierkegaard and Modern Christians.* Oxford: 1947, 1-52.

710. "Choose, leap and be free." *Times Literary Supplement* 45 (1946):109-111.

711. Clive, Geoffrey. "The sickness unto death in the underworld: A study of nihilism." *Harvard Theological Review* 51 (1958):135-167. [Kierkegaard, Dostoievsky, Kafka]

712. Clive, G. "Seven types of offence [in nineteenth century and contemporary literature]. *Lutheran Quarterly* 10 (1958):11-25.

713. Coates, J. B. "Sören Kierkegaard." *Fortnightly Review* 167 (1950):243-250.

714. Cochrane, A. C. "On the anniversaries of Mozart, Kierkegaard, and Barth." *Scottish Journal of Theology* 9 (1956):251-263.

715. Cochrane, Arthur C. *The Existentialists and God. Being and the Being of God in the Thought of Sören Kierkegaard, Karl Jaspers, Martin Heidegger, Jean-Paul Sartre, Paul Tillich, Etienne Gilson, Karl Barth.* Philadelphia: Westminster Press, 1956. 174p.

716. Collins, James D. "The fashionableness of Kierkegaard." *Thought* 22 (1947):211-215.

717. Collins, James D. "The mind of Kierkegaard: The problem and the personal outlook." *Modern Schoolman* 26 (1948):1-22.

718. Collins, James D. "The mind of Kierkegaard: The spheres of existence and the romantic outlook." *Modern Schoolman* 26 (1949):121-147.

719. Collins, James D. "The mind of Kierkegaard: Becoming a Christian in Christendom." *Modern Schoolman* 26 (1949): 293-322.

720. Collins, James D. "Three Kierkegaardian problems. 1-3. 1:. . .; 2: The ethical view and its limits; 3. The nature of the human individual." *New Scholasticism* 22 (1948):370-416; 23 (1949):3-37; 147-185.

721. Collins, James D. "Kierkegaard and Christian philosophy." *The Thomist* 14 (1951):441-465.

722. Collins, James D. "Sören Kierkegaard." In his
The Existentialists. A Critical Study. Chicago: Regnery,
1952.

723. Collins, James D. "The relevance of Kierkegaard."
Commonweal 62 (1955):439-442

724. Collins, James Daniel. "Faith and reflection in
Kierkegaard." *Journal of Religion* 37 (1957):10-19.

725. Comstock, W. R. "Aspects of aesthetic existence:
Kierkegaard and Santayana." *International Philosophical
Quarterly* 6 (1966):189-213.

726. Cook, F. J. Raymond. "Kierkegaard's literary art."
Listener 72 (1964):713-714.

727. Copleston, Frederick C. "Kierkegaard." In his
History of Philosophy, 7. London: Burns and Oates, 1963,
335-350.

728. Crites, Stephen. "Pseudonymous authorship as art and
as act." In *Kierkegaard: A Collection of Critical Essays.*
Josiah Thompson, ed. Garden City: Doubleday & Co., Anchor
Books, 183-229.

729. Croxall, Thomas Henry. "The Christian doctrine of
hope and the Kierkegaardian doctrine of 'the moment'."
Expository Times 56 (1945):292-295.

730. Croxall, Thomas H. "Man's inner condition: A study
in Kierkegaard." *Philosophy* 22 (1947):252-255.

731. Croxall, Thomas H. "The importance of Kierkegaard."
Danish Foreign Office Journal (1948):30-33.

732. Croxall, Thomas H. "Kierkegaard as seen by an
Englishman." *Danish Foreign Office Journal* (1955):11-14.

733. Cumming, Robert D. "Existence and communication."
Ethics 65 (1955):79-101.

734. Curtis, Jerry L. "Heroic commitment, or the dialectics
of the leap in Kierkegaard, Sartre, and Camus." *Rice University Studies* 59 (1973):17-26.

735. Daise, Benjamin. "Kierkegaard and the absolute
paradox." *Journal of the History of Philosophy* 14 (1976):
63-68.

736. Dargan, Edwin Charles. "Soren Kierkegaard." In his
A History of Preaching, 2. New York: Hodder & Stoughton,
1912, 423-429.

737. Demant, V. A. "Soren Kierkegaard: Knight of faith."
Nineteenth Century 127 (1940):70-77.

738. Dewey, Bradley Rau. "Kierkegaard and the blue
testament." *Harvard Theological Review* 60 (1967):391-409.

739. Dru, Alexander. "Kierkegaard: A great Christian
thinker." *Listener* 54 (1955):841-842.

740. Dru, Alexander. "Reply with rejoinder." *Dublin
Review* 221 (1948):183-185.

741. Drucker, P. F. "The unfashionable Kierkegaard."
Sewanee Review 57 (1949):587-602. Reprinted in his
Men, Ideas and Politics. New York: Harper, 1971, 50-65.

742. Dunstan, J. Leslie. "Kierkegaard and Jeremiah."
Andover Bulletin 47 (1955):17-24. (Kierkegaard centennial
issue.)

743. Dupré, Louis K. "Kierkegaard: Melancholy Dane."
America 94 (1956):689-690.

744. Eller, Vernard. "Fact, faith, and foolishness:
Kierkegaard and the new quest." *Journal of Religion* 48
(1968):54-68.

745. Eller, Vernard. "Existentialism and the brethren."
Brethren Life and Thought 5 (1960):31-38.

746. Eller, Vernard. "Kierkegaard knew the Brethren! Sort
of." *Brethren Life and Thought* 8 (1963):57-60.

747. Evans, C. Stephens. "Mis-using religious language:
Something about Kierkegaard and 'the myth of God incarnate'."
Religious Studies 15 (1979):139-158.

748. Evans, C. Stephens. "Kierkegaard: Belief as existen-
tially necessary." In his *Subjectivity and Religious Belief:
A Historical, Critical Study*. Grand Rapids (Michigan):
Christian Univ. Press, 1978, 74-122 and passim.

749. Fabro, Cornelio. "The problem of desperation and
Christian spirituality in Kierkegaard." *Kierkegaardiana*
4 (1962):63-69.

750. Fausset, Hugh I' Anson. "Kierkegaard and the present
age." *Aryan Path* 13 (1942):259-263. Reprinted in his
Poets and Pundits: A Collection of Essays. London: Cape,
1947; New Haven: Yale Univ. Press, 1947, 205-222.

751. Fay, Thomas A. "Communication of truth and the
existential dialectic in the thought of Kierkegaard."
The Personalist 53 (1972):161-169.

752. Fenger, Henning. "Kierkegaard--A literary approach."
Scandinavica 3 (1964):1-16.

753. Ferrie, W. S. "Sören Kierkegaard: Hamlet or Jeremiah?"
Evangelical Quarterly 8 (1936):142-147.

754. Fitzer, Joseph. "Liturgy and comedy: Some Kierkegaardian reflections." *Downside Review* 52 (1972-73):588-602.

755. Fleissner, E. M. "Legacy of Kierkegaard."
New Republic 133 (1955):16-18.

756. Forgey, Wallace. "A pastor looks at Kierkegaard."
Andover Newton Bulletin 47 (1955):32-39.

757. Forrest, William. "A problem in values: The Faustian
motivation in Kierkegaard and Geothe." *Ethics* 63 (1953):
251-261.

758. Forshey, Gerald. "Pharaoh, Kierkegaard, and black
power." *Christian Advocate* 12 (1968):7-8.

759. Fowler, Albert. "Waters from his own well."
University of Kansas City Review 22 (1955):89-92.

760. Fox, Michael. "Will the real S. Kierkegaard please
step forward?" *Queen's Quarterly* 83 (1976):367-374.

761. Galati, Michael. "A rhetoric for the subjectivist in
a world of untruth: The tasks and strategy of Sören Kierkegaard." *QJS* 55 (1969):372-380.

762. Gallagher, T. "Sören Kierkegaard." In *Existentialist
Thinkers and Thought.* F. Patka, ed. New York: Phil. Libr.,
1962, 75-92.

763. Gardiner, Patrick. "Kierkegaard's two ways." *Proceedings of the British Academy* 54 (1968):207-229.

764. Geismar, Eduard. "Sören Kierkegaard." *American-
Scandinavian Review* 17 (1929):591-599.

765. Genêt. "Letter from Paris." *New Yorker* 11 (1964):170.

766. Gerber, Rudolph J. "Kierkegaard, reason, and faith."
Thought 44 (1969):29-52.

767. Gilson, Etienne. "Sören Kierkegaard." In his
Being and Some Philosophers. (1949) 2d ed., corrected and
enlarged, Toronto: Pontifical Institute of Mediaeval Studies,
1952.

768. Gilson, Etienne, Langan, T., and Maurer, A. A.
"Sören Kierkegaard." In their *Recent Philosophy. Hegel to
the Present.* Random House, 1966, 69-78.

769. Gimblett, Charles. "Sören Kierkegaard: A strange
saint." *London Quarterly and Holborn Review* 180 (1955):
280-282.

770. Glenn, John D., Jr. "Kierkegaard on the unity of comedy and tragedy." *Tulane Studies in Philosophy* 19 (1970):41-53.

771. Glicksberg, Charles I. "The aesthetics of nihilism." *University of Kansas City Review* 27 (1960):127-130.

772. Glicksberg, Charles I. "The Kierkegaardian paradox of the absurd." In his *The Tragic Vision in Twentieth-Century Literature*. Carbondale (Illinois): Southern Illinois Univ. Press, 1963, 18-28.

773. Golding, Henry J. "Kierkegaard: A neglected thinker." *Standard* 12 (1926):142-148.

774. Goulet, D. A. "Kierkegaard, Aquinas, and the dilemma of Abraham." *Thought* 32 (1957):165-188.

775. Graef, H. C. "Prophets of doom." *Catholic World* 182 (1956):202-206.

776. Graham, D. Aelred. "Introducing Christianity into Christendom. An impression of Sören Kierkegaard." *Clergy Review* 24 (N.S.) (1944):535-541. Reprinted in his *Christian Thought and Action*. New York: Harcourt, 1958, 145-154.

777. Gregory, T. S. "Kierkegaard: The prophet of now." *Listener* 36 (1942):717-719.

778. Gregory, T. S. "Kierkegaard: The only philosopher?" *Listener* 36 (1946):798. [See Ratcliffe, no. 950]

779. Gregory, T. S. "Kierkegaard: The prophet of now." *Current Religious Thought* 10 (1950):7-11.

780. Grene, Marjorie. "Kierkegaard: The philosophy." *Kenyon Review* 9 (1947):48-69.

781. Grene, Marjorie. "Sören Kierkegaard: The self against the system." In *Dreadful Freedom*. Chicago: Univ. of Chicago Press, 1959, 15-40.

782. Grieve, Alexander. "Sören Kierkegaard." *Expository Times* 19 (1908):206-209.

783. Grieve, Alexander. "Sören Kierkegaard." In *Encyclopedia of Religion and Ethics*, 133. James Hastings and John A. Selbie, eds. London, 1926. [See Hastings, no. 793]

784. Griffith, Gwilym O. "Kierkegaard." In his *Interpreters of Man. A Review of Secular and Religious Thought from Hegel to Barth*. London: Lutterworth, 1943, 25-41 and passim.

785. Gumbiner, Joseph Henry. "Sören Kierkegaard." In his
Existentialism and father Abraham. Commentary 5 (1948):
143-148 and passim.

786. Hall, T. "Contra Kierkegaard." *Theology Today* 27
(1970):71-75.

787. Hamburger, M. "A refusal to review Kierkegaard."
In *Art as Second Nature: Occasional Pieces, 1950-1974*.
New York: Carionet New Press, dist. by Dufour, 1975. 156p.
[The last years of Kierkegaard]

788. Hamilton, Kenneth M. "Created soul--eternal spirit:
A continuing theological thorn." *Scottish Journal of
Theology* 19 (1966):23-34.

789. Hannay, Alastair. "A kind of philosopher: Comments
in conncetion with some recent books on Kierkegaard."
Inquiry 18 (1975):354-365. [See Kleinman, no. 850]

790. Haroutunian, Joseph. "Protest to the Lord." *Theology
Today* 12 (1955):295-296.

791. Harper, Ralph. "Two existential interpretations."
Philosophy and Phenomenological Research 5 (1945):392-400.

792. Harper, Ralph. *The Seventh Solitude. Metaphysical
Homelessness in Kierkegaard, Dostoevsky, and Nietzsche.*
Baltimore: Johns Hopkins Press, 1967. 153p.

793. Hastings, James, and Selbie, John, eds. *Encyclopaedia
of Religion and Ethics*. 1926. [See Grieve, no. 782]

794. Heinecken, M. J. "Kierkegaard as Christian."
Journal of Religion 37 (1957):20-30.

795. Heinemann, F. H. "The existential Christian." In
Existentialism and the Modern Predicament. New York:
Harper Torchbooks, 1958, 30-46 and passim.

796. Heinemann, F. H. "Origin and repetition." *Review of
Metaphysics* 4 (1950):201-214.

797. Heiss, R. *Hegel, Kierkegaard, Marx. Three Great
Philosophers Whose Ideas Changed the Course of Civilization.*
Trans. from the German by E. B. Garside. Boston (Massachu-
setts): Seymour Lawrence, 1975, 438p.; New York: Dell, Dell
Paperbacks.

798. Held, Matthew. "The historical Kierkegaard: Faith or
gnosis." *Journal of Religion* 37 (1957):260-266.

799. Henriksen, Aage. "Kierkegaard's reviews of literature."
Orbis Litterarum 10 (1955):75-83. [Symposion Kierkegaard-
ianum]

800. Herbert, R. "God-man." *Religious Studies* 6 (1970):
157-174.

801. Heschel, Abraham Joshua. "The Kotzter and Kierkegaard."
In his A *Passion for Truth*. New York: Farrar, Straus and
Giroux, 1973, 85-115 and passim.

802. Hess, Mary W. "Three Christians in literature:
Browning, Kierkegaard, Heine." *Christianity Today* 8 (1964):
13-15.

803. Heywood, J. Thomas. "Logic and existence in Kierkegaard." *Journal of the British Society for Phenomenology*
2 (1971):3-11.

804. Hill, B. Victor. *Education and the Endangered
Individual. A Critique of Ten Modern Thinkers.* New York:
Teachers College Press, 1974. 322p.

805. Hill, E. F. F. "Kierkegaard: The man and his thought."
World Review (1948):58-62.

806. Hirst, Désirée. "An honest man." In *Vues sur Kierkegaard*. Henein and Wahba, eds. 1955, 62-84.

807. Hoffding, Harald. "Sören Kierkegaard." In his
A *History of Modern Philosophy. A Sketch of the History of
Philosophy from the Close of the Renaissance to Our Own Day.*
Trans. from the German ed. by B. E. Meyer. London and
New York: Macmillan, 1900; reg. repr. ibid., Humanities
Press, 1950; reg. repr. ibid., Dover, 1955.

809. Hoffding, Harald. "Sören Kierkegaard." In his
A *Brief History of Modern Philosophy.* Authorized trans. by
Charles Finley Sanders. New York, 1931.

810. Hoffding, Harald. "Sören Kierkegaard." In his
Outlines in Psychology. Trans. by Mary E. Lowndes.
London: Macmillan, 1891. (Macmillan's Manuels for Students:
psychology.)

811. Hoffman, W. Michael. "Kierkegaard as philosophical
poet." *Midwest Journal of Philosophy* 5 (1977):21-30.

812. Holder, F. L. "Advance beyond Socrates." *Encounter*
31 (1970):235-240.

813. Holmer, Paul L. "Kierkegaard, a religious author."
American-Scandinavian Review 33 (1945):147-152.

814. Holmer, Paul L. "Kierkegaard and religious proposi-
tions." *Journal of Religion* 35 (1955):135-146.

815. Holmer, Paul L. "Kierkegaard and kinds of discourse."
Middelelser fra Sören Kierkegaard Selskabet 4 (1954):1-5.

816.   Holmer, Paul L.   "On understanding Kierkegaard."
Orbis Litterarum 10 (1955):93-106.

817.   Holmer, Paul L.   "Kierkegaard and the sermon."
Journal of Religion 38 (1957):1-9.

818.   Holmes, Roger W.   "The problems of philosophy in
the Twentieth Century."   *Antioch Review* 22 (1962):287-296.

819.   Hong, H.   "Sören Kierkegaard as a Christian philosopher."   *Scottish Journal of Theology* (1941).

820.   Hong, Howard V.   "The comic, satire, irony, and
humor: Kierkegaardian reflections."   In *Midwest Studies in
Philosophy, 1: Studies in the History of Philosophy.*
Peter A. French, Theodore E. Uehling, Jr., and Howard K.
Wettstein, eds.   Morris: Univ. of Minnesota, 1976, 98-105.
136p.

821.   Hook, Sidney.   "Two types of existential religion and
ethics."   *Partisan Review* 26 (1959):58-63.

822.   Hopper, S. R.   "Modern Diogenes: A Kierkegaardian
crotchet."   In *Religion and Culture: Essays in Honor of
Paul Tillich.*   W. Leibrecht, ed.   New York: Harper, 1959,
91-112.

823.   Horgby, Ingvar.   "Immediacy--subjectivity--revelation."
Inquiry 8 (1965):84-117.

824.   Horn, Robert L.   "On understanding Kierkegaard understanding [reply to R. Kroner]."   *Union Seminary Quarterly
Review* 21 (1966):341-345.

825.   Horton, William.   "British theological leadership."
Christendom 1 (1936):515-524.

826.   Hubbeling, H. G.   "Logical reconstructivism as a
metaphilosophical method of interpretation and discussion."
Philosophica 16 (1975):51-64.

827.   Hubben, William.   "Sören Kierkegaard."   In his
*Four Prophets of Our Destiny: Kierkegaard, Dostojevsky,
Nietzsche, Kafka.*   New York: Macmillan, 1952, 1-41.

828.   Hubben, William.   *Four Prophets of Our Destiny:
Kierkegaard, Dostoievsky, Nietzsche, Kafka.*   New York:
Macmillan, 1952, viii-170p.; *Dostoevsky, Kierkegaard,
Nietzsche and Kafka.   Four Prophets of Our Destiny.*
New York: Collier Books, 1962, 188p.

829.   Hustwit, Ronald.   "Some notes on what Kierkegaard calls
'an ideal interpretation'."   *Ohio Journal of Religious
Studies* 3 (1975):55-60.

830. Huszar, George de. "Preface to Kierkegaard." *South Atlantic Quarterly* 48 (1949):100-106.

831. Idinopulos, T. A. "The theology of the individual: Sören Kierkegaard." In *The Erosion of Faith*. Chicago: Quadrangel Books, 1971, 30-58.

832. Jacobson, Nolan Pliny. "The predicament of man in Zen Buddhism and Kierkegaard." *Philosophy East and West* 2 (1952):238-253.

833. Jagal, Ernest. "Malicious philosophers of science." *Partisan Review* 10 (1943):40-57.

834. James, Ingli. "The autonomy of the work of art: Modern criticism and the Christian tradition." *Sewanee Review* 70 (1962):296-318.

835. Jaspers, Karl. "The importance of Nietzsche, Marx, and Kierkegaard in the history of philosophy." Trans. by Stanley Godman. *Hibbert Journal* 49 (1951):226-234; "The importance of Kierkegaard." Trans. by Erwin W. Geissman. *Cross Currents* 2 (1952):5-16.

836. Jaspers, Karl. "Origin of the contemporary philosophical situation (the historical meaning of Kierkegaard and Nietzsche)." In his *Reason and Existenz. Five Lectures*. Trans. with an introduction by William Earle. New York: The Noonday Press, a div. of Farrar, Straus and Giroux, 1955, 19-50.

837. Jensen, Alfred Dewey. "Dr. Johnson, Kierkegaard, and Gingell's dilemma." *Sophia* (Australia) 15 (1976):7-12.

838. Jones, Llewellyn. "The transmigration of Kierkegaard." *Humanist* 2 (1942):21-27.

839. Johannesson, Eric O. "Isak Kinesen, Soren Kierkegaard, and the present age." *Books Abroad* 36 (1962):20-24.

840. Johnson, Howard. "The Diety in time: An introduction to Kierkegaard." *Theology Today* 1 (1945):517-536.

841. Kaufmann, R. J. "A poetry for Sisyphus." *Prairie Schooner* 40 (1966):23-43.

842. Kaufmann, Walter. "A hundred years after Kierkegaard. II: Kierkegaard." *Kenyon Review* 18 (1956):182-211.

843. Kaufmann, Walter. "Kierkegaard." In *From Shakespeare to existentialism. Studies in Poetry, Religion and Philosophy*. Boston: Beacon Press, 1959, 161-189.

844. Kean, Charles D. *The Meaning of Existence*. New York, 1947. [Christianity in the light of Kierkegaardian existentialism.]

845. Kellenberger, James. "The language-game view of religion and religious certainty." *Canadian Journal of Philosophy* 2 (1972):255-275.

846. Kern, Edith Goldenberg. *Existential Thought and Fictional Technique: Kierkegaard, Sartre, Beckett.* New Haven (Connecticut), London: Yale Univ. Press, 1970. 261p.

847. "Kierkegaard." *Sign* 25 (1946):28.

848. Killinger, John. "Existentialism and human freedom." *English Journal* (1962):303-312.

849. Kleinman, J. "Kierkegaard. The mad bank-note." *Dialogue. Journal of Phi Sigma Tau* (Milwaukee, Wisconsin) 18 (1975-76):1-3.

850. Kleinman, Jackie. "Kierkegaard--some unfinished business." *Inquiry* 19 (1976):486-492. [Re: A. Hannay's "A kind of philosopher. . ." *Inquiry* (1975). See no. 789]

851. Klemke, E. D. "Logicality versus alogicality in the Christian faith." *Journal of Religion* 38 (1958):107-115.

852. Klemke, E. D. "Some misinterpretations of Kierkegaard." *Hibbert Journal* 57 (1959):259-270.

853. Krieger, Murray. "Tragedy and the tragic vision." In *The Tragic Vision: Variations on a Theme in Literary Interpretation*. New York: Holt, 1960, 1-21.

854. Kuhn, Helmut. "Champions of forgetfulness. The historicist and the either-or philosopher." In his *Freedom Forgotten and Remembered*. Chapel Hill: Univ. of North Carolina Press, 1943, 14-21 and passim.

855. Kuhn, Helmut. "Existentialism and metaphysics." *Review of Metaphysics* 1 (1947):37-60.

856. Kuhn, Helmut. *Encounter with Nothingness. An Essay on Existentialism*. Hinsdale (Illinois): Regnery, 1949, 13-20, 29-30, 67-68, 124-129. (Humanist Library, 2.)

857. Larsen, Robert E. "Kierkegaard's absolute paradox." *Journal of Religion* 42 (1962):34-43.

858. Leendertz, W. "Soren Kierkegaard: An interpretation." *Mennonite Quarterly Review* 23 (1949):203-231.

859. LeFevre, Perry D., ed. *The Prayers of Kierkegaard* (with a new interpretation of his life and thought). Chicago: Univ. of Chicago Press, 1963. 244p.

860. LeFevre, P. D. "Snare of truth." *Pastoral Psychology* 19 (1968):33-44.

861. Lenning, Per. "The dilemma of 'grace alone'."
Dialog 6 (1967):108-114.

862. Levertoff, P. "On some reflections on Kierkegaard."
Quest 45.

863. Levi, Albert William. "A hundred years after Kierkegaard. I: The three masks." *Kenyon Review* 18 (1956):
169-182.

864. Levy, G. E. "Kierkegaard's significance as a
'corrective'." *Colgate-Rochester Divinity School Bulletin*
19 (1942).

865. Lewis, Edwin. A *Philosophy of the Christian Revelation*. New York: Harper, 1940; London: Epworth, 1948.

866. Livingston, G. H. "Kierkegaard and Jeremiah." *Asbury
Seminarian* 11 (1957):46-61.

867. Lönning, P. "Dilemma of 'grace alone'." *Dialog* 6
(1967):108-114.

868. Lönning, P. "Salvation and politics [editorial]."
Lutheran World 18 (1971):268-271.

869. Löwith, Karl. "On the historical understanding of
Kierkegaard." *Journal of Philosophy* 38 (1941):677-678;
Review of Religion 7 (1943):227-241.

870. Löwith, Karl. "Nature, history, and existentialism."
Social Research 19 (1952):79-94.

871. Lowrie, Walter. "Kierkegaard." *Church Review* 2
(1941):8-10.

872. Lowrie, Walter. "Translators and interpreters of
Sören Kierkegaard." *Theology Today* 12 (1955-56):312-327.

873. Lowrie, Walter. "Qualified retraction and unqualified
apology." *Theology Today* 16 (1959):267.

874. Lubac, Henri de. *The Drama of Atheist Humanism*.
London: Sheed & Ward, 1949.

875. Lucas, Ernest. "Sören Kierkegaard." *Holborn Review*
157 (1932):7-17.

876. Lund, Margaret. "The single ones." *The Personalist*
41 (1960):15-24.

877. MacGillvray, Arthur, S. J. "The melancholy Dane:
Sören Kierkegaard." *Catholic World* 163 (1946):338-342.

878. Mackey, Louis H. "Sören Kierkegaard: The poetry of inwardness." In *Existential Philosophers: Kierkegaard to Merleau-Ponty*. George A. Schrader, Jr., ed. New York: McGraw-Hill, 1967, 45-108.

879. Mackey, L. "Philosophy and poetry in Kierkegaard." *Review of Metaphysics* 23 (1969):316-332.

880. Mackintosh, Hugh Ross. "A great Danish thinker." *Expository Times* 13 (1902):404.

881. Mackintosh, Hugh Ross. "Theology of paradox." In *Types of Modern Theology: Schleiermacher to Barth*. New York: Scribner, 1939, 218-262.

882. MacRae, D. G. "The Danish malady." *Life & Letters Today* 47 (1945):85-90.

883. Malantschuk, G. "Kierkegaard and the totalitarians." *American-Scandinavian Review* 34 (1946):246-248.

884. Mantripp, J. C. "Sören Kierkegaard." *London Quarterly and Holborn Review* 164 (1939):237-243; 268-294.

885. Marcuse, Herbert. *Reason and Revolution. Hegel and the Rise of Social Theory*. London, New York & Toronto: Oxford Univ. Press, 1941, 262-267.

886. Maritain, Jacques. "From existential existentialism to academic existentialism." *Sewanee Review* 56 (1948): 210-229.

887. Martensen, H. *Christian Ethics*. Trans. from the Danish with the sanction of the author by C. Spence. Edinburgh: Clark, 1873, 217-236. (Clark's Foreign Theological Library, series 3, vol. 39.)

888. Martin, Vincent. *Existentialism: Kierkegaard, Sartre and Camus* (Compact Studies). Washington: Thomist Press, 1962. 48p.

889. Marsh, James L. "The two Kierkegaards." *Philosophy Today* 16 (1972):313-322.

890. Masur, G. "Founding and destroying fathers." In *Prophets of Yesterday*. New York: Macmillan, 1961, 38-105.

891. McCarthy, Vincent A. "Melancholy and religious melancholy in Kierkegaard." *Kierkegaardiana* 10 (1977): 152-165.

892. McEachran, F. "The significance of Sören Kierkegaard." *Hibbert Journal* 44 (1946):135-141.

893. McFadden, R. "Nuclear dilemma, with a nod to Kierkegaard." *Theology Today* 17 (1961):505-518.

894. McInerny, Ralph. "Ethics and persuasion: Kierkegaard's existential dialectic." *Modern Schoolman* 33 (1956):219-239.

895. McInerny, Ralph M. "Kierkegaard and speculative thought." *New Scholasticism* 40 (1966):23-35.

896. McInerny, Ralph. "The ambiguity of existential metaphysics." *Laval Théologique et Philosophique* 12 (1956): 120-124.

897. McKeon, Richard. "The philosophy of Kierkegaard." *New York Times Book Review* 25 (1945).

898. McKinnon, Alastair. "Kierkegaard: 'Paradox' and irrationalism [abstract]." *Journal of Philosophy* 62 (1965): 651-652.

899. McKinnon, Alastair. "Kierkegaard: 'Paradox' and irrationalism." *Journal of Existentialism* 7 (1967):401-416.

900. McKinnon, Alastair. "Believing the 'paradoks': A contradiction in Kierkegaard?" *Harvard Theological Review* 61 (1968):633-636.

901. McKinnon, Alastair. "The central works in Kierkegaard's authorship." *Revue Internationale de Philosophie* 27 (1973):84-94.

902. McKinnon, Alastair. "Theological focus in Kierkegaard's *Samlede Woerker*: Some basic data." *SRC* 4 (1974): 58-62.

903. McKinnon, Alastair. "The increase of Christian terms in Kierkegaard's *Samlede Vaerker*." *Kierkegaardiana* (1974): 147-162.

904. McKinnon, Alastair. "Paradox and faith in Kierkegaard." In *The Challenge of Religion Today*. John King-Farlow, ed. The Canadian Contemporary Philosophy Serie. New York: Science History Publications, 1976.

905. McMinn, J. B. "Value and subjectivity in Kierkegaard." *Review and Expositor* 53 (1956):477-488.

906. McPherson, Thomas. "Second great Commandment: Religion and morality." *Congregational Quarterly* 35 (1957):212-222.

907. Merlan, Philip. "Toward the understanding of Kierkegaard." *Journal of Religion* 23 (1943):77-90.

908. Merlan, Philip. "Must we reinterpret Kierkegaard?" *Journal of Religion* 53 (1973):48-64.

909. Mesnard, Pierre. "The character of Kierkegaard's philosophy." *Philosophy Today* 1 (1957):84-89.

910. Michalson, Gordon Elliott. "Dramatic approach to
Christianity." *Christendom* 9 (1944):462-475.

911. Miller, Samuel H. "Kierkegaard: Then and now."
Andover Newton Bulletin 47 (1955):5-11.

912. Minear, Paul S. "The church: Militant or triumphant?"
Andover Newton Bulletin 47 (1955):25-31. (Kierkegaard
centennial issue.)

913. Minear, Paul S. "Thanksgiving as a synthesis of the
temporal and the eternal." *Anglican Theological Review*
38 (1956):4-14.

914. Moore, W. G. "Kierkegaard and his century." *Hibbert
Journal* 36 (1938):568-582.

915. Moore, W. G. "Recent studies of Kierkegaard."
Journal of Theological Studies 40 (1939):225-231.

916. Muggeridge, Malcolm. "Books." *Esquire* 70 (1968):30.

917. Muggeridge, Malcolm. "Sören Kierkegaard: 1813 to 1955."
In his *A Third Testament*. Boston-Toronto: Little, Brown and
Co., a Time-Life television book, 1976, 118-145.

918. Munz, Peter. "Sum qui sum." *Hibbert Journal* 50
(1952):143-152.

919. Murphy, John L. "Faith and reason in the teaching of
Kierkegaard." *American Ecclesiastical Review* 145 (1961):
233-265.

920. Nageley, Winfield E. "Kierkegaard's Archimedean
point." In *Contemporary Philosophic Thought*, 3.
H. E. Kiefer, ed. New York: State Univ. of New York Press,
1970, 163-180.

921. Nageley, Winfield E. "Kierkegaard's irony in the
Diapsalmata." *Kierkegaardiana* 6 (1967):51-75.

921a. Nelson, Clifford A. "The dimension of inwardness in
Christianity." *Augustana Quarterly* 21 (1941):125-144.

922. Neumann, Harry. "Kierkegaard and Socrates on the
dignity of man." *The Personalist* 48 (1967):453-460.

923. Niebuhr, Reinhold. "Coherence, incoherence, and
Christian faith." *Journal of Religion* 31 (1951):155-168.

924. Nielsen, H. A. "Kierkegaard's metaphysical crochet."
Proceedings of the American Catholic Philosophical Association
46 (1972):123-132.

925. Norborg, Sv. *Varieties of Christian Experience*.
Minneapolis (Minnesota): Augsburg, 1937, 113-115 and passim.

926. Noyce, Gaylord B. "Wounded by Christ's sword."
Interpretation 8 (1954):433-443.

927. O'Donnell, William G. "Kierkegaard: The literary
manner." *Kenyon Review* 9 (1947):35-47.

928. Ofstad, Harald. "Morality, choice, and inwardness."
Inquiry 8 (1965):33-72.

929. Oke, C. Clare. "Kierkegaard as major prophet."
Expository Times 62 (1950-51):61-62. [See Stewart, no. 1004]

930. Oliver, W. Donald. "The concept and the thing."
Journal of Philosophy 33 (1936):69-80.

931. O'Mara, Joseph. "Kierkegaard revealed." *Dublin
Studies* 38 (1949):447-456.

932. Otani, Masaru. "Introduction to Kierkegaard."
Meddelelser fra Sören Kierkegaard Selskabet 5 (1955):3-5.

933. Otani, Masaru. "Introduction to Kierkegaard."
(Howard A. Johnson's lectures in Japan.) *Meddelelser fra
Sören Kierkegaard Selskabet* 5 (1955):3-5.

934. Otani, Masaru. "Something about Kierkegaard's inner
history." *Orbis Litterarum* 10 (1955):191-195.

935. Otani, Masaru. "Self-manifestation of 'freedom in
anxiety' by Kierkegaard." *Orbis Litterarum* 22 (1967):
393-398.

936. Pedersen, Bertel. "Fictionality and authority: A
point of view for Kierkegaard's work as an author."
Modern Language Notes 89 (1974):938-956.

937. Pelikan, Jaroslav. *From Luther to Kierkegaard: A
Study of the History of Theology.* St. Louis: Concordia
Press, 1950. 178p.

938. Pelikan, Jaroslav. *Human Culture and the Holy.
Essays on the True, the Good and the Beautiful. Kierkegaard,
Paul, Dostoevsky, Luther, Nietzsche [and] Bach.* London:
Student Christian Movement Press, 1959. 172p.

939. Percy, Walker. "The message in the bottle." *Thought*
34 (1959):405-433.

940. Perkins, Frances. *The Roosevelt I Knew.* New York:
Viking, 1946.

941. Perkins, Robert L. "Persistent criticisms--Misinter-
pretations of Sören Kierkegaard's ethical thought." In
Mem. XIII Congr. Intern. Filos. 7:377-388.

942. Perkins, Robert L. "Kierkegaard's epistemological preferences." *International Journal for Philosophy of Religion* 4 (1973):197-217.

943. Phillips, Dewi Z. *Faith and Philosophical Inquiry.* London: Routledge & Kegan Paul, 1970, viii-277p. [Kierkegaard's notion of subjectivity, the relation of God and Christian conception of love.]

944. Pittenger, W. Norman. "Sören Kierkegaard." *Anglican Theological Review* 38 (1956):1-3.

945. Pomerleau, Wayne P. "The accession and dismissal of an upstart handmaid." *Monist* 60 (1977):213-227.

946. Pope, R. Martin. "Impressions of Kierkegaard." *London Quarterly Review* 166 (1941):17-24.

947. Popkin, Richard H. "Theological and religious scepticism." *Christian Scholar* 39 (1956):150-158.

948. "Queues for Kierkegaard." *Times Educational Supplement* 2554 (1964):1149.

949. Rasmussen, Dennis. *Poetry and Truth.* The Hague: Mouton, 1974. 121p.

950. Ratcliffe, S. K. "Kierkegaard, the only philosopher?" *Listener* 36 (1946):755.

951. Read, Herbert. "Kierkegaard." In his *A Coat of Many Colours. Occasional Essays.* London: Routledge, 1945, 248-258.

952. Reed, Walter J. *Meditations on the Hero. A Study of the Romantic Hero in Nineteenth Century Fiction.* New Haven: Yale Univ. Press, 1974.

953. Reinhardt, Kurt Frank. *Existentialist Revolt: The Main Themes and Phases of Existentialism: Kierkegaard, Nietzsche, Heidegger, Jaspers, Sartre, Marcel.* With an app. on existentialist psychotherapy. Milwaukee: Bruce, 1952, vii-245p.; 2d ed. New York: Ungar, 1960, 281p.

954. Reinhold, Hans A. "Sören Kierkegaard: Great Christian of the Nineteenth Century." *Commonweal* 35 (1942):608-611.

955. Riding, Laura. "Sören Kierkegaard." *Times Literary Supplement* 36 (1937):275.

956. Riviere, William T. "Introducing Kierkegaard." *Christian Century* 56 (1939):1164-1166.

957. Riviere, William T. "Interpretation of Kierkegaard. A reply to H. N. Wieman." *Christian Century* 56 (1939): 444-446. [See Wieman, no. 1046]

958. Roberts, David E. "Kierkegaard." In *Existentialism and Religious Belief*. New York: Oxford Univ. Press, 1959, 61-144.

959. Roberts, David E. "A review of Kierkegaard's writings." *Review of Religion* 7 (1943):300-317.

960. Robertson, J. G. **"Sören Kierkegaard."** *Modern Language Review* 9 (1914):500-513; revised in his *Essays and Addresses on Literature*. London: Routledge, 1935, 227-244.

961. Rohatynn, Dennis A. "Kierkegaard and his critics." In his *Two Dogmas of Philosophy and Other Essays in the Philosophy of Philosophy*. Cranbury: Fairleigh Dickinsen Univ. Press, 1977.

962. Rohde, Peter P. "Kierkegaard and our time." *Arena* (1949):84-94.

963. Rosenberg, H. "The riddles of Oedipus." In *Act and the Actor: Making the Self*. Cleveland Pub. Co., 1970, 58-73.

964. Rowell, Ethel M. "The interplay of the past and present." *Hibbert Journal* 41 (1943):355-360.

965. Rougement, Denis de. "Kierkegaard revealed in his irony." *Arizona Quarterly* 1 (1945):4-6.

966. Rougement, Denis de. "Two Danish princes: Kierkegaard and Hamlet," and "Dialectic of the myths (1) Meditation at the fabulous crossroads." In *Love Declared. Essays in the Myth of Love*. Trans. from the French by Richard Howard. New York: Pantheon Books, 1963, 77-98 and 109-162.

967. Rougement, Denis de. "Kierkegaard." In *Dramatic Personages*. Trans. from the French by Richard Howard. New York: Holt, 1964, 27-74.

968. Said, Edward W. "Molestation and authority in narrative fiction." In *Aspects of Variation. Selected Papers from the English Institute*. J. Hillis Miller, ed. New York: Columbia Univ. Press, 1971, 47-68. [Incl. disc. of Kierkegaard, Marx, and Vico in relat. to requisite conditions for fiction.]

969. Sartre, Jean-Paul. "Kierkegaard, the singular universal." In *Between Existentialism and Marxism*. Trans. from the French by John Mathews. London: New Left Books; New York: Pantheon Books, 1974, 141-169.

970. Savage, Donald S. "Genius or apostle." *Changing World* No. 6:20-31.

971. Schacht, Richard. "Kierkegaard on 'truth is sub-jectivity' and 'the leap of faith'." *Canadian Journal of Philosophy* 2 (1972-73):297-313.

972.   Schacht, Robert.   "Kierkegaard on 'truth is subjectivity' and 'the leap of faith'," and "Kierkegaard's
phenomenology of spiritual development." In his *Hegel and
After. Studies in Contemporary Philosophy Between Kant
and Sartre.* Univ. of Pittsburgh Press, 1975, 119-134 and
135-174.

973.   Scott, Nathan A.   "A Kierkegaard's strait gate."   In
his *Mirrors of Man in Existentialism.*   Collins & World,
1978, 25-59.

974.   Seaver, George.   "Denmark's dead man." *Nineteenth
Century* 139 (1946):287-291.

975.   Sechi, Vanina.   "Art, language, creativity and Kierkegaard." *Humanitas* (Duquesne Univ.) 5 (1969):81-97.

976.   Sechi, Vanina.   "The poet." *Kierkegaardiana* 10 (1977):
166-181.

977.   Sigard, Ran.   "The existentialism of Kierkegaard."
In *Studies in Existentialism* [in Hebrew]. Jerusalem:
The Bialik Institute, 1975.   282p.

978.   Sjursen, Harold P.   "Method and perspective when
reading Kierkegaard." *Kierkegaardiana* 8 (1971):199-211.

979.   Sjursen, Harald P.   "The comic apprehension." *Midwest
Studies in Philosophy* 1 (1976):108-113.

980.   Skinner, J. E.   "Philosophical megalomania."
Theology and Life 9 (1966):146-159.

981.   Slaate, H. A.   "Kierkegaard's introduction to American
Methodists: A tribute." *The Drew Gateway* 30 (1960):161-167.

982.   Smith, Constance J.   "The single one and the other."
Hibbert Journal 46 (1948):315-321.

983.   Smith, Elwyn Allen.   "Kierkegaard and dogmatic
theology: An epistemological impasse." *Evangelistic
Quarterly* (1945):106-123.

984.   Smith, John E.   "The revolt of existence." *Yale
Review* 43 (1953-54):364-371.

985.   Smith, Vincent E.   "Kierkegaard's descent to the
individual." In *Idea-Men of Today.* Milwaukee: Bruce, 1950,
238-264.

986.   Sobosan, Jeffrey G.   "One hand clapping. . .A study
of the paradoxical in *Lear* and Kierkegaard." *Laval
Théologique et Philosophique* 30 (1974):47-53.

987. Solomon, Robert C. "Sören Kierkegaard: Faith and the subjective individual." In *From Rationalism to Existentialism. The Existentialists and Their Nineteenth-Century Backgrounds*. New York: Harper & Row, 1972, 69-104.

988. Sontag, Frederick. "Kierkegaard and the search for a self." *Journal of Existentialism* 7 (1967):443-457.

989. Soper, David Wesley. "Kierkegaard: The Danish Jeremiah." *Religion in Life* 13 (1944):522-535.

990. "Sören Kierkegaard: Danish moralist and author." *Review of Reviews* 9 (1894):236.

991. "Sören Kierkegaard: Prophet with honor." *Christian Century* 80 (1963):943.

992. Sponheim, Paul R. "Kierkegaard and the suffering of the Christian man." *Dialog* 3 (1964):199-206.

993. Sponheim, Paul R. "Christian coherence and human wholeness." In *The Future of Empirical Theology*. Fred Berthold, Jr. and B. E. Meland, eds. Chicago: Univ. of Chicago Press, 1969, 195-220.

994. Stack, George J. "Kierkegaard and potentiality, existence, and possibility." *Agora* (Potsdam, N.Y.) 22 (1972):50-64.

995. Stack, George J. "Kierkegaard's existential categories." *The Personalist* 57 (1976):18-33.

996. Stack, George J. "Kierkegaard. The self and ethical existence." *Ethics* 83 (1972-73):108-125.

997. Standley, N. V. "Kierkegaard and man's vocation." *The Vocation Guidance Quarterly* (Washington) 20 (1971): 119-122.

998. Stanley, Rupert. "Sören Kierkegaard." *New-Church Magazine* (1947):23-27.

999. Starkoff, C. "The election: Choice of faith." *Review of Religion* 24 (1965):444-454.

1000. Steere, Douglas V. "Discovering Kierkegaard." *Christendom* 3 (1938):146-151.

1002. Steere, Douglas V. "Sören Kierkegaard and purity of heart." In *Doors into Life through Five Devotional Classics*. New York: Harper, 1948.

1003. Stengren, G. L. "Connatural knowledge in Aquinas and Kierkegaardian subjectivity." *Kierkegaardiana* 10 (1977):182-189.

1004. Stewart, H. L. "Sören Kierkegaard as major prophet of the XIXth century," and "Kierkegaard as major prophet." *Expository Times* 61 (1949-50):271-273; 62 (1950-51):284-285.

1005. Stewart, R. W. "A neglected prophet." *Expository Times* 38 (1927):520-521.

1006. Stewart, R. W. "Is church like a theatre?" *Expository Times* 62 (1950):27-28.

1007. Sulzbach, Marian Fuerth. "Time, eschatology, and the human problem." *Theology Today* 7 (1950):321-330.

1008. Swenson, David F. "Sören Kierkegaard." *Scandinavian Studies and Notes* 6 (1920-21):1-41.

1009. Swenson, David F. "Sören Kierkegaard." *Scandinavian Studies* 6 (1923):1-41.

1010. Swenson, David F. "The 'existential dialectic' of Kierkegaard." (Abstracts of papers to be read at the 38th annual meeting of the Eastern division of the American Philosophical Association, Wesleyan Univ., 1938.) *Journal of Philosophy* 35 (1938-39):684-685.

1011. Swenson, David F. "The anti-intellectualism of Kierkegaard." *Philosophical Review* 25 (1916):567-586. Reprinted in *The Presence of Kierkegaard in Contemporary American Life*. L. L. Lawson, ed. Metuchen (New Jersey): Scarecrow Press, 1970, 23-42.

1012. Taylor, Mark C. "Language, truth and indirect communication." *Tijdschrift voor Filosofie* 37 (1975):74-88.

1013. "The 'offence' of the God-man: Kierkegaard's way of faith." *Times Literary Supplement* 36 (1937):229-230.

1014. Thomas, G. F. "Christian existentialism: Kierkegaard." In his *Religious Philosophies of the West*. New York: Scribners, 1965, 290-336.

1015. Thomas, J. Heywood. "The christology of Sören Kierkegaard and Karl Barth." *Hibbert Journal* 53 (1954-55): 280-288.

1016. Thomas, J. Heywood. "Logic and existence in Kierkegaard." *Journal of the British Society of Phenomenology* 2 (1971):3-11.

1017. Thomas, J. M. Lloyd. "The modernness of Kierkegaard." *Hibbert Journal* 45 (1947):309-320.

1018. Thompson, Josiah. "The master of irony." In *Kierkegaard: A Collection of Critical Essays*. Josiah Thompson, ed. Garden City: Doubleday/Anchor Books, 103-163.

1019. Thomsen, Eric H. "That tremendous Dane." *Religion in Life* 2 (1933):247-260.

1020. Thomte, Reidar. "New reflections on the Great Dane." *Discourse* 6 (1963):144-155.

1021. Thulstrup, Niels. "Theological and philosophical Kierkegaardian studies in Scandinavia, 1945-1953." *Theology Today* 12 (1955):297-312. (Trans. by Paul Holmer.)

1022. Tillich, Paul. "The breakdown of the universal synthesis." In *Perspectives on Nineteenth and Twentieth Century Protestant Theology.* New York: Harper, 1967, 136-207.

1023. Tyler, P. "Hamlet's cell." In *Every Artist His Own Scandal: A Study of Real and Fictive Heroes.* Horizon Press, 1969, 121-188.

1024. Unamuno, Miguel de. *The Tragic Sense of Life in Men and Peoples.* Trans. by J. E. Crawford Flitch with an introductory essay by Salvador de Madariaga. London: Macmillan, 1921.

1025. Untermyer, Louis. "Sören Kierkegaard." In *Makers of the Modern World.* New York: Simon and Schuster, 1955, 7-11.

1026. Updike, John. "The fork." *New Yorker* 42 (1966): 115-118, 121-124, 128-130, 133-134.

1027. Updike, John. "The rubble of footnotes bound into Kierkegaard." [Abst. article available from Scholar's Press, Missoula, MT.] Crowley, Sue M. *American Academy of Religion* 45 (1977):359.

1028. Ussher, Arland. *Journey Through Dread. A Study of Kierkegaard, Heidegger, and Sartre* [Copyright 1955]. New York: Biblo & Tannen, 1968. 160p.

1029. Utterback, Sylvia W. "Kierkegaard's inverse dialectic." *American Academy of Religion, Philosophy of Religion and Theology, Proceedings* (1976):4-16.

1030. Van de Pitte, Frederick P. "Kierkegaard's 'approximation'." *The Personalist* 52 (1971):483-498.

1031. Versfeld, Martin. "Kierkegaard and metaphysics." In *The Mirror of Philosophers.* New York-London: Sheed & Ward, 1960, 44-70.

1032. Vick, George R. "A new 'Copernican revolution'." *The Personalist* 52 (1971):630-642. [Kierkegaard and Heidegger on poetic discourse.]

1033. Wadia, A. R. "Sören Kierkegaard." *Aryan Path* 35 (1964):446-450.

1034.   Wahba, Magdi.   "The spasm and the fever."   In
Vues sur Kierkegaard.   Henein and Magdi Wahba, eds.
Paris, 1955, 98-106.

1035.   Wahl, Jean.   "The philosophy of Sören Kierkegaard."
In *A Short History of Existentialism*.   Trans. from French
by Forrest William and Stanley Maron.   New York: The Philosophical Library, 1949, 1-9.

1036.   Wahl, Jean.   *Philosophies of Existence. An Introduction to the Basic Thought of Kierkegaard, Heidegger,
Jaspers, Marcel, Sartre*.   Trans. from French by F. M. Lory.
London: Routledge & Kegan Paul; New York: Schocken Books,
1969, 126p.

1037.   Wahl, Jean.   "Freedom and existence in some recent
philosophies."   *Philosophy and Phenomenological Research*
8 (1948):538-556.

1038.   Walker, Jeremy.   "The paradox in *Fear and Trembling*."
Kierkegaardiana 10 (1977):133-151.

1039.   Webb, Clement C. J.   "Apropos de Kierkegaard."
Philosophy 18 (1943):68-74.

1040.   Wells, William W.   "Two issues in the interpretation
of Kierkegaard's works."   *Modern Schoolman* 54 (1977):363-368.

1041.   Westphal, Merold.   "Kierkegaard and the logic of
insanity."   *Religious Studies* 7 (1971):193-211.

1042.   Westphal, Merold.   "Kierkegaard as prophetic
philosopher."   *Christian Scholar's Review* 7 (1977):109-118.

1043.   White, W.   "Kierkegaardian privacy; a note on faith,
conscience, and rules."   *Encounter* 34 (1973):372-381.

1044.   Whittemore, Robert C.   "Of history, time, and
Kierkegaard's problem."   *Journal of Religious Thought*
11 (1954):134-155.

1045.   Widenman, Robert.   "Kierkegaard's terminology--and
English."   *Kierkegaardiana* 6 (1968):113-130.

1046.   Wieman, Henry Nelson.   "Interpretation of Kierkegaard."
Christian Century 56 (1939):444-446.   [See Riviere, no. 957]

1047.   Wild, John.   "Kierkegaard and classic philosophy."
Journal of Philosophy 35 (1938-39):685-686; *Philosophical
Review* 49 (1940):536-551.

1048.   Wilde, J. T., and Kummel, W. B., trans. and eds.
*The Search for Being.   Essays from Kierkegaard to Sartre
on the Problem of Being*.   New York: Twayne, 1962.   556p.

1049. Williams, Forrest. "A problem in values: The Faustian motivation in Kierkegaard and Goethe." *Ethics* 63 (1952-53): 251-261.

1050. Willimon, William H. "Kierkegaard on preachers who become poets." *Worship* 49 (1975):107-112.

1051. Wilson, Colin. "Kierkegaard." In *Religion and the Rebel*. Boston: Houghton Mifflin, 1957, 232-241.

1052. Winkel-Horn, Frederik. *History of the Literature of the Scandinavian North from the Most Ancient Times to the Present*. Revised by the author and trans. by Rasmus B. Andersen. With a bibliography of. . .books in the English language relating to Scandinavian countries. . . . Chicago: Griggs, 1884, 286-288.

1053. Wrighton, B. "Thoughts on Kierkegaard." *Arena* 1 (1933):317.

1054. Zweig, P. "A genius for unsavoriness." *Nation* 207 (1968):283-284.

FRENCH

1055. Alain [Pseud.: E. Charlier]. "Difficultés de Kier-kegaard." *Combat* (Paris) (10.11.1955); *La Table Ronde* (1955):88-90.

1056. Anonymous. "Un nouveau courant de pensée. D'où il vient." *Semaine Economique* (2.1.1948).

1057. Anonymous. "Ce que nous devons à Kierkegaard [Jean Wahl, Gabriel Marcel, Jean Beaufret, Brice Parain, F. Alquié, Aimé Patri, Jean Lacroix]. *Figaro Littéraire* (12.11.1955).

1058. Assaad-Mikhaïl, Fawzia. "Mort de l'homme et subjec-tivité [Kierkegaard, Nietzsche]. *Revue de Métaphysique et de Morale* 73 (1968):430-461.

1059. Aubenque, Pierre. "Préface" to *Etudes sur* In Vino Veritas *de Kierkegaard*. Denise Chaplain.   (Annales de l'Université de Besançon, 69). Paris: Les Belles Lettres, 1965. 102p.

1060. Bannour, Wanda. "Kierkegaard." In *La Philosophie et l'histoire*, ch. 9, vol. 5 in *Histoire de la Philosophie: Idées, Doctrines*. François Chatelet, ed. Paris: Hachette, 1972-73.

1061. Basch, Victor. "Un individualiste religieux, Sören Kierkegaard." In *Essais d'Esthétique, de Philosophie et de Littérature*. Paris: Alcan, 1934, 268-315.

1062. Beaufret, Jean. *Introduction aux Philosophies de l'Existence. De Kierkegaard à Heidegger.* Paris, 1971. 213p.

1063. Bellessort, André. "Le crépuscule d'Elseneur." In *A Travers les Pays et les Livres. Huit articles.* Paris: Perrin, 1926 (ii-299p.), 1-60.

1064. Bespaloff, R. *Cheminements et Carrefours. Julien Green; André Malraux; Gabriel Marcel; Kierkegaard; Chestov devant Nietzsche.* Paris: Vrin, 1938, xi-241p.

1065. Billeskov Jansen, F. J. *L'Age d'Or.* Deux conférences faites à la Sorbonne. . . . Copenhague: Munksgaard, 1953, 21-28.

1066. Billeskov Jansen, F. J. "Les grands romans philosophiques de Kierkegaard." *Revue Univ. Bruxelles* 13 (1960-61): 175-197.

1067. Billeskov Jansen, F. J. "Essai sur l'art de Kierkegaard." *Orbis Litterarum* 10 (1955):18-27. [Symposion Kierkegaardianum]

1068. Billeskov Jansen, F. J. "Le climat philosophique du Danemark au temps de Kierkegaard." In *Kierkegaard et al Philosophie Contemporaine.* Johs. Witt-Hansen, ed. *Danish Yearbook of Philosophy* 1 (1971):16-21. [Discussions, 21-36]

1069. Blanchet, Charles. "Kierkegaard ou la foi sauvage." *Esprit* 39 (1971):916-928.

1070. Blin, Georges. "L'alternative kierkegaardienne." *Les Temps Modernes* 1 (1946):737-750.

1071. Bonnefoy, Yves. "La passion et l'objet." In *Vues sur Kierkegaard.* Henein and M. Wahba, eds. Paris, 1955, 19-21.

1072. Bosc, Jean. "La pensée protestante. Kierkegaard." *Foi et Vie* 37 (1936):181-187.

1073. Brandt, Frithiof. "Sören Kierkegaard." *Le Nord* 4 (1941):295-301.

1074. Brandt, Frithiof. "Soren Kierkegaard comme Actéon." *Orbis Litterarum* 10 (1955):28-35. [Symposion Kierkegaardianum]

1075. Brandt, Frithiof. "Ce qu'il y a de réalité dans les oeuvres de Sören Kierkegaard." *Revue Philosophique* 63 (1938):257-277. (Conférence faite à la Sorbonne le 4 Mai 1938.)

1076. Brun, Jean. "Kierkegaard penseur tragique." *Etudes Philosophiques* 18 (1963):323-332.

1077. Brunner, Fernand. "Signification de Kierkegaard."
In *Mélanges offerts à H. Corbin*. Seyyed Hossein, ed.
Nasr (Wisdom of Persia). Tehran: Institute of Islamic
Studies; Montreal: McGill Univ., 1977, 521-537.

1078. Burnier, André. "La pensée de Kierkegaard." *Revue
de Théologie et de Philosophie* 31 (1943):101-113.

1079. Caron, Jacques. "Dialectique de la communication chez
Kierkegaard." *Philosophiques* 3 (1976):167-181.

1080. Cattaui, Georges. "Kierkegaard le précurseur."
In *Vues sur Kierkegaard*. Henein and Wahba, eds. Paris,
1955, 45-49.

1081. Chestov, Leon (Sjestov, Lev). "Dans le taureau de
Phalaris. (Le savoir et la liberté.) Trad. par B. de
Schloezer. *Revue de Philosophie* 58 (1933):18-60; 252-308.

1082. Clair, André. "L'homme malade et la santé comme
tâche, selon Kierkegaard (à suivre); (suite et fin).
Revue des Sciences Philosophiques et Théologiques 54 (1970):
489-515; 619-635.

1083. Clair, André. "Lire Kierkegaard." *Esprit* 39 (1971):
903-915.

1084. Clair, André. "Détruire l'illusion: Note sur un
thème Kierkegaardien." *Revue Philosophique de Louvain* 70
(1972):43-62.

1085. Clair, André. "Médiation et répétition. Le lieu de
la dialectique kierkegaardienne." *Revue des Sciences
Philosophiques et Théologiques* 59 (1975):38-78 [Résumé,
Summary, 78].

1086. Clair, André. "Enigme nietzschéenne et paradoxe
kierkegaardien." *Revue Théologie et de Philosophie* (1977):
196-221.

1087. Colette, Jacques. "Chronique kierkegaardienne."
Revue Nouvelle 37 (1963):181-188.

1088. Colette, Jacques. "Bulletin d'histoire de la
philosophie: Kierkegaard." *Revue des Sciences Philosophiques
et Théologiques* 54 (1970):654-680.

1089. Colette, Jacques. "Etudes kierkegaardiennes récentes."
Revue Philosophique de Louvain 70 (1972):116-130.

1090. Colette, Jacques. "Le désir d'être soi et la
fonction du père chez Kierkegaard." *L'Inconscient: Revue
de Psychanalyse* 5 (1968):131-155.

1091. Colette, Jacques. "Musique et sensualité: Kierkegaard
et le *Don Juan* de Mozart." *La Vie Spirituelle* 126 (1972):
33-45.

1092. Colette, Jacques. "Kierkegaard." In *Histoire de la Philosophie*. III: Du XIXe siècle à nos jours. Publiés sous la direction dYvon Beleval. (Encyclopédie de la Pléiade, 38). Paris: Gallimard, 1974, 85-96.

1093. Congar, M. J. "Bulletin d'histoire des doctrines chrétiennes: Kierkegaard." *Revue des Sciences Philosophiques et Théologiques* 22 (1933):551-552.

1094. Congar, M. J. "L'actualité de Kierkegaard." *La Vie Intellectuelle* 6 (1934):9-36.

1095. Corbin, H. "Témoignage à Kierkegaard." *Le Semeur* (Dec. 1932).

1096. Cornu, Michel. "Actualité de Kierkegaard." *Revue de Théologie et de Philosophie* (1971):428-437.

1097. Delacroix, Henri. "Sören Kierkegaard. Le christianisme absolu à travers le paradoxe et le désespoir." *Revue de Métaphysique et de Morale* 8 (1900):459-484.

1098. Derycke, Gaston. "Du nouveau sur Kierkegaard." *Cassandre* (Bruxelles)(9.5.1943).

1099. Diem, H. "Kierkegaard et la postérité." *Revue d' Histoire et de Philosophie Religieuses* 46 (1966):1-16.

1100. Duquesne, Marcel. "Kierkegaard cet incompris." In *Universitas*. Numéro spécial, *Mélanges de Sciences Religieuses* 34 (1977):173-186. Lille: Facultés Catholiques, 1977.

1101. Fardoulis-Lagrange, Michel. "Pile et face." In *Vues sur Kierkegaard*. Henein and Wahba, eds. Paris, 1955.

1102. Flam, L. "Sören Kierkegaard (1813-1963)." *Revue Univ. Bruxelles* 15 (1962-63):392-397.

1103. Fondane, Benjamin. "Héraclite le Pauvre, ou nécessité de Kierkegaard." *Cahiers du Sud* 22 (1935):757-770.

1104. Fondane, Benjamin. "Chestov et Kierkegaard et le serpent." In *La Conscience Malheureuse*. Paris, 1936, 229-257.

1105. Fondane, Benjamin. "Le lundi existentiel et le dimanche de l'histoire." In *L'existence*. Essais par Albert Camus, Benjamin Fondane etc. . Paris: Gallimard, 1945, 25-53. (Collection Métaphysique I.)

1106. Fouchet, Max-Pol. "Au pays de Kierkegaard." *Carrefour* (Paris) (2.1.1947).

1107. Fruchon, Pierre. "Kierkegaard et l'historicité de la foi. Autopsie de la foi et temporalité." *Recherches de Sciences Religieuses* 61 (1973):321-351 [Summary, 352].

1108. Gandillac, Maurice de. "Kierkegaard, le Pascal du
Nord." *La Revue Universelle* 59 (1934):371-376.

1109. Gateau, Jean J. "Soeren Kierkegaard (1813-1855)."
Bibliotèque Universelle et Revue de Genève 2 (1929):14-16.

1110. Geismar, Ed. "La victoire sur le doute chez Sören
Kierkegaard." *Revue d'Histoire et de Philosophie Religieuses*
6 (1926):38-59.

1111. Gignoux, Victor. "La philosophie de Kierkegaard."
In *Cours de Philosophie 3: La Philosophie Existentielle.*
Paris: Institut Viète, 1950, 10-13; 2d ed. ibid. 1955.

1112. Gignoux, Victor. *La Philosophie Existentielle*
[S. Kierkegaard, Jaspers, Heidegger, J.-P. Sartre, G. Marcel,
R. le Senne] [1950]. 2d ed., Paris: Lefèbvre, 1955. 92p.

1113. Gillet, L. "Dieu et lumière." In *Vues sur Kierkegaard.* Henein and Wahba, eds. Paris, 1955, 91-97.

1114. Goldmann, Lucien. In *Kierkegaard Vivant.* Paris:
Gallimard, 1966, 125-164.

1115. Groethuysen, B. "Mythes et portraits." *Les Essais*
23 (1947):191-202.

1116. Gusdorf, Georges. "Kierkegaard (1813-1855)." In
Les Philosophes Célèbres. Ouvrage publié nous la direction
de M. Merleau-Ponty. Paris: Edition Lucien Mazenod, 1956,
242-248.

1117. Hanssens, Patrick. "Éthique et foi. Quelques
réflexions inspirées par S. Kierkegaard." *Nouvelle Revue
Théologique* 109 (1977):360-380.

1118. Heidegger, Martin. "La fin de la philosophie et la
tâche de la pensée." In *Kierkegaard Vivant.* Paris:
Gallimard, 1966, 167-204.

1119. Hoch, Jules. "Sören Kierkegaard." *La Grande Revue*
23 (1902):603-622.

1120. Höffding, Harald. "Sören Kierkegaard, 5 Mai 1813-
5 Mai 1913. (Discours prononcé le 5 Mai 1913 à l'Université de Copenhague). *Revue de Métaphysique et de Morale*
21 (1913):713-732.

1121. Hohlenberg, J. "Kierkegaard tel qu'il était."
La Table Ronde (1955):16-32.

1122. Holm, Sören. "L'être comme catégorie de l'éternité."
Orbis Litterarum 10 (1955):84-92.

1123. Huber, G. "Comment les philosophies de l'existence
se sont-elles approprié la pensée kierkegaardienne."
In *Danish Yearbook of Philosophy* 8 (1971):37-42 [Discussions
42-64].

1124. Jaspers, Karl. "Actualité de Kierkegaard." Trad. de
l'allemand par Hélène Naef. *La Table Ronde* 95 (1955):53-65.
In his *Bilans et Perspectives*. Ed. Desclée, de Brouwer.

1125. Jaspers, Karl. In *Kierkegaard Vivant*. Paris:
Gallimard, 1966, 81-93.

1126. Jeannine, B. "Sören Kierkegaard, le moraliste danois."
La Nouvelle Revue 15 (1893).

1127. Jolivet, Régis. *Les Doctrines Existentialistes de
Kierkegaard à J.-P. Sartre*. Paris: Fontenelle, 1948. 372p.

1128. Jolivet, Régis. "Kierkegaard, penseur existentiel."
In *Danish Yearbook of Philosophy* 8 (1971):194-200.

1129. Kofoed-Hansen, H. P. "Notice sur la vie et les
oeuvres de S. A. Kierkegaard." In *Sören Kierkegaard: En
Quoi l'Homme de Génie Diffère-t-il de l'Apôtre?* Copenhagen,
1886, 3-8.

1130. Klossowski, Pierre. *Sade, Mon Prochain* (suivi de
deux essais sur Kierkegaard et Georges Bataille). Paris:
Ed. du Seuil, 1947. 206p. (Coll. "Pierres Vives".)

1131. Lapassade, Georges. "Le deuil de la philosophie:
Kierkegaard et Marx." *Etudes Philosophiques* (1963):333-341.

1132. Lavelle, Louis. "La philosophie. L'individu et
l'absolu." *Le Temps* (1936):3 (Feuilleton).

1133. Lavelle, Louis. "La vrai visage de Kierkegaard."
La Table Ronde (1955):73-75.

1134. Le Blond, J. M. "Christianisme et souffrance. En
souvenir de S. Kierkegaard." *Etudes* 288 (1956):381-395.

1135. Lefèbvre, Henri. "Le Don Juan du Nord." *Europe* 46.

1136. Lögstrup, K. E. "Le néant et l'action 'Kierkegaard'."
In *Danish Yearbook of Philosophy* 8 (1971):159-167
[Discussions 167-180].

1137. Lombardi, F. "Kierkegaard aujourd'hui." In *Danish
Yearbook of Philosophy* 8 (1971):135-140 [Discussions 140-158].

1138. Maheu, René. "Allocution." In *Kierkegaard Vivant*.
Colloque organisé par l'Unesco à Paris, 23 avril 1964.
Paris: Gallimard, 1966, 9-19.

1139. Malantschuk, G. "L'observateur psychologique."
Trad. du danois par Marguerite Gay. *La Table Ronde* (1955):
48-52.

1140. Malevez, Léopold. "Subjectivité et vérité chez
Kierkegaard et dans la théologie chrétienne." *Mélanges
Joseph Maréchal II*. Bruxelles: Ed. Universelle, 1950;
Paris: Desclée de Brouwer, 1950, 408-423.

1141. Marcel, Gabriel. "Kierkegaard et ma pensée." In
Kierkegaard Vivant. Paris: Gallimard, 1966, 64-80.

1142. Maury, Lucien. In *Les Scandinaves et nous*. Paris,
1947, 29.

1143. Mesnard, Pierre. "Comment définir la philosophie de
Kierkegaard?" *Revue d'Histoire de Philosophie Religieuses*
35 (1955):393-403.

1144. Mesnard, Pierre. "Kierkegaard aux prises avec la
conscience française." *Revue de Littérature Comparée*
29 (1955):453-477.

1145. Mesnard, Pierre. "Le 'journal' de Kierkegaard a-t-il
une valeur philosophique?" *Etudes Philosophiques* (1963):
299-314.

1146. Mitrani, Nora. "La beauté du diable." In *Vues sur
Kierkegaard*. Henein and Wahba, eds. Paris, 1955, 50-57.

1147. Paci, Enzo. "Kierkegaard vivant et la véritable
signification de l'histoire." In *Kierkegaard Vivant*.
Paris: Gallimard, 1966, 111-124.

1148. Petit, Paul. "Fragment d'une lettre sur Kierkegaard."
Deucalion. Cahiers de Philosophie 1 (1940):245-248.

1149. Preiss, Th. "Le message de Kierkegaard." *Le Semeur*
(1933).

1150. Preiss, Th. "A propos de Kierkegaard." *Revue
d'Histoire et de Philosophie Religieuses* 16 (1936):46-64.

1151. Prenter, Regin. "L'homme, synthèse du temps et de
l'éternité d'après Sören Kierkegaard." *Studia Theologica*
2 (1948):5-20.

1152. Rennes, Jacques. *Libre Humanisme. Réponse à Pascal,
Kierkegaard et aux Existentialistes*. Saint-Vaast-la-Houghe:
Manche, L'Amitié par le livre, 1947. 164p.

1153. Ricoeur, Paul. "Philosopher après Kierkegaard."
Revue de Théologie et de Philosophie 13 (1963):303-316.

1154. Romeyer, Blaise. "Auto-critique de Kierkegaard."
Giornale di Metafisica 6 (1951):394-407.

1155.   Romeyer, Blaise. "La raison et la foi au service de la pensée. Kierkegaard devant Augustin." *Archivio di Filosofia* 18 (1952):7-41 (184-217).

1156.   Rougemont, Denis de. "Nécessité de Kierkegaard." *Foi et Vie* 35 (1934):605-620. (Notice biographique, 602-604.)

1157.   Rougemont, Denis de. "Forme et transformation ou l'acte selon Kierkegaard." *Hermes* (Jan. 1936).

1158.   Rougemont, Denis de. *Les Personnes du Drame* (Ramuz, Claudel, Gide, Luther, Goethe, Kafka, Kierkegaard). New York, 1944; Neufchatel: A la Baconnnière, 1945, 219p. (Kierkegaard, Introduction, 51-55; Trois rapsodies sur des thèmes empruntés à Kierkegaard, 55-104.)

1159.   Sartre, Jean-Paul. "L'universel singulier." In *Kierkegaard Vivant*. Paris: Gallimard, 1966, 20-63. Reprinted in his *Situations X*. "Kierkegaard." In *Situations VIII-IX*. Paris: Gallimard, 1972 [Unesco colloquium, April 1964].

1160.   Saurat, D. "Kierkegaard." *Marsyas* (Nov. 1935).

1161.   Savin, Maurice. "En lisant Kierkegaard 1951-1955." *La Table Ronde* (1955):33-42.

1162.   Schuwer, L. "Un témoin de la vie intérieure." *Hippocrate* (Paris) (Fev. 1934).

1163.   Sentein, François. "Le secret professionel. Un personnage impossible." *Arts* (29.9.1954).

1164.   Soliman, Lotfallah. "Correspondence (à Magdi Wahba)." In *Vues sur Kierkegaard*. Henein and Wahba, eds. Paris, 1955, 107-108.

1165.   Serrand, A.-Z. "Etre ou ne pas être [A propos d'un article où Henning Hoirup pousse un parallèle entre Kierkegaard et Grundtvig, *Theology Today* (1955):328-342, et d'un compte rendu, *ibid.*, 380-388, par H. A. Johnson de: S. Kierkegaard, *On Authority and Revelation*]. *Vie Intellectuelle* (1955):101-107.

1166.   Starobinski, Jean. "Les masques du pécheur et les pseudonymes du chrétien [Kierkegaard]. *Revue de Théologie et de Philosophie* 13 (1963):334-346.

1167.   Tisseau, P. H. "Vie de Sören Kierkegaard." *La Table Ronde* (1955):9-15.

1168.   Tieghem, Paul van, ed. *Répertoire Chronologique des Littératures Modernes*. Paris, 1935.

1169.   Vergote, Henri-Bernard. "Dialectique de la Communication." *Revue de Métaphysique et de Morale* 76 (1971): 53-60.

1170. Vergote, Henri-Bernard. "La pureté du coeur chez Sören Kierkegaard." *Études Philosophiques* (1972):503-524 [Résumé, Summary, 503].

1171. Viallaneix, Nelly. "Sören Kierkegaard: La voix et l'ouie (à propos des *Quatre Discours Édifiants* de 1843). *Études Philosophiques* 24 (1969):211-224.

1172. Viallaneix, Nelly. "Kierkegaard retrouvé." *Études Théologiques et Religieuses* (Montpellier) 52 (1977):197-204.

1173. Villadsen, Pierre. "Note" in *Sören Kierkegaard: Vie et Règne de l'Amour*. Paris, 1946, 5-6.

1174. Villard, Jean. "Kierkegaard et la communication de l'existence." *Revue de Théologie et de Philosophie* (1973): 250-254.

1175. Wahl, Jean. "Kierkegaard: L'angoisse et l'instant." *La Nouvelle Revue Française* 20 (1932):634-655.

1176. Wahl, Jean. "Sur quelques catégories kierkegaardiennes: l'Existence, l'Individu isolé, la Pensée subjective." *Recherches Philosophiques* 3 (1933-34):171-202.

1177. Wahl, Jean. "Subjectivité et transcendance." *Bulletin de la Societé Française de Philosophie* 37 (1937): 161-163.

1178. Wahl, Jean. "Pompes pour Kierkegaard." *Mercure de France* 348 (1963):171.

1179. Wahl, Jean. *Petite Histoire de "l'Existentialisme," Suivie de Kafka et Kierkegaard. Commentaires*. Paris: Club Maintenant, 1947. 131p.

1180. Wahl, Jean. *Esquisse pour une Histoire de l'Existentialisme de Kierkegaard et Kafka*. Textes de Kafka et Max Brod trad. par Hélène Zylberberg. Paris: l'Arche, 1949, 157p. *Esquisse pour une Histoire de l'Existentialisme de Kierkegaard à Kafka, Heidegger, Sartre*. Paris: l'Arche, 1949, 160p.

1181. Wahl, Jean. In *Kierkegaard Vivant*. Paris: Gallimard, 1966, 205-212.

1182. Wahl, Jean. In *La Pensée de l'Existence*. Paris: Flammarion. Bibliotèque de Philosophie Scientifique, 1951, 5-58.

1183. Wahl, Jean. In *Les Philosophies de l'Existence*. Paris: Armand Colin, 1954, 15; 22-39.

GERMAN

1184. Aall, Anathon. "Sören Kierkegaard." In Friedrich
Ueberweg's *Grundriss der Gesch. der Philosophie*. 5. Theil:
Die Phil. des Auslandes v. Beg. des 19. Jahrh.s bis auf die
Gegenwart. 12 Aufl., hrsg. von T. K. Oesterreich. Berlin,
1928, xiii-260, 262-264, 270.

1185. Achelis, Th. "Sören Kierkegaard." *Allgemeine
Zeitung* (München) 109 (1906):339-340.

1186. Achelis, Th. "Sören Kierkegaard." *National Zeitung*
(Berlin) (13.7.1905).

1187. Adam, Julie. "Eine Philosophie der Pflicht."
Die Wage 14 (1911):158.

1188. Adorno, Theodor W. "Kierkegaard noch einmal: Zum
hundertundfünfzigsten Geburtstag." *Neue Deutsche Hefte*
95 (1963):5-25.

1189. Adrian, Joseph. "Kierkegaards Bedeutung für die
Gegenwart nach Griesebach." *Wissen und Glauben* 24 (1927):
288-292.

1190. Adrian, Joseph. "Kierkegaard." *Zeitschrift für den
katholischen Religionsunterricht an höheren Lehranstalten*
5 (1928):308.

1191. Ahfeldt, Clemens. "Zur Erinnerung an Sören Kierkegaard." *Kirchliche Zeitschrift der Synode von Iowa* (Chicago)
(1915).

1192. Allemand, Beda. *Ironie und Dichtung. Fr. Schlegel,
Novalis, Solger, Kierkegaard, Nietzsche, Thomas Mann.*
Pfullingen: Neske, 1956.

1193. Anonymous. "Streiflichter auf die neueste Geschichte
des Protestantismus. Die religiöse Bewegung in den skandi-
navischen Ländern. I. Dänemark: Zustände, Ecclesiolae,
Baptistern und Mormonen; Grundtvig, Dr. Kierkegaard."
Historisch-Politische Blätter für das katholische Deutschland
(München) 38 (1856):1-30.

1194. Anonymous. "Sören Kierkegaard." *Basler Nachrichten*
(9.4.1910).

1195. Anonymous. "Nero und die Schwermut. Sören Kierkegaard." *Psyche* (Heidelberg) 2 (1948-49):321-326.

1196. Anonymous. "Wie ein Knabe aus Kopenhagen das Denken
lernte." *Sonntagsblatt* (hesg. von Hanns Lilje) (Hannover)
3 (1950):6.

1197. Anonymous. "Das Wort Kierkegaards." *Neue Wege* (Blätter für den Kampf der Zeit) (Zürich) 48 (1954):591-592.

1198. Anz, Wilhelm. "Philosophie und Glaube bei Sören Kierkegaard. Über die Bedeutung der Existenzdialektik für die Theologie." *Zeitschrift für Theologie und Kirche* 51 (1954):50-105.

1199. Anz, Wilhelm. "Die religiöse Unterscheidung. Ueber das Verhältnis von Dichtung u. Existenzdialektik bei Sören Kierkegaard." *Orbis Litterarum* 10 (1955):5-17.

1200. Anz, Wilhelm. "Fragen der Kierkegaardinterpretation, II." *Theologische Rundschau* 26 (1960):44-79, 168-205.

1201. Baeumler, Alfred. "Gedanken über Kierkegaard." *Nationalsozialistische Monatshefte* 5 (1934):167-180. Also in his *Studien zur deutschen Geistesgeschichte*. Berlin, 1937, 78-98.

1202. Bahr, H.-E. "Der Widerspruch zwischen Christlichem und Aesthetischem als Konstruktion Kierkegaards." *Kerygma und Dogma* 6 (1960):86-103.

1203. Barth, Heinrich. "Kierkegaard, der Denker. Vier Vorlesungen." *Zwischen den Zeiten* (München) 4 (1926): 194-234.

1204. Barth, Karl. In *Die protestantische Theologie im 19.Jahrhundert. Ihre Vorgeschichte und ihre Geschichte*. Zürich: Evangel. Verlag, 1947.

1205. Baerthold, A. *Eine Verfasser-Existenz eigner Art*. Aus seinen Mittheilungen zusammengestellt. Halberstadt: Frantz'sche Buchh., 1873, viii-174p.

1206. Bärthold, A. *Was Christentum ist. Zur Verständigung über diese Frage*. Gütersloh: Bertelsmann, 1884. 51p.

1207. Bärthold, A. *Die Wendung zur Wahrheit in der modernen Kulturentwicklung*. Gütersloh: Bertelsmann, 1885. 80p.

1208. Bärthold, A. *Persönlichkeit in ihrer Verwirklichung der Ideale*. Gütersloh: Bertelsmann, 1886, viii-141p.

1209. Bärthold, A. "Entgegnung." *Theologische Literaturzeitung* 12 (1887):93.

1210. Bärthold, A. "Theologische Würdigung von Sören Kierkegaard." *Das Pfarrhaus* 4 (1887):116-123.

1211. Bärthold, A. "Aus Kierkegaard zur Sache Schrempfs. *Die Christliche Welt* 7 (1893):293-295.

1212. Bärthold, A. "Ein Jünger Jesu (Sören Kierkegaard)."
Die Christliche Welt 7 (1893):318-321.

1213. Bärthold, A. "Zur Bekanntschaft mit Sören Kierkegaard." *Die Christliche Welt* 7 (1893):595-597 (Korte
Bemaerkn. t. 14 forskell. Vaerker).

1214. Baumann, Julius. "Kierkegaard." In *Deutsche und
ausserdeutsche Philosophie der letzten Jahrzehnte dargestellt
und beurteilt*. Gotha, 1903, 490-494.

1215. Beck, A. Fr. "Übersichtliche Darstellung des jetzigen
Zustandes der Theologie in Dänemark." *Theologische Jahrbücher* (Tübingen) 3 (1844):497-536.

1216. Beck, Maximillian. In *Von der Existenz der Philosophen.
Philosophische Hefte* (Berlin) 1 (1928):3-4 (Sonderheft über
Heidegger: *Sein und Zeit*).

1217. Bense, Max. "Sören Kierkegaard und der deutsche
Geist." In his *Vom Wesen deutscher Denker, oder Zwischen
Kritik und Interpretation*. München, 1938, 99-129.

1218. Bense, Max. "Einleitung. Über Leben und Wirken
Sören Kierkegaards." In Kierkegaard's *Entweder-Oder*.
Übers. von Chr. Schrempf. Leipzig, 1939, vii-xxxix.

1219. Bense, Max. *Leben im Geist*. Hamburg: Hoffmann &
Campe, 1942. 91p. (Geistiges Europa. Bücher über geistige
Beziehungen europäischer Nationen.)

1220. Besch, Johannes. "Sören Kierkegaards Bedeutung."
Die Reformation (Berlin) 4 (1905).

1221. Besch, Johannes. "Sören Kierkegaards Angriffe gegen
die Christenheit." *Die Reformation* (Berlin) 12 (1913).

1222. Besch, Johannes. "Kierkegaard." In *Sprecher Gottes
in unserer Zeit*. Stuttgart: Steinkopf, 1919 (152p.), 105-143.

1223. Besch, Johannes. "Zur Frage der Beschäftigung mit
Sören Kierkegaard." *Zeitschrift für Pastoraltheologie*
(Göttingen) 27 (1931):332-337.

1224. Billeskov Jansen, F. J. "Kierkegaard und die Nach-
welt." *Ausblick* 25 (1974):3-9.

1225. Bochinger, Richard. "Das Gesicht der Zeit."
Zeitwende (München) 24 (1952-53):112-116.

1226. Boehlich, Walter. "Kierkegaard als Verführer."
Merkur 7 (1953):1075-1088.

1227. Boehlich, Walter. "Sören, Prinz von Dänemark."
Der Monat 6 (1954):628-634.

1228. Bohlin, Torsten. "Kierkegaard als Apologet." *Wort und Tat* (1921):1.

1229. Bohlin, Torsten. "Drei Kierkegaardbücher." *Zeitschrift für Kirchengeschichte* 49 (N.F. 12) (1930):247-255.

1230. Bohlin, Torsten. "Der Geist macht lebendig. Ein Beitrag zum Verständnis von Kierkegaards Glaubensauffassung." *Zeitschrift für Systematische Theologie* 16 (1939-40):456-461.

1231. Bohlin, Torsten. "Angst, Verzweiflung und Glaube, Ein Beitrag zum Verständnis der Sündenauffassung bei Kierkegaard." *Glaube und Ethos* (Festschrift für Georg Wehrung). Stuttgart, 1940, 141-151.

1232. Bohnenblust, Gottfried. "Sören Kierkegaard [Sonnet]." In *Gedichte*. Frauenfeldt, 1912.

1233. Bohnenblust, Gottfried. "Sören Kierkegaard." *Die Furche* (Berlin) 4 (1913):20. S. K. portr. som kunstbilag, 41.

1234. Bohnenblust, Gottfried. "Sören Kierkegaard." *Neue Zürcher Zeitung* (6.5.1913):125.

1235. Bonus, Arthur. "Vom Unterschied der lebendigen Werke [S. Kierkegaards] und der philologischen und ästhetisch-technischen Dokumente." *Die Christliche Welt* 19 (1905):755-759.

1236. Bonus, Arthur. "Die beiden Kierkegaards zur Passionszeit." *Die Kunstwart* 24 (1911):29-34.

1237. Bonus, Arthur. "Eine Mystifikation über Kierkegaard." *Die Christliche Welt* 19 (1915):458-462.

1238. Borelius, Hilma. In *Die nordischen Literaturen* (Handbuch der Literaturwissenschaft, hrsg. v. Oskar Walzel). Potsdam, 1931, 74-75.

1239. Branczik, Leo. "Sören Kierkegaard, der asketische Don Juan. Zu seinem 100. Geburtstage am 5 Mai 1913." *Der Merker* 4 (1913):334-337.

1240. Brand, W. "Christentumsverkündigung nach Sören Kierkegaard." *Der alte Glaube* 7 (1905-06):1-3.

1241. Brandes, Georg. *Sören Kierkegaard: Ein literarisches Charakterbild*. Hildesheim/New York: Georg Olms, 1975. 240p. [Photo reprint of 1879 "Autorisierte deutsche Ausgabe."]

1242. Brandes, Georg. "Weltliteratur." *Das Literarische Echo* 2 (1899-1900):4.

1243. Brandes, Georg. "Sören Kierkegaard (1877)." In *Skandinavische Persönlichkeiten. Zweiter Teil*. München, 1902, 258-445 (Ges. Schr. 3).

1244. Brandes, Georg. *Kierkegaard und andere skandinavische Persönlichkeiten.* Dresden: Reissner, 1924. 566p. (Ges. Schriften, Bd. 3).

1245. Brandes, Georg. In *Hauptströmungen der Literatur des neunzehnten Jahrhunderts.* Vom Verfasser neubearbeitete endgültige Ausgabe. Bd. 6, Berlin, 1924.

1246. Brandt, Frithiof. "Der Vater des Existentialismus." *Freie Presse* (Buenos Aires) (10.11.1955).

1247. Brandt, Frithiof. "Kierkegaard und das europaische Denken." *Die Furche* (Wien) (12.11.1955).

1248. Brausewetter, Arthur. "Sören Kierkegaard." *Neue Preussische Kreuzzeitung* (Berlin) (3.8.1921).

1249. Brecht, Franz Josef. "Die Situation der gegenwärtigen Philosophie." *Neue Jahrbücher für Wissenschaft und Jugenbildung* 6 (1930):42-58 (om S. K. passim).

1250. Brecht, Franz Josef. "Die Kierkegaardforschung in letzten Jahrfünft." *Literarische Berichte aus dem Gebiete der Philosophie* (Erfurt) (1931):5-35.

1251. Brecht, Franz Josef. "Kierkegaards philosophiegeschichtliche Stellung." *Aus Unterricht und Forschung* (Stuttgart) (1934):222-234.

1252. Brechtken, Josef. "Die Dominanz der Praxis im Christlichen. Dargestellt am Beispiel Sören Kierkegaard." *Tijdschrift voor Filosofie* 36 (1974):61-77.

1253. Bremer, Fredrika. *Leben im Norden. Eine Skizze. Morgen-Wachen. Ein Glaubensbekenntnis.* Aus dem Schwedischen. Von Fredrika Bremer. Leipzig: Brockhaus, 1858. 115p. (Ges. Schriften, 20 Bd.)

1254. Brod, Max. "Kierkegaard." *Die Neue Rundschau* (32. Jahrg. der freien Bühne) 1 (1921):403-418.

1255. Brod, Max. "Kierkegaard, Heidegger, Kafka." *L'Arche* 21 (1946):44-55.

1256. Brod, Max. In *Diesseits und Jenseits.* Zürich: Mondial, 1947.

1257. Brömse, Heinrich. "Die ästhetische Lebensauschauung bei Kierkegaard." *Vossische Zeitung* (Berlin) (31.3.1911).

1258. Brömse, Heinrich. "Die ästhetische Lebensanschauung bei Kierkegaard." *Zeitung für Literatur, Kunst und Wissenschaft* (Beilage des Hamburger Correspondent) (31.3.1912).

1259. Bruckner, Nicolaus. "Sören Kierkegaard." *Saarbrücker Zeitung* (1930).

1260. Brunner, Emil. "Die Botschaft Sören Kierkegaards."
Neue Schweizer Rundschau (Zürich) 23 (1930):84-99.

1261. Brunner, Emil. "Begegnung mit Kierkegaard." Der
Lesezirkel (Zürich) 17 (1929):21.

1262. Buber, Martin. Der Frage an den Einzelnen. Berlin,
1936. 124p. ("Der Einzige" und der Einzelne, 9-27;
Der Einzelne und sein Du, 29-44; Der Einzelne und das offenl.
Wesen, 45-59.)

1263. Buber, Martin. "Von einer Suspension des Ethischen."
In Gottesfinsternis. Betrachtungen zur Beziehung zwischen
Religion und Philosophie. Zürich: Manesse, 1953, 138-144.

1264. Buchner, Eberhard. "Sören Kierkegaard." Strassburger
Post (3.5.1913).

1265. Buchner, Eberhard. "Sören Kierkegaard." Dredsner
Anzeiger (4.5.1913).

1266. Buchner, Eberhard. "Sören Kierkegaard." St. Peters-
burger Zeitung (Montagsblatt) (1913).

1267. Cappelörn, Niels Jörgen. "Kierkegaards eigener
'Gesichtspunkt': 'Vorwärts zu leben, aber rückwärts zu
verstehen'." Neue Zeitschrift für Systematische Theologie
und Religionsphilosophie 17 (1975):61-75.

1268. Carlsen, Fredrik. "Sören Kierkegaard." Hochland
5 (1907):66-78.

1269. Christensen, Arild. "Zwei Kierkegaardstudien 1:
Ethische und dogmatische Problematik im Begriff der Angst
2: Eigentlicher und uneigentlicher Augenblick. Zwei
Beiträge zur Anthropologie Johannes' des Verführers."
Orbis Litterarum 10 (1955):36-49.

1270. Christensen, Arild. "Der junge Kierkegaard als
Schriftstellerpersönlichkeit und die Persönlichkeitsauffassung
in den Frühwerken." Orbis Litterarum 18 (1963):26-47.

1271. Claeson, Kristian. In Zeitschrift für die gesammte
lutherische Theologie und Kirche, 1864, 309-310.

1272. Cohn, Jonas. In Die Philosophie im Zeitalter des
Spezialismus (Nachkantische Philosophie, 2. Hälfte).
Leipzig und Berlin: Teubner, 1925 (130p.), 93-97. (Die
Gesch. d. Philos., 7. Th. Aus Natur-u. Geisteswelt, Bd. 747.)

1273. Colette, Jacques. "Die Philosophie des Willens, das
Christentum und die ethische Mitteilung bei Sören Kierke-
gaard." Übersetzung von Reiner Schürmann. Philosophisches
Jahrbuch 84 (1977):277-292.

1274. Cuesow, Hans. "Sören Kierkegaard, der christliche
Denker aus Dänemark." *Kirche und Volk* 1 (1946):2.

1275. Dallago, Carl. "Eine Auseinandersetzung [A propos
Theodor Haecker, "den Konvertiten"]. *Der Brenner* 7 (1922):
176-217.

1276. Dallago, Carl. "Augustinus, Pascal und Kierkegaard."
Der Brenner 6 (1921):642-734.

1277. Dallago, Carl. *Der grosse Unwissende.* Innsbruck,
1924 (650p.), 424-552. Augustinus, Pascal und Kierkegaard.
ptr. after *Der Brenner* 6 (1921):642-734.

1278. Dennert, E., ed. *Klassiker der religiösen Weltan-
schauung: 1: Kant, Kierkegaard, Kingsley.* Berlin, 1909.

1279. Dessauer, Ph. "Sören Kierkegaards Dialektik der
menschlichen Existenz." *Die Schildgenossen* (Rothenfels)
18 (1939):181-208.

1280. Deuser, H. *Sören Kierkegaard, die paradoxe Dialektik
des politischen Christen.* München: Kaiser, 1974. 254p.

1281. Diem, Hermann. "Zur Psychologie der Kierkegaard-
Renaissance." *Zwischen den Zeiten* 10 (1932):216-248.

1282. Diem, Hermann. "Christliche Gestalten. Sören Kierkegaard." *Frankfurter Zeitung* (4.11.1934).

1283. Diem, Hermann. "Sören Kierkegaard." In *Festschrift
an Rudolf Bultmann.* Stuttgart und Köln: Kohlhammer, 1949,
34-47.

1284. Diem, Hermann. "Um Kierkegaard." *Evangelische
Theologie* 9 (1949-50):526-528.

1285. Diem, Hermann. "Kierkegaard und sein Jahrhundert."
Zeitwende. Die neue Furche 26 (1955):727-736.

1286. Diem, Hermann. "Sokrates in Dänemark." *Schweizer
Monatshefte* (Zurich) 35 (1955-56):422-431.

1287. Diem, Hermann. "Dogmatik und Existenzdialektik bei
Sören Kierkegaard." *Evangelische Theologie* 15 (1955):
402-506.

1288. Diem, Hermann. "Dogmatik und Existenzdialektik bei
Sören Kierkegaard." *Orbis Litterarum* 10 (1955):50-65.

1289. Doctor, Herta. "Verwischte Spuren. Auf der Suche
nach Sören Kierkegaard." *Die Welt* (23.3.1950).

1290. Dollinger, Robert. "Was bleibt von Sören Kierkegaard?" *Deutsches Pfarrerblatt* (Essen) 55 (1955):481-484,
510-512.

1291. Droop, Fritz. "Sören Kierkegaard." *Mannheimer*
Tageblatt no. 122 (1913).

1292. Droop, Fritz. "Kierkegaard und die Frauen."
Hamburger Fremdenblatt no. 204 (1913).

1293. Droop, Fritz. "Sören Kierkegaard." *Berliner Tage-*
blatt no. 268 (1913).

1294. Droop, Fritz. "Sören Kierkegaard." *Masken*. Halbmonatsschr. des Düsseldorfer Schauspielhauses 9 (1914):
243-247.

1295. Eilers, Edgar. "Das geistige Jahr. Untersuchungen
und Interpretationen zu s. relig. Struktur in Vergleich
mit Sören Kierkegaard." Ph.D., München Universität, 1951,
278p.

1296. Eisenhuth, Heinz Erich. *Der Begriff des Irrationalen*
als philosophisches Problem. Ein Beitrag zur existenzialen
Religionsbegrundung. Göttingen: Vandenhoeck & Ruprecht,
1931, ix-274p. (Studien zur systematischen Theologie,
Heft 8.) (Der Begriff des Existentialen in seiner philosophischen Bedeutung und Geschichte. 1: Die philosophische
Bedeutung des Begriffs des Existentialen, 218-222;
2: Existenz und Wirklichkeit bei Kierkegaard, 222-229;
3: Kritik an Kierkegaard vom existentialen Denken aus,
230-233.)

1297. Eisler, Rudolf. In *Philosophen-Lexikon. Leben,*
Werke und Lehren der Denker. Berlin, 1912, 349-350.

1298. Eldersch, Ludwig. "Ein gothisches Genie." *Neues*
Oesterreich (Wien) (6.11.1955).

1299. Elert, Werner. In *Der Kampf um das Christentum*.
Geschichte der Beziehungen zwischen dem evangelischen
Christentum in Deutschland und das allgemeine Denken seit
Schleiermacher und Hegel. München, 1921 (viii-513p.),
431-434.

1300. Engel, Otto. "Sören Kierkegaard." *Stuttgarter Neues*
Tageblatt no. 531 (1930).

1301. Engelbrecht, Kurt. "Sören Kierkegaard." *Kölnische*
Zeitung no. 613 (1930).

1302. Ernst, Paul. In *Ein Credo I-II*. Berlin: Meyer &
Jessen, 1912 (viii-235-221p.). Neue Ausgabe, hrsg. von
K. A. Kutzbach. München: G̃ Müller, 1935, II, 197-200.

1303. Fahrenbach, Helmut. *Die gegenwärtige Kierkegaard-*
Auslegung in der deutschprachigen Literatur von 1948 bis
1962 (Philosophische Rundschau Beiheft 3). Tübingen:
J. C. B. Mohr, 1962. 82p.

1304. Fauteck, Heinrich. "Pedantische Notizen zu einer
Kierkegaard-Ausgabe." *Neue Rundschau* 78 (1967):352-356.

1305. Feldkeller, Paul. "Sören Kierkegaard." *Königsberger
Allgemeine Zeitung* no. 530 (1930).

1306. Feldkeller, Paul. "Sören Kierkegaard. Zu seinem
120. Geburtstag." *Stuttgarter Neues Tageblatt* (5.5.1933).

1307. Fischer-Manpoteng, F. C. In *Menschsein als Aufgabe.
Stufen der Selbstbesinnung im Leben des Einzelnen.*
Heidelberg, 1928.

1308. Franken, J. Christiann. "Die psychologische Kritik
Kierkegaards." In *Kritische Philosophie und dialektische
Theologie. Prolegomena zu einer philosophischen Behandlung
des Problems der christlichen Gemeinschaft.* Amsterdam:
H. J. Paris, 1932, x-439p.), 71-80.

1309. Friedrich, Paul. "Sören Kierkegaard als ethischer
Erzieher. Eine Studie." *Pädagogisches Archiv* 48 (1906):
650-662.

1310. Friedrich, Paul. "Sören Kierkegaard als ethischer
Erzieher." In *Deutsche Renaissance. Gesamm. Aufsätze.*
Bd. 1-2. Leipzig: Zenion-Verlag, 1911 und 1913.

1311. Gabriel, Leo. *Existenzphilosophie. Von Kierkegaard
zu Sartre.* Wien: Herold, 1950, 416p. *Existenzphilosophie.
Kierkegaard, Heidegger, Jaspers, Sartre.* Dialog d. Posi-
tionen 2, vollst. überarb. u. erg. Aufl. Wien, München:
Herold-Verlag, 1968, 369p.

     book review:
     Endre von Ivanka, *Scholastik* 27 (1952):400-408.

1312. Gabriel, Leo. "Sören Kierkegaard. Zu seinem 100.
Todestag." *Oesterreichische neue Tageszeitung* (Wien)
(10.11.1955).

1313. Gabriel, Leo. "Der religiöse Skandal. Sören Kier-
kegaard-Gedanken zum 100. Todestag des 'prognostischen
Genies' Europas." *Salzburger Nachrichten* (11.11.1955).

1314. Gaudig, Hugo. "Sören Kierkegaard." *Kirchliche
Monatsschrift* 5 (1885):133, 202, 298, 352, 430ff.

1315. Geismar, Eduard. "Sören Kierkegaard." *Zeitschrift
für systematische Theologie* 3 (1925):3-49.

1316. Geismar, Eduard. "Der Einfluss deutschen Geistes
auf Sören Kierkegaard." *Deutsch-nordische Zeitschrift*
2 (1929):15-22 (Festnummer).

1317. Geismar, Eduard. In *Die Religion in Geschichte und
Gegenwart.* Bd. 3, 2. Aufl., 1929, 747-751.

1318. Geismar, Eduard. "Einleitung." *Sören Kierkegaard:
Religion der Tat*. Leipzig, 1930, vii-xiii.

1319. Geismar, Eduard. "Sören Kierkegaards Bedeutung für
Frömmigkeit und Theologie." *Banater Monatshefte*. Zeitschrift fur deutsches Geistesleben, Temesvór (1936-37):
179-182.

1320. Geismar, Eduard. "Sören Kierkegaards Bedeutung für
Frömmigkeit und Theologie." *Ekklesia*. Eine Sammlung von
Selbstdarstellungen der christlichen Kirchen, 2: Die
skandinavischen Länder. Die Kirche in Dänemark. Bd. II.
Leipzig, 1937, 127-141.

1321. Gemmer, Anders. "Religionsphilosophische Grundgedanken bei Kierkegaard." *Geisteskultur (Comenius-
Gesellschaft)* 34 (1925):19-27.

1322. Gemmer, Anders. "Die Lebensphilosophie Sören Kierkegaards." *Philosophie und Leben* 2 (1926):293-297.

1323. Gerber, Hans Erhard. *Nietzsche und Goethe. Studien
zu einem Vergleich* (Sprache und Dichtung, 78). Bern-
Stuttgart: Verlag Paul Haupt, 1954. 151p.

1324. Gerken, Alexander. "O.F.M., Theologie und Existenz
bei Kierkegaard." *Wissenschaft und Weisheit* 32 (1969):
19-38.

1325. Gerlach, H. M. "Spätburgerliche Philosophie und
Konservatismus." *Deutsche Zeitschrift für Philosophie*
24 (1976):603-617.

1326. Gieseler, Franz. "Zur Würdigung Sören Kierkegaards.
Eine Entgegnung mit Nachschrift (von Paul Graue)." *Die
christliche Welt* 12 (1898):411-417.

1327. Goes, E. "Kierkegaards Sendung an die Gegenwart."
Der Protestant 4 (1900):6-8.

1328. Grässe, J. G. Th. In *Geschichte der Poesie Europas
und der bedeutendsten aussereuropäischen Länder vom Anfang
des 16. Jahrhunderts bis auf die neueste Zeit*. Leipzig,
1848, p. 979.

1329. Grau, R. Fr. "Mitteilungen aus Sören Kierkegaard."
Beweis des Glaubens 28 (N.F. 13) (1892):358-360, 426-436.

1330. Grisebach, E. In *Die Grenzen des Erziehers und
seine Verantwortung*. Halle: M. Niemeyer, 1924 (xxi-333p.),
xi-xxi.

1331. Guardini, Romano. "Der Ausgangspunkt der Denkbewegung Sören Kierkegaards." *Hochland* 24 (1927):12-33.

1332. Guardini, Romano. "Kierkegaards Idee des absoluten Paradoxes." *Die Schildgenossen* 9 (1919):191.

1333. Haecker, Theodor. "F. Blei und Kierkegaard." *Der Brenner* 4 (1914).

1334. Haecker, Theodor. "Kierkegaard am Fusse des Altars." *Der Brenner* 7 (1923):71-85.

1335. Haecker, Theodor. "Sören Kierkegaard." *Hochland* 22 (1925):188-212.

1336. Haecker, Theodor. "Sören Kierkegaard." In *Christentum und Kultur*. München: Kösel, 1927 (273p.), 66-114.

1337. Haecker, Theodor. In *Tag- und Nachtbucher 1939-1945*. Mit einem Vorwort hrsg. von Heinrich Wild. München: Kösel, 1949, 59, 77, 293, 301, and passim.

1338. Haenchen, Ernst. "Das neue Bild Kierkegaards." *Deutsche Theologie* 3 (1936):273-287. Forts. m. titlen: Das neue Kierkegaardbild, *ibid.*, 298-329; 376-394.

1339. Haenchen, Ernst. "Kampf um Kierkegaard." *Deutsches Volkstum* 18 (1936):670-678.

1340. Hafner, Gotthilf. "Sören Kierkegaard." *Wu. W.* 11 (1956):277-280.

1341. Hammel, W. "Die 'naturliche Religion' bei Newman und die 'Religiosität A' bei Kierkegaard." In *Newman Studien*. Hrsg. von H. Fries und W. Becker (Veröffentlichungen des Cardinal Newman Kuratoriums). 2. Folge. Nürnberg: Glock und Lutz, 1954, 21-46.

1342. Hansen, Chr. "Leben und Charakteristik des Verfassers." In *Zur Selbstprüfung* [1862], 1-21. 2. Aufl., Erlangen, 1869, 1-21.

1343. Hansen, S. "Die Bedeutung des Leidens für das Christusbild Sören Kierkegaards." *Kerygma und Dogma* 2 (1956):1-28.

1344. Havenstein, Eduard. "Auslandische Denker: Sören Kierkegaard." *Jahresberichte für neuere deutsche Literaturgeschichte* 24 (1915):699-700.

1345. Heinsoeth, Heinz, and Windelband, W. *Lehrbuch der Geschichte der Philosophie*. Hrsg. von Heinz Heimsoeth. Tübingen: Mohr & Siebeck, 1935 (xxxix-642p.), xxxiii, 533, 588, 600-602.

1346. Heinemann, Fritz. In *Neue Wege der Philosophie. Eine Einführung in die Philosophie der Gegenwart*. Leipzig: Quelle & Meyer, 1929 (xxviii-434p.).

1347. Heiss, Robert. "Sören Kierkegaards Bild vom Menschen."
Blätter für deutsche Philosophie 10 (1936):225-239.

1348. Heiss, Robert. Die grossen Dialektiker des 19.
Jahrhunderts. Hegel, Marx, Kierkegaard. Köln: Kiepenheuer
& Witsch, 1963. 437p.

1349. Hermann, Ulrich. "Deutsche Bücher zu Kierkegaard."
Eckart N.F. 2 (1926):145.

1350. Hessen, Johannes. In Religionsphilosophie.
Bd. 1: Methoden und Gestalten der Religionsphilosophie.
Bd. 2: System der Religionsphilosophie. Essen & Freiburg
i Br.: Hv. Chamier, 1948.

1351. Heubaum, Alfred. "Sören Kierkegaard." Preussische
Jahrbücher 90 (1897):50-86.

1352. Heuch, J. C., and Plitt, G. "Sören Aabye Kierkegaard." Zeitschrift für die gesammte lutherische Theologie
und Kirche 25 (1864):295-309; 309-310.

1353. Hevesi, Ludwig. "Ein ironischer Don Juan." Pester
Lloyd (Budapest) no. 234 (1904).

1354. Himmelstrup, J. "Einige Gegenbemerkungen zu Schott-
laenders Kritik." Philosophischer Anzeiger 4 (1929-30):
42-50.

1355. Hirsch, Emanuel. "Zum Verständnis von Kierkegaards
Verlobungszeit (Kierkegaard-Studien, 1. Stück)." Zeitschrift
für systematische Theologie 5 (1927):55-75.

1356. Hirsch, Emanuel. "Kierkegaards Erstlingsschrift
(Kierkegaard-Studien, 2. Stück)." Zeitschrift für systematische Theologie 8 (1930):90-144.

1357. Hirsch, Emanuel. "Eine Meditation Kierkegaards."
Deutsche Theologie 1 (1934):373.

1358. Hirsch, Emanuel. "Sören Kierkegaard." Suddeutsche
Monatshefte 32 (1935):296-305.

1359. Hirsch, Emanuel. "Sören Kierkegaard." In Der Weg
der Theologie. Stuttgart: W. Kohlhammer, 1937 (128p.
Sammlung von Aufsätze), 108-124.

1360. Hirsch, Emanuel. "Sören Kierkegaards dialektische
Kritik am idealistischen Christenumsverständnis." In
Die Umformung des christlichen Denkens in der Neuzeit.
Ein Lesebuch. Tübingen: Mohr & Siebeck, 1938 (vi-343p.),
319-343.

1361. Hirsch, Emanuel. In Geschichte der neueren evangel-
ischen Theologie im Zusammenhang mit den allgemeinen
Bewegungen des europäischen Denkens. 1-5. Gütersloh:
C. Bertelsmann, 1949-54.

1362. Hirsch, Emanuel. "Der Kirchensturm von Kopenhagen.
Sören Kierkegaards Angriff auf Christenheit, Kirche und
Ortodoxe." *Sonntagsblatt.* 6 (1953):7-9.

1363. Hirsch, Emanuel. "Kierkegaards Sprache und Stil."
In *Sören Kierkegaard 1855-1955. Zum Kierkegaard-Gedenkjahr
vorgelegt.* Düsseldorf & Köln: Diederichs, 1955, 12-17.

1364. Hoffding, Harald. "Sören Kierkegaard in Dänemark
im 19. Jahrhundert." *Archiv für Geschichte der Philosophie*
2 (1889):(49-74) 64-68.

1365. Hoffmann, Karl. "Kierkegaard als Denker." In
Zur Litteratur und Ideengeschichte. 12 Studien. Charlottenburg, 1908 (viii-165p.), 26-49.

1366. Hoffmann, Karl. "Kierkegaard." *Die Gegenwart* 67
(1905):247-252.

1367. Hohlenberg, Johannes. "Sören Kierkegaard und unsere
Zeit." *Universitas* 1 (1950):463-465.

1368. Holm, Sören. "Holberg, Grundtvig, Kierkegaard,
drei dänische Denker." *Neue Zeitschrift für systematische
Theologie* 7 (1965):49-61.

1369. Horn, Fr. Winkel. In *Gesch. der Literatur des
skandinavischen Nordens von den ältesten Zeiten bis auf
die Gegenwart.* Leipzig: B. Schlicke, 1880 (viii-404p.),
259-261.

1370. Horn, Fr. Winkel. "Sören Aabye Kierkegaard."
Allgemeine Encyklopädie der Wissenschaften und Künste
(Leipzig) II. Section: Theil 35 (1884):24-28.

1371. Hübscher, Arthur. *Von Hegel zu Heidegger. Gestalten
und Probleme* (Reclams Universal-Bibliothek, 8651/8654).
Stuttgart: Reclam, 1961. 278p.

1372. Hürlimann, Otto. "Kierkegaard." *Der Aufbau* (Zürich)
30 (1949):4-9, 17-20, 25-27, 33-35.

1373. Jaspers, Karl. "Kierkegaard und Nietzsche: Leiden
oder Lust als letztes." In *Psychologie der Weltanschauungen.*
Berlin: Jul Springer, 1919 (xii-428p.), 225-226. 2. durchgeseh. Aufl. ibid. 1922 (xiii-486p.), 255-256. "Der Geist
zwischen Vereinzelung und Allgemeinheit: Das Individuum und
das Allgemeine. Das Offenbarwerden." Ibid. 1922, 370-381.
3. Unveränd. Aufl. ibid. 1954.

1374. Jaspers, Karl. "Herkunft der gegenwärtigen philosophischen Situation (Die geschichtliche Bedeutung Kierkegaards und Nietzsches). In *Vernunft und Existenz. Fünf
Vorlesungen, 25.-29. März 1935.* Groningen: J. B. Walters,
1935 (115p.), 1-28.

1375. Jaspers, Karl. "Kierkegaard. 1951." In *Rechenschaft und Ausblick. Reden und Aufsätze*. München: R. Piper, 1951, 115-133.

1376. Jaspers, Karl. "Kierkegaard." *Der Monat* 3 (1951): 227-236.

1377. Jaspers, Karl. "Kierkegaard, Leben und Werk." *Universitas* 6, II (1951):1057-1070.

1378. Jaspers, Karl. "Kierkegaard." *Neubau* 7 (1952): 95-99.

1379. Jentsch, Karl. "Sören Kierkegaard." *Die Zukunft* 12 (1904):87-95.

1380. Jessen, E. A. F. "Sören Kierkegaard." In *Die Hauptströmungen des religiösen Lebens der Jetztzeit in Dänemark*. Gütersloh: C. Bertelsmann, 1895 (vi-176p.), 79-96.

1381. Jorgensen, Alfred Th. "Sören Kierkegaard." *Theologisches Literaturblatt* 34 (1913):385-389.

1382. Joest, Wilfried. "Zur Auseinandersetzung mit Kierkegaard." *Verkündigung und Forschung* [Für] 1951-52 (1953-54): 225-244.

1383. Kampmann, Theoderich. "Kierkegaard als religiöser Erzieher." *Theologie und Glaube* (Paderborn) 39 (1949):31-56.

1384. Kampmann, Th. "Mensch und Christ in der Welt Sören Kierkegaards." *Akademisch. Bonifatius Korrespondent* 53 (1938):51-67.

1385. Kampmann, Th. "Kierkegaards Werke deutsch." *Theologie und Glaube* 42 (1952):358-362.

1386. Kassner, Rudolf. "Kierkegaards fünfundsiebzigster Todestag." *Die Literarische Welt* 6 (1930).

1387. Kassner, Rudolf. *Sören Kierkegaard.* Heidelberg: C. Pfeffer, 1949. 67p.

1388. Kassner, Rudolf. "Sören Kierkegaard," and "Das Gottmenschentum und der Einzelne." In *Essays*. Insel-Verlag, 1913.

1389. Kassner, Rudolf. "Sören Kierkegaard. Eine Einleitung zu einer französischen Übersetzung seines Tagebuchs." *Frankfurter Zeitung* 72 (1927):1-3.

1390. Keller, Adolf. "Kierkegaards Wirkung auf die Welt." *Deutsche Allgemeine Zeitung* (Berlin) (15.6.1937).

1391. Kesseler, Kurt. "Sören Kierkegaard und die Philosophie der Innerlichkeit." *Die Wartburg* 13 (1914).

1392. Kesser, Arnim. "Sören Kierkegaard." *Der neue Merkur*
2 (1924):536-544.

1393. Kober, F. "Beck, Kierkegaard und Stanger als Zuchtmeister auf Christus." *Allgemeine evang.-luth. Kirchenzeitung* 58 (1925):183-185.

1394. Korff, Friedrich Wilhelm. "Hermetische Hermeneutik
und ideologische Ontologie im Gefolge Sören Kierkegaards.
Ein Betrag zur Typologie aktueller Gesinnung." *Studium
Generale* 24 (1971):865-905.

1395. Korff, Friedrich Wilhelm, und Ries, Wiebrecht.
"Um Kierkegaards Verbindlichkeit." *Philosophische Rundschau*
18 (1972):242-266.

1396. Korff, Friedrich Wilhelm. "Kierkegaards Nachmütze."
Neue Rundschau 85 (1974):270-277.

1397. Kränzlin, Gerhard. "Sören Kierkegaard." In
Existenzphilosophie und Panhumanismus. Scheldorf am
Kochelsee: Brunnen, 1950, 7-37.

1398. Kraus, Wolfgang. "Der Philosoph des christlichen
Paradox." *Oberösterreichische Nachrichten* (Linz) (11.11.
1955); *Volkszeitung* (Klagenfurt) (13.11.1955).

1399. Krauss, Stephan. "Die Konflikt-Ideologie des dänischen
Philosophen Sören Kierkegaard (1813-1855)." In *Der seelische
Konflikt. Psychologie und existentiale Bedeutung*.
Stuttgart: F. Enke, 1933 (viii-125p.), 53-58, 82, 99, 118.

1400. Kronig, G. "Sören Kierkegaard." *Bremer Kirchliche
Monatsschrift* (N. F. des Bremer Kirchenblattes) 1 (1929):
188-195.

1401. Kühner, Karl. "Sören Kierkegaard." *Der Volkserzieher*
(Berlin) 16 (1912):95-96.

1402. Kütemeyer, W. "Nachwort" in Sören Kierkegaard's
Der Begriff der Ironie. München, 1929, 341-369.

1403. Kütemeyer, W. "Nachwort" in Sören Kierkegaard's
Christliche Reden. Jena, 1929, 414-423.

1404. Kütemeyer, W. "Sören Kierkegaard und der 'Korsar'."
Deutscher Almanak für 1930, 1: Leipzig: Reclam, 1930, 176-193;
Die Brücke (1931):176-193.

1405. Kütemeyer, W. "Vorwort" in Sören Kierkegaard's
Der einzelne und die Kirche. Berlin, 1934, 5-33.

1406. Kütemeyer, W. "Nachwort" in Sören Kierkegaard's
Das Evangelium der Leiden. 2 Aufl. München, 1936, 115-124.

1407. Kuhn, Helmut. In *Begegnung mit dem Nichts. Ein Versuch über die Existenzphilosophie.* Tübingen: Mohr, 1950.

1408. Landmann, Michael. "Kierkegaard--der Denker der innerlichen Wahrheit." *Universitas* 20 (1965):1171-1179.

1409. Landmann, Michael. "Phänomenologie, Kierkegaard, Marxismus." *Neue Rundschau* 86 (1975):461-472.

1410. Larsen, K. Olesen. "Sören Kierkegaard--Zeuge der Wahrheit." *Sonntagsblatt* (1955):12-13.

1411. Lehmann, Eduard. "Einleitung. Sören Kierkegaard 5. Maj 1813-11. Nov. 1855." In *Sören Kierkegaard.* Berlin, 1913, 7-24 (Klassiker der Religion, 8 & 9 Bd.).

1412. Lehmann, J. "Zur Würdigung Kierkegaards." *Evangelische Kirchenzeitung* 75 (1901):795-798, 825-828.

1413. Leisegang, Hans. "Hegel, Marx, Kierkegaard. Zum dialektischen Materialismus und zur dialektischen Theologie." *Blick in die Wissenschaft* 1 (1948):128-138. *Hegel, Marx, Kierkegaard. Zum dialektischen Materialismus und zur dialektischen Theologie.* Berlin, 1948. 41p.

1414. Lilienfein, Heinrich. "Sören Kierkegaard, der Denker der Leidenschaft." *Das literarische Echo* 14 (1911-12): 371-378.

1415. Lilienfein, Heinrich. "Sören Kierkegaard." *Neues Tageblatt* (Stuttgart) (5.5.1913).

1416. Lilienfein, Heinrich. "Zu Sören Kierkegaard." *Die Literatur* 31 (1928-29):143-145.

1417. Lindström, Valter. "Kierkegaards bewaffnete Neutralität." *Orbis Litterarum* 10 (1955):148-155.

1418. Löwith, Karl. In *Von Hegel zu Nietzsche. Der revolutionäre Bruch im Denken des 19. Jahrhunderts. Marx und Kierkegaard* [1941]. 2. Aufl. Zürich-Wien: Europa, 1950; 5. Aufl. Stuttgart: Kohlhammer, 1964, 464p.

1419. Löwith, Karl. "Jener Einzelne: Kierkegaard." *Merkur* 10 (1956):147-162.

1420. Lögstrup, K. E. *Auseinandersetzung mit Kierkegaard.* (Kontroverse um Kierkegaard und Grundtvig, K. E. Lögstrup and Götz Harbsmeier, eds.) Münich: Chr. Kaiser, 1968. ["Mit Erweiterungen für die deutsche Ausgabe aus dem Dänischen übersetzt von Rosemarie Lögstrup."]

1421. Lukács, Georg. "Kierkegaard." *Deutsche Zeitschrift für Philosophie* 1 (1953):286-314. Also in *Der Zerstörung der Vernunft. Der Weg des Irrationalismus von Schelling zu Hitler.* Berlin: Aufbau-Verlag, 1957.

1422. Lunding, Erik. *Adalbert Stifter; mit einem Anhang über Kierkegaard und die existentielle Literaturwissenschaft.* Copenhagen: Nyt Nord. Forl., 1946. (Studien zur Kunst und Existenz). (131-150).

1423. Lütke, Moritz. In *Kirchliche Zustände in den skandinavischen Ländern Dänemark, Norwegen, Schweden. Mittheilungen aus der Gegenwart.* Bevorwortet von Dr. Kraft. Elberfeld: Friederichs, 1864 (viii-144p.), 45-58.

1424. Malantschuk, G. "Das Verhältnis zwischen Wahrheit und Wirklichkeit in S. Kierkegaards existentiellem Denken." *Orbis Litterarum* 10 (1955):166-177. [Symposion Kierkegaardianum]

1425. Malantschuk, Gregor. "Die Begriffe Immanenz und Transzendenz bei Sören Kierkegaard." *Neue Zeitschrift für systematische Theologie* 19 (1977):225-246.

1426. Malantschuk, Gregor. "Sören Kierkegaard und das kollaterale Denken." *Zeitschrift für philosophische Forschung* 24 (1970):3-16.

1427. Marck, Sigfried. "Existentielle Dialektik. 1. Die dialektische Theologie. Kierkegaard, Barth, Gogarten, Emil Brunner." In *Die Dialektik in der Philosophie der Gegenwart.* 1. Halbbd. Tübingen: Mohr & Siebeck, 1929, vi-166p.

1428. Marcuse, Ludwig. "Sören Kierkegaard: die Überwindung des romantischen Menschen." *Die Dioskuren* 2 (1923):194-237.

1429. Martensen, H. L. In *Die christliche Ethik.* Allgemeiner Theil. Gotha, 1871, 305-333.

1430. Martensen, H. L. *Aus meinem Leben I-III.* Aus dem Dänischen von A. Michelsen. Karlsruhe & Leipzig: H. Reuther, 1883-84 (vi-v-267-176-260p.). S. K.: III, 12-24.

1431. Martensen, Hans L. "Kierkegaard und die Situationsethik." *Scholastik* 26 (1951):556-564.

1432. Messer, August. "Gedanken Kierkegaards." *Philosophie und Leben* 6 (1930):47-50.

1433. Mettler, Artur. "Nachfolge und Reich Gottes: Sören Kierkegaard (1813-1855) und Christoph Blumhardt (1842-1919)." *Reformatio* 17 (1969):139-151.

1434. Meyer, Hans. In *Systematische Philosophie.* Bd. 1: Allgem. Wissenschaftstheorie und Erkenntnislehre. Padeborn: Schöningh, 1955.

1435. Meyer, Richard M. "I. La Mennais. Sören Kierkegaard. II. Ludwig Feuerbach. Max Stirner." *Vossische Zeitung* (Sonntagsbeilage, Berlin) (1895):5-8, 4-9.

1436. Michel, Ernst. "Sören Kierkegaard." *Die Tat* 5 (1913):138-144.

1437. Michel, Ernst. "Sören Aabye Kierkegaard." *Lexikon für Theologie und Kirche* 5 (1933):946-948.

1438. Michelsen, Alex. "Sören Aabye Kierkegaard." *Realencyklopädie für protestantische Theologie und Kirche* 2 (1880):664-670.

1439. Monrad, M. J. *Denkrichtungen der neueren Zeit. Eine kritische Rundschau.* Deutsche, vom Verfasser selbst besorgte, Bearbeitung. Bonn: E. Weber, 1879 (viii-284p.), 47-57, 58-67.

1440. Müller, Johannes. "Sören Kierkegaard." *Hammer* 3 (1904):559-562.

1441. Mumbauer, Johannes. "Sören Kierkegaard." *Hochland* (1913):184-194.

1442. Neuenschwander, Ulrich. *Gott im neuzeitlichen Denken, II: Henri Bergson, Ernst Bloch, Martin Buber, Hermann Cohen, Ludwig Feuerbach, Johann Gottlieb Fichte, Georg Friedrich Wilhelm Hegel, Martin Heidegger, Karl Jaspers, Sören Kierkegaard, Karl Marx, Friedrich Nietzsche, Jean-Paul Sartre, Max Scheler, Friedrich Wilhelm Joseph Schelling* (Gütersloher Taschenbücher Siebenstern, 244). Gütersloh: Gütersloher Verlagshaus Mohn, 1977. 244p.

1443. Neumann, Johannes. "Kierkegaards Liebeskonflikt." *Psyche* 2 (1948-49):327-370.

1444. Neumann, Johannes. "Kierkegaards *Pfahl im Fleisch.*" *Internationale Zeitschrift für Individual-Psychologie* 18 (1949):7-14.

1444a. Neumann, Johannes. "Kierkegaard zwischen Protestantismus und Katholizismus." *Deutsches Pfarrerblatt* 50 (1950): 227-230.

1445. Neumann, Johannes. "Sören Kierkegaards Individuationsprozess nach seinen Tagebüchern." *Zeitschrift für Psychotherapie und medizinische Psychologie* 2 (1952):152-168.

1446. Niebergal, Friedrich. "Predigttypen und Predigtaufgaben der Gegenwart 5: Kierkegaard, Barth und Thurneysen, Dehn, Ehrhard." *Die christliche Welt* 39 (1925):738-743.

1447. Niedermeyer, Gerhard. "Sören Kierkegaard." *Neuwerk* 12 (1930):130-136.

1448. Nielsen, Fredrik. "Sören Aabye Kierkegaard." *Realencyklopädie für protestantische Theologie und Kirche* 3 (1901):278-282.

1449. Nigg, Walter. *Religiöse Denker: Kierkegaard-Dosto-jewsky-Nietzsche-Van Gogh.* Berlin-München: Gebr. Weiss, 1952. 420p.

1450. Nippold, Friedrich. "Sören Kierkegaard." In *Handbuch der neuesten Kirchengesch. seit der Restauration von 1814.* Elberfeld: R. L. Friderichs, 1867 (xv-484p.), 458-460.

1451. Noack, Hermann. "Kierkegaard und unsere Zeit." *Hamburger Fremdenblatt* (30.5.1925).

1452. Nostiz, Osw von. "Kierkegaard und der Verführer." *Begegnung* 5 (1950):132-134.

1453. Nostiz, Osw von. "Kierkegaards Dämon." *Wirtschafts-Zeitung* 4 (1909):9.

1454. Nussbächer, Konrad. "Der 'existierende Denker' Sören Kierkegaard." *Klingsor* 1: Kronstadt [(Brasov) Rumaenien] (1924):23-28.

1455. Obenauer, K. J. In *Die Problematik des ästhetischen Menschen in der deutschen Literatur.* München, 1933.

1456. Obenauer, K. J. In *Der ästhetische Mensch in der neueren deutschen Literatur. Zeitschrift für Deutschkunde* 44 (1930):369-379 (375-376).

1457. Ogiermann, Helmut. "Kierkegaard." *Orientierung* 15 (1951):99-101, 113-115.

1458. Paganus [Pseud.]. "Kierkegaards *Augenblick.*" *Das freie Wort* (1910):630-638.

1459. Pape, W. "S. Aa. Kierkegaard. Skizze seines Lebens und Wirkens." *Der Beweis des Glaubens* 14 (1878):169-189.

1460. Paulsen, Anna. "Sören Kierkegaard zum Gedächtnis." *Kirche in der Zeit* 10 (1955):244-245.

1461. Paulsen, Anna. "Religiosität oder Glaube. Eine Einführung in Sören Kierkegaard." *Schule und Evangelium* (Stuttgart) 1 (Vortrag 25.5.1926). Sonderdr. ibid. 1927, 19p.

1462. Paulsen, Anna. "Die Auswirkung Sören Kierkegaards in der Existenzphilosophie heute." *Die Stimme der Gemeinde.* Monatsschr. d. Bekennenden Kirche 2 (1950):13-14.

1463. Paulsen, Anna. "Noch einmal der andere Kierkegaard." *Evangelische Theologie* 11 (1951-52):561-571.

1464. Paulsen, Anna. "Auf Spuren Kierkegaards." *Almanach auf das Jahr des Herrn 1952.* Hamburg: Wittig, [1951], 78-85.

1465. Paulsen, Anna. "Das Verhältnis des Erbaulichen zum
Christlichen: Zum Problem der *Erbaulichen Reden* Sören
Kierkegaards." In *Kierkegaardiana* 6 (1967):97-106.

1466. Paulsen, Anna. "Was heisst existieren." In
Kierkegaardiana 8 (1971):182-192.

1467. Petersen, C. "Sören Kierkegaard." *Evangelische
Kirchenzeitung* no. 13, 14, 15 (1911).

1468. Pfister, Oskar. In *Das Christentum und die Angst*.
Zürich: Artemis, 1944, 19-21.

1469. Pfister, Rudolf. "Zur Existenzdialektik Sören
Kierkegaards." *Neue Schweizer Rundschau* N.F. 20 (1952):
112-117.

1470. Pieper, Annemarie. "Die Bedeutung des Begriffs
'Existenzkategorie' im Denken Kierkegaards." *Zeitschrift
für philosophische Forschung* 25 (1971):187-201.

1471. Pieper, Annemarie. "Sören Kierkegaard. Inter-esse
Zwischen Theorie und Praxis." *Philosophische Rundschau*
24 (1977):129-145.

1472. Planck, Reinhold. "Von Luther zu Kierkegaard. Ein
von der Zensur verbotener Artikel." *Die christliche Welt*
35 (1919):164-169.

1473. Platzhoff, Eduard. "Sören Kierkegaard." *Theologische
Rundschau* 4 (1901):135-148, 179-187, 219-226.

1474. Plitt, G. "S. A. Kierkegaard. Skizzirt von J. C.
Heuch. Nachtrag. Noch ein Wort aus dem Norden über
Kierkegaard." Mittgetheilt von G. Plitt. *Zeitschrift für
die gesammte lutherische Theologie und Kirche* 25 (1864):
295-309, 309-310.

1475. Poppenberg, Felix. "Don Juan imaginaire." *Die
Nation* 21 (1903-04):395-398.

1476. Quehl, Ryno. "Dr. Sören Kierkegaard wider die
dänische Staatskirche, mit einem Hinblick auf Preussen."
In *Aus Dänemark*. Berlin: Decker, 1856 (xxix-380p., 3 Ab-
bildungen), 277-306; Anhang. III. Zusätze, 368-380.

1477. Rehm, Walter. "[I. P.] Jacobsen, [S. K.] und die
Schwermut." In *Experimentum medietatis*. *Studien zur
Geistes- und Literaturgeschichte des 19.Jahrhunderts*.
München: Rinn, 1947, 184-239.

1478. Rehm, Walther. "Mottostudien: Kierkegaards Motti."
Beträge zu Philosophie und Wissenschaft 4 (1962):267-300.

1479. Reisner, Erwin. "Kierkegaard und seine Bedeutung für das philosophische Denken unserer Zeit." *Neue deutsche Hefte*. Beiträge zur europäischen Gegenwart 2 (1955):661-672.

1480. Rest, Walter. "Die kontroverstheologische Relevanz Sören Kierkegaards." *Catholica*, Jahrbuch für Kontroverstheologie 9 (1952-53):81-94.

1481. Rest, Walter. "Auslandische Werke über Kierkegaard." *Catholica* 9 (1952-53):150-151.

1482. Rest, Walter. "Zum Verständnis Sören Kierkegaards." *Die Kirche in der Welt* 8 (1955):43-46.

1483. Reuter, Hans. "Zum Gedächtnis Kierkegaards. I-II." *Protestantenblatt* 46 (1913):611-614, 670-673.

1484. Richter, Liselotte. "Konstruktives und Destruktives in der neuesten Kierkegaard-Forschung." *Theologische Literaturzeitung* 77 (1952):141-148.

1485. Richter, Liselotte. "Sören Kierkegaard." In Kierkegaard's *Die Leidenschaft des Religiösen. Eine Auswahl aus Schriften und Tagebüchern*. Stuttgart: Reclam, 1953, 3-15.

1486. Richter, Liselotte. "Kierkegaard und das Zeitalter der Technokratie." *Zeichen der Zeit* (1955):402-406.

1487. Richter, Liselotte. "Sören Kierkegaard in Berlin." *Jahrbuch für brandenburgische Landesgeschichte* 6 (1955): 10-16.

1488. Richter, Liselotte. "Sören Kierkegaard schreibt an Kinder." *Eckart-Jahrbuch* (1955056):94-105.

1489. Rohrmoser, Günter. "Ernst oder ironie?--Eine Zwischenbemerkung zur Interpretation Kierkegaards." *Archiv für Geschichte der Philosophie* 44 (1962):75-86.

1490. Roos, H. "Sören Kierkegaard und die Kenosis-Lehre." In *Kierkegaardiana* 2:54-60.

1491. Rusche, Helga. "Sören Kierkegaard, ein Leben in der Nachfolge Christi." *Der junge Mann* 3 (1951):15-17.

1492. Ruttenbeck, W. "Glaube und Schrift. Eine Betrachtung im Anschluss an S. Kierkegaard." *Der Geisteskampf der Gegenwort* 65 (1929):254-263.

1493. Ruttenbeck, Walter. "Kierkegaard, der christliche Denker und sein Werk." *Studien zur Geschichte der Theologie und der Kirche* 25 (1929).

1494. Ruttenbeck, Walter. "Zur neuesten Kierkegaard-Literatur." *Zeitschrift für Kirchengeschichte* 53 (1934):695-701.

1495. Sawatzki, Günther. "Promenade in Kopenhagen."
Sonntagsblatt (1955):9-10.

1496. Sawatzki, Günther. "Falsche Autorität und echte
Nachfolge." *Sonntagsblatt* (1955):11.

1497. Schäfer, Klaus. "Kierkegaard--Kirchenvater der
Wertlehre: Bemerkungen zu E. Tielschs Untersuchung
'Kierkegaards Glaube'." In *Kierkegaardiana* 6 (1967):152-180.

1498. Schelderup, Harald. In *Gesch. der philosophischen
Ideen von der Renaissance bis zum Gegenwart.* Übers. v.
Leixner von Grünberg. Berlin & Leipzig: de Gruyter, 1929
(viii-232p.), 125-129.

1499. Schlötermann, Heinz. *Vom göttlichen Urgrund. Acht
Gespräche über das Christentum von Meister Eckhart bis
Berdiajew* [Eckhart, Nikolaus von Kues, J. Böhme, F. W. J.
von Schelling, F. E. D. Schleiermacher, S. Kierkegaard,
N. Berdiajew, R. Otto.] Hamburg: Meiner, 1950. 279p.

1500. Schlüter, Wilhelm. "Sören Kierkegaard." *Deutschland*
4 (1906):417-427.

1501. Schneider, R., Hausmann, M., and Thielecke, H.
"Begegnung mit Kierkegaard." *Eckart* 25 (1956):115-121.

1502. Schnell, Jenny. "Sören Kierkegaard." *Pastoraltheologie* 33 (1937):228-232.

1503. Schrempf, Christoph. "Sören Kierkegaard und sein
neuester Beurteiler." *Evangelische Kirchenzeitung* 16 (1886).

1504. Schrempf, Christoph. "Sören Kierkegaards Stellung
zu Bibel und Dogma." *Zeitschrift für Theologie und Kirche*
1 (1891):179-229.

1505. Schrempf, Christoph. "Sören Kierkegaard." *März* 6
(1912):52-56, 90-97.

1506. Schrempf, Christoph. In *Die Religion in Geschichte
und Gegenwart* (1912):1095-1103.

1507. Schrempf, Christoph. "Sören Kierkegaard." *Christliche Freiheit* 29 (1913):309ff., 323.

1508. Schrempf, Christoph. "Abschied von Sören Kierkegaard."
Der Diederichs-Löwe 3 (1929):138-141.

1509. Schrey, H. H. "Die Ueberwindung des Nihilismus bei
Kierkegaard und Nietzsche." *Zeitschrift für systematische
Theologie* 21 (1950):50-68.

1510. Schubart, W. "Sören Kierkegaard." *Schweizerische
Monatschefte für Politik und Kultur* 21 (1941-42):20-27.

1511. Schückler, Georg. "Das Anliegen Sören Kierkegaards."
Begegnung 5 (1950):323-327.

1512. Schückler, Georg. "Sören Kierkegaard und sein
Anliegen." *Neue Ordnung* 5 (1951):152-161.

1513. Schückler, Georg. "Kierkegaard Stellung zu Luther
und zu Kirche." *Neue Ordnung* 5 (1951):429-438.

1514. Schulz, Walter. "Interpretatorische Hinweise auf
die Philosophie Kierkegaards, Nietzsches und Heideggers."
In *Die Vollendung des deutschen Idealismus in der Spät-
philosophie Schellings*. Stuttgart: Kohlhammer, 1955, 274-290.

1515. Schulz, Walter. "Existenz und System bei Sören
Kierkegaard." In *Wesen und Wirklichkeit des Menschen*.
Festschrift fur Helmut Plessner. Hrsg. von Klaus Ziegler.
Göttingen: Vanden Hoeck & Ruprecht, 1957, 107-128.

1516. Schulze-Maizier, Fr. "Vom Sinn der rechten Mitte."
Deutsche Rundschau 66 (1940):101-106 (om K., 103-104).

1517. Schumann, Max. "Sören Kierkegaard." *Xenion* 6 (1913):
70-77.

1518. Söe, N. H. "Der Quidam des Experiments als religiöser
Typus." *Orbis Litterarum* 10 (1955):259-267. [Symoposion
Kierkegaardianum]

1519. Sorainen, Kalle. "Einige Beobachtungen im Bezug auf
die lateinischen Übersetzungen Sören Kierkegaards aus dem
griechischen Neuen Testament." In *Kierkegaardiana* 9 (1974):
56-74.

1520. Stammer, Martin. "Sören Kierkegaard." *Neue kirchliche
Zeitung* 24 (1913):412-428.

1521. Steffen, Albert. "Kierkegaard und die Gegenwart."
Das Geotheanum (Dornach, Schwiez) 10 (1931):83.

1522. Steiger, L. "Unzeitgemässer Kierkegaard." *Evange-
liche Theologie* 29 (1969):244-266.

1523. Stisser, W. "Hat Sören Kierkegaard uns heute etwas
zu sagen?" *Deutsches Pfarrerblatt* 43 (1939).

1524. Storck, M. "Sören Kierkegaard und wir." *Geisteskampf
der Gegenwart* (1933):339-343.

1525. Strodtmann, Adolf. "Sören Kierkegaard. Seine Theorien
und sein Einfluss auf die schriftstellerische Produktion
[in Dänemark]." In *Das geistige Leben in Dänemark. Streif-
züge auf den Gebieten der Kunst, Literatur, Politik und
Journalistik des skandinavischen Nordens*. Berlin: Gebr.
Pastel, 1873 (xvi-266p.), 95-126.

1526. Strodtmann, Adolf. "Sören Kierkegaard. Nach einer
Charakteristik seiner literarischen Thätigkeit von
G. Brandes." Beilage zur *Allgemeine Zeitung* 81 (1878):278,
279-281, 283, 3., 5., 6., 8. & 10.10, 4069-4070, 4101-4104,
4118-4120, 4143-4144, 4173-4175.

1527. Tagger, Theodor. "Note zu Kierkegaard." *Die Schau-
bühne* 12 (1916):374.

1528. Theunissen, Gert H. "Sören Kierkegaard. Das Christentum unter vier Augen." *Rheinischer Merkur* 10 (1955):7.

1529. Theunissen, Gert H. "Sören Kierkegaard--und wir
heute." In *Sören Kierkegaard 1855-1955. Zum Kierkegaard-
Gedenkjahr vorgelegt.* Düsseldorf-Köln: Diederichs, 1955,
3-11.

1530. Thielicke, Helmut. *Das Verhältnis zwischen dem
ethischen und dem ästhetischen. Eine systematische Untersuchung.* Leipzig: Felix Meiner, 1932, xv-262p. Phil. Diss.
Erlangen, 1932.

1531. Thielicke, Helmut. In *Theologische Ethik I-II.*
Tübingen: Mohr, 1951-55.

1532. Thrändorff, Ernst. "Sören Kierkegaard in der Schul-
Kirchengeschichte." *Monatsblätter für den evangelische
Religionsunterricht* 14 (1921):24-38.

1533. Thust, Martin. "Der ästhetische Mensch. Erste Einführung in den Geist Sören Kierkegaards." *Preussische
Jahrbücher* 190 (1922):49-63.

1534. Thust, Martin. "Das Marionettentheater Sören Kierkegaards." *Zeitwende* 1 (1925):18-38.

1535. Thust, Martin. "Sören Kierkegaard und die wissenschaftliche Theologie." *Zeitwende* (1927):173.

1536. Troeltsch, Ernst. *Zur religiösen Lage, Religionsphilosophie und Ethik.* Tübingen: Mohr & Siebeck, 1913,
Ges. Schriften 2, xi-866p. (Om S. K., 293-294 & passim.)

1537. Unger, Rudolf. "Kierkegaard, der religiöse Prophet
des Nordens. Worte erster Einführung. *Der Wächter* 7
(1924):468-494. Also in *Aufsätze zur Literatur- und Geistesgeschichte.* Berlin: Juncker & Dünnhaupt, 1929 (viii-238p.),
122-162.

1538. van Radenborgh, G. "Wie beantwortet Kierkegaard die
Frage nach der rechten Verkündigung?" *Neue Zeitschrift für
systematische Theologie* 4 (1962):158-196.

1539. Vetter, August. *Frömmigkeit als Leidenschaft: Eine
Deutung Kierkegaards.* München: Karl Alber Freiburg, 1963.

1540. Vielhaber, Hiltgart. "Sören Aabye Kierkegaard."
Sozialistische Monatshefte 17 (19) (1913):542-549.

1541. Wagner-Simon, Therese. "Sören Kierkegaard."
Schweizer Rundschau 48 (1948):505-519.

1542. Wahl, Jean. In *Vom Nichts vom Sein und von unserer
Existenz. Versuch einer kleinen Geschichte des Existential-
ismus.* In die deutsche Sprache übertr. von Dominique Bernard.
Augsburg & Basel: Die Brigg, 1954.

1543. Warmuth, Kurt. "Soeren Kierkegaard--ein Seelsorger
für die Seelsorger." *Archiv für Geschichte der Philosophie*
30 (N.F. 23) (1917):111-138.

1544. Warmuth, Kurt. "Sören Kierkegaard, ein Prophet der
Innerlichkeit." *Allgemeine evangelische-lutherische Kirchenzeitung* 58 (1925):742-745. Also in: *Der Tag* (Paderborn)
no. 160 (1925); *Köningsberger Allgemeine Zeitung* Lit.-Beilage
59 (1925); *Tägliche Rundschau* (6.10.1925); *Der Geisteskampf
der Gegenwart* 62 (1926):108-113; *Neues Sächsisches Kirchenblatt* 33 (1926):109-112; *Monatsschrift für Pastoraltheologie*
24 (1928):276-280.

1545. Warmuth, Kurt. "Sören Kierkegaard in der Gegenwart."
Theologische Blätter 20 (1941):226-241.

1546. Weidenmann, J. "Sören Kierkegaard, 1813-1855."
Reformierte Schweiz (1953):374-376.

1547. Weigert, Edith. "Sören Kierkegaards Gemütsschwank-
ungen." *Psyche* H. 14 (1960-61):608-616.

1548. Weischedel, W. "Sören Kierkegaard und die christliche
Verkündigung." *Bausteine* 41 (1934):2-15.

1549. Wenzel, Fritz. "Lobpreis auf die Liebe Gottes.
Kierkegaards Bedeutung für unsere Zeit." *Kirche* 3 (1948):3.

1550. Wenzel, Fritz. In *Der Einzelne und die Gemeinschaft.
Eine Beitrag zur Philosophie der Kulturkrise.* Ohlau i Schl.:
H. Eschenhagen, 1935 (vi-84p.), 24-52. Phil. Diss. Breslau,
1935.

1551. Wernle, Paul. "Sören Kierkegaard." *Basler Nachrichten* (11.5.1912).

1552. Weymann-Weyhe, W. "Sören Kierkegaard und die
christliche Existenz." *Die Kirche in der Welt* 2 (1949):
223-226.

1553. Wien, Alfred. "'Jener Einzelne'. Zur Einführung in
das Studium Kierkegaards." *Leipziger Zeitgeist* no. 1 (1913).

1554. Wien, Alfred. "Sören Kierkegaard. Zur 100.Wieder-
kehr von Kierkegaards Geburtstag am 5.Mai 1913. Ein Lebensbild." *Westermanns ill. deutsche Monatshefte* 57 (1913):
428-434.

1555. Wien, Alfred. "Echo der Zeitschriften." *Das literarische Echo* 15 (1913):1138-1139.

1556. Wien, Alfred. "Sören Kierkegaard." *Deutsche Zeitung*
(1921), Unterhaltungs-Beilage no. 430, 432, 434, 24.9,
10.10 & 24.10.

1557. Wilde, Frank-Eberhard. "Sein und Wirklichkeit
[Kierkegaard]." In *Kierkegaardiana* 8:193-198.

1558. Winkel Horn, Fr. In *Gesch. der Literatur des skandinavischen Nordens von den ältesten Zeiten bis auf die
Gegenwart.* Leipzig: B. Schlicke, 1880 (viii-404p.), 259-261.

1559. Winkel Horn, Fr. "Sören Aabye Kierkegaard." *Allgemeine Excyklopädie der Wissenschaften und Künste.* Leipzig,
II. Section: Theil 35 (1884):24-28.

1560. Winkler, Robert. "Die Eigenart des theologischen
Erkennens. Ein Beitrag zum Problem der Existenz."
Zeitschrift für systematische Theologie 9 (1931-32):277-318
(om S. K., 287-290).

1561. Winkler, Robert. "Kierkegaard, Katholizismus und
Protestantismus." *Christentum und Wissenschaft* (1930).

1562. Woerner, Roman. "Sören Kierkegaard." *Das literarische
Echo* 9 (1907):511-516.

1563. Wotton, Henry. "Drei klassische Verführer."
Xenion 4 (1911):1-6.

1564. Wust, Peter. *Die Dialektik des Geistes.* Augsburg:
Benno Filser, 1928, xv-752p. (om S. K., 31, 183-189, 586-589,
614f., 734).

1565. Wust, Peter. *Ungewissheit und Wagnis.* Salzburg &
Leipzig, 1937.

1566. Wust, Peter. *Der Mensch und die Philosophie. Ein-
führung in die Hauptfragen der Existenzphilosophie.*
Mit einem Vorwort und Nachwort des Herausgebers Augustin
Borgolte. Münster: Regensberg, 1947. 151p.

1567. Zenker, E. V. "Sören Kierkegaard--Philosophie und
Liebe." *Freie Welt* 4 (1925):15-23, 12-18, 19-24, 14-20.

1568. Zillesen, Alfred. "Vom Umindividualisieren der
Individualität." *Christliche Freiheit* 13 (1913):434-437.

ITALIAN

1569. Abbagnano, Nicola. In *Storia della Filosofia* [1946]. 2d ed. II. Torino: Unione Tipografico, 1950, 179-193.

1570. Abbagnano, Nicola. "Kierkegaard e il sentiero della possibilità." In *Studi Kierkegaardiani*. A cura di Cornelio Fabro. Brescia: Morcelliana Editrice, 1957, 9-28.

1571. Armellini, Rina Anna. *Genesi ed evoluzione dell' angoscia esistenzialista*. [Profili di Kierkegaard, Dostojewskiy, Kafka, Sartre e Camus.] (Centro di Cultura Aldo, Masieri, Rovigo.) Numero speciale della Rivista *La Sorgente*, 1950. 47p.

1572. Banfi, A. "La Riforme e il pensiero europeo Kierkegaard." *Coscienza* (1926).

1573. Battaglia, F. "Kierkegaard tra il singolo e Dio." In *Il Problema Morale Nell'esistenzialismo*. Bologna: Zuffi, 1946, 202p.; 2d ed. ibid. 1949, vii-314p.

1574. Bellisario, Vincenzo. "Il dramma di Kierkegaard." *Rivista di Filosofia Neo-Scolastica* 34 (1942):127-136.

1575. Bobbio, Noberto. "Kierkegaard e noi." *Rivista del movimento 'Comunita'* 4 (1950):54-55.

1576. Borgese, G. A. "Don Giovanni in Danimarca." In *La Vita e il Libro. Saggi di Letteratura e di Cultura Contemporanea*. Bologna: Zanichelli, 1927. 322p.

1577. Brancatisano, Fortunato. "Angoscia e inquietudiné in Sören Kierkegaard." *Noesis* 1 (1946):291-316.

1578. Buonaiuti, Ernesto. "Ancora Kierkegaard." *Religio* 13 (1937):366-367.

1579. Cantoni, Remo. "L'eredità spirituale di Sören Kierkegaard." In *Studi Kierkegaardiani*. A cura di Cornelio Fabro. Brescia: Morcelliana Editrice, 1957, 93-104.

1580. Carlini, Armando. In *Avviamento allo Studio della Filosofia*. Nuova [4a] ed. Firenze, 1936, p. 249.

1581. Castelli, Ferdinando. "Sören Kierkegaard suscitatore di realtà eterne e invisibili." *Civilta Cattolica* 127 (II) (1976):456-463.

1582. Chestov, Leon (Sestov, Lev). "Dio e l'amore." In Kierkegaard's *Lo Specchio della Parola*. A cura di Cornelio Fabro e E. Valenziani. Firenze: Fussi, 1948, 1-26.

1583. Chiesa, Mario. "Cinque esistenzialisti [Kierkegaard, Dostoievski, Barth, Marcel, Berdiaeff]. *Rivista Rosminiana* 44 (1950):67-74.

1584. Collins, James. "Fede e riflessione in Kierkegaard."
In *Studii Kierkegaardiana*. A cura di Cornelio Fabro.
Brescia: Morcelliana Editrice, 1957, 105-123.

1585. Cortese, Alessandro. "L' 'organico' culturale
(paragrafi kierkegaardiani)." *Ve P.* 48 (1965):132-144.

1586. Cortese, Alessandro. "Soeren Aabye Kierkegaard,
abbozzo sulla sua vita." *Ve P.* 48 (1965):38-54.

1587. Cortese, Alessandro. "La domanda su Kierkegaard
(La lotta tra il vecchio e il nuovo negocio del sapone)."
Archivio di Filosofia 1 (1968):143-158.

1588. Cortese, Alessandro. "Il Pastore Adler: Della
libertà religiosa in Kierkegaard." *Archivio di Filosofia*
2 (1968):629-646.

1589. Cortese, Alessandro. "Il Pastore A. P. Adler o
della libertà religiosa in Kierkegaard." Contributi dell'
Istituto di Filosofia, I (1969):81-113 (Pubblicazioni dell'
Universita Cattolica del Sacro Cuore III, 14).

1590. Cortese, Alessandro. "Filosofia, pena e tempo.
La coscienza della pena in Kierkegaard." In *Il Mito della
Pena*. *Archivio di Filosofia* (1967):469-481.

1591. Cristaldi, Mariano. "Sören Kierkegaard e trauma
della testimonianza." In Kierkegaard's *La Neutralità
Armata e il Piccolo Intervento* (Filosofia e tempo presente,
2). A cura di Mariano Cristaldi e Gregor Malantschuk.
Messina: A. M. Sortino, 1972, 11-92.

1591a. Cristaldi, Rosario Vittorio. "Kierkegaard o della
testimonianza impossibile [A proposito di S. Kierkegaard,
La Neutralita Armata. . .; e di M. Cristaldi, *Problemi di
Storiografia. . .*]. *Teoresi* 32 (1977):233-246.

1592. D'Agostino, Francesco. "La fenomenologia dell'uomo
giusto: Un parallelo tra Kierkegaard e Platone." *Rivista
Internazionale di Filosofia del Diritto* 49 (1972):153-172.

1593. Dottori, Riccardo. "La testimonianza di Kierkegaard."
In *Informazione e Testimonianza*. *Archivio di Filosofia*
(1972):55-66.

1594. Fabro, Cornelio. "Kierkegaard, poeta-teologo dell'
Annunciazione." *Humanitas* 3 (1948):1025-1034.

1595. Fabro, Cornelio. "Critica di Kierkegaard all'Otto-
cento." *Atti del XV Congressonazionale di Filosofia. . .*
1948. Messina-Firenze: D'Anna, 1949, 375-385.

1596. Fabro, Cornelio. "Attualità e ambiguità dell'opera
Kierkegaardiana." *Orbis Litterarum* 10 (1955):66-74.
[Symposion Kierkegaardianum]

1597. Fabro, Cornelio. "La fenomenologia della fede--
Ambiguità della fede in Soeren Kierkegaard." *Archivio di
Filosofia* (1957):187-197. [Il compito della fenomenologia.]

1598. Fabro, Cornelio. "La missione di Kierkegaard."
Ethica 8 (1969):169-180.

1599. Fabro, Cornelio. "La *pistis* aristotelica nell'opera
di Sören Kierkegaard." *Proteus* 5 (1974):3-24.

1600. Fabro, Cornelio. "Kierkegaard, Cristianesimo tragico
o dramatico?" *Humanitas* (Brescia) 31 (1976):532-537.

1601. Francia, E. "Il significato di Sören Kierkegaard."
Studium, Rivista Universitaria 31 (1935):334-341.

1602. Francia, E. "Preludio su Kierkegaard." *Frontespizio*
no. 3 (1938).

1603. Gab, G. [Gabetti, Guiseppe]. "Sören Aabye Kierkegaard." *Enciclopedia Italiana* 20 (1933):193-194.

1604. Gavazzeni, G. "Kierkegaard, il Don Giovanni e la
musica." *Rassegna d' Italia* (Milano) (1947).

1605. Gozzini, M. "La tragedia dell'io in Sören Kierkegaard." *L'Ultima* (Firenze) no. 34, 35 (1948).

1606. Gristaldi, Mario. "Materialismo storico ed esistenzialismo: Kierkegaard e Marx." *Humanitas* 4 (1949):1043-1046.

1607. Höffding, Harald. "Un discendente di Amleto. Sören
Kierkegaard." *Leonardo*, Rivista d'idee 4 (1906):67-79.

1608. Höffding, Harald. In *Compendio di Storia della
Filosofia Moderna*. Versione italiana di Ludovico Limentani
1923 . 3d ed., Milano: Bocca, 1946, 219-222 (Piccola
Biblioteca di Scienze Moderne, 237).

1609. Höffding, Harald. *Storia della Filosofia Moderna*.
Indicazioni bibliografiche a cura di D. Bigalli e P. Rossi.
Trad. del tedesco di P. Martinetti. Vol. I: Dal Rinascimento
a Leibniz. Vol. II: Da Locke a Kierkegaard. Firenze:
Sansoni, 1970.

1610. Jansen, F. J. Billeskov. "I grandi romanzi filosofici
di Kierkegaard." In *Studi Kierkegaardiani*. A cura di
Cornelio Fabro. Brescia: Morcelliana Editrice, 1957, 67-92.

1611. Jaspers, Karl. "Chi è Kierkegaard?" (Trad. di
Maurizio Malaguti.) *Ethica* 8 (1969):81-90.

1612. Koch, Carl. "Sören Kierkegaard." Traduzione di
Ragnhild Lund. *Il Rinnovamento* 2 (1908):27-42.

1613.   Lazzarini, Renato. "Logica esistenzialistica e
logica agonistica in Kierkegaard." *Atti del Congresso
Internazionale di Filosofia*, Roma, 1946. Vol. 2, Milano:
Castellani, 1948, 313-319.

1614.   Licciardello, P. Nello. "Itinerari dell'esistenzialismo romantico. S. Kierkegaard." *Teoresi* 15 (1960):
25-42.

1615.   Liotta, R. "L'educazione della possibilita in
S. Kierkegaard." *Prospettive Pedagogiche* 5 (1968):204-213.

1616.   Lombardi, Franco. "Alcune riflessioni su Kierkegaard
ed altre poche cose. In *Kierkegaard e Nietzsche*. *Archivio
di Filosofia* 1953, No. 2: Milano-Roma: Bocca, 1953, 105-113.

1617.   Lombardi, R. "Sören Kierkegaard, uno pensatore
triste." *La Civiltà Cattolica* no. 2254 (1944).

1618.   Lombardi, R. "Il momento religioso nel pensiero
Kierkegaardiana." *La Civiltà Cattolica* no. 2258 (1944).

1619.   Losacco, Michele. In *Lineamenti di Storia di Filosofia ad uso delle Scuole Medie*. Napoli: Loffredo, 1931,
p. 227.

1620.   Löwith, Karl. *Da Hegel a Nietzsche*. Torino: Einaudi,
1949. 637p. (Biblioteca di Cultura Filosofica, 9.)

1621.   Löwith, Karl. "Kierkegaard: 'Quel singolo'." In
Studi Kierkegaardiani. A cura di Cornelio Fabro. Brescia:
Morcelliana Editrice, 1957, 181-201.

1622.   Lowrie, Walter. "Sören Kierkegaard." *Religio* 11
(1935):1-15.

1623.   Mancini, Italo. *Filosofi Esistenzialisti*. (Pubbl.
dell'Università di Urbino. Serie di Lettere e Filosofia,
18.) Urbino: Argalia Editore, 1964. 276p.

1624.   Masi, Giuseppe. "Storicità e cristianesimo in Kierkegaard." *Archivio di Filosofia* 1953, No. 2: Milano-Roma:
Bocca, 1953, 115-132.

1625.   Melchiorre, Virgilio. "Metafisica e storia in Sören
Kierkegaard." *Sapienza* 8 (1955):203-221.

1626.   Milano, A. "Il 'divenire di Dio' in Hegel, Kierkegaard e San Tomasso d'Aquino." In *San Tomasso e il Pensiero
Moderno*. *Saggi*. Roma: Pont. Accad. Romana di San Tomasso
d'Aquino. Città Nuova, 1974, 284-294.

1627.   Paci, E. "Personalità ed esistenza nel pensiero
di Kierkegaard." In *Pensiero, Esistenza, e Valore*.
Milano-Messina: Principato, 1940, vii-197p.

1628. Paci, E. "Studi sur Kierkegaard." *Studi Filosofici* 1 (1940).

1629. Paci, Enzo. "Ironia, demoniaco ed eros in Kierkegaard (in: Kierkegaard e Nietzsche. . .)." *Archivio di Filisofia* No. 2, Milano-Roma: Bocca, 1953, 71-103.

1630. Paci, Enzo. "Il cammino della vita [Kierkegaard]." *Aut-Aut* (1954):111-126.

1631. Paci, Enzo. "Storia ed apocalisse in Kierkegaard (in: Apocalisse e Insecuritas). *Archivio di Filisofia* No. 2, Milano: Frat Bocca, 1954, 141-162.

1632. Paci, Enzo. "Kierkegaard contro Kierkegaard." *Aut-Aut* (1954):269-301.

1633. Paci, Enzo. "Angoscia e relazione in Kierkegaard." *Aut-Aut* (1954):363-376.

1634. Paci, Enzo. "Ripetizione ripresa e rinascita in Kierkegaard." *Giornale Critico della Filosofia Italiana* 33 (1954):313-340.

1635. Parente, P. "Il vero volto di Kierkegaard." *Osservatore Romano* (1952):3.

1636. Pareyson, Luigi. "Kierkegaard e la poesia d'occasione." *Rivista di Estetica* 10 (1965):248-255.

1637. Pastore, A. "Il messagio di Sören Kierkegaard." *Logos* no. 1-2 (1943). Reprinted in his *La Volontà dell' Assurdo. Storia e Crisi dell'Esistenzialismo.* Milano: Bolla, 1948. 237p.

1638. Pedersen, Peder. "Copenhagen [Pseud.: Walter Lowrie]: Un panegirico [sullo Kierkegaard]." *Religio* 14 (1938):81-85.

1639. Pellegrini, Alessandro. "Il 'sistema' e gli eretici [Hegel og Kierkegaard]. *Archivio di Storia della Filosofia Italiana.*

1640. Pelloux, Luigi. "Un nuovo testo di Kierkegaard." *Studium* 1 (1946):239-240.

1641. Preti, Giulio. "Kierkegaard, Feuerbach e Marx." *Studi Filosofici* 10 (1949):187-208.

1642. Riconda, Giuseppe. "L 'eredità di Kierkegaard e la teologia dialettica nel suo significato speculativo." *Filosofia* 25 (1974):215-232.

1643. Rollier, M. A. "*L'Ora* di Sören Kierkegaard." *Gioventu Cristiana* no. 10 (1931).

1644. Ruggiero, Guido. In *Filosofia del Noveccento*. *Appendice a La Filosofia Contemporanea* [1933]. 4. ed. Bari: Laterza, 1950 [1949].

1645. Sciacca, M. F. "L'esperienza etico-religiosa di Sören Kierkegaard." *Logos* 20 (1937):121-128.

1646. Sciacca, G. M. *L'esperienza Religiosa e l'io in Hegel e Kierkegaard*. Palerma: Palumbo, 1948. 60p.

1647. Spera, Salvatore. "Il mito di Faust. Aspirazioni letterarie, riflessioni filosifiche, preoccupazioni religiose del giovane Kierkegaard." *Archivio di Filosofia* (1974): **309-339**. [E. Castelli, Nota conclusiva, 340.]

1648. Stella, Fernando. "Kierkegaard: un uomo in presenza di Dio." *Raccolta di Studi e Ricerche* (Bari) 2 (1978): 331-341.

1649. Turoldo, D. "Kierkegaard e le soglie del Regno." *Il Ragguaglio Librario* (Milano) (3.3.1946).

1650. Vircillo, Domenico. "Ambiguità e fede in Kierkegaard, Nietzsche e Kafka." *Sapienza* 26 (1973):27-69.

SPANISH

1651. Artola, José Maria. "Situación y sentido del pensamiento hegeliano en la actualidad." *Estudios Filosóficos* 22 (1973):349-384.

1652. Blackham, H. J. *Seis Pensadores Existencialistas. Kierkegaard, Nietzsche, Jaspers, Marcel, Heidegger, Sartre.* Trad. del inglés y notas bibliográficas por Ricardo Jordana (Libros Tau, 3). 2d ed. Barcelona: Oikos-Tau, 1967. 194p.

1652a. Brandt, Frithiof. "Sören Kierkegaard y la filosofia internacional." *La Nación* (11.11.1955).

1653. Carrasco de la Vega, Rubén. "Origen del existencialismo: Alma y doctrina de Kierkegaard." *Kollasuyo* (La Paz) 10 (1951):50-61.

1654. Cassini de Vázquez, María Cristina. "Kierkegaard, el caballero de la fe." *Sapientia* 27 (1972):273-284.

1655. Castellani, Leonardo. *De Kierkegaard a Tomas de Aquino*. Buenos Aires: Editorial Guadalupe, 1974. 264p.

1656. Chiodi, Pietro. *El Pensamiento Existencialista. Kierkegaard, Jaspers, Heidegger, Marcel, Sartre, Merleau-Ponty, Abbagnano, Paci.* Trad. al español por Héctor Rogel (Manuales UTEHA, no. 138/138a, Sección 7, Filosofía). México: Unión Tipográfica Editorial Hispanoamericana, 1962, v-193p.

1657. Ciarlo, H. O. "La noción de instante y presencia en
Kierkegaard." *Philosophia* (Mendoza) (1961):34-43.

1658. Daniel-Ropa, H. "Un Pascal protestante: Sören
Kierkegaard." *Folia Humanística* 3 (1965):385-390.

1659. Delacroix, H. "Estudio critico sobre Kierkegaard."
(Dat.: Julio de 1900.) *Prosas de Sören Kierkegaard*. Madrid,
1918, 43-99.

1660. Elizalde, S. "Kierkegaard, mensaje de sinceridad
religiosa." *Mensaje* (Santiago de Chile) 8 (1959):180-184.

1661. Fabro, Cornelio. "Kierkegaard, precursor del desper-
tar cristiano." *Arbor* 13 (1949):111-124.

1662. Fabro, Cornelio. "La critica de Kierkegaard al
octocientos." *Sapientia* (La Plata) 5 (1950):9-18.

1663. Farré, Luis. *Unamuno, William James y Kierkegaard*.
Cuadernos Hispano-americanos 20 (1954):279-299.

1664. Gabriel, Leo. *Filosofía de la existencia. Kierkegaard, Heidegger, Jaspers, Sartre. Diálogo de las posi-
ciones*. Traducido del alemán por Luis Pelayo Arribas
(Biblioteca de autores cristianos, 352). Madrid: La Editorial
Católica, 1974. 352p.

1665. Gabriel de Sotiello. O. F. M. Cap., Cristianismo
y mundanidad. Algunos aspectos del pensamiento religioso
de Kierkegaard." *Naturaleza y Gracia* (Salamanca) 3 (1956):
93-118.

1666. Giordani, Mário Curtis. "Kierkegaard, pensador
religioso." *Vozes* (Petrópolis) 56 (1962):335-349.

1667. Höffding, Harald. "Sören Kierkegaard." *Prosas de
Sören Kierkegaard*. Madrid, 1918, 1-42.

1668. Jolivet, Régis. "El pensamiento de Kierkegaard."
Sapientia 4 (1949):32-40.

1669. Jolivet, Régis. *Las Doctrines Existencialistas desde
Kierkegaard a Jean-Paul Sartre*. Trad. española de Arsenio
Pacios. Madrid: Editorial Gredos. Manuales universitarios,
1950; trad. del francés por A. Pacio. 4a ed. Madrid: Gredos,
1969, 409p.

1670. Larrañeta, Rafael. "La existencia como encrucijada
dialéctica entre la filosofia y la fe. Un estudio sobre
Sören Kierkegaard." *Estudios Filosóficos* 24 (1975):337-381;
25 (1976):17-70.

1671. Leal, J. Tarcísio. "Diálogo com Kierkegaard."
Latinoamérica (México) 6 (1954):322-327.

1672. Löwith, Karl. *De Hegel a Nietzsche. La Quiebra Revolucionara del Pensamiento en el Siglo XIX. Marx y Kierkegaard.* Trad. de Emilio Estiú. 2d ed. Buenos Aires: Sudamericana, 1974. 612p.

1673. Marion, Francisco Jarauta. "Soeren Kierkegaard. Pensador subjetivo religioso." *Logos. Revista de Humanidades* (Cali) (1973):25-48.

1674. Massuh, Victor. "Dos libros sobre Kierkegaard." *Notas y Estudios de Filosofía* 4 (1953):255-259.

1675. Padilla, Tarcisio M. "Kierkegaard y la 'philosophie de l'esprit'." *Estudios* (Madrid) 20 (1964):377-396.

1676. Perez Marchand, M. L. "Sören Kierkegaard, 1813-55." *Asomante* 12 (1956):6-36.

1677. Plazaola, Juan. "Estética y religión en Kierkegaard." *Estudios* 32 (1974):301-319.

1678. Rodríguez Rosado, Juan José. *La Aventura de Existir.* Pamplona: Ed. Universidad de Navarra, 1976. 225p.

1679. Sabanes, J. R. "El lugar de Kierkegaard in la filosofía." *Cuadernos Teológicos* (Buenos Aires) (1956): 17-25.

1680. San Miguel, José R. "En torno a Kierkegaard: posibilidad y sentido de una teología en el existencialismo." *Crisis* 4 (1957):433-445.

1681. Shein, L. J. "El concepto kierkegaardiano de temor en relación con el yo." *Folia Humanística* 15 (1977):297-306.

1682. Solary, L. F. "Influencia de Kierkegaard en la filosofia actual." *La Prensa* (Lima) (7.7.1942).

1683. Stack, George J. "Repetición constructiva versus repetición negativa [Kierkegaard versus psicoanálisis]." *Folia Humanística* 16 (1978):123-137.

1684. Vasseur, Alvaro Armando. "La potencia tragica. Don Javier de Urrazuno." In *Gloria. Aventuras Peregrinas.* Madrid: Editorial América, 1919, 229-243. (Biblioteca Andrés Bello, 57.)

1685. Vázques, Mária Cristina Cassins de. "Kierkegaard, el caballero de la fe." *Sapientia* 27 (1972):273-284.

1686. Vidiella, J. *De Kierkegaard a Sartre. El Existencialismo* (Marabú Zas, 83). Barcelona: Bruguera, 1963. 147p.

1687. Virasoro, Manuel. "Un espión al servicio de Dios: Kierkegaard." *Ciencia Fe* 13 (1957):509-515.

1688. Wahl, Jean. In *La Filosofías de la Existencia*. Trad. Alejandro Sanvisens. Barcelona: Vergara Editorial, 1956.

PORTUGUESE

1689. Barbuy, H. "Kierkcgaard e o desespero religioso." *Revista Brasileira de Filosofía* 6 (1956):22-37.

1690. Bó, E. T. "Kierkegaard e a filosofia actual." *Revista Brasileira de Filosofía* 6 (1956):59-69.

1691. Brandt, Frithiof. "Sören Kierkegaard e a filosofia universal." *Revista Portuguesa de Filosofía* 14 (1958): 245-249. [Filosofia europeia contemporânea.]

1692. Brandt, Frithiof. "Sören Kierkegaard e la filosofia universal." *O Tempo* (São Paulo) (1.11.1955); *A província do Pará* (Brasil) (11.11.1955); *Folha do Norte* (Brasil) (11.11.1955).

1693. Ferreira, V. "Notas sobre Kierkegaard." *Revista Brasileira de Filosofía* 1 (1951):490-494.

1694. Jolivet, Régis. *As Doctrinas Existencialistas*. Trad. del francés por A. de Q. V. e Lencastre. Porto, 1953.

1695. Niner, Elaine Cecília. "Sören Kierkegaard e a problemática humana." *Convívium S. P.* 8 (1969):14-32.

1696. Reale, Miguel. "Kierkegaard, o seu e o nosso tempo." *Revista Brasileira de Filosofía* 6 (1956):181-191.

1697. Washington, L. "Vida, obra e mensagem de Kierke- gaard." *Revista Brasileira de Filosofía* 6 (1956):3-21.

CATALAN

1698. Estelrich y Artigues, Joan. "El sentiment trágic de S. Kierkegaard." *Revista* (Barcelona), 1918.

1699. Höffding, Harald. "Sören Kierkegaard." (Trad. de J. Estelrich.) *Quaderns d'Estudi* (Barcelona) (1918):87-94.

DUTCH, SCANDINAVIAN AND OTHER LANGUAGES

1700. Anonymous. "Sören Kierkegaard." *Nederlandsch Tijdschrift voor Psychologie en Grenzgebiete* (Amsterdam) 1 (1934).

1701. Appeldoorn, J. G. "Sören Kierkegaard." *Theologisch
Tijdschrift* (Leiden) 34 (1900):227-260.

1702. Bergman, Bo. *Predikare.* Stockholm: Bonnier, 1967.

1702a. Bergman, Samuel Hugo. "Kierkegaard's existential
philosophy." In *Dialogical Philosophy from Kierkegaard to
Buber* [in Hebrew]. Jerusalem: Bialik Institute, 1974. 288p.

1703. Born, Eric von. "Tanke och handling hos Kierkegaard
[Thought and action in Kierkegaard]." *Var Lösen* 47 (1956):
283-285.

1704. Brandell, G. "Människouppfattningen hos Sören
Kierkegaard och e Goethes Faust." *Religion oc Kultur*
25 (1954):100-103.

1705. Brandt, Frithiof. "Sören Kierkegaard, groot Deens
denker, wiens taal eeuw na zijn dood begrepen wordt.
Levens-filosoof, christelijk denker en vorlooper van modern
existentialisme." *Leeuwarder Courant* (10.11.1955).

1706. Brandt, Frithiof. "Sören Kierkegaard en de internationale wijsbegeerte." *Vrij Nederland* (12.11.1955).

1707. Broonkhorst, A. J. "Kierkegaard--van zonderling
toot een der grootste denker." *Het Vaderland* (11.11.1955).

1708. Cappelörn, Niels Jörgen. "Et hidtil ukendt brev fra
Kierkegaard til den kendte 'Hr. Kold i Fredensborg'."
Kierkegaardiana 9 (1974):267-270.

1709. Cappelörn, Niels Jörgen. "Fire 'nye' Kierkegaard-
dedikationer: Lidt til belysning af Kierkegaards forhold
til R. Nielsen og J. P. Mynster." *Kierkegaardiana* 9 (1974):
248-266.

1710. Cappelörn, Niels, Jörgen. "Et Forsog Pa En Bestemmelse
Af Begrebet Forargelse Hos Sören Kierkegaard." *Dansk
Teologisk Tidsskrift* 38 (1975):197-229.

1711. Chantepie de la Saussaye. "Over Christendom en
Cultuur (Augustinus, Rousseau, Schleiermacher, Vinet,
Kierkegaard)." *Onze Eeuw* 13 (1913):217ff.

1712. Daniëls, Z. M. F. "(O. P.): Het strenge Christendom
van Sören Kierkegaard, I-III." *Het Centrum* (Utrecht)
(29.11; 2.12; 6.12.1911).

1713. *Denkers van deze tijd. Kierkegaard, Nietzsche, Barth,
Niebuhr, Sartre, Bultmann.* Uitgeg. in opdracht van de
Christelijk-nationale bibliotheek. 2. druk. Franeker:
T. Wever, 1954. 328p. [Voor deelnemers aan de Chr.-nat.
bibl.]

1714. Dijkstra, R. "Sören Kierkegaard, 1813-1855."
Bloesen en Vrucht (Groningen) 4 (1914-15):627-641.

1715. Delfgaauw, Bernard. *Wat is Existentialisme? Kier-kegaard, Marcel, Jaspers, Heidegger, Sartre.* 7e herziene
druk. Baarn: Het Wereldvenster, 1969. 130p.

1716. Delfgaauw, Bernard. "Jacob Nieuwenhuis en het
deense denken ten tijde van Kierkegaard." *Algemeen
Nederlands Tijdschrift voor Wijsbegeerte en Psychologie*
68 (1976):190-197.

1717. Dokter, T. "Sören Kierkegaard." *Onder eigen Vaandel*
(Wageningen) 14 (1939):37-56.

1718. Dupré, L. "S. Kierkegaard. Schets van zijn inner-
lijke ontwikkeling." *Streven* 9 (1955-56):217-225.

1719. Esser, P. H. In *Levensapecten. Essays. Bergson,
Pascal, Kierkegaard, Dostojewski.* Zutphen: Ruys, 1946
(130p.), 51-90.

1720. Fenger, Henning. "'Mestertyven'--Kierkegaards första
dramatiske forsög." *Edda* 71 (1971):331-339.

1721. Flam, Leopold. *De Krisis van de Burgerlike Moraal.
Van Kierkegaard tot Sartre.* Antwerpen: Uitgeverej 'Ontwikkeling', 1956. 176p.

1722. Flam, Leopold. "Sören Kierkegaard, de Ketter (1813-
1855)." *NVT* 11 (1957):408-421.

1723. Flam, Leopold. "Kierkegaard (1813-1963), I-II."
Dialoog 3 (1962-63):241-261; 4 (1963-64):1-12.

1724. Flam, Leopold. "Sören Kierkegaard (1813-1963)."
Revue Univ. Bruxelles 15 (1962-63):392-397.

1725. Flam, Leopold. "Flitsen." *NVT* 16 (1963):774-778.

1726. Flam, Leopold. "Kierkegaard (geboren op 5 Mei 1813)."
TVUB 5 (1963):204-216.

1727. Flam, Leopold. "De onmogelijke liefde van Sören
Kierkegaard." *Dialoog* 6 (1965-66):232-249.

1728. Gajdenko, P. "K'erkegor i filosofkso-èsteticeskie
istoki èkzistencializma." *V. Lit.* 11 (1967):133-157.
[Kierkegaard and the philosophical-esthetic sources of
existentialism.]

1729. Gjerlöff, Einar. "Sören Kierkegaards tungsindskom-
pleks." *Natuurwetenschappelijk Tijdschrift* 437 (1967):
313-339.

1730. Grooten, J. "Het problem der 'onrechtstreekse mede-
deling' bij Kierkegaard." *Handelingen van het Twintigste
Vlaamse Filologencongres*, Antwerpen 7.-9. April 1953.
Leuven: Pauwels, 1953, 260-263.

1731. Gustafsson, Berndt. "Kierkegaard och kyrkoaret
[Kierkegaard and the ecclesiastical year]. *Svensk Teologisk
Kvartalskrift* 34 (1958):96-110.

1732. Gyllensten, Lars. "Sören Kierkegaard [The Sören
Kierkegaard point of view]." *Prisma* (Suède) (1950):72-73.

1733. Haitjema, Th. L. "Paradoxaal, naar niet anti-intel-
lectualistisch." *Nieuwe Theologische Studiën* (Groningen)
7 (1924):129-143.

1734. Hansen, Holger. "Omkring Sören Kierkegaard. Syns-
punkter og problemer [About S. Kierkegaard. Points of view
and problems]." *Ord och Bild* 62 (1953):547-558.

1735. Hansen, Knud. "Sören Kierkegaard og nutiden." In
*Revolutionaer Samvittighed: Udvalgte Taler og Essays om
Karl Marx og Sören Kierkegaard*. Copenhagen: Gyldendal,
1965, 89-150.

1736. Havelaar, Just. "Kierkegaard im Kampf mit sich
selbst." *De Stem* (Arnhem) 3 (1923):177-181.

1737. Hedenius, Ingemar. "Om Sören Kierkegaard." *Ord och
Bild* 73 (1964):206-220.

1738. Heiss, Robert. *Hegel, Kierkegaard, Marx. De Grote
Dialectische Denkers van de Negentiende Eeuw*. Vertaald
door M. Mok (Aulaboeken, 418). Utrecht, Antwerpen: Het
Spectrum, 1969. 408p.

1739. Hepp, Valentin. "Sören Aabye Kierkegaard." *Chris-
telijke Encyclopaedie voor Het Nederlandsche Volk* (Kampen)
31 (1927):383-386.

1740. Heyerdahl, G. Borsand. "Sören Kierkegaard." In
Estetikk. Fra Platon til vare Dager. Truls Winther, ed.
Oslo: Tanum/Norli, 1977.

1741. Hielkema, M. "Kierkegaard, lang vergeten, weer
actueel. Boeteprediking na 'n eeuw international herleefd."
Het Vrije Volk (11.11.1955).

1742. Holm, Sören. "Sören Kierkegaard." In *Filosofien
i det Nittende Aarhundrede*. Copenhagen: Munksgaard, 1967,
171-191.

1743. Holm, Sören. "Kierkegaard först--og Grundtvig saa."
Nederlands Theologisch Tijdschrift 71 (1970):102-109.

1744. Ishizu, T. "Le fondement de la pensée de Kierkegaard: mécanisme, fonction et source de la mélancolie
[en japonais, rés. angl.]. *Bunka* 19 (1955):1-18.

1745. Jensen, Jörgen B. "Gentagelser." *Studenterkredsen*
(Copenhagen) 36 (1968-69):21-29.

1746. Jensen, Povl. Johs. "S. Kierkegaard og demokratiet:
En skitse." *Kierkegaardiana* 10 (1977):70-84.

1748. Kofoed, Niels. "Kierkegaards syn pa myten som udtryk
for erkendelse." In *Myte og Intellekt*. Copenhagen: Munksgaard, 1968, 55-92. (Munksgaardserien 24.)

1749. Koppang, Ole. "Sören Kierkegaards hemmelige note
[The secret notes of S. Kierkegaard]." *Kirke og Kultur*
58 (1953):176-179.

1750. Lavrin, Janko. "Soeren Kierkegaard." *Sodobnost*
16 (1968):718-727.

1751. Leemans, Victor. "Kierkegaardiana." *Kultuurleven*
21 (1954):376-378.

1752. Leemans, Victor. "De wordingsjaren van Sören
Kierkegaard." *Tijdschrift voor Philosophie* 17 (1955):
623-661. [Sommaire, 661-662.]

1753. Leemans, Victor. "Kierkegaard en onze tijd."
D. Warande Belf. (1956):386-391.

1754. Leendertz, W. "Naar aanleiding van een nieuwen
preekenbundel." *Stemmen des Tijds* 8 (1919):25-43.

1755. Leendertz, W. "Sören Kierkegaard." *Nederlands
Theologisch Tijdschrift* 10 (1955):65-75.

1756. Leendertz, W. "Sören Kierkegaard, Deens filosoot en
theoloog." *Algemeen Handelsblad* (Amsterdam) (9.11.1955).

1757. Lindström, Valter. "Kierkegaardrenässansen [The
renaissance of Kierkegaard]." *Teologinen Aikakauskirja*
(1952):65-80.

1758. Lindström, Valter. "Kierkegaards tolkning av
sjalvfornekelsen sasom kristendomens livsform [K's interpretation of self-denial as the essence of Christianity]."
Svensk Teologisk Kvartalskrift (1950):326-334.

1759. Lögstrup, K. E. "Kierkegaards tale om andsforholdets
fordoblelse: En tolkning." In *Kunst og Etik*. 2d ed.
Copenhagen: Gyldendal, 1967, 157-165. [Orig. pub. 1961.]

1760. Lund, Birgit. "Ole Lund Kierkegaards forfatterskab:
Personskildring/Motiv/Stil." In *Moderne Dansk Bornelitter-
atur*. Gunnar Jakobsen, et al., eds. Copenhagen: Forum,
1975, 227-237.

1761. Lund, Mogens. "Er 'Begrebet Angest' kun filosofi?"
Tidehverv 41 (1967):33-41.

1762. Malantschuk, Gregor. "Begreberne Immanens og
Transcendens hos Sören Kierkegaard." *Kierkegaardiana* 9
(1974):104-132.

1763. Malantschuk, G. "Begrebet det helige hos Sören
Kierkegaard." *Kierkegaardiana* 10 (1977):85-94.

1764. Marees van Swinderen, J. D. "Sören Kierkegaard."
Leven en Werken (Amsterdam) 2 (1917):408-434.

1765. Meranaios, Kostis. "Papadiamontes-Kierkegaard: To
Aisthima kai he Philosophia tis Zois." *Kritika Phylla*
14 (1974):94-99; 15 (1975):167-174.

1766. Müller, P. "Sören Kierkegaards forstaelse af
teodiceproblemet, belyst ud fra hans skildring af Job-
skikkelsen." *Dansk Teologisk Tidsskrift* 32 (1969):199-217.

1767. Müller, Paul. "Betingelser for meddelelsen af det
kristelige hos Sören Kierkegaard." *Dansk Teologisk
Tidsskrift* 36 (1973):25-43.

1768. Müller, Paul. "Tvivlens former og deres rolle i
erkendelsen af det historiske: En studie i Sören Kierkegaards erkendelsesteori." *Dansk Teologisk Tidsskrift*
37 (1974):177-216.

1769. Müller, Paul. "Grundprincipperne i Sören Kierkegaards meddelelsesdialektik og deres anvendelse i forfatterskabet." *Dansk Teologisk Tidsskrift* 41 (1978):123-133.

1770. Müller, Paul. "Kierkegaard--humanismens taenker."
Dansk Teologisk Tidsskrift 42 (1979):66-74.

1771. Nordentoft, Kresten. "Noget om Kierkegaard, Freud
og Marx." *Kredsen* 41 (1973):1-8.

1772. Oosterbaan, J. A. "De enkeling en het algemene in
het denken van Sören Kierkegaard." *Algemeen Nederlands
Tijdschrift voor Wijsbegeerte en Psychologie* 55 (1962-63):
123-136.

1773. Otani, Hidehito. "Thought-method of S. Kierkegaard.
Methodological sense of conceptions of 'subjectivity' and
'irony'." [En japonais.] *Philosophy* (Tokyo) no. 29 (1953)
[rés. anglais, 4-5].

1774. Pedersen, A. Benned. "Öjeblikket." *Tidehverv*
(Copenhagen) 43 (1969):101-106.

1775. Pedersen, A. Benned. "Uendelighedens dobbelt-
bevaegelse." *Tidehverv* 51 (1977):53-59.

1776. Pedersen, Jörgen. "Sören Kierkegaards bibelsyn."
Kierkegaardiana 9 (1974):23-55.

1777. Pedersen, Olaf. *Van Kierkegaard tot Sartre.*
Vertaald door Johan Winkler. Amsterdam: Het Wereldvenster,
1951, 166p.; 3e druk. Baarn: Het Wereldvenster, 1956, 159p.

1779. Petander, Signe Svanöe. "Kierkegaard og kvinnen."
Studiekamraten 47 (1965):88-90.

1780. Pont, Joh W. "Sören Kierkegaard." *Stemmen uit de
Luthersche Kerk in Nederland* (Amsterdam) 2 (1896):97-125.

1781. Rispens, J. A. "Sören Kierkegaard. Met naschrift
door Just Havelaar." *De Stem* (Arnhem) 4 (1924):56-67.

1782. Rohde, H. P. "Om Sören Kierkegaard som bogsamler:
Studier i hans efterladte papirer og böger paa Det kongelige
Bibliotek." *Fund og Forskning i Det Kongelige Biblioteks
Samlinger* 8. Copenhagen: D. B. K., 1961, 79-127. [English
Summary]

1783. Sikken, W. In *Het Compromis als Zedelijk Vraagstuk.*
Assen, 1937.

1784. Sikken, W. "Honderd jaar geleden overleed Sören
Kierkegaard." *Nieuwe Rotterdamsche Courant* (5.11.1955).

1785. Slok, Johs. "Afmytologisering af Kierkegaard."
Dansk Teologisk Tidsskrift 40 (1977):120-127.

1786. Smit, Gabriel. "Kierkegaard, den enkeling voor Gods
aanschijn." In *Hedendaagse Visies op Den Mens.* J. Peters,
ed. Herleen: Winants, 1950, 20-38.

1787. Söe, N. H. "Om begrebet 'Barmhjertighed' hos Sören
Kierkegaard." In *Festskrift til Sören Holm.* Peter Kemp, ed.
Copenhagen: Nyt Nordesk Forlag, 1971, 43-52.

1788. Sörensen, Villy. "Sören Kierkegaard og det folkelige,"
and "Sören Kierkegaard og det eksistentielle." In *Mellem
Fortid og Fremtid: Kronikker og Kommentarer.* Copenhagen:
Gyldendal, 1969, 98-103 and 104-109.

1789. Thulstrup, Maria Mikulová. "Sören Kierkegaards
martyrbegreb." *Dansk Teologisk Tidsskrift* 27 (1964):100-113.

1790. Thulstrup, Maria Mikulová. "Kierkegaards mode med
mystik gennem den spekulative idealisme." *Kierkegaardiana*
10 (1977):7-69.

1791. Ukkola, Helge. "Kuolematon Kierkegaard [The immortal
Kierkegaard]." *Valvoja* (1954):107-112.

1792. Ukkola, Helge. "Tyhjentymätön Kierkegaard."
Helsingin Sanomat (1970):21. ["Inexhaustible K."]

1793. van Munster, H. A. "Een analyse van Kierkegaards proefschrift." *Tijdschrift voor Philosophie* 18 (1956): 347-380. [Summary, 380.]

1794. Van den Beld, A. "Over Kierkegaards notie van de suspensie van het ethische." *Bijdragen* 39 (1978):424-439. [Summary, 439.]

1795. Vanderveken, Johan. "De Deensche denker Sören Aabye Kierkegaard." *Volk en Kultuur* 2 (1942):18ff.

1796. Vandiest, Julien. "Hegel, Nietzsche en Kierkegaard?" *De Nieuwe Stem* 20 (1965):385-407; 465-479.

1797. Verhofstadt, E. "Een gestalte in het werk van Kierkegaard." *NVT* (1957):1061-1075.

1798. Waals, Jacqueline E. v. d. "Kierkegaard I-II." *Onze Eeuw* (Haarlem) 21 (1921):171-189; 274-295.

1799. Walgrave, J. H. "Sören Kierkegaard. Zijn denken een experiment met de mensheid." *De Maasbode* (Rotterdam) (10.11.1955).

1800. Walravens, Else. "Eenzaamheid en gemeenschap in de filosofie van Soeren Kierkegaard, I-II." *Dialoog* 11 (1970-71):143-156, 187-207; 12 (1971-72):189-197.

1801. Zweerman, Th. "De vertroosting der wijsbegeerte." *Tijdschrift voor Filosofie* 38 (1976):3-55.

CHAPTER 4:
Studies
of Individual Works
by Sören Kierkegaard

1802. Babelon, André. "Introduction" to *In Vino Veritas*. Paris, 1933, 7-38.

1803. Barthelme, Birgit. "A view of Julien Sorel, the protagonist of 'The Red and the Black,' with reference to *The Concept of Irony*." In *Kierkegaardiana* 10, Niels Thulstrup, ed. Copenhagen: C. A. Reitzels Boghandel, 1977, 246-252.

1804. Baerthold, A. "Vorwort" to *Zwölf Reden*. Halle, 1875, iii-vii.

1805. Baerthold, A. "Vorbemerkungen" to *Einübung in Christentum*. Halle, 1878, iii-viii.

1806. Bärthold, A. "Vorwort" to *Die Krankheit zum Tode*. Halle, 1881, iii-vii.

1807. Bärthold, A. *Geleitbrief für Sören Kierkegaard*: Ein Bisschen Philosophie. Leipzig: Fr. Richter, 1890. 14p.

1808. Battaglia, Felice. "Etica e religione nel *Diario* di Kierkegaard." *Studi Kierkegaardiana*. A cura di Cornelio Fabro. Brescia: Morcelliana Editrice, 1957, 29-65.

1809. Battaglia, F. "*Diario II*." *Giornale di Metafisica* 8 (1953):488-493.

1810. Beck, Samuel J. "Abraham, Kierkegaard: *Either, Or*." *Yale Review* 62 (1972):59-75.

1811. Bellezza, Vito A. "Lo specchio della parola" di Kierkegaard. In his *L' Esistenzialismo Cristiano*. Quaderno dell' *Archivio di Filosofia* 18 (1949):120-123.

1812. Bense, Max. "Einleitung. Über Leben und Wirken
Sören Kierkegaards." In his *Entweder-Oder*, übers. von Chr.
Schrempf. Leipzig, 1939, vii-xxxix.

1813. Bespaloff, Rachel. "Notes sur la *Répétition* de Kier-
kegaard." Trad. du danois par P. H. Tisseau. *Revue de
Philosophie* 59 (1934):335-363; reprinted in *Cheminements et
Carrefours*. Paris, 1938, 101-144.

1814. Bespaloff, Rachel. "En marge de *Crainte et Tremblement*
de Kierkegaard." *Revue de Philosophie* 60 (1935):43-72;
reprinted in *Cheminements et Carrefours*. Paris, 1938, 145-188.

1815. Bogen, James. "Kierkegaard and the 'Theological
Suspension of the Ethical'." *Inquiry* 5 (1962):305-317.
[Ref. is to *Fear and Trembling*.]

1816. Bonus, Arthur. "Vom Unterschied der lebendigen
Werke [S. Kierkegaards] und der philologischen und ästhetisch-
technischen Dokumente." *Christliche Welt* 19 (1905):755-759.

1817. Bortolaso, G. "*Briciole di Filosofia*. . .A cura di
C. Fabro." *Civilta Cattolica* 114 (1963):455-463.

1818. Bragstad, William R. "Luther's influence on *Training
in Christianity*." *Lutheran Quarterly* (1976):257-271.

1819. Brandt, Frithiof. "Introduction" to *Ou Bien*. . .*Ou
Bien*. Paris, 1943, ix-xviii.

1820. Brock, Erich. "Neue Tagebücher Kierkegaards."
Neue Züricher Zeitung (1931).

1821. Broichstetten, Horst. "Nachwort" to *Das Tagebuch eines
Verführers*. Berlin, 1917, 247-255.

1822. Brunkhorst, F. "Kierkegaards Angriff auf die Christenheit." *Monatsschrift für Pastoraltheologie* 21 (1925):132-141.

1823. Capel, Lee M. "Introduction" and "Notes" to
The Concept of Irony. (With constant reference to Socrates.)
New York: Harper & Row, 1966, 442p.; London: Collins.

1824. Cappelörn, Niels Jörgen. "Kierkegaards eigener
'Gesichtspunkt': 'Vorwärts zu leben, aber rückwärts zu ver-
stehen'." *Neue Zeitschrift für systematische Theologie und
Religionsphilosophie* 17 (1975):61-75.

1825. Cavell, Stanley. "Kierkegaard's 'On Authority and
Revelation'." In *Must We Mean What We Say: A Book of Essays*.
Cambridge, 1976; orig. pub. New York: Scribners, 1969.

1826. Channing-Pearce, M. "*Repetition*: A Kierkegaardian
Study." *Hibbert Journal* 41 (1942-43):361-364.

1827. Chaplain, Denise. *Etude sur "In Vino Veritas" de Kierkegaard*. (Annales littéraires de l'Université de Besançon, 69.) Paris: Les Belles Lettres, 1964.

1828. Clive, Godffrey. "The sickness unto death in the underworld: A study of nihilism." *Harvard Theological Review* 51 (1958):135-167.

1829. Crites, Stephen. "Introduction" and "Notes" to *Crisis in the Life of an Actress, and Other Essays on Drama*. New York: Humanities Press, 1967, 154p.; London: William Collins.

1830. Crocker, Sylvia F. "Sacrifice in Kierkegaard's *Fear and Trembling*." *Harvard Theological Review* 68 (1975): 125-139.

1831. Cruickshank, A. "Theology and Kierkegaard's *Post-script*." *Church Quarterly* 1 (1969):206-211.

1832. Cuvelier, Fernand. "Préface" to *Le journal d'un séducteur*." Trad. du danois. (Les maudits de la litterature mondiale, 6.) Kalmthout-Anvers: Beckers, 1969. 231p.

1833. Daise, Benjamin. "Kierkegaard's pseudonymous works." Ph.D., The University of Texas at Austin, 1973, 216p. *Dissertation Abstracts* 34: 6040A.

1834. Desjardins, R. "Un traité de Kierkegaard sur l'amour du prochain." *Revue d' Ascétique et de Mystique* 38 (1962): 83-105.

1835. Deuser, Hermann. "Der 1 Index-Band Zu Kierkegaards *Papirer*."   *Neue Zeitschrift für systematische Theologie und Religionsphilosophie* 18 (1976):246-249.

1836. Dewey, Bradley R. "The erotic-demonic in Kierkegaard's *Diary of the Seducer*."   *Scan* 10 (1971):1-24.

1837. Dewey, Bradley R. "Sören Kierkegaard's *Diary of the Seducer*: A history of its use and abuse in international print." *Fund og Forskning i Det kongelige Biblioteks Samlinger* 20 (1973):137-157.   Summary in Danish, 162-164.

1838. Diem, Hermann. "Nachwort" to *Zur Überwindung des Nihilismus*. Stuttgart, 1946, 59-69.

1839. Dietrichson, Paul. "Introduction to a reappraisal of *Fear and Trembling*." *Inquiry* 12 (1969):236-245.

1840. Dollinger, Robert. "Zur Einführung" to *So Spricht Sören Kierkegaard*. Berlin, 1930, 5-11.

1841. Donier, R. "*Crainte et Tremblement* par Sören Kierkegaard." *Vie Intellectuelle* 10 (1935):374-382.

1842. Dorner, Albert. "Vorrede" to *Leben und Walten der Liebe*. Leipzig, 1890, iii-xiii.

1843. Droop, Fritz. "Einleitung" to *Auswahl aus seinen Bekenntnissen und Gedanken*. München, 1914, v-xxxii.

1844. Dunstan, J. Leslie. "The Bible in *Either/Or*." *Interpretation* 6 (1952):310-320.

1845. Englund, Claes. "Kring Kierkegaards *Krisen og en Krise i en Skuespillerindes Liv*." *Ord och Bild* 70 (1961): 54-60.

1846. Evangelista, Naomi. "Kierkegaard's *Repetition*: An essay in understanding." *Philippine Studies* (Manila) 23 (1976):76-88.

1847. Fabro, Cornelio. "La critica di Kierkegaard alla dialettica hegeliana nel *Libro su Adler*." *Giornale Critico della Filosofia Italiana* 9 (1978):1-32.

1848. Fabro, Cornelio. "Introduzione" to *Diario I* (1834-1848). Brescia, 1948, vii-cxxv.

1849. Fabro, Cornelio. "La religiosità di Kierkegaard nel suo *Diario*." *Humanitas* 3 (1948):209-216.

1850. Fauteck, Heinrich. "Kierkegaard - ein konservativer Revolutionar. Zum Abschluss der deutschen Ausgabe seiner *Tagebücher*." *Neue Rundschau* 86 (1975):141-151.

1851. Ferlov, Knud. "Prefazione" to *In Vino Veritas*. Lanciano, 1910, 3-12.

1852. Ferlov, Knud. "Introduction" to *Riens philosophiques*. Paris, 1937, 7-45.

1853. Fruchon, P. "Kierkegaard et l'historicité de la foi: la vision de l'historique, illusion et vérité [Les Miettes philosophiques]." *Recherches de Sciences Religieuses* 60 (1972):329-363.

1854. Garelick, Herbert M. *The Anti-Christianity of Kierkegaard. A Study of* Concluding Unscientific Postscript." 's Gravenhage: Martinus Nijhoff, 1965, vii-73p.

1855. Gateau, Jean J. "Introduction" to *Traité du désespoir*. Paris, 1932, 7-48.

1856. Geismar, Eduard. "Einleitung" to *Die Reinheit des Herzens*, 2 Aufl. Munchen, 1926, 3-9.

1857. Geismar, Eduard. "Einleitung" to *Religion der Tat*. Leipzig, 1930, vii-xiii.

1858. Graue, Paul. "Sören Kierkegaards Angriff auf die Christenheit." Christliche Welt 12 (1898):147-150, 170-179, 195-202.

1859. Gerdes, Hayo, tr. Die Tagebücher, I-V. Düsseldorf: Diederich, 1962-74, 445p., 358p., 348p., 422p. ["Anmerkungen," I:355-416; II:249-280: III:319-344; IV:313-334; V:389-409.]

1860. Gillhoff, Gerd. "Introduction" to Diary of a Seducer. Trans. from the Danish. New York: Frederick Ungar, 1969. 181p.

1861. Gleiss, Otto. "Vorwort" to Entweder-Oder I. Theil. Leipzig, 1885, v-vii.

1862. Gleiss, Otto. "Enleitung" to Entweder-Oder 2. Aufl. Dresden & Leipzig, 1904, v-xii.

1863. Goetz, Diego Hanns. "Über Sören Kierkegaard: In Vino Veritas und Unterschiedliche Gedanken über die Ehe gegen Einwendungen." In his Das Vaterunser der Liebenden. Wien: Herald, 1952, 59-160.

1864. Gottsched, H. "Nachwort" to Furcht und Zittern. Wiederholung. 2. verbesserte Aufl. Jena, 1909, 205-209.

1865. Gottsched, H. "Vorwort" to Buch des Richters. Jena & Leipzig, 1905, 1-9.

1866. Gottsched, H. "Nachwort" to Die Krankheit zum Tode. Jena, 1911, 130-131.

1867. Griffith, Gwilym O. "Kierkegaard on Faith: A Study of Fear and Trembling." Hibbert Journal 42 (1943):58-63.

1868. Griffith, Richard M. "Repetition: Constantine (S.) Constantius." Journal of Existential Psychiatry 2 (1962): 437-448.

1869. Grieve, Alexander. "Sören Kierkegaard. A study of the third section of his Stadia Upon Life's Way." Expository Times 19 (1907-08):206-209.

1870. Grossart, Friedrich. "Grundmotiv und Aufbau der pseudonyme Schriften Kierkegaards." Deutsche Vierteljahrs- schrift für Literaturwissenschaft und Geistesgeschicht 19 (1941):139-182.

1871. Guirguis, Renée. "Notes sur La Répétition. Henein & Wahba, eds., Vues sur Kierkegaard. 1955, 22-25.

1872. Guardini, Romano. Ritratto della malinconia (Vom Sinn der Schwermut) [Contiene passi scelti da opere di S. A. Kierkegaard]. Versione dal tedesco [e dal danese] di Romana Guarnieri [1952]. 2d ed., Brescia: Morcelliana, 1954. 67p. (Fuochi III. serie.)

1873. Haecker, Theodor. "Nachwort" to *Kritik der Gegenwart.*
Innsbruck, 1914, 62-87.

1874. Haecker, Theodor. "Vorwort" to *Der Pfahl im Fleisch.*
Innsbruck, 1914, 5-21.

1875. Haecker, Theodor. "Nachowrt" to *Der Begriff des Auser-*
wählten. Hellerau, 1917, 335-421.

1876. Haecker, Theodor. "Nachwort" to *Am Fusse des Altars.*
München, 1922, 67-87.

1877. Haecker, Theodor. "Kierkegaard *Am Fusse des Altars.*"
Der Brenner 7 (1923):71-85.

1878. Haecker, Theodor. "Vorwort" to *Die Tagebücher,* 1 Bd.
Innsbruck, 1923, v-viii.

1879. Haecker, Theodor. "Sören Kierkegaards *Altarreden.*"
In his *Christentum und Kultur.* München: Kösel, 1927 (273p.),
115-134.

1880. Haecker, Theodor. "Vorwort" to *Religiöse Reden,*
2 Aufl. Leipzig, 1936, 9-11.

1881. Haecker, Theodor. "Nachwort" to *Kritik der Gegenwart.*
Basel, 1946, 76-106.

1882. Hamilton, Kenneth. "Man: Anxious or guilty? A second
look at Kierkegaard's *The Concept of Dread.*" *Church and*
Society 46 (1963):293-299.

1883. Hamilton, Kenneth M. "Man: Anxious or guilty? A
second look at Kierkegaard's *The Concept of Dread.*" *Christian*
Scholar 46 (1963):293-299.

1884. Hennemann, Gerhard. "Die christliche und die sokra-
tische Definition der Sunde. Nach Sören Kierkegaards Schrift
Die Krankheit zum Tode." *Deutsches Pfarrerblatt* 52 (1952):
611-613.

1885. Herzog, Johannes. "Abwehr von Sören Kierkegaards
Angriff auf die Christenheit. Ein Beitrag zur Verständnis
der Mission Kierkegaards an die evangelische Kirche."
Zeitschrift für Theologie und Kirche 8 (1898):271-340; 341-381.

1886. Hess, Mary W. "The dilemma in Kierkegaard's *Either/Or.*"
Journal of Philosophy 42 (1945):216-219.

1887. Hirsch, Emanuel. "Die Stellung von Kierkegaards
Entweder-Oder in der Literatur- und Geistesgeschichte."
In his *Wege zu Kierkegaard.* Berlin: Die Spur, 1968, 9-19.

1888. Hirsch, Emanuel. "Kierkegaards Erstlingsschrift."
(Kierkegaard-Studien, 2. Stück.) *Zeitschrift für systematische*
Theologie 8 (1930):90-144.

1889. Hong, Howard. "The Kierkegaard papers." *Tri Quar-terly* 16 (1969):100-123.

1890. Hubbeling, H. G. "Als het ogenblik in de tijd eens beslissende betekenis had. . .Een kritisch-logische analyse van Kierkegaards argumentatie in het eerste hoofdstuk van de *Wijsgerige Kruimels*." *Bijdragen* 34 (1973):383-396. [Summary: "Suppose the moment in time had a decisive signifi-cance. . .A critical logical analysis of Kierkegaard's argu-mentation in the first chapter of the *Philosophical Frag-ments*," 396-397.]

1891. Huber, Hans. "Einleitung" to *Furcht und Beben*. Wiesbaden, 1935, vii-xlviii.

1892. Hutchings, P. A. "Conjugal faithfulness." In Royal Institute of Philosophy. *Human Values*, Godfrey Vesey, ed. London: Harvester Press, dist. by Humanities Press, 1978, 61-85. [*Either/Or*]

1893. Jaurata Marion, F. "El problema fundamental del *Postscriptum* de Soeren Kierkegaard." *Stromata* 31 (1975): 299-311.

1894. Johnson, Ralph H. "Kierkegaard on philosophy." *Dialogue* 17 (1978):442-455. [*Concluding Unscientific Post-script*]

1895. Jones, Joe R. "Some remarks *On Authority and Revela-tion* in Kierkegaard." *Journal of Religion* 57 (1977):232-251.

1896. Kassner, Rudolf. "Sören Kierkegaard. *Aphorismen*." *Neue Rundschau* (Freie Bühne) 17 (1906):513-543.

1897. Kassner, Rudolf. "Sören Kierkegaard. Aus seinem Tagebuch." In his *Motive. Essays*. Berlin: S. Fischer, 1906 (190p.), 1-76.

1898. Kassner, Rudolf. "Sören Kierkegaard. Introduction." [à *Fragments d'un Journal*] Trad. par Alix Guillain. *Commerce* 12 (1927):153-154; 165-202.

1899. Kauer, Edmund Th. "Nachwort" to *Das Tabebuch eines Verführers*. Berlin, 1928, 285-287.

1900. Kloeden, Wolfdietrich von. "Sören Kierkegaards *Der Begriff Angst* im Kursunterricht der gymnasialen Oberstufe." *Kierkegaardiana* 10 (1977):253-261.

1901. Kroner, Richard D. "Kierkegaard's *Either/Or* today." *Union Review* (1944):23-26.

1902. Kütemeyer, W. "Nachwort" to *Der Begriff der Ironie*. München, 1929, 341-369.

1903. Kütemeyer, W. "Nachwort" to *Christliche Reden*. Jena, 1929, 414-423.

1904. Kütemeyer, W. "Vorwort" to *Der einzelne und die Kirche*. Berlin, 1934, 5-33.

1905. Kütemeyer, W. "Nachwort" to *Das Evangelium der Leiden*, 2. aufl. München, 1936, 115-124.

1906. Langan, Th. "*The Concept of Irony*." *Theological Studies* 28 (1967):592-595.

1907. Langlois, Jean. "Essai sur *Crainte et Tremblement* de Soeren Kierkegaard." *Sciences Ecclésiastiques* 6 (1954): 25-50.

1908. Langlois, Jean. "Essai sur *Crainte et Tremblement* de Soeren Kierkegaard." *Annales de l'ACFAS* (Montreal) 20 (1954):140-144.

1909. Larsen, K. Olesen. "Zur Frage des Paradoxbegriffes in *Philosophische Brocken* und *Abschliessende unwissenschaftliche Nachschrift*." *Orbis Litterarum* 10 (1955):130-147. [Tysk tekst]

1910. LeFevre, Perry. "The Hong translation of Kierkegaard's *Papirer*: Winner of the National Book Award for Translation, 1968." *Journal of Religion* 50 (1970):69-78.

1911. Lindstrom, Valter. "A contribution to the interpretation of Kierkegaard's book: *The Works of Love*." *Studia Theologica* 6 (1952):1-29.

1912. Logstrup, K. E. "Auseinandersetzung mit Kierkegaards *Leben und Walten der Liebe*." *Studia Theologica* 7 (1953-54): 86-103.

1913. Lowrie, Walter. "Introduction" and "Notes" to *The Concept of Dread*. Trans. by W. Lowrie. 2d ed., Princeton (New Jersey): Princeton Univ. Press, 1967. 154p.

1914. Lowrie, Walter. "Editor's Introduction" to *Repetition*. Harper Torchbooks, 1964, 7-28.

1915. Lowrie, Walter. "Preface" and "Notes" to *On Authority and Revelation: The Book on Adler, or a Cycle of Ethico-Religious Essays*. Princeton (New Jersey): Harper Torchbooks, 1966, xli-l.

1916. Mackey, Louis. "Kierkegaard's lyric of faith: A look at *Fear and Trembling*." *Rice Institute Pamphlet* 47 (1960): 30-47.

1917. Mackey, Louis. "The view from Pisgah: A reading of *Fear and Trembling*." In Josiah Thompson, ed. *Kierkegaard: A collection of Critical Essays*. Garden City: Doubleday, Anchor Books, 394-428. "Some versions of the aesthete: Kierkegaard's *Either/Or*." *Rice University Studies* 50 (1964):39-54.

1918. Marsh, James L. "A *Concluding Scientific Postscript*." *Southwestern Journal of Philosophy* 6 (1975):159-171.

1919. McInerny, Ralph. "A Note on the Kierkegaardian *Either/Or*." *Laval Théologique et Philosophique* 8 (1952): 230-242.

1920. McKinnon, A. "Theological focus in Kierkegaard's *Samlede Vaerker*. Some basic data." *Studies in Religion* (Toronto) 4 (1974):58-62.

1921. McKinnon, A. "The increase of Christian terms in Kierkegaard's *Samlede Vaerker*." L. Lawson, ed. *Kierkegaard's Presence in Contemporary American Life*. Metuchen (New Jersey): Scarecrow Press, 1970, 147-162.

1922. McKinnon, A. "Theological focus in Kierkegaard's authorship." *Studies in Religious Criticism* 4:58-62.

1923. McKinnon, A. "The central works in Kierkegaard's authorship." *Revue Internationale de Philosophie* 27 (1973): 84-94.

1924. Mesnard, Pierre. "Le *Journal* de Kierkegaard a-t-il une valeur philosophique?" *Etudes Philosophiques* 18 (1963): 299-314.

1925. Messineo, A. "Il *Diario* de Sören Kierkegaard." *Civiltà Cattolica* 99 (1948):164-167.

1926. Montanari, Primo. "Intorno alle *Briciole di Filosofia* e *Postilla non Scientifica* di Kierkegaard." *Studia Patavina* 12 (1965):143-145.

1927. Morra, Gianfranco. "La sospensione della morale secondo S. A. Kierkegaard." *Ethica* 1 (1962):121-137.

1928. Muller, John D. "Between the aesthetic and the ethical: Kierkegaard's *Either/Or*." *Philosophy Today* 23 (1979):84-94.

1929. Nagley, Winfield E. "Kiergaard's irony in the *Diapsalmata*." *Kierkegaardiana* 6 (1966):51-75.

1930. Nagley, W. E. "*The Concept of Irony*." *Journal of the History of Ideas* 29 (1968):458-464.

1931. Neumann, Johannes. "Sören Kierkegaards Individuations-prozess nach seinen *Tagebüchern*." *Zeitschrift für Psycho-therapie und Medizinische Psychologie* 2 (1952):152-168.

1932. Nielsen, E. Brandt. "Den store bog om Adler af Sören Kierkegaard." *Praesteforeningens Blad* 60 (1970):785-790.

1933. O'Connor, D. "*The Concept of Irony*." *The Heythrop Journal* 9 (1968):76-79.

1934. Oden, Thomas C. "Introduction" to *Parables of Kierke-gaard*. T. C. Oden, ed. Princeton: Princeton Univ. Press, 1978, vii-vxiii.

1935. Outka, G. H. "Religious and moral duty: Notes on *Fear and Trembling*." In G. H. Outka and J. P. Reeder, eds. *Religion and Morality*. Anchor Books, 1973, 204-254.

1936. Paci, Enzo. "Il significato dell'introduzione Kierke-gaardiana al "*Concetto dell'angoscia*." *Rivista di Filosofia* 45 (1954):392-398.

1937. Paulsen, Anna. "Das Verhältnis der Erbaulichen zum Christlichen: Zum Problem der *Erbaulichen Reden* Sören Kier-kegaards." In *Kierkegaardiana* 6. Copenhagen: Munksgaard, 1966, 97-106.

1938. Petit, Paul. "Préface" to *Postscriptum aux Miettes Philosophiques*. Paris: Mesmil, 1941, v-ix.

1939. Petit, Paul. "Préface" to *Les Miettes Philosophiques*. Paris, 1947, 9-32.

1940. Prini, Pietro. "Kierkegaard e la filosofia come giornale intimo." *Archivio di Filosofia* (1959):73-90. [La Diaristica filosofica]

1941. Pupi, A. "*Briciole di filosofia*. . .a cura di C. Fabro, I-II." *Rivista di Filosofia Neoscolastica* 55 (1963):652-658.

1942. Redaelli, Luigi. "Introduzione" to *Il Diario del Seduttore*. Torino, 1910, v-xxiii; 3d ed. Milano, 1942, v-xix; 4h ed. Milano, 1948, v-xix.

1943. Richter, Liselotte. "Sören Kierkegaard." In *Die Leidenschaft des Religiösen. Eine Auswahl aus Schriften und Tagebüchern*. Stuttgart: Reclam, 1953, 3-15.

1944. Richter, Liselotte. "Sören Kierkegaard schreibt an Kinder." *Eckart-Jahrbuch* (1955-56):94-105.

1945. Roberts, David E. "*Works of Love*: A review article." [A propos des oeuvres de Kierkegaard: *Works of Love; For Self-examination; Judge for Yourselves!; Attack upon "Christendom"* et *A Kierkegaard Anthology*. R. Bretall, ed.] *Review of Religion* 12 (1948):382-403.

1946. Rollier, M. A. "*L'Ora* di Sören Kierkegaard." *Gioventu Cristiana* No. 10 (1931).

1947. Rossi, Eugenio Augusto. "Premessa" to *I gigli dei campi e gli uccelli del cielo*. Milano, 1945, 5-19.

1948. Russell, Bruce. "What is the ethical in *Fear and Trembling*?" [J. Bogen, *Kierkegaard and the "Theological Suspension of the Ethical"*.] *Inquiry* 18 (1975):337-343.

1949. Saathoff, Albrecht. "Kierkegaards *Erbauliche Reden*." *Monatsschrift für Pastoraltheologie* 12:177-183.

1950. Sack, Max. "*Die Verzweiflung*. Eine Untersuchung ihres Wesens und ihrer Entstehung. Mit einem Anhang." In *Krankheit zum Tode*. Kallmünz: Lassleben, 1930 (vi-136p.), 107-135.

1951. Salmona, Bruno. "La socialità nel *Diario* di Kierkegaard." *Sapienza* 11 (1958):409-423.

1952. Santuri, Edmund. "Kierkegaard's *Fear and Trembling* in logical perspective." *Journal of Religious Ethics* 5 (1977): 225-247.

1953. Schaeder, Hans Heinrich. "Vorbemerkung" to *Über den Begriff der Ironie*. München & Berlin, 1929, iii-ix.

1954. Schauder, K. "Existenz zwischen Glauben und Kritik. Die Geschichte eines inneren Lebens. Zur Neuausgabe der *Tagebücher* Sören Kierkegaards." *Reformatio* (Olten) 25 (1976):171-175.

1955. Schlegel, W. "*Entweder/Oder*, II." *Philosophischer Literaturanzeiger* 11 (1958):268-271.

1956. Schrag, C. O. "Note on Kierkegaard's teleological suspension of the ethical." *Ethics* 70 (1959):66-68.

1957. Schrempf, Christoph. "Vorrede; Einleitung" to *Zur Psychologie der Sünde, der Bekehrung und des Glaubens*. Leipzig, 1890, vii-x; xi-lvi.

1958. Schrempf, Christoph. "Einleitung" to *Agitatorische Schriften und Aufsätze 1851-1855*. Stuttgart, 1896, xiii-xxiv.

1959. Schrempf, Christoph. "Vorwort; Nachwort" to *Der Augenblick*. 2. Aufl. Jena, 1909, v-vi; 155-171.

1960. Schrempf, Christoph. "Nachwort" to *Abschliessende unwissenschaftliche Nachschrift*. 2. Teil. Jena, 1910, 305-314.

1961. Schrempf, Christoph. "Sören Kierkegaards *Angriff auf die Christenheit*." *Die Wahrheit* 5 (1895):121-124.

1962. Schrempf, Christoph. "Nachwort" to *Der Begriff der Angst*. Jena, 1912, 164-173.

1963. Schrempf, Christoph. "Nachwort" to *Entweder-Oder*. 2. Teil. Jena, 1913, 309-329.

1964. Schrempf, Christoph. "Nachwort" to *Stadien auf dem Lebensweg*. Jena, 1914, 459-479.

1965. Schrempf, Christoph. "Nachwort" to *Zur Selbstprüfung*. Jena, 1922, 191-199.

1966. Schrempf, Christoph. "Nachwort" to *Der Gesichtspunkt für meine Wirksamkeit als Schriftsteller*. Jena, 1922, 171-182.

1967. Schrempf, Christoph. "Nachwort" to *Leben und Walten der Liebe*. Jena, 1924, 397-408.

1968. Schufreider, Gregory J. "The logic of the absurd (in Kierkegaard's *Concluding Unscientific Postscript*). *Philosophy Archives* 5 (1979):21p.

1969. Short, John. "The *Journals* of Sören Kierkegaard." *Theology* 41 (1940):36-43.

1970. Sontag, Frederick. "Introduction" to *On Authority and Revelation. The Book on Adler*. Harper Torchbooks, 1966, vii-xl.

1971. Soraine, N. Kalle. "Bildersprache und Sympolismus im *Begriff der Ironie*." In *Kierkegaardiana*, 6. Niels Thulstrup, ed. Copenhagen: Munksgaard, 1967, 30-50.

1972. Stack, George J. "The inward journey: Kierkegaard's *Journals and Papers*." *Philosophy Today* 23 (1979):170-195. [Essay: Review--article of English trans. of first 4 vols. of Kierkegaard's *Journals and Papers*.]

1973. Stack, George J. "Review of Kierkegaard's *Journals and Papers* (Vols. 5-8). *International Studies in Philosophy* (forthcoming 1980).

1974. Stobart, Mabel Annie. "The *Either/Or* of Sören Kierkegaard [sic]." *Fortnightly Review* N.S. 71 (1902):53-60.

1975. Thulstrup, Marie. "Les *Oeuvres de l'Amour*de Kierkegaard en regard du Nouveau Testament." 10 (1955):268-279. [Symposion Kierkegaardianum]

1976. Thulstrup, Niels. "Introduction" to *Philosophical Fragments, or, A Fragment of Philosophy*, by Johannes Climacus [pseud.]. Trans. rev. and commentary trans. by Howard H. Hong. 2d ed. Princeton (New Jersey): Princeton Univ. Press, 1967, xcvii-260p.

1977. Tisseau, P.-H. "*L'Adolphe* de B. Constant et la *Répétition* de Kierkegaard." *Revue de Littérature Comparée* 13 (1933):239-258.

1978. Tisseau, P.-H. "Avant-propos" to *Le Banquet*. Paris, 1933, 1-16.

1979. Tisseau, P.-H. "Introduction" to *La Répétition*. Paris, 1933, 1-22.

1980. Tisseau, P.-H. "Note du traducteur" to *Pour un examen de conscience*. Bazoges-en-Pareds, 1934, 5-7.

1981. Tisseau, P.-H. "Introduction" to *Ce que nous apprennent les lis des champs et les oiseaux du ciel*. Paris, 1935, 7-32.

1982. Tisseau, P.-H. "Note du traducteur" to *La pureté du coeur*. Bazoges-in Pareds, 1935, 7-8.

1983. Tisseau, P.-H. "Introduction" to *L'École du Christianisme*. Bazoges-en-Pareds, 1936, v-ix.

1984. Tisseau, P.-H. "Avant-propos" to *Point de vue explicatif de mon oeuvre*. Bazoges-en-Pareds, 1940, 5-10.

1985. Tisseau, P.-H. "Avant-propos" to *Les stades sur le chemin de la vie. Coupable?--non coupable?* Bazoges-en-Pareds, 1942, 5-10.

1986. Trillhaas, Wolfgang. "Neuausgabe der Werke Kierkegaards." *Die Sammlung* 6 (1951):430-431.

1987. Ulrich, Hermann. "Vorbemerkung" to *Die Tagebücher 1832-1839*. 2. Teil (Auswahl). Berlin, 1930, 5-12.

1988. Updike, John. "The Fork [i.e., Sören Kierkegaard]." *The New Yorker* (1966):115-134. [Esp. on R. G. Smith, ed. and tr. *The Last Years: Journals, 1853-1855*. London: Collins; New York: Harper & Row, 1965.]

1989. Valanziani, E. "Introduzione" to *La Ripetizione*. Milano, 1945, 5-13.

1990. Van de Pitte, Frederick P. "Kierkegaard's *Approximation*." *The Personalist* 52 (1971):483-498.

1991. Van Dijk, Is. "Inleiding" to *Keur uit de Werken*. Haarlem, 1905, i-xv.

1992. Venator, F. "Vorwort" to *Aus den Tiefen der Reflexion*. Zweibrücken i. Pfalz, 1901, 3-8.

1993. Vergote, Henri-Bernard. "Dialectique de la communication Texte de Sören Kierkegaard ." (S. Kierkegaard's *Papirer* viii-2, 86-89) introduit par H.-B. Vergote. *Revue de Métaphysique et de Morale* 76 (1971):53-76.

1994. Vergote, Henri-Bernard. "Kierkegaard dans le rôle de 'Privat-Docent'." *Revue de Métaphysique et de Morale* 76 (1971):53-60. [Art. introd. tr. (60-76) of two lectures on the dialectics of communication, written 1874.]

1995. Viallaneix, Nelly. "Sören Kierkegaard: la voix et l'ouie (A propos des *Quatre Discours Édifiants* de 1843). *Études Philosophiques* (1969):211-224.

1996.   Viestad, H. J.   "Sören Kierkegaards *Papirer* i ny og foroket utgave."   *Norsk Theologisk Tidsskrift* 70 (1970): 177-183.

1997.   Wahl, Jean.   "Introduction" to Kierkegaard's *Le Concept d'Angoisse*.   Paris, 1935, 1-37.

1998.   Walker, Jeremy.   "The paradox in *Fear and Trembling*." In *Kierkegaardiana*, 10.   Niels Thulstrup, ed.   Copenhagen: C. A. Reitzels Boghandel, 1977, 133-151.

1999.   Walker, Jeremy D. B.   *To Will One Thing: Reflections on Kierkegaard's* Purity of Heart.   Montreal: McGill Univ. Press, 1972.   167p.

2000.   Wasmuth, E.   "*Die Krankheit zum Tode* und Anderes." *Theologische Revue* 59 (1963):32-35.

CHAPTER 5:
Entries Arranged
by Proper Names

Abraham

2001. Chryssides, George D. "Abraham's faith." *Sophia*
12 (1973):10-16.

2002. Gordis, Robert. "The faith of Abraham: A note on
Kierkegaard's 'teological suspension of the ethical'."
Judaism 25 (1976):414-419.

2003. Goulet, Denis A. "Kierkegaard, Aquinas, and the
dilemma of Abraham." *Thought* 32 (1957):165-188. [Inter-
pretation of Genesis, Chap. 22.]

2004. Grangier, Edouard. "Abraham, oder Kierkegaard, wie
Kafka und Sartre ihn sehen." *Zeitschrift für Philosophische
Forschung* 4 (1949-50):412-421.

2005. Gumbiner, Joseph Henry. "Existentialism and Father
Abraham." *Commentary* 5 (1948):143-148.

2006. Harrelson, Walter J. "Kierkegaard and Abraham."
Andover Bulletin 47 (1955):12-16. (Kierkegaard centennial
issue.)

2007. Mesnard, P. "Kierkegaard et l'utilisation existentielle de la figure d'Abraham." *Cahiers Sioniens* 5 (1951):
121(213)-140(232). [Abraham, Père des Croyants]

2008. Mesnard, Pierre. "Die Gestalt Abrahams bei Kierkegaard." *Bibel und Kirche*. Organ des katholischen
Bibelwerkes (Stuttgart) (1952):88-95.

2009. Sokel, Walter H. "Kleists 'Marquise von O', Kierkegaards 'Abraham' und Musils 'Tonka': Drei Stufen des Absurden in seiner Beziehung zum Glauben." In *Robert Musil: Studien zu seinem Werk*. Karl Dinklage et al., eds. Hamburg: Rowohlt, 1970, 57-70.

Adler, Alfred P.

2010. Cortese, Alessandro. "Il pastore Adler. Della libertà religiosa in Kierkegaard." *Archivio di Filosofia* (*L'Ermeneutica della Libertà Religiosa*) (1968):629-646.

2011. Cortese, Alessandro. "Il pastore A. P. Adler o della libertà religiosa in Kierkegaard." *Contributi dell'Inst. di Filosofia* 1 (1969):81-113. [Pubblicazioni dell'Univ. Cattolica del Sacro Cuoro III, 14.]

2012. Fabro, Cornelio. "La critica di Kierkegaard alla dialettica Hegeliana nel 'libro su Adler'." *Giornale Critico della Filosofia Italiana* 57 (1978):1-32.

2013. West, George K. "Kierkegaard and Adler. A Comparison of the Categories of Life as Seen by Both Authors and the Consequent Implications for Therapy." Ph.D., Florida State Univ., 1975, 274p. *Dissertation Abstracts* 37 (1976): 138A.

Adorno, Theodor W.

2014. Buck-Morss, Susan. *The Origin of Negative Dialectics. Theodor W. Adorno, Walter Benjamin and the Frankfurt Institute*. New York: The Free Press, 1977, 114-123 and passim.

Andersen

2015. Betz, Werner. "Andersen und Kierkegaard." In *Festschrift für Walter Baethe*. Kurt Rudolph et al., eds. Weimar: Böhlau, 1966.

2016. van Munster, H. A. "Kierkegaards kritiek op Andersen. De verhouding tussen persoon en situatie." *Algemeen Nederlands Tijdschrift voor Wijsbegeerte en Psychologie* 50 (1957-58):82-89.

Antigone

2017.   Fauteck, Heinrich.   "Kierkegaards Antigone."   *Skan-
dinavistik* 4 (1974):81-100.

2018.   Hirsch, Emanuel.   "Kierkegaards Antigone und Ibsens
Frau Atving."   In *Gestalt Gedanke Geheimnis: Festschrift
für Johannes Pfeiffer zu seinem 65.Geburtstag.*   Berlin:
Die Spur, 1967, 167-181.

2019.   Rehm, Walther.   "Kierkegaards Antigone."   *Deutsche
Vierteljahrsschrift für Literaturwissenshaft und Geistes-
geschichte* (Halle) 28 (1953):1-39.   Also in *Begegnungen und
Probleme.   Studien zur Deutschen Literaturgeschichte.*
Bern: Franche, 1958, 274-316.

Aquinas (see Thomas Aquinas)

Arendt, Hannah

2020.   Lafer, Celso.   "Da dignidade do politica: Hannah
Arendt."   *Discurso* 3 (1972):185-198.

Aristotle

2021.   Durkan, John.   "Kierkegaard and Aristotle: A parallel."
Dublin Review 213 (1943):136-148.

2022.   Fabro, C.   "La *pistis* aristotelica nell'opera di
S. Kierkegaard."   *Proteus* 5 (1974):3-24.

2023.   Rohatyn, Dennis.   "A note on Aristotle and Kierkegaard."   *Classical World* 65 (1971-72):130-131.

2024.   Stack, George.   "Aristotle and Kierkegaard's existential ethics."   *Journal of the History of Philosophy*
12 (1974):1-19.

2025.   Stack, George J.   "Aristotle and Kierkegaard's
Concept of Choice."   *Modern Schoolman* 46 (1948):11-23.

2026.   Stack, George J.   "Aristoteles y Kierkegaard: Concepto
de posibilidad humana, I-II."   *Folia Humanistica* 10 (1972):
15-33, 137-149.

2027.   Stack, George J.   "Aristoteles y las categorias
existenciales de Kierkegaard."   *Folia Humanistica* 9 (1971):
1029-1041.

2028. Widenman, Robert. "Some aspects of time in Aristotle
and Kierkegaard." In *Kierkegaardiana* 8 (1971):7-22.

Auden, W. H.

2029. Auden, W. "A preface to Kierkegaard." *New Republic*
110 (1944):683-686.

2030. Callan, Edward. "Auden and Kierkegaard: The artistic
framework of *For the Time Being*." *Christian Scholar*
48 (1965):211-223.

2031. Callan, Edward. "Auden's *New Year Letter*: A new
style of architecture." *Renascence* 16 (1963):13-19.

2032. James, William C. "Anthropological poetics: Auden's
typology of heroism." In *Kierkegaardiana* 10 (1977):239-245.

2033. Replogle, Justin. "Auden's Religious Leap."
Wisconsin Studies in Contemporary Literature 7 (1966):47-75.

2034. Seymour, Betty Jean. "The Dyer's Hand: Kierkegaardian Perspectives on Person, Word, and Art Re-discovered
in W. H. Auden." Ph.D., Duke Univ., 1975, 155p.
Dissertation Abstracts 36 (1975):4583A.

2035. Whitehead, Lee M. "Art as Communion: Auden's *The Sea
and the Mirror*." *Perspective* 14 (1966):171-178.

Augustine

2036. Dallago, Carl. "Augustine, Pascal und Kierkegaard."
In his *Der grosse Unwissende*." Innsbruck, 1924 (650p.),
424-552. Originally published in *Der Brenner* 6 (1921):
642-734.

2037. Manasse, E. M. "Conversion and liberation: A comparison of Augustine and Kierkegaard." *Review of Religion*
7 (1943):361-383. [M. bibliogr.]

2038. Romeyer, Blaise. "La raison et la foi au service de
la pensée. Kierkegaard devant Augustin." *Archivio di
Filosofia* 18 (1952):cah. 2, 7-41 (184-217).

Ayer, A. J.

2039. Jones, Charles Edwin. "The Theory of Truth as
Subjectivity in Kierkegaard, Compared with Theories of
Truth in Blanshard and Ayer." Ph.D., Univ. of Arkansas,
1973, 190p. *Dissertation Abstracts* 34 (1973):2699A.

Barth, Karl

2040. Bridel, Philippe. "Theologie de Vinet et Barthisme."
Revue de Théologie et de Philosophie 24 (1936):87-91.

2041. Brinkschmidt, Egon. *Sören Kierkegaard und Karl Barth.*
Neukirchen-Vluyn: Neukirchener Verlag, 1971. 171p.

2042. Buonaiuti, E. "Carlo Barth e la 'teologia della
crise'." *La Nuova Europa* 2 (1945).

2043. Engelbrecht, Barend Jacobus. "Die Tijdsstruktuur
in die Gedagtekompleds: Hegel--Kierkegaard--Barth."
Diss. Theol., Groningen, 1949, 83p. (Groninger schrijfkamer)

2044. Fabro, Cornelio. "Kierkegaard e K. Barth."
Studi Francescani 55 (1958):155-158.

2045. Gemmer, Anders, and Messer, August. *Sören Kierkegaard und Karl Barth.* Stuttgart: Strecker & Schröder,
1925, xii-307p. (I: Sören Kierkegaard. Sein Leben und
sein Werk. Von Anders Gemmer. 1-133; II: Karl Barth.
Von August Messer. 135-302.)

2046. Jorgensen, K. E. J. "Karl Barth in the light of
Danish theology." *Lutheran Church Quarterly* 6 (1931):
175-181.

2047. McKinnon, Alastair. "Barth's relation to Kierkegaard: Some further light." *Canadian Journal of Theology*
13 (1967):31-41.

2048. Navarria, Salvatore. *Sören Kierkegaard e l'Irrazionalismo di Karl Barth.* Palermo: Palumbo, 1943. 248p.
(Ricerche filosofiche. Collezione Renda, 3.)

2049. Rechtmann, H. J. "Sören Kierkegaards Einfluss auf
Karl Barth und sein Kreis." *Kölnische Volkszeitung*
(14.7.1928).

2050. Söe, N. H. "Karl Barth og Sören Kierkegaard." In
Kierkegaardiana 2 (1957):55-64.

2051. Thomas, John Heywood. "The Christology of Sören
Kierkegaard and Karl Barth." *Hibbert Journal* 53 (1955):
280-288.

Bayle, Pierre

2052. Jossua, Jean-Pierre. *Pierre Bayle ou l'Obsession du Mal*. Paris: Aubier-Montaigne, 1977. 190p.

Beckett, Samuel

2053. Rosen, Steven J. *Samuel Beckett and the Pessimistic Tradition*. New Brunswick (New Jersey): Rutgers Univ. Press, 1976. [Compares Beckett and Kierkegaard]

Berdiaev, Nicholas

2054. Berdiaev, Nicholas. In his *Solitude and Society*. Trans. from Russian by George Reavey. London: Bles, 1939; New York: Scribner, 1939.

Bergson, Henri

2055. Catteau, Georges. "Bergson, Kierkegaard, and mysticism." (Trans. by A. Dru.) *Dublin Review* 97 (1933):70-78.

2055a. Ferlov, Knud. "De Kierkegaard a Bergson." *Les Nouvelles Litteraires* 8 (1928):3. (Hommage a Henri Bergson.)

2056. Rose, Mary C. "Three Hierarchies of Value: A Study in the Philosophies of Value of Henri Bergson, Alfred North Whitehead, and Soeren Kierkegaard." Ph.D., The Johns Hopkins Univ., 1949. 310p.

Blake, William

2057. Scrimgeour, J. R. "Great example of horror and agony: A comparison of Sören Kierkegaard's demoniacally despairing individual with William Blake's spectre of Urthono." *Scandinavian Studies* 47 (1975):36-41.

Blei, F.

2058. Haecker, Theodor.   "F. Blei und Kierkegaard."
Der Brenner 4 (1914).

Blondel, Maurice

2059. Henrici, Peter. "Maurice Blondel di fronte alla
filosofia tedesca." *Gregorianum* 56 (1975):615-638.

Bloy, León

2060. O'Malley, Frank. "The passion of León Bloy."
Review of Politics 10 (1948):100-115.

Blumhardt, Christoph

2061. Mettler, Artur. "Nachfolge und Reich Gottes: Sören
Kierkegaard (1813-1855) und Christoph Blumhardt (1842-1919)."
Reformatio 17 (1968):139-151.

Bonaventura

2062. Mollo, Gaetano. "Fede e ragione: Un raffronto tra San
Bonaventura e S. Kierkegaard." In *San Bonaventura Maestro
di Vita Francescana e di Sapienza Cristiania*.
Miscellanea Francescana 75 (1975):721-732.

Bradley, F. H.

2063. Clive, Geoffrey H. "The Connection Between Ethics
and Religion in Kant, Kierkegaard, and F. H. Bradley."
Ph.D., Harvard Univ., 1975.

Brandes, Georg

2064. Krüger, Paul, ed. *Correspondance de Georg Brandes. Lettres Choisies et Annotées.* I–II. Copenhaque: Rosenkilde and Bagger, 1952–56. Reg. Notes et références I–II, ibid.

2065. M [pseud.]. "S. Kierkegaard og Dr. G. Brandes." *Dansk Kirketidende* 34 (1879):509–513.

2066. Seidlin, Oskar. "Georg Brandes." *Journal of the History of Ideas* 3 (1942):415–442.

2067. Strodtmann, Adolf. "Sören Kierkegaard. Nach einer Charakteristik seiner literarischen Thätigkeit, von G. Brandes." Beilage zur *Allgemeine Zeitung* 81 (1878): 4069–4070, 4102–4104, 4118–4120, 4143–4144, 4173–4175.

Bretschneider, K. G.

2068. Thulstrup, Niels. "Kierkegaard og K. G. Bretschneider." In *Festskrift Til Sören Holm.* Peter Kemp, ed. Copenhagen: Nyt Nordisk Forlag, 1971, 31–42.

Brightman, Edgar S.

2069. Soper, William Wayne. "The Self and its World in Ralph Barton Perry, Edgar Sheffield Brightman, Jean-Paul Sartre and Soeren Kierkegaard." Ph.D., Boston Univ., 1962, 563p. *Dissertation Abstracts* 23 (1962):1042.

Brooks, Cleanth

2070. Bové, Paul A. "Cleanth Brooks and modern irony: A Kierkegaardian critique." *Boundary* 4 (1976):727–749.

Browning, Robert

2071. Hess, Mary Whitcomb. "Browning: An English Kierkegaard." *Christian Century* 79 (1962):569–571.

2072.   Hess, Mary Whitcomb.   "Browning and Kierkegaard as heirs of Luther." *Christian Century* 80 (1963):799-801.

Brunner, Emil

2073.   Grant, M. C.   "Power of the unrecognized 'blik': Adam and humanity according to Sören Kierkegaard and Emil Brunner." *Studies in Religion* 7 (1978):47-52.

Buber, Martin

2074.   Mueller, Robert William.   "A Critical Examination of Martin Buber's Criticisms of Soeren Kierkegaard." Ph.D., Purdue Univ., 1974, 228p. *Dissertation Abstracts* 35 (1974): 3816A.

2075.   Petras, John W.   "God, man and society, the perspectives of Buber and Kierkegaard." *Journal of Religious Thought* 23 (1966-67):119-128.

2076.   Shearson, William Arrindell.   "The Notion of Encounter in Existentialist Metaphysics: An Inquiry into the Nature and Structure of Existential Knowledge in Kierkegaard, Sartre, and Buber." Ph.D., Univ. of Toronto (Canada), 1970. *Dissertation Abstracts* 32 (1971):3374A.

2077.   Zeigler, Leslie.   "Personal existence: A study of Buber and Kierkegaard." *Journal of Religion* 40 (1960): 80-94.

Bultmann, Rudolf

2078.   Arendt, R. P.   "Der Begriff des Wunders besonders im Hinblick auf Bultmann und Kierkegaard." *Neue Zeitschrift für Systematische Theologie und Religionsphilosophie* 12 (1970):146-164.

2079.   Collet, Jacques.   "Kierkegaard, Bultmann et Heidegger." *Revue des Sciences Philosophiques et Théologiques* 44 (1965):597-600.

2080.   Kuhlmann, Gerhardt.   "Zum theologischen Problem der Existenz. Fragen an Rudolf Bultmann." *Zeitschrift für Theologie und Kirche* 37 N.F. (1929):28-57.

2081.   Wolf, Herbert C.   *Kierkegaard and Bultmann: The Quest of the Historical Jesus*. Minneapolis: Augsburg, 1965. 100p.

Calvin

2082. Schilder, Klaas. *Zur Begriffsgeschichte des 'Paradoxon' mit besonderer Berücksichtigung Calwins und das nach-Kierkegaardschen 'Paradoxon'.* Kampen: J. J. Kok, 1933, 472p. Phil. Diss. Erlangen, 1933.

Camus, Albert

2083. Curtis, J. L. "Heroic commitment, or the dialectics of the leap in Kierkegaard, Sartre, and Camus." *Rice Univ. Studies* (Houston, Texas) 59 (1973):17-26.

2084. Hanna, Thomas L. "The Lyrical Existentialists: The Common Voice of Kierkegaard, Nietzsche, and Camus." Ph.D., Univ. of Chicago, 1960. 135p.

2085. Harrow, K. "Caligula, a study in aesthetic despair." *Contemporary Literature* 14 (1973):31-48.

2086. Reichenback, Bruce. "Camus, and Kierkegaard: A contrast in existential authenticity." *University College Quarterly* 5 (1976):223-240; *Christian Scholar's Review* 5 (1976):223-240.

2087. Skjoldager, Emanuel. "Camus og Kierkegaard." *Kirke og Kultur* (Oslo) 74 (1969):360-369.

Carlyle, Thomas

2088. Timmerman, John H. "Feet of Clay--Concepts of Heroism in the Works of Carlyle, Dickens, Browning, Kierkegaard and Nietzsche." Ph.D., Ohio Univ. *Dissertation Abstracts* 34 (1974):5933A.

2089. Wilson, John R. *"Signs of the Times* and *The Present Age:* Essays of crisis." *Western Humanities Review* 26 (1972):369-374. [Similarities between Carlyle and Kierkegaard.]

Chateaubriand, François

2090. Grimsley, Ronald. "Romantic melancholy in Chateaubriand and Kierkegaard." *Comparative Literature* 8 (1956): 227-244.

Chestov, Leo

2091. Fondane, Benjamin. "Kierkegaard, Chestov et le serpent." *Les Cahiers du Sud* (Marseille) 21 (1934): 534-554; reprinted in his *La Conscience Malheureuse*. Paris, 1936, 229-257.

Christ

2092. Bianchi, Cirillo. "Cristo scandalo della ragione e oggetto della fede secondo Kierkegaard." *Rivista Rosminiana* 68 (1974):316-321.

2093. Boyer, Charles. "Le Christ de Kierkegaard." *Doctor Communis* 29 (1976):21-53.

2094. Cortese, Alessandro. "Dell'infallibilità come messagio di Cristo in Sören Kierkegaard." *Archivio di Filosofia* (1970):603-613.

2095. Dallago, Carl. *Der Christ Kierkegaards*. Innsbruck: Brenner-Verlag, 1922. 80p.

2096. Fischer, Hermann. *Die Christologie des Paradoxes: Zur Herkunft und Bedeutung des Christusverständnisses Sören Kierkegaards*. Göttingen: Vandenhoeck & Ruprecht, 1970. 134p.

2097. Gerdes, Hayo. *Das Christusbild. Sören Kierkegaards Verglichen mit die Christologie Hegels und Schleiermachers*. Düsseldorf: Kiederichs, 1960. 216p.

2098. Gerdes, Hayo. *Das Christusverständnis des jungen Kierkegaard. Ein Beitrag zur Erläuterung der Paradox-Gedankens*. Itzehoe: Verlag Die Spur, 1962. 89p.

2099. Gerdes, Hayo. *Der geschichtliche biblische Jesus oder der Christus der Philosophen. Erwägungen zur Christologie Kierkegaards, Hegels und Schleiermachers*. 2. Aufl. Berlin: Verlag Die Spur, 1974. 230p.

2100. Kober, W. "Beck, Kierkegaard und Stanger als Zuchtmeister auf Christus." *Allgemeine Evangelisch-Lutherische Kirchenzeitung* 58 (1925):183-185.

2101. Lindström, Valter. "La théologie de l'imitation de Jésus-Christ chez Sören Kierkegaard." Pour le centenaire de la mort de Kierkegaard. Trad. de l'allemand par Jean Carrère. *Revue d'Histoire et de Philosophie Religieuse* (Strasbourg) 35 (1955):379-392.

2102. Marchesi, Angelo. "Due scelte di fronte a Cristo:
Kierkegaard e Nietzsche." In *Il Cristo dei Filosofi Atti
del XXX Convegno di Gallarate, 1975*. Brescia: Morcelliana,
1976, 149-166.

2103. Müller, Mogens. "Historikerens Jesus, Den historiske
Jesus og kirkens Kristus-forkyndelse." [And in German,
"Der Jesus der Historiker, der Historische Jesus."]
Dansk Teologisk Tidsskrift 38 (1975):81-104; *Kerygma und
Dogma* 22 (1976):277-298.

2104. Niedermeyer, Gerhard. "Das Dogma von der Person
Jesu Christi in seinem Verhältnis zum persönlichen Heilsglauben. Zum Andenken Sören Kierkegaards 100.Geburtstag
(5.Mai 1813)." *Die Furche* (Berlin) Hefte zur Furche (1913):
25p.

2105. Niedermeyer, Gerhard. "Christuserlebnis Sören
Kierkegaards. I." *Evangelische Religiöse Unterricht*
52 (1941):71-77.

2106. Ruttenbeck, Walter. "Das Christusbild Kierkegaards
in seinen Grundzügen." *Der Geisteskampf der Gegenwort*
(Gütersloh) 61 (1925):5-12.

2107. Sessa, Piero. "La persona di Cristo nel pensiero
di S. Kierkegaard." *Scuola Cattolica* 93 (1965):223-238.

2108. Sponheim, Paul R. *Kierkegaard on Christ and
Christian Coherence*. New York: Harper & Row, 1968.

2109. Widmer, Gabriel. "Kierkegaard et le Christ."
Revue de Théologie et de Philosophie 13 (1963):273-291.

2110. Wolf, H. C. "Kierkegaard and the quest of the
historical Jesus." *Lutheran Quarterly* 16 (1964):3-40.

Collins, James

2111. Holmer, Paul Leroy. "James Collins and Kierkegaard."
Middelelser fra Sören Kierkegaard Selskabet 5 (1954):1-8.

Clough

2112. Nadel, Ira Bruce. "Kierkegaard and Clough."
Victorian Institute Journal 6 (1977):43-47.

Conrad, Joseph

2113. Smith, Joyce Carol Oates. "The existential comedy of Conrad's youth." *Renascence* 16 (1963):22-28.

Constant, Benjamin

2114. Tisseau, Paul-Henri. "*L'Adolphe* de B. Constant et la *Répétition* de Kierkegaard." *Revue de Littérature Comparée* 13 (1933):239-258.

Corsair (See also Goldschmidt)

2115. Anonymous. "Die Karikaturen des *Korsaren* gegen Kierkegaard." *Die Literarische Welt* (Berlin) 6 (1930): 3-4.

2116. Bredsdorff, Elias. *Corsaren, Goldschmidt og Kierkegaard.* Copenhagen: Corsaren, 1977, 2d rev. ed.

2117. Kütemeyer, W. "Sören Kierkegaard und der *Korsar.*" *Deutscher Almanak* für 1930, I: Leipzig: Reclam, 1930, 176-193.

2118. Kütemeyer, W. "Sören Kierkegaard und der *Korsar.*" *Die Brücke* (1931):176-193.

2119. Niedermeyer, Gerhard. "Sören Kierkegaard und der *Korsar.*" *Zeitwende* (München) 2 (1926):449-463.

Descartes, René

2120. Grimsley, Ronald. "Kierkegaard and Descartes." *Journal of the History of Philosophy* 4 (1966):31-41.

2121. Löwith, Karl. "Descartes' vernünftiger Zweifel und Kierkegaards Leidenschaft der Verzweiflung." In *Congrès Descartes* [IX. Congrès Internationale de Philosophie]. Raymond Bayer, ed. Paris: Études Cartésiennes, 1937, fasc. I, parte 1., 74-79.

Dinesen, Isak

2122. Johannesson, E. O. "Isak Dinesen, Sören Kierkegaard, and the present age." *Books Abroad* 36 (1962):20-24.

Don Juan (See also Mozart)

2123. Borgese, G. A. "Don Giovanni in Danimarca." In his
*La Vita e il Libro. Saggi di Letteratura e di Cultura
Contemporanea*. Bologna: Zanichelli, 1927. 322p.

2124. Fenger, Henning. "Prise de conscience esthétique de
Kierkegaard: *Don Juan*." *Orbis Litterarum* 27 (1972):224-228.
[Mozart]

2125. Gavazzeni, G. "Kierkegaard, il Don Giovanni e la
musica." *Rassegna d' Italia* (Milano) (1947).

2126. Grimsley, Ronald. "The Don Juan theme in Molière
and Kierkegaard." *Comparative Literature* 6 (1954):316-334.

2127. Heckel, Hans. *Das Don Juan-Problem in der neueren
Dichtung*. Stuttgart: J. B. Metzler, 1915, 171p. (Bres-
lauer Beiträge zur Literaturgesch., N.F. 47). Phil. Diss.
Breslau, 1915 (S. Kierkegaard, 118-141).

2128. Klossowski, Pierre. "Don Juan selon Kierkegaard."
Acephale I (Paris) (1937):27-32.

2129. Poppenberg, Felix. "Don Juan imaginaire."
Die Nation 21 (1903-04):395-398.

2130. Prather, Kieran. "Kierkegaard's symbolic use of
Don Giovanni." *Journal of Aesthetic Education* 12 (1978):
51-63.

2131. Rauch, Leo. "Kierkegaard ve-Don Giovanni."
Bikoret-u-Parshanut 6 (1974):11-16. [Kierkegaard and Don
Giovanni. Summary in English, viii-ix.]

2132. Sauvage, Micheline. "L'ombre d'un séducteur:
Kierkegaard et Don Juan." *La Table Ronde* November (1957):
108-113.

2133. Svendsen, Hans Jörgen. "Daemon og menneske: Don
Juan og AEstetiker A. i Sören Kierkegaards *Enten-Eller*." In
Indfaldsvinkler. Copenhagen: Gyldendal, 1964, 40-57.

Dostoevsky, Fyodor

2134. Chestov, Leon (Sjestov, Lev). "Kierkegaard et
Dostoiewsky." (Les voix qui clament dans le désert).
Conférence. Trad. par B. de Schloezer. *Cahiers du Sud*
23 (1936):179-200.

2135. Chestov, Leon (Sjestov, Lev). "Kierkegaard y
Dostoyewsky." *Sur* (Buenos Aires) 5 (1935):7-39.

2136. Chestov, Leon (Sjestov, Lev). "Kierkegaard und
Dostojewski." *Deutsche Beiträge*. Eine zweimonatsschrift,
2 (München) (1948):324-343.

2137. Čiževskyi, Dmitrij. *O Dostojevskom* (Über Dostojevskij. Eine Sammelschrift, hrsg. von A. L. Béma).
Praha, 1929 (162p.), 9-38 (om S. Kierkegaard, passim).
[Zum Doppelgangerproblem bei Dostojevskij. Versuch einer
philosophischen Interpretation.]

2138. Čiževskyi, Dmitrij. "Zum Doppelgangerproblem bei
Dostojevskij. Versuch einer philosophischen Interpretation." *Dostojevskij-Studien*. Gesammelt und herausgegeben
von D. Cizevskyi. Reichenberg: Stiepel, 1931 (116p.),
19-50 (om S. Kierkegaard 45, 48-50). Veröffentlichungen
der Slavistischen Arbeitsgemeinschaft an der Deutschen
Universität in Prag. I. Reihe: Untersuchungen, Heft 8.

2139. Clive, Geoffrey. "The sickness unto death in the
underworld: A study of nihilism [Kierkegaard-Dostoevsky]."
Harvard Theological Review 51 (1958):133-167.

2140. Greenway, John L. "Kierkegaardian doubles in
Crime and Punishment." *Orbis Litterarum* 33 (1978):45-60.

2141. Lieb, Fritz. "Das Problem des Menschen bei
Dostojewskij. Versuch einer theologischen Exegesis [Sören
Kierkegaard]." *Orient und Occident*. Blätter fur Theo-
logie, Ethik und Soziologie (Leipzig) 3 (1930):22-40.

2142. Migliorini, Giulio. "Diritto e società in Kierkegaard e in Dostojevskij." *Rivista Internazionale di
Filosofia del Diritto* 38 (1961):474-490.

2143. Onasch, Konrad. "Gleichzeitigkeit und Geschichte:
Randbermerkungen zum Vergleich Dostojevskijs mit Kierkegaard. Erhard Peschke zum 65.Geburtstag." *Zeitschrift
für Religions- und Geistesgeschichte* 25 (1973):46-57.

2144. Pondrom, Cyrena N. "Two demonic figures: Kierkegaard's Merman and Dostoevsky's Underground Man." *Orbis
Litterarum* 23 (1968):161-177.

2145. Thomassen, Einar. "Kierkegaard og Dostojevskij."
Dansk Udsyn (1953):309-330.

2146. Thomassen, Einar. "Kierkegaard og Dostojevskij."
Edda 42 (1955):246-265.

Duns Scotus

2147. Gneo, Corrado. "L'Opzione radicale come fondamento
dell'essere e Duns Scoto." *Aquinas* 14 (1971):125-132.

Eliot, T. S.

2148. Hanzo, Thomas. "Eliot and Kierkegaard: 'The meaning
of happening' in *The Coctail Party*." *Modern Drama* 3
(1960):52-59.

Emerson, Ralph Waldo

2149. Fromm, Harold. "Emerson and Kierkegaard: The
problem of historical Christianity." *Massachusetts Review*
9 (1968):741-752.

2150. Lee, Roland F. "Emerson through Kierkegaard: Toward
a definition of Emerson's theory of communication."
English Literary History 24 (1957):229-248.

Eucken

2151. Rudde, Gerhard. "Kierkegaard und Eucken als Volkserzieher." *Württemburger Zeitung*. Schwabenspiegel
(Stuttgart) 19 (1925):153.

Faulkner, William

2152. Bedell, George C. *Kierkegaard and Faulkner.
Modalities of Existence*. Baton Rouge: Louisiana State
Univ. Press, 1972. 261p.

Faust

2153. Clair, André. "Le mythe de Faust et le concept kierkegaardien de démoniaque." *Revue Philosophique de Louvain* 77 (1979):24-49. [Résumé, Abstract, 49-50]

2154. Spera, Salvatore. "Il mito di Faust. Aspirazioni letterarie, riflessioni filosofiche, preoccupazioni religiose del giovane Kierkegaard." *Archivio di Filosofia* (1974):309-339. [E. Castelli, Nota conclusiva, 340]

Feuerbach

2155. Brun, Jean. "Feuerbach et Kierkegaard." *Cahiers du Sud* 50 (1963):34-43.

2156. Elrod, John W. "Feuerbach and Kierkegaard on the self." *Journal of Religion* 56 (1976):348-365.

2157. Matrai, L. "Three antagonists of Hegel: Feuerbach, Kierkegaard, Marx." In *Danish Yearbook of Philosophy* 8 (1971):115-119. [Discussions, 119-134]

2158. Preti, Giulio. "Kierkegaard, Feuerbach e Marx." *Studi Filosofici* (Milano) 10 (1949):187-208.

2158a. Sannwald, Adolf. "Kierkegaard und Feuerbach in der Abhängigkeit von und im Kampf mit der idealistischen Dialektik." In his *Der Begriff der "Dialektik" und die Anthropologie*. Eine Untersuchung über das Ich-Verständnis in der Philosophie des deutschen Idealismus und seiner Antipoden. München, 1931, 215-270. (Forschungen zur Gesch. und Lehre des Protestantismus. R. 3, Bd. 4.)

Fichte, Johann Gottlieb

2159. Schulz, W. *Johann Gottlieb Fichte. Soren Kierkegaard*. Pfullingen: Neske, 1977. 77p.

Freud, Sigmund

2160. Adler-Vonessen, Hildegard. "Angst in der Sicht von S. Kierkegaard, S. Freud und M. Heidegger." *Psyche* (Heidelberg) 25 (1971):692-715. [Summary, 714]

2161. Cole, J. Preston. *The Problematic Self in Kierkegaard and Freud.* New Haven (Connecticut), London: Yale
Univ. Press, 1971. 244p.

2162. Marcuse, Ludwig. "Zwei Diagnosen der Angst. Kierkegaard und Freud." *Der Monat* 8 (1955):28-38.

2163. Stack, George J. "Repetition in Kierkegaard and
Freud." *The Personalist* 58 (1977):249-260.

Frisch, Max

2164. Manger, Philip. "Kierkegaard in Max Frisch's novel
Stiller." *German Life and Letters* 20 (1967):119-131.

Gentile, Giovanni

2165. Vettori, V. "Giovanni Gentile tra Kierkegaard e
Marx." *Città di Vita* (Firenze) 9 (1954):685-691.

Ghazali

2166. Kassian, H. "Existentialist tendencies in Ghazali
and Kierkegaard (within the framework of theological
existentialism)." *Islamic Studies* 10 (1971):103-128.

Goethe (See also Faust)

2167. Anonymous. "Liebe und Ehe. Kierkegaard über
Goethe." *Der Christliche Student* (Tübingen) (1949):49--55.

2168. Bienenstock, Max. "Sören Kierkegaard und sein
Urteil über Goethe (dat. 10.Juni 1912)." *Neue Jahrbücher
für das Klassische Altertum, Geschichte und Deutsche
Literatur und für Padagogik* (Leipzig und Berlin) 29 (1912):
443-448.

2169. Closs, August. "Goethe (1749-1832) und Kierkegaard
(1813-1855): Gleichwichtige Mitte und *Entweder-Oder*."
Etudes Germaniques 4 (1949):278-290.

2170. Closs, August. "Goethe and Kierkegaard." *Modern
Language Quarterly* 10 (1949):264-280.

2171. Closs, August. "Goethe and Kierkegaard." In
Medusa's Mirror. Studies in German Literature. London:
Cresset Press; New York: Dufour, 1957, 96-112.

2172. Gerber, Hans Erhard. *Nietzsche und Goethe. Studien
zu einem Vergleich* (Sprache und Dichtung, 78). Bern-
Stuttgart: Verlag Paul Haupt, 1954. 151p.

2173. Kahn, L. W. "Goethes Iphigenie, Kleists Amphitryon
und S. Kierkegaard." *Monatshefte für Deutschen Unterricht*
(Madison, Wisconsin) 39 (1947).

2174. Oppel, Horst. "Kierkegaard und Goethe." *Deutsche
Vierteljahrsschrift für Literaturwissenschaft und Geistesgeschichte* 16 (1938):126-159.

2175. Roos, Carl. *Kierkegaard og Goethe*. Copenhagen:
Gad, 1955. 231p.

2176. Roos, Carl. "Zu Goethe-Lekture Kierkegaards, I:
Die Romane." *Orbis Litterarum* 10 (1955):214-235.
[Symposion Kierkegaardianum]

2177. Steffensen, Steffen. "Kierkegaard und Goethe."
Nerthus 3 (1972):19-55.

2178. Williams, Forest. "A problem in values: The Faustian
motivation in Kierkegaard and Geothe." *Ethics* 63 (1953):
251-261.

Gogarten

2179. Jacob, Gunther. "Der Geistesbegriff bei Gogarten
und Kierkegaard." *Die Christliche Welt* 43 (1929):68-73.

Goldschmidt

2180. Bredsdorff, Elias. *Corsaren, Goldschmidt og Kierkegaard*. 2d rev. ed. Copenhagen: Corsaren, 1977.

Grabbe

2181. Christenden, Arild. "Titanismus bei Grabbe und
Kierkegaard." *Orbis Litterarum* 14 (1959):184-205.

Greene, Graham

2182. Evans, Robert O. "Existentialism in Greene's
The Quiet American. Modern Fiction Studies 3 (1957):
241-248.

2183. Noxon, James. "Kierkegaard's stages and *A Burnt-out
Case!* [Graham Greene]." *Review of English Literature*
(Leeds) 3 (1962):90-101.

Grundtvig, Nikolai F. S.

2184. Albeck, Gustav, and Michelsen, William, eds.
Grundtvig-Studier, 1973. Copenhagen: Danske Boghandleres
Kommissionantalt, 1973. 239p.

2185. Allen, E. L. "Grundtvig and Kierkegaard."
Congregational Quarterly 24 (1946):205-212.

2186. Anonymous. *Kopenhagener Zeitung* 1 (1856). [Sören
Kierkegaard and N. F. S. Grundtvig]

2187. Bukdahl, Jörgen. "Grundtvig og Kierkegaard."
Kierkegaardiana 9 (1974):196-219. [Also in his *Tordenvejret og Gentagelsen.*]

2188. Christensen, M. G. "Grundtvig and Kierkegaard."
Lutheran Quarterly 2 (1950):441-446.

2189. Höirup, Henning. "Grundtvig and Kierkegaard: Their
views of the Church." Trans. by Johannes Knudsen.
Theology Today 12 (1955):328-342.

2190. Holm, Sören. "Grundtvig und Kierkegaard. Parallelen
und Kontraste." *Zeitschrift für Systematische Theologie*
(Berlin) 23 (1954):158-176.

2191. Holm, Sören. "Holberg, Grundtvig, Kierkegaard,
drei dänische Denker." *Neue Zeitschrift für Systematische
Theologie* 7 (1965):49-61.

2192. Holm, Sören. *Grundtvig und Kierkegaard. Parallelen
und Kontraste.* (Übers. aus dem dänischen Manuskript von
Günther Jungbluth). Köbenhavn: Nyt Nordisk Forlag;
Tübingen: Katzmann, 1956, 101p.

2193. Jones, Llewellyn. "Kierkegaard or Grundtvig?"
Christian Century 49 (1952):588-589, 674-675.

2194. Klein, E. F. "Zwei Danen, Kierkegaard und Grundtvig." In his *Zeitbilder aus der Kirchengeschichte für die christliche Gemeinde*. Bd. I-II. Berlin: Acker-Verlag, 1. Th. 1911; 2. Th. 1912; 3. Th. 1913; 4. Th. 1927.

2195. *Kontroverse um Kierkegaard und Grundtvig*. Hrsg. von Knud Ejler Lögstrup und Götz Harbsmeier. I: *Das Menschliche und das Christliche*. Beitr. z. Einf. in d. Diskussion um Kierkegaard und Grundtvig. München: Kaiser, 1966. 140p.

2196. *Kontroverse um Kierkegaard und Grundtvig*. Hrsg. von Knud Ejler Lögstrup, auseinandersetzung mit Kierkegaard. Mit Erw. f. d. dt. Ausg. aus d. Dän. übers. von Rosemarie Lögstrup. München: Kaiser, 1968. 248p.

2197. *Kontroverse um Kierkegaard und Grundtvig*. Hrsg. von Knud Ejler Lögstrup und Götz Harbsmeier. Bd. III: *Götz Harbsmeier, Wer is der Mensch? Alternativen zu Kierkegaard* (Kontroverse um Kierkegaard und Grundtvig, 3). Göttingen: Vandenhoeck und Ruprecht, 1972. 245p.

2198. Lehmann, Ed. "Deux réformateurs du protestantisme danois: Sören Kierkegaard et Grundtvig." *Revue d'Histoire et de Philosophie Religieuses* 11 (1931):499-505.

2199. Lindhardt, P. G. *Konfrontation: Grundtvigs praedikener i kirkearet 1845-55 pa baggrund af Kierkegaards angreb pa den danske kirke og den "officielle" kristendom*. Copenhagen: Akademisk Forlag, 1974. 200p. ["Indledning," 5-19; "Grundtvigs praedikener," 21-188; "Kommentar," 189-206; "Efterskrift," 207-217.]

2200. Lindhardt, P. G. "Kierkegaard og Grundtvig." *Dansk Udsyn* 37:147-161 [no year given].

2201. Lund, Herman. "Sören Kierkegaard [and N. F. S. Grundtvig]." *Le Temoignage*. Journal de l'Eglise de la Confession d'Augsbourg (Paris) (1877).

2202. Malantschuk, Gregor. "Grundtvig og Kierkegaard: Et Grundtema I Joergen Bukdahl; Tordenvejret og Gentagelsen." *Dansk Teologisk Tidsskrift* 38 (1975):139-143.

2203. Nauman, St. Elmo H., Jr. "The Social Philosophies of Soeren Kierkegaard and Nikolai Frederik Severin Grundtvig." Ph.D., Boston Univ., 1969, 224p. *Dissertation Abstracts* 30 (1969):2081A.

2204. Paulsen, Anna. "Kontroverse um Grundtvig und Kierkegaard." In *Kierkegaardiana* 6 (1968):150-159.

2205. Serrand, A.-Z. "Etre ou ne pas être." *Vie Intell-*
ectuelle (1955):101-107. [A propos d'un article où
Henning Höirup pousse un parallèle entre Kierkegaard et
Grundtvig, *Theology Today* (1955):328-342, et d'un compte
rendu, *ibid.*, 380-388, par H. A. Johnson de: S. Kierkegaard, *On Authority and Revelation.*]

2206. Steffensen, Steffen. "Grundtvig und Kierkegaard."
Ausblick (Lübeck) 1 (1950):49-50.

2207. Thaning, Kay. "Lindhardts bog om Grundtvig og
Kierkegaard." *Praesteforeningens Blad* 65 (1975):641-648,
657-663.

2208. Toftdahl, Hellmut. "Debatten om Grundtvig og
Kierkegaard: En kritisk gennengag." In *Grundtvig-Studier*,
1969. Copenhagen: Danske Boghandleres Kommissionantalt,
1969, 47-86.

2209. Toftdahl, Hellmut. "Grundtvig og Sören Kierkegaard." *Kierkegaardiana* 7 (1973):30-49. [Summary in
English, 225-232.]

2210. Weltzer, Carl. *Grundtvig og Sören Kierkegaard.*
Copenhagen: Gyldendal, 1952. 192p.

Haecker, Theodor

2211. Mumbauer, Johannes. "Die neuen Tertulliane.
(Sören Kierkegaard und Theodor Haecker)." *Literarischer
Handweiser* 58 (1922):545-550.

Hamann, Johann Georg

2212. Anonymous. "Hamann und Kierkegaard." *Die Brücke.*
Uebersetzungen aus der Weltpresse. (Essen) (1950):13.

2213. Nadler, Käte. "Hamann und Hegel." *Logos* 20 (1931):
259-285.

2214. Paresce, E. "Hume, Hamann, Kierkegaard e la filosofia della credenza." *Rivista Internazionale di Filosófia
del Diritto* no. 4 (1949).

2215. Schulze-Maizier, Fr. "Johann Georg Hamann und
Sören Kierkegaard." *Die Tat* 28 (1936):605-619.

2216. Smith, Ronald Gregor. "Hamann and Kierkegaard."
In *Kierkegaardiana* 5 (1964):52-67. Niels Thulstrup, ed.
Copenhagen: Munksgaard.

2217. Smith, Ronald Gregor. "Hamann und Kierkegaard."
In *Zeit und Geschichte Dankesgabe an Rudolf Bultmann zur
80.Geburtstag.* Herausgegeben von Erich Dinkle. Tübingen:
J. C. B. Mohr, 1964.

2218. Smith, Ronald Gregor. "Hamann Renaissance."
Christian Century 67 (1960):768-769.

2219. Steffensen, Steffen. "Kierkegaard und Hamann."
Orbis Litterarum 22 (1967):399-417.

2220. Thulstrup, Niels. "Incontro di Kierkegaard e
Hamann." In *Studi Kierkegaardiani.* A cura di Cornelio
Fabro. Brescia: Morcelliana, 1957, 323-357.

2221. Weber, H. E. "Zwei Propheten des Irrationalismus.
Johann G. Hamann und S. Kierkegaard als Bahnbrecher der
Theologie des Christusglaubens." *Neue Kirchliche Zeit-
schrift* 28 (1917):23-58, 77-125.

Hamlet (See also Shakespeare)

2222. Bellessort, André. "Le crépuscule d'Elseneur
[Hamlet and S. Kierkegaard]." *Revue des Deux Mondes*
84 (1914):49-83.

2223. Boehlich, Walter. "Sören, Prinz von Dänemark."
Der Monat 6 (1954):628-634. [Kierkegaard and Hamlet]

2224. Börge, Vagn. "Kierkegaard und Hamlet." *Wissenschaft und Weltbild* 23 (1970):50-58.

2225. Madariaga, Salvador de. "Noch einmal: Kierkegaard
und Hamlet. War Hamlet melancholisch?" *Der Monat* 6
(1954):625-628.

2226. McCarty, Robert Eugene. "The Wonder-Wounded Hearer:
The Problem of Communication in Kierkegaard's Authorship
and Its Application to an Understanding of *Hamlet.*"
Dissertation Abstracts 28 (1977):2814A.

2227. Rougemont, Denis de. "Hamlet et Kierkegaard. Deux
princes danois." *Preuves* no. 24 (1953).

2228. Rougemont, Denis de. "Kierkegaard and Hamlet: Two
Danish Princes." *Anchor Review* 1 (1955):109-127.

2229. Rougemont, Denis de. "Two Danish princes: Kierke-
gaard and Hamlet." In *Love Declared. Essays in the
Myth of Love.* Trans. from French by Richard Howard.
New York: Pantheon Books, 1963, 77-98.

2230. Rougemont, Denis de. "Kierkegaard und Hamlet."
Der Monat 5 (1953):115-124.

2231. Silveira, Paulo da. "Ao correr da pena. A ponte
que perdeu a outra margem [S. Kierkegaard and Hamlet]."
Jornal do Commercio Rio de Janeiro (14.7.1949).

Hansen, Martin A.

2232. Schow, H. W. "Kierkegaardian perspectives in
Martin A. Hansen's *The Liar*." *Critique* 15 (1974):53-65.

Hartmann, Eduard von

2233. Monachus [pseud.]. *Relative Absoluta? oder der Weg
zur Geistesfreiheit und freien Liebe. Traumphantasien.*
Leipzig: Th. Dieter, 1899.

Hegel, F. W.

2234. Ansbro, John Joseph. "Kierkegaard's Critique of
Hegel--An Interpretation." Ph.D., Fordham Univ., 1964,
356p. *Dissertation Abstracts* 25 (1964):3615.

2235. Anz, Wilhelm. "Hegel und Kierkegaard." In his
Humanismus und Christentum. Hamburg, 1955, 27-33.

2236. Artola, José Maria. "Situacion y sentido del
pensamiento hegeliano en la actualidad." *Estudios
Filosóficos* 22 (1973):349-384.

2237. Baeumler, Alfred. "Hegel und Kierkegaard." *Deutsche
Vierteljahrsschrift für Literaturwissenschaft und Geistesgeschichte* 2 (1924):116-130. Also in his *Studien zur
deutschen Geistesgeschichte*. Berlin, 1937, 54-70.

2238. Bense, Max. *Hegel und Kierkegaard. Eine prinzipielle Untersuchung*. Köln: Staufen, 1948. 82p.

   book reviews:
   Helmuth Dempe, *Philosophische Literaturanzeiger* 3
      (1951):36-39;
   Wilfried Joest, *Theologische Literaturzeitung* 75
      (1950):533-538;
   Friederich Grossart, *Philosophische Studien* 2 (1950):
      217-221.

2239. Bense, Max. *Hegel y Kierkegaard. Una Investigación de Principios*. Trad. de Guillermo Floris Margadant (Colección Cuardernos, 28). México: UNAM, 1969. 81p.

2240. Bogen, James. "Remarks on the Kierkegaard-Hegel controversy." *Synthèse* 13 (1961):372-389.

2241. Borgia. *Presentazione di Bruno Widmar* (Hegel, Kierkegaard). Galatina: Editrice Salantina, 1971. 134p.

2242. Castellana, Wanda. "La crisi del modello hegeliano in Soeren Kierkegaard." In *Saggi e Ricerche di Filosofia*. A cura di Ada Lamacchia. Lecce: Edizioni Milella, 1972 (121p.), 41-51.

2243. Chestov, Leon (Sjestov, Lev). "Job ou Hegel? Apropos de la philosophie existentielle de Kierkegaard." [Trad. par B. de Schloezer.] *La Nouvelle Revue Française* 23 (1935):755-762.

2244. Christiansen, Lars. "Die Kategorie der Geschichte bei Hegel und bei Kierkegaard." *Nerthus* 3 (1972):57-71.

2245. Cirell Czerna, R. "A experiência romântica em Kierkegaard e Hegel." *Revista Brasileira de Filosofia* 6 (1956):38-58.

2246. Collins, James D. "Kierkegaard's critique of Hegel." *Thought* 18 (1943):74-100.

2247. Collins, James D. "The mind of Kierkegaard: The attack upon Hegelianism." *Modern Schoolman* 26 (1949): 219-251.

2248. Crites, Stephen. *In the Twilight of Christendom: Hegel vs. Kierkegaard on Faith and Religion*. (AAR Studies in Religion 2). Chambersburg: American Academy of Religion. 1972. 109p.

2249. *Die Hegelsche Linke*. Texte aus den Werken von Heinrich Heine, Arnold Ruge, Moses Hess, Max Stirner, Bruno Bauer, Ludwig Feuerbach, Karl Marx und Sören Kierkegaard ausgewählt und eingeleitet von Karl Löwith. Stuttgart-Bad Cannstatt: Friedrich Fromman Verlag (Günther Holzboog), 1962. 288p.

2250. Earle, William. "Hegel and some contemporary philosophies." *Philosophy and Phenomenological Research* 20 (1960):352-364.

2251. Fabro, Cornelio. "La dialettica della libertà e l'assoluto (per un confronto fra Hegel e Kierkegaard)." In *Kierkegaard e Nietzsche*. Scritti di E. Paci, C. Fabro, F. Lombardi, G. Masi, V. A. Bellezza, P. Valori, T. Morretti Costanzi, R. Cantoni, A. Santucci. *Archivio di Filosofia* no. 3 (1953). Milano-Roma: Fratelli Bocca, 1953, 45-69.

2252. Fabro, Cornelio. "Kierkegaard critico di Hegel." In *Incidenza di Hegel. Studi raccolti nel Secondo Centenario della Nascità del Filosofo*. A cura di Fulvio Tessitore. Napoli: Morano, 1970 (1140p.), 499-563.

2253. Gigante, M. "Il messaggio esistenziale di Kierkegaard e la filosofia hegeliana." *Asprenas* (Napoli) 17 (1970):392-412.

2254. Guarda, Victor. *Kierkegaardstudien: Mit besonderer Berücksichtigung des Verhältnisses Kierkegaards zu Hegel*. (Beihefte zur Zeitschrift für Philosophische Forschung 34). Meisenheim: Hain, 1975, viii-98p.

2255. Hagen, Edward von. *Abstraktion und Konkretion bei Hegel und Heidegger*. Bonn: Bouvier, 1969. 108p.

2256. Hansen, Olaf. "The Problem of Alienation and Reconciliation. A Comparative Study of Marx and Kierkegaard in the Light of Hegel's Formulation of the Problem." Ph.D., Princeton Theological Seminary, 1956, 449p. *Dissertation Abstracts* 35 (1975):4680A.

2257. Heiss, Robert. *Hegel, Kierkegaard, Marx. De grote dialectische Denkers van de negentiende eeuv*. Vertaald door M. Mok. 2d druk. Utrecht, Antwerpen: Het Spectrum, 1971. 408p.

2258. Holm, Sören. "Sören Kierkegaard og Hegel." *Nordisk Tiskrift* 44:68-81.

2259. Hyppolite, Jean. "Hegel et Kierkegaard dans la pensée française contemporaine." In *Figures de la Pensée Philosophique. Ecrits* (1931-1968), Vol. I. Paris: Presses Universitaires de France, 1971, 196-208.

2260. Joest, Wilfried. "Hegel und Kierkegaard." *Theologische Literaturzeitung* 75 (1950):533-538.

2261. Joest, Wilfried. "Hegel und Kierkegaard. Bemerkungen zu einer prinzipiellen Untersuchung." In *Sören Kierkegaard*. Hrsg. von Heinz H. Schrey. Darmstadt: Wissenschaftliche Buchgesellschaft, 1971, 81-89.

2262. Johansen, Udo. "Kierkegaard und Hegel." *Zeitschrift für Philosophische Forschung* 7 (1953):20-53.

2263. Karowski, Walter. "Kierkegaard über Hegel." *Zeitschrift für Systematische Theologie* 15 (1938):602-616.

2264. Kroner, Richard J. "Kierkegaard or Hegel?" *Revue Internationale de Philosophie* 6 (1952):79-96.

2265. Kroner, Richard J. "Kierkegaards Hegelverständnis." *Kant-Studien* 46 (1954-55):19-27.

2266. Kroner, Richard J. "Kierkegaard's understanding of Hegel." *Union Seminary Quarterly Review* 21 (1966):233-244; Reply. R. L. Horn. 21 (1966):341-345.

2267. Leisegang, Hans. *Hegel, Marx, Kierkegaard. Zum dialekt. Materialismus und zur dialekt. Theologie.* Berlin: Wissenschaftliche Editionsgesellschaft, 1948. 41p.

2268. Lessing, Arthur. "Hegel and existentialism: On unhappiness." *The Personalist* 49 (1968):61-77.

2269. Limentani, Ludovico. "Sören Kierkegaard. Polemica antihegeliana." In his *Il Pensiero Moderno. Storia della Filosofia da R. Descartes a H. Spencer.* Milano, 1930, 542-549.

2270. Majoli, Bruno. "La critica ad Hegel in Schelling e Kierkegaard." *Rivista Filosofia Neo-Scolastica* 46 (1954): 232-263.

2271. Marck, Sigfried. "Die Religionsphilosophie der Romantik: Hegel und Kierkegaard." *Jahresbericht der Schlesische Gesellschaft für Vaterländische Kultur* 100. Bericht, 1927, 105-106.

2272. Marion, F. J. "Kierkegaard frente a Hegel." *Pensamiento* 31 (1975):387-406.

2273. Marsh, James L. "Hegel and Kierkegaard: A Dialectical and Existential Contrast." Ph.D., Northwestern Univ. *Dissertation Abstracts* 32 (1971):3371A.

2274. Mátrai, L. "Three antagonists of Hegel: Feuerbach, Kierkegaard, Marx." In *Danish Yearbook of Philosophy* 8 (1971):115-119. [Discussions, 119-134]

2275. McKinnon, Alastair. "Similarities and differences in Kierkegaard's accounts of Hegel." In *Kierkegaardiana* 10 (1977):117-131.

2276. McLaughlin, Wayman Bernard. "The Relation Between Hegel and Kierkegaard." Ph.D., Boston Univ., 1958, 346p. *Dissertation Abstracts* 19 (1958):1788.

2277. Melchiorre, Virgilio. "Kierkegaard ed Hegel. La polemica sul 'punto di partenza'." In *Studi Kierkegaardiani.* A cura di Cornelio Fabro. Brescia: Morcelliana, 1957, 253-266.

2278. Müller, Ernst. "Das Hegelbild der Gegenwart." *Dichtung und Volkstum* (N.F. des Euphorion) 38 (1937): 252-265. (S. Kierkegaard, 261-263.)

2279. Mueller, G. "Kierkegaard y Hegel." *Revista de la Universidad de Buenos Aires* 4 (1949):353-387.

2280. Müller, Philip. "Kierkegaard lecteur de Hegel."
Studia Philosophica 33 (1973):157-171.

2281. Nadler, Käte. Der dialektische Widerspruch in
Hegels Philosophie und das Paradoxon des Christentums.
Leipzig: Felix Meiner, 1931, viii-143p. Phil. Diss. Kiel,
1931.

2282. Niecikowski, Jerzy. "Stirner, Kierkegaard--krytycy
Helga." Archiwum Historii Filozofi i Mysli Spotecznej
13 (1967):141-171. [Summary in German]

2283. Pellegrini, Alessandro. "Il 'sistema' e gli
heretici [Hegel and Kierkegaard]." Archivio di Storia
della Filosofia Italiana 4 (1935):159-165.

2284. Perkins, Robert Lee. "Kierkegaard and Hegel: The
Dialectical Structure of Kierlegaard's Ethical Thought."
Ph.D., Indiana Univ., 1965. Dissertation Abstracts 26
(1965):2809.

2285. Perkins, Robert Lee. "The family: Hegel and
Kierkegaard's Judge Wilhelm." Hegel-Jahrbuch (Meisenheim/
Glan) (1967):89-100.

2286. Perkins, Robert Lee. "Hegel and Kierkegaard: Two
critics of romantic irony." In Hegel in Comparative
Literature. Frederick G. Weiss, ed. Review of National
Literature 1 (1970):232-254.

2286a. Perkins, Robert Lee. "Beginning the system:
Kierkegaard and Hegel." In Akten XIV. Intern. Kongr.
Philos. 6:478-485.

2287. Pomerleau, Wayne P. "Perspectives on Faith and
Reason. Studies in the Religious Philosophy of Kant,
Hegel and Kierkegaard." Ph.D., Northwestern Univ., 1977,
266p. Dissertation Abstracts 38 (1978):5531A.

2288. Poole, Roger C. "Hegel, Kierkegaard and Sartre."
New Blackfriars 47 (1966):532-541.

2289. Reuter, Hans. S. Kierkegaards religionsphilosophische Gedanken im Verhältnis zu Hegels religionsphilosophischen System. Leipzig: Quelle and Mayer, vi-131p.
(Abhandlungen zur Philosophie und ihrer Geschichte, hrsg.
von R. Falckenberg, 23).

2290. Ramsey, Robert Paul. "Existenz and the existence
of God: A study of Kierkegaard and Hegel." Journal of
Religion 28 (1948):157-176.

2291. Read, Lawrence McKim. "Hegel and Kierkegaard: A
Study in Antithetical Concepts of the Incarnation."
Ph.D., Columbia Univ., 1967, 212p. Dissertation Abstracts
28 (1967):1852A.

2292.   Reinhardt, Kurt F.   "The cleavage of minds: Kierkegaard and Hegel." *Commonweal* 24 (1936):523-524.

2293.   Ringleben, Joachim. *Hegels Theorie des Sünde. Die
Subjektivitäts-logische Konstruktion eines theologischen
Begriffs.* Berlin-New York: de Gruyter, 1977.

2294.   Ritschl, D.   "Kierkegaards kritik an Hegels logik.
Zu Sören Kierkegaards 100. Todestag." *Theologische Zeitung*
11 (1955):437-465. [See Thulstrup, no. 2303]

2295.   Rudolph, Arthur W.   "The concept of man in Hegel
and Kierkegaard." *ITA Humanidades* (São José dos Campos)
8 (1972):55-71.

2296.   Sciacca, G. M.   *L'esperienza religiosa e l'io in
Hegel e Kierkegaard.* Palermo: Palumbo, 1948. 60p.

2297.   Sliogeris, A[rvydas].   "Buties problema G. Hegelio
ir S. Kjerkegoro filosofijoje." *Problemos* 19 (1977):23-24.
[Existential problems in philosophy of Hegel and Kierkegaard. English and Russian summaries.]

2298.   Start, Lester J.   "Kierkegaard and Hegel." Ph.D.,
Syracuse Univ., 1953.

2299.   Stavrides, Maria Margareta.   "The Concept of Existence in Kierkegaard and Heidegger." Ph.D., Columbia Univ.,
1952, 205p. *Dissertation Abstracts* 12:641.

2300.   Taylor, Mark C.   "Journeys to Moriah: Hegel vs.
Kierkegaard." *Harvard Theological Review* 70 (1977):305-326.

2301.   Taylor, Mark C.   "Love and forms of spirit. Kierkegaard vs. Hegel." In *Kierkegaardiana* 10 (1977):95-116.
Copenhagen: C. A. Reitzels Boghandel.

2302.   Theunissen, Michael.   "Die Dialektik der Offenbarung.
Zur Auseinandersetzung Schellings und Kierkegaards mit
Religionsphilosophie Hegels." *Philosophisches Jahrbuch*
72 (1964-65):134-160.

2303.   Thulstrup, Niels.   "Kierkegaards Verhältnis zu
Hegel." *Theologische Zeitschrift* 13 (1957):200-226.
[Reply to article by D. Ritschl. See no. 2294.]

2304.   Thulstrup, Niels.   "Sören Kierkegaard, historien de
la philosophie de Hegel." *Tijdschrift voor Filosofie*
27 (1965):521-572.

2305.   Thulstrup, Niels.   *Kierkegaards Verhältnis zu Hegel
und zum spekulativen Idealismus 1835-1846: Historisch-
analytische Untersuchung.* Stuttgart: Kohlhammer, 1972.
320p.

2306.   Tweedie, Donald F., Jr.   "The Significance of Dread
in the Thought of Kierkegaard and Heidegger."   Ph.D.,
Boston Univ., 1954.

2307.   Van der Hoeven, J.   "Kierkegaard en Marx als dialectische critici van Hegel, I-II."   *Philosophia Reformata*
34 (1969):84-100; 35 (1970):101-118; 36 (1971):125-150.
[Summary, 150-154]

2308.   Vandiest, Julien.   "Hegel, Nietzsche en Kierkegaard."
De Nieuwe Stem 20 (1965):385-407, 465-479.

2309.   Vobis, Bonaventura.   "Hegel, Marx und Kierkegaard
in ihrem Beitrag zum Thema 'Der Einzelne und die Gemeinschaft'."   *Franziskanische Studien* 35 (1953):87-90.

2310.   Wahl, Jean.   "Hegel et Kierkegaard."   *Revue Philosophique* 56 (1931):321-380.

2311.   Wahl, Jean.   "Hegel et Kierkegaard."   Verhandlungen
des *dritten Hegelkongresses* vom 19. bis 23. April 1933 in
Rom.   Im Auftr. des internat. Hegelbundes hrsgeg. von
B. Wigersma.   Tubingen, 1934, 235-249.

2312.   Whittemore, Robert C.   "Pro Hegel, contra Kierkegaard."   *Journal of Religious Thought* 13 (1956):131-144.

2313.   Zweerman, Th.   "De vertroosting der wijsbegeerte."
Tijdschrift voor Filosofie 38 (1976):3-55.

Heidegger, Martin

2314.   Brod, Max.   "Kierkegaard, Heidegger, Kafka."
L'Arche 21 (1946):44-55.

2315.   Brod, Max.   "Kierkegaard, Heidegger, Kafka."
Prisma.   Kulturzeitschrift (München) 1 (1947):17-20.

2316.   Carlini, Armando.   "Il problema dell'interiorità
nel Kierkegaard e nello Heidegger, Kierkegaard: I.   L'angoscia e il peccato.   II.   L'angoscia e l'instante.--Martin
Heidegger: Che cos'è la metafisica?"   In *Il Mito del
Realismo*.   Firenze, 1936, 57-85.

2317.   Collet, Jacques.   "Kierkegaard, Bultmann et Heidegger."   *Revue des Sciences Philosophiques et Théologiques*
49 (1965):597-600.

2318.   De Feo, Nicola Massimo.   *Kierkegaard, Nietzsche,
Heidegger (Laocoonte)*.   Milano: Silva, 1964.   279p.

2319. Driscoll, Giles. "Heidegger's ethical monism."
New Scholasticism 42 (1968):497-510.

2320. Fondane, Benjamin. "Martin Heidegger sur les routes
de Kierkegaard et de Dostoievski." In *La Conscience
Malheureuse*. Paris, 1936 (306p.), 169-198.

2321. Henry, J. "The term 'primitive' in Kierkegaard and
Heidegger." In *The Concept of the Primitive*. Ashley
Montagu, ed. Free Press, 1968, 212-228.

2322. Hübscher, Alfred. "Der Existenzbegriff bei
Heidegger, Sartre und Kierkegaard." *Kirchenblatt für die
Reformierte Schweiz* 105 (1949):194-199.

2323. Ishizu, Shoji. "Shukyo no konkyo ni kansuru Kenkyu:
Kirukegoru to Haidegga no Ginmi ni sotte [A study of the
ground of religion: In Kierkegaard and Heidegger]."
Tohoku Daigaku Bungaku-bu Kenkyu Nempo (Sendai) 8 (1957):
171-221.

2324. Katayama, Masanao. "Shi ni tsuite--Haidegga to
Kirukegoru [On death--Heidegger and Kierkegaard]."
Kirukegour Kenkyu, 10, Rikkyo Daigaku Kirisutokyo Gakkai,
Tokyo, 1968, 95-119.

2325. Lögstrup, K. E. *Kierkegaards und Heideggers Exis-
tenzanalyse und ihr Verhältnis zur Verkündigung*. Berlin:
Blaschker, 1951. 127p.

2326. Löwith, Karl. "Grundzüge der Entwicklung der
Phänomenologie zur Philosophie und ihr Verhältnis zur
protestantischen Theologie [Heidegger and Kierkegaard]."
Theologische Rundschau N.F. 2 (1930):26-64; 333-361.

2327. Stack, George J. "Concern in Kierkegaard and
Heidegger." *Philosophy Today* 13 (1969):26-35.

2328. Stack, George J. "The language of possibility and
existential possibility." *Modern Schoolman* 50 (1972-73):
159-182.

2329. Stern, Guenther. "On the pseudo-concreteness of
Heidegger's philosophy." *Philosophy and Phenomenological
Research* 8 (1948):337-370.

2330. Vick, George R. "A new 'Copernican revolution'."
The Personalist 52 (1971):630-642. [Kierkegaard and
Heidegger on poetic discourse.]

2331. Vogt, Annemarie. *Das Problem des Selbstseins bei
Heidegger und Kierkegaard*. Giessen: H. & J. Lechte, 1936,
61p. Phil. Diss. Giessen, 1936.

2332. Wahl, Jean. "Heidegger et Kierkegaard." *Recherches
Philosophiques* 2 (1932-33):349-370.

2333. Waelhens, H. de. "Kierkegaard et Heidegger." In *La Philosophie de Martin Heidegger*. Louvain: Éd. de l'Institut Supérieur de Philosophie, 1942, xi-379p. Réimpress. ibid., 1946, 330-352.

2334. White, Carol Jean. "Time and Temporality in the Existential Thought of Kierkegaard and Heidegger." Ph.D., Univ. of California, Berkeley, 1976, 369p. *Dissertation Abstracts* 38 (1977):853A.

2335. Wyschogrod, Michael. *Kierkegaard and Heidegger. The Ontology of Existence*. New York: Humanities Press; London: Routledge & Kegan Paul, 1964, xii-156p.

Heine, Heinrich

2336. Hess, Mary A. "A last century liberal: Heinrich Heine." *Catholic World* 183 (1956):281-285.

Herzen

2337. Blackham, Harold J. "The comparison of Herzen with Kierkegaard: A comment." *Slavic Review* 25 (1966):213-217. [See Davison and Lambert, nos. 2338, 2339]

2338. Davison, R. M. "Herzen and Kierkegaard." *Slavic Review* 25 (1966):191-209.

2338a. Davison, R. M. "Reply." *Slavic Review* 25 (1966): 218-221.

2339. Lambert, E. "Herzen or Kierkegaard." *Slavic Review* 25 (1966):210-214.

Hesse, Hermann

2340. Jansen, Peter. "Asthetisches Sein und ethische Existenz. Hermann Hesses *Glasperlenspiel* und Kierkegaard." *Stimmen der Zeit* 195 (1977):402-414.

2341. Jansen, Peter. "Essere estetico ed esistenza etica (Hermann Hesse e Kierkegaard)." *Letture* 33 (1978):501-512.

Hirsch, Emanuel

2342. Steffensen, Steffen. "Emanuel Hirsch als Kierke-
gaard-Übersetzer." *Meddelelser fra Sören Kierkegaard
Selskabet* (Köbenhavn) 4 (1953):6-7.

Höffding, Harald

2343. Sorainen, Kalle. "Kierkegaard und Höffding."
Orbis Litterarum 10 (1955):245-251. [Symposion Kierke-
gaardianum]

Holstrup

2344. Bruun, Andersen K. "Kierkegaard og Holstrup [Kier-
kegaard and Holstrup]." *Gads Danske Magasin* 45 (1951):
233-244.

Hotho

2345. Barfoed, Niels. "Hotho und Kierkegaard." *Orbis
Litterarum* 22 (1967):378-386.

Hugel, Baron von

2346. Michalson, Gordon Elliott. *Baron von Hugel and
Sören Kierkegaard. A Comparison of Similarities and
Differences in Their Statements of the Christian Religion.*
Madison (New Jersey): Drew Theological Seminary, 1946.
365p.

Hugo, Victor

2347. Grimsley, Ronald. "Hugo, Kierkegaard and the
character of Nero." *Revue de Littérature Comparée* 32
(1958):230-236.

Hume, David

2348. Popkin, Richard H. "Hume and Kierkegaard." *Journal of Religion* 31 (1951):274-281.

Husserl, Edmund

2349. Spiegelberg, Herbert. "Husserl's phenomenology and existentialism." *Journal of Philosophy* 57 (1960):62-74.

2350. Valori, Paolo. "Husserl e Kierkegaard [in *Kierkegaard e Nietzsche*. Scritti di E. Paci, C. Fabro, F. Lombardi, G. Masi, V. A. Bellezza, P. Valori, T. Moretti Costanzi, R. Cantoni, A. Santucci.]." *Archivio di Filosofia* (Milano-Roma) no. 2 (1953):191-200.

2351. Vancourt, R. "Deux conceptions de la philosophie: Husserl et Kierkegaard." *Mélanges de Science Religeuse* 2:193-234.

Ibn 'Arabi

2352. Askari, Muhammad Hasan. "Orient et Occident: Ibn 'Arabi et Kierkegaard." Trad. de l'ourdou par André Guimbretière. Suivi de: *Quelques Réflexions*, par Jean Wahl. *Revue de Métaphysique et de Morale* 68 (1963):1-18, 19-24.

Ibsen, Henrik

2353. Bukdahl, Jörgen. "Arricia og Rom: Kierkegaard, og Ibsens gennembrud med *Brand*." In *De to Spor*. Erik Vagn Jensen, ed. Copenhagen: Gyldendal, 1976, 114-137.

2354. Chesnais, P. G. la. "Ibsen disciple de Kierkegaard?" *Edda* 21 (1934):355-410.

2355. Düwel, Hans. *Der Entwicklungsgedanke in Sören Kierkegaards* Entweder-Oder *und in Henrik Ibsens* Komödie der Liebe [Vervielfältigt nur im]. Auszug: Rostock: Winterberg, 1920. Phil. Diss. Rostock, 1919.

2356. Halvorsen, Wendell Q. "Ibsen and Kierkegaard." *Union Seminary Quarterly Review* 2 (1946):13-17.

2357. Hems, John M. "Abraham and Brand." *Philosophy* 39 (1964):137-144.

2358. Hirsch, Emanuel. "Kierkegaards Antigone und Ibsens Frau Atving." In *Gestalt Gedanke Geheimnis: Festschrift für Johannes Pfeiffer zu seinem 65. Geburtstag.* Berlin: Die Spur, 1967, 167-181. Reprinted in his *Wege zu Kierkegaard.* Berlin: Die Spur, 1968, 34-53.

2359. Lund, Mary Graham. "The existentialism of Ibsen." *The Personalist* 41 (1960):310-317.

2360. Magnino, Bianca. "Enrico Ibsen e Sören Kierkegaard." *Nuova Antologia* 7 Ser. (Roma) 258 (336) (1928):298-311. (Nel Centenario Ibseniano, II).

2361. Möhring, Werner. "Ibsens Abkehr von Kierkegaard." *Edda* 15 (1928):43-71.

2362. Möhring, Werner. *Ibsen und Kierkegaard.* Leipzig: Mayer & Müller, 1928, 59-140. Phil. Diss. Berlin, 1928.

2363. Möhring, Werner. *Ibsen und Kierkegaard.* Leipzig: Mayer & Müller, viii-187p. (Palaestra, 160).

2364. Muret, Maurice. "Un précurseur d'Henrik Ibsen; Sören Kierkegaard." *La Revue de Paris* 8 (1901):98-122.

2365. Rappoport, Angelo S. "Ibsen, Nietzsche and Kierke- gaard. I-II." *New Age* 3 (1908):408-409; 428-429.

2366. Stobart, Mabel A. "New light on Ibsen's *Brand.*" *Fortnightly Review* N.S. 66 (1899):227-239.

2367. Unamuno y Jugo, Miguel de. "Ibsen y Kierkegaard (Salamanca, Marzo de 1907)." In *Mi Religion y Otros Ensayos Breves.* Madrid, 1910, 67-75. (Biblioteca Renacimiento. Prieto y co.)

2368. Wood, Forrest, Jr. "Kierkegaardian light on Ibsen's *Brand.*" *The Personalist* 51 (1970):393-400.

James, William

2369. Evans, Charles Stephen. "Subjective Justifications of Religious Belief. A Comparative Study of Kant, Kierke- gaard, and James." Ph.D., Yale Univ., 1974, 285p. *Dissertation Abstracts* 35 (1975):4611A.

2370. Farré, Luis. "Unamuno, William James y Kierkegaard." *Cuadernos Hispano-Americanos* (1954):64-88.

2371. Gilmartin, Thomas V. "Soul-Sickness. A Comparison of William James and Sören Kierkegaard." Ph.D., Graduate Theological Union, 1974, 321p. *Dissertation Abstracts* 36 (1976):6763A.

Jaspers, Karl

2372. Dufrenne, M., et Ricoeur, P. *Karl Jaspers et la Philosophie de l'Existence*. Préface de Karl Jaspers. Paris: Éd. du Seuil, 1947. 399p. (Collections Esprit.)

2373. Fabro, Cornelio. "Jaspers et Kierkegaard." *Revue des Sciences Philosophiques et Théologiques* 37 (1953): 209-252.

2374. Schrag, Oswald O. *Existenece, Existenz, and Trans-cendence: The Philosophy of Karl Jaspers*. Pittsburgh (Pennsylvania): Duquesne Univ. Press, 1971. 251p.

2375. Sperna Weiland, J. *Philosophy of Existence and Christianity. Kierkegaard's and Jaspers' Thoughts on Christianity* (Philosophia Religionis, III). Assen: Van Gorcum and Co., 1951. 144p.

2376. Wahl, Jean. "Le problème du choix, l'existence et la transcendance dans la philosophie de Jaspers." *Revue de Métaphysique et de Morale* 41 (1934):405-444.

Jeremiah

2377. Dunstan, J. Leslie. "Kierkegaard and Jeremiah." *Andover Newton Bulletin* 47 (1955):17-24.

Job

2378. Müller, Paul. "Sören Kierkegaards forstaelse af teodicé-problemet, belyst ud fra hans skildring af Job-skikkelsen." *Dansk Teologisk Tidsskrift* 32 (1969):199-217.

Jung, Carl

2379. Bertelsen, Jes. *Ouroboros: En Undersogelse af Selvets Struktur*. Copenhagen: Borgens Forlag, 1974. 158p. [Diss. Univ. of Aarhus. On some elements of Jungian psychology, with constant reference to Kierkegaard.]

2380. Hitchkock, John. "A Comparison of 'Complementarity' in Quantum Physics with Analogous Structures in Kierke-gaard's Philosophical Writings, from a Jungian Point of View." Ph.D., Graduate Theological Union, 1975, 363p. *Dissertation Abstracts* 36 (1976):6764A.

2381. Sobosan, Jeffrey G. "Kierkegaard and Jung on the self." *Journal of Psychology and Theology* 3 (1975):31-35.

Kafka, Franz

2382. Billeter, Fritz. *Das Dichterische bei Kafka und Kierkegaard. Ein typologischer Vergleich*. Winterthur: Keller, 1965. 206p.

2383. Boisdeffre, Pierre de. "Kierkegaard et Kafka." *Revue de Paris* (1955):138-142.

2384. Edwards, Brian F. M. "Kafka and Kierkegaard: A reassessment." *German Life and Letters* 20 (1967):218-225.

2385. Egon Hessel, R. A. "Kierkegaard und Kafka." In *Kierkegaard-Studiet*, International Edition (Osaka, Japan) 3 (1966):11-16.

2386. Grangier, E. "Abraham, oder Kierkegaard, wie Kafka und Sartre ihn sehen." *Zeitschrift Philosophische Forschung* 4 (1950):412-420.

2387. Hopper, Stanley R. "Kafka and Kierkegaard: The function of ambiguity." *American Imago* 35 (1978):93-105.

2388. Merrill, Reed B. "Infinite absolute negativity: Irony in Kierkegaard and Kafka." *Comparative Literature* 16 (1979):222-236.

2389. Rahv, Philip. "Kafka's hero." *Kenyon Review* 1 (1939):60-74.

2390. Vircillo, Domenico. "Ambiguità e fede in Kierkegaard, Nietzsche e Kafka." *Sapienza* 26 (1973):27-69.

2391. Wahl, Jean. *Petite Histoire de "l'Existentialisme", Suivie de Kafka et Kierkegaard. Commentaires*. Paris: Club Maintenant, 1947. 131p.

2392. Wahl, Jean. *Esquisse pour Une Histoire de l'Existentialisme, Suive de Kierkegaard et Kafka*. Textes de Kafka et Max Brod trad. par Hélène Zylberberg. Paris: l'Arche

2393. Wahl, Jean. "Kierkegaard and Kafka." Trans. by Lienhard Bergel. In *The Kafka Problem*. Angel Flores, ed. New York: New Directions, 1946, 262-275.

2394. Winkler, R. O. C. "The significance of Kafka." *Scrutiny* 7 (1938):354-360.

Kant, Immanuel

2395. Abbagnano, Nicola. "Filosofia della possibilità. Kant e Kierkegaard." In *Esistenzialismo Positivo*. 2d ed. Torino: Taylor, 1948, 31-33.

2396. Baeumler, Alfred. "Kierkegaard und Kant über die Reinheit des Herzens." *Zwischen den Zeiten* 3 (1925): 182-187. Reprinted in his *Studien zur deutschen Geistesgeschichte*. Berlin, 1937, 71-77.

2397. Berberich, Gerta. *La Notion Métaphysique de la Personne chez Kant et Kierkegaard*. Fribourg (Suisse): St. Paul, 1942. 81p. Diss. Fribourg (Suisse) lettres.

2398. Brunner, Emil. "Das Grundproblem der Philosophie bei Kant und Kierkegaard. Vortrag vor der Kantgesellschaft in Utrecht, Dezember 1923." *Zwischen den Zeiten* 2 (1924): 31-46.

2399. Clive, Geoffrey H. "The Connection Between Ethics and Religion in Kant, Kierkegaard, and F. H. Bradley." Ph.D., Harvard Univ., 1953.

2400. Evans, Charles Stephen. "Subjective Justifications of Religious Belief. A Comparative Study of Kant, Kierkegaard, and James." Ph.D., Yale Univ., 1974, 285p. *Dissertation Abstracts* 35 (1975):4611A.

2401. Gill, Jerry H. "Kant, Kierkegaard, and religious knowledge." *Philosophy and Phenomenological Research* 28 (1967):188-204.

2402. Peck, William Dayton. "On Autonomy: The Primacy of the Subject in Kant and Kierkegaard." Ph.D., Yale Univ., 1974, 297p. *Dissertation Abstracts* 35 (1974): 3063A.

2403. Schrader, George A. "Kant and Kierkegaard on duty and inclination." *Journal of Philosophy* 55 (1968):688-701.

2404. Tielsch, E. "Kierkegaards Ethik im Verhältnis zur 'klassischen' Ethik, insbesondere der Kants." In *Festschrift H. J. de Vleeschauwer*. (Communications of the Univ. of South Africa.) Pretoria: Publications Committee of the Univ. of South Africa, 1960 (232p.), 131-149.

Keats

2405. Ruotolo, L. "Keats and Kierkegaard: The tragedy of two worlds." *Renascence* 16 (1964):175-190.

2406. Will, Frederick. "A confrontation of Kierkegaard and Keats." *The Personalist* 43 (1962):338-351.

Kierkegaard, Henrietta

2407. Thompson, Josiah. "Sören Kierkegaard and his sister-in-law Henrietta Kierkegaard." *Fund og Forskning* 12 (1965): 101-120.

Kleist

2408. Kahn, L. W. "Goethes Iphigenie, Kleists Amphitryon und S. Kierkegaard." *Monatshefte für Deutschen Unterricht* (Madison, Wisconsin) 39 (1947).

2409. Kim, J.-J. "Kierkegaard et Kleist, poètes tragiques." *La Table Ronde* (1955):82-85.

2410. Sokel, Walter H. "Kleist's Marquise of O, Kierkegaard's Abraham, and Musil's Tonka: Three stages of the absurd as the touchstone of faith." *Wisconsin Studies in Contemporary Literature* 8 (1967):505-516.

Lagarde

2411. Rolffs, E. "Kierkegaard und de Lagarde, zwei religiöse Kritiker der Volkskirche. Zu Lagardes 50. Todestag (22. Dez.)." *Zeitschrift für Systematische Theologie* 18 (1941):384-403.

Laing, Ronald

2412. Sugerman, S. "Sin and madness; a study of the self in Sören Kierkegaard and Ronald Laing." *The Drew Gateway* 41 (1970):48-49.

Larsen, K. O.

2413. Jepsen, Holger. "En Kierkegaard parafrase." *Dansk Udsyn* 48 (1968):370-384. [About K. Olesen Larsen's interpretation.]

Lavelle, Louis

2414. Delfgaauw, Bernard. *Het Spiritualistische Existen-tialisme van Louis Lavelle*. Amsterdam: Proefschr (Noord-Hollandsche Uitgevers), 1947. 137p.

Leibniz

2415. Grimsley, Ronald. "Kierkegaard and Leibniz." *Journal of the History of Ideas* 26 (1965):383-396.

2416. Nedergaard-Hansen, Leif. *Bayle's og Leibniz' Dröf-telse af Theodicé-Problemet. En Idéhistorisk Redegörelse.* Med nogle traek af denne debats avspejling i dansk filo-soferen fra Holberg til Kierkegaard. Avec un résumé français [Le problème de la théodicée traité par Bayle et Leibniz]. I. del: Bayle. II. del: Leibniz. Köbenhavn: Munksgaards Forlag, 1965, 482p. et 263p.

2417. Sorainen, Kalle. "Kierkegaard und Leibniz." *Ajatus* 17 (1953):177-186.

2418. Viallaneix, Nelly. "Kierkegaard, lecteur de Leibniz." *Critique* (Paris) 25 (1969):895-914.

Leopardi

2419. Giampiccoli, G. "Kierkegaard e Leopardi." *Gioventù Cristiana* no. 2-3 (1940).

Lessing

2420. Baerthold, A. *Lessing und die Objective Wahrheit, aus Sören Kierkegaards Schriften zusammengestellt.* Halle, 1877, vii-99p.

2421. Campbell, R. "Lessing's problem and Kierkegaard's answer." *Scottish Journal of Theology* 19 (1966):35-54.

2422. Colette, Jacques. "Kierkegaard et Lessing." *Revue des Sciences Philosophiques et Théologiques* 44 (1960): 2-39.

2423. Lunding, Erik. "Lessing und Kierkegaard." *Orbis Litterarum* 2 (1944):158-187.

2424. Requadt, P. "Lessing, Schlegel, Kierkegaard."
Neue Schweizer Rundschau 22 (N.F. 1) (1933):103-108.

Lichtenberg

2425. Oksenhalt, Svein. "Kierkegaard's Lichtenberg: A
Reconsideration." *Proceedings of the Pacific Northwest
Conference on Foreign Languages* 16 (1965):50-56.

Lindhardt

2426. Thaning, Kay. "Lindhardts bog om Grundtvig og
Kierkegaard." *Praesteforeningens Blad* 65 (1975):641-648,
657-663.

Löwenhjelm, Harriet

2427. Arb, Siv. "Harriet Löwenhjelm och Sören Kierkegaard." *Ord och Bild* 49 (1960):491-503.

Lukács, George

2428. Hunsinger, G. "Marxist view of Kierkegaard; George
Lukács on the intellectual origins of fascism." *Union
Seminary Quarterly Review* 30 (1974):29-40.

Luther, Martin

2429. Bohlin, Torsten. "Luther, Kierkegaard und die dia-
lektische Theologie I-III." Übers. von Anne Marie
Sundwall-Hoyer. *Zeitschrift für Theologie und Kirche*
N.F. 7 (1926):163-198; 268-279.

2430. Bragstad, William R. "Luther's influence on
Training in Christianity. Lutheran Quarterly (1976):
257-271.

2431. Brun, Jean. "Kierkegaard et Luther." *Revue Métaphysique et de Morale* 75 (1970):301-308.

2432. Congar, M. J. "Kierkegaard et Luther (Extrait de
la Vie intellectuelle du 25. Nov. 1934)." *Foi et Vie* 35
(1934):712-717.

2433. Geismar, Eduard. "Kierkegaard und Luther." *Zeitschrift für Pastoraltheologie* (Göttingen) 25 (1929):
227-241.

2434. Geismar, Eduard. "Wie urteilte Kierkegaard über
Luther?" *Jahrbuch d. Luther-Gesellschaft* (Luther-Jahrb.)
10 (1928):1-27.

2435. Hess, Mary W. "What Luther meant by faith alone."
Catholic World 199 (1964):96-101.

2436. Laporte, André. *Trois témoins de la Liberté: Erasme
de Rotterdam, Martin Luther, Soeren Kierkegaard.* Genève
1949, 128 + 4p. (dactylogr.) + 1 annexe: Théses et épithèses. (Thèse bach. theol.).

2437. Lögstrup, K. E. "Die Kategorie und das Amt der
Verkündigung im Hinblick auf Luther und Kierkegaard."
Evangelische Theologie 9 (1949-50):249-269.

2438. Mortensen, Viggo. "Luther og Kierkegaard." In
Kierkegaardiana 9 (1974):163-165.

2439. Planck, Reinhold. "Von Luther zu Kierkegaard. Ein
von der Zensur verbotener Artikel." *Die Christliche Welt*
33 (1919):164-169.

2440. Reuter, Hans. "Kierkegaard und Luther." *Die Stud-
ierestube* (Langensalza) 16 (1918):442-451.

2441. Schükler, G. "Kierkegaards Stellung zu Luther und
zur Kirche." *Neue Ordnung* (Köln) 5 (1951):429-438.

Mailer, Norman

2442. Schrader, George A. "Norman Mailer and the despair
of defiance." *Yale Review* 51 (1961):267-280.

Malantschuk, Gregor

2443. Dewey, B. R. "Gregor Malantschuk, Kierkegaard's
serving interpreter." *Religion in Life* 40 (1971):74-84.

Mann, Thomas

2444. Lewalter, Chr., and Paeschke, Hans. "Thomas Mann
und Kierkegaard." *Merkur* 3 (1949):925-936.

2445. Paci, Enzo. *Relazioni e Significati, II: Kierkegaard e Thomas Mann* (Saggi, 2). Milano: Lampugnani Nigri,
1965. 341p.

2446. Rehder, Helmut. "Thomas Mann--and Kierkegaard?
Some reflections on irony and a letter." In *Saga og Sprak:
Studies in Language and Literature.* John M. Weinstock, ed.
Austin (Texas): Pemberton Press, 1972, 291-300.

Marcel, Gabriel

2447. Marcel, Gabriel. "Points d'interrogation."
La Table Ronde (1955):76-78.

Maritain, Jacques

2448. Maritain, Jacques. "Le champion du singulier
(Fragment d'un essai sur Kierkegaard)." *Recherches et
Débats* cahier n. 19 (1957).

2449. Maritain, Jacques. In *Court Traité de l'Existence
et de l'Existante.* Paris: Hartmann, 1947. [S. Kierke-
gaard]

Marcuse, Herbert

2450. Marcuse, Herbert. "Kierkegaard." In *Reason and
Revolution. Hegel and the Rise of Social Theory.* London
New York and Toronto: Oxford Univ. Press, [1941], 262-267.

Martensen

2451. B. [Pseud.]. Martensen und Kierkegaard." *Nordisches
Telegraph* 2 (1850):1095-1096.

Marx, Karl

2452. Allen, E. L. "Kierkegaard and Karl Marx." *Theology*
40 (1940):117-121.

2453. Arendt, Hannah. "Tradition and modern age."
Partisan Review 21 (1954):53-75.

2454. Arendt, Hannah. "Marx, Kierkegaard et Nietzsche."
Preuves (1962):14-29.

2455. Brechtken, Josef. "Wahrheit in Praxis. Ein Vergleich christlicher Existenzialogie mit der materialis-
tischen Ontologie der Praxis und die Frage nach der
konsequenz (Kierkegaard oder Marx)." *Tijdschrift voor
Filosofie* 37 (1975):391-419.

2456. Bukdahl, Jörgen K. "Kierkegaard mellem ideologi og
Utopi II: Problemer og perspektiver i de senere ars
Marxistisk inspirerede Kierkegaard-loesning." *Dansk
Teologisk Tidsskrift* 40 (1977):31-56.

2457. Fackre, Gabriel Joseph. "Comparison and Critique
of the Interpretations of Dehumanization in the Thought
of Sören Kierkegaard and Karl Marx." Ph.D., Univ. of
Chicago, 1962.

2458. Fabro, Cornelio. *Tra Kierkegaard et Marx*. Firenze:
Vallecchi, 1952. 242p.

2459. Fabro, Cornelio. "Kierkegaard e Marx." Atti del
Congresso Internazionale di Filosofia, promosso dall'Isti-
tuto di Studi Filosofici. Vol. I: *Il Materialismo Storico*.
Milano: Castellani, 1947, 3-16.

2460. Fabro, Cornelio. "Kierkegaard y Marx. Versión del
italiano por Alma Novella Marani." *Sapientia* (La Plata)
7 (1952):257-267.

2461. Forrester, D. B. "The attack on Christendom in Marx
and Kierkegaard." *Scottish Journal of Theology* (London)
25 (1972):181-196.

2462. Frandsen, Hans E. A. *Historieproblemet hos Kierkegaard og den unge Marx*. (Poetik 26). Roskilde: Universitetsforlag, 1976. 90p.

2463. Gristaldi, Mario. "Materialismo storico ed esistenzialismo: Kierkegaard e Marx." *Humanitas* 4 (1949):
1043-1046.

2464. Hansen, Olaf. "The Problem of Alienation and Reconciliation. A Comparative Study of Marx and Kierkegaard in
the Light of Hegel's Formulation of the Problem." Ph.D.,
Princeton Theological Seminary, 1956, 449p. *Dissertation
Abstracts* 35 (1975):4680A.

2465. Jaspers, Karl. "The importance of Nietzsche, Marx
and Kierkegaard in the history of philosophy." Trans. by
Stanley Godman. *Hibbert Journal* 49 (1950-51):226-234.

2466. Lapassade, Georges. "Le deuil de la philosophie:
Kierkegaard et Marx." *Études Philosophiques* 18 (1963):
333-341.

2467. Leconte, Henry. "A la recherche d'un Anti-Marx."
Masses no. 8 (1933).

2468. Leisegang, Hans. "Hegel, Marx, Kierkegaard. Zum
dialektischen Materialismus und zur dialektischen Theologie." *Blick in die Wissenschaft* 1 (1948):128-138.

2469. Löwith, Karl. "L'achèvement de la philosophie
classique par Hegel et sa dissolution chez Marx et Kierkegaard." *Recherches Philosophiques* 4 (1934-35):232-267.

2470. Löwith, Karl. *Von Hegel zu Nietzsche. Der Revolutionäre Bruch im Denken d. 19. Jahrhundert. Marx und
Kierkegaard.* 4 Aufl. Stuttgart: Kohlhammer, 1958. 464p.

2471. Nenning, Günther. "Sören Kierkegaard und Karl
Marx." *Neue Zeit* (Graz) (6.11.1955).

2472. Rohrmoser, G. "Kie Religionskritik von Karl Marx
im Blickpunkt der Hegelschen Religionsphilosophie."
Neue Zeitschrift für Systematische Theologie 2 (1960):
44-64.

2473. Thieme, Karl. "Durch Kierkegaard zu Karl Marx."
Zeitschrift für Religion und Sozialismus (Karlsruhe)
1 (1929):27-33.

2474. Van der Hoeven, J. "Kierkegaard en Marx als
dialectische critici van Hegel, I-III." *Philosophie
Reformata* 34 (1969):85-100; 35 (1970):101-118; 36 (1971):
125-154. [Summary in English, 36:150-154.]

Melville, Herman

2475. Anderson, Betty C. "The Melville-Kierkegaard
syndrome." *Rendezvous* 3 (1968):41-53.

2476. Bowen, James K. "'Crazy Arab' and Kierkegaard's 'melancholy fantastic'." *Research Studies* (Washington State University) 37 (1969):60-64. [Kierkegaard and Melville]

2477. Ishag, Saada. "Herman Melville as Existentialist: An analysis of *Typee, Mardi, Moby Dick*, and *The Confidence Man*." *Emporia State Research Studies* 14 (1965):5-41, 60-62.

Molière

2478. Grimsely, Ronald. "The Don Juan theme in Molière and Kierkegaard." *Comparative Literature* 6 (1954):316-334.

Möller, Poul Martin

2479. Henningsen, B. *Poul Martin Möller oder die dänische Erziehung des Sören Kierkegaard*. Eine krit. Monographie mit e. ersten Übers. seiner Abhandlung über d. *Affectation*. Frankfurt am Main: Akademisch Verlagsgesellschaft, 1973. 134p.

2480. Jones, W. Glyn. "Sören Kierkegaard and Poul Martin Möller." *Modern Language Review* 60 (1965):73-82.

2481. Sinding, Vilhelm. "Note biographique sur un héros de Kierkegaard: Le modele du Séducteur [P. L. Möller]." *Revue de Métaphysique et de Morale* 74 (1969):106-115.

2482. Vergotte, Henri-Bernard. "Poul Martin Moeller et Soeren Kierkegaard." *Revue de Métaphysique et de Morale* 75 (1970):452-476.

Mozart, Wolfgang A. (See also Don Juan)

2483. Anonymous. "Ein Mozart-Evangelist [S. Kierkegaard]." *Hamburger Nachrichten* (26.1.1906).

2484. Börge, Vagn. *Kierkegaard und das Theater, mit besonderer Rücksicht auf Mozarts* Don Juan. Wien: Hans Riel (provisorische Ausgabe), 1947. (Die Kunst des Theaters und des Films, Theater- und Filmwissenschaftliche Schriftenreihe, Folge 8.)

2485. Clive, Geoffrey. "The demonic in Mozart." *Music and Letters* 37 (1956):1-13.

2486.   Croxall, Thomas H.   "Kierkegaard and Mozart."
Music and Letters 26 (1945):151-158.

2487.   Erhardt, Otto.   "Don Juan, Mozart and Kierkegaard."
Die Scene 7 (1917):97-101.

2488.   Fabro, Cornelio.   "Estetica mozartiana nell'opera
di Kierkegaard."   In *Atti III Congress Internationale
Estetica*.   Torino: Istituto di Estetica di Torino, 1957,
706-710.

2489.   Fenger, Henning.   "Prise de conscience esthétique
de Kierkegaard: *Don Juan*."   *Orbis Litterarum* 27 (1972):
224-228.   [Mozart]

2490.   Hamilton, William.   Daring to be the enemy of God:
Some reflections on the life and death of Mozart's Don
Giovanni."   *Christian Scholar* 46 (1963):40-54.

2491.   Schutz, Alfred.   "Mozart and the philosophers."
Social Research 23 (1956):219-242.

2492.   Turner, W. J.   "Kierkegaard, la musica y Mozart."
Asomante (San Juan) 1 (1945).

2493.   Wutzky, Anna-Charlotte.   "Sören Kierkegaard und
Mozart.   Zum 75. Todestag Sören Kierkegaards am 11. November 1930."   *Zeitschrift für Musik* (Regensburg) 97 (1930):
913-917.

Musil, Robert

2494.   Sokel, W. H.   "Kleist's Marquise of O, Kierkegaard's
Abraham, and Musil's Tonka: Three stages of the absurd as
the touchstone of faith."   *Wisconsin Studies in Contemporary
Literature* 8 (1967):505-516.   Reprinted in *Robert Musil:
Studien zu seinem Werk*.   Karl Dinklage et al., eds.
Hamburg: Rowohlt, 1970, 57-70.

Musset, Alfred de

2495.   Tisseau, Paul-Henri.   "La 'Confession' de Musset et
le 'Banquet' de Kierkegaard."   *Revue de Littérature
Comparée* 14 (1934):491-511.

Nero

2496. Grimsley, Ronald. "Hugo, Kierkegaard and the character of Nero." *Revue de Littérature Comparée* 32 (1958):230-236.

Newman

2497. Becker, W. "Der Überschritt von Kierkegaard zu Newman in der Lebensentscheidung Theodor Haeckers." *Newman-Studien* (Nürnberg) 1 (1948):251-270.

2498. Brechtken, Josef. *Kierkegaard, Newman. Wahrheit und Existenzmitteilung* (Monographien zur philosophischen Forschung, 66). Meisenheim a. Glan: Hain, 1970. 234p.

2499. Fabro, Cornelio. "Le problème de l'église chez Newman et Kierkegaard." *Revue Thomiste* 77 (1977):30-90.

2500. Hammel, W. "Die 'natürliche Religion' bei Newman und die 'Religiosität A' bei Kierkegaard." In *Newman Studien*. Hrsg. von H. Fries und W. Becker (Veröffentlichungen des Cardinal Newman Kuratoriums). 2. Folge. Nürnberg: Glock und Lutz, 1954. 389p.

2501. Przywara, Erich. "Kierkegaard-Newman." *Newman Studien* 1 (1948):77-101.

Nielsen, Rasmus

2502. Asmussen, Eduard. "Sören Kierkegaard und Rasmus Nielsen." In *Entwicklungsgang und Grundprobleme der Philosophie Rasmus Nielsens*. Flensburg, 1911 (107p.), 16-25. Phil. Diss. Erlangen.

Nietzsche, Friedrich

2503. Assaad-Mikhail, Fawzia. "Nietzsche et Kierkegaard. Des possibilités d'une interprétation nietzschéenne de Kierkegaard (Dialogue des morts-vivants)." *Revue de Métaphysique et de Morale* 71 (1966):463-482.

2504. Assaad-Mikhail, Fawzia. "Nietzsche et Kierkegaard." *Revue de Métaphysique et de Morale* 72 (1967):463-482.

2505. Assaad-Mikahil, Fawzia. "Mort de l'homme et subjectivité [Kierkegaard, Nietzsche]." *Revue de Métaphysique
et de Morale* 73 (1968):430-461.

2506. Assaad-Mikhail, Fawzia. "Kierkegaard interprète de
Nietzsche." *Revue de Métaphysique et de Morale* 78 (1973):
45-87.

2507. Balthasar, Hans Urs von. "Kierkegaard und Nietzsche."
In *Prometheus. Studien zur Geschichte des deutschen
Idealismus* (1937; m. titel: *Der deutsche Idealismus*).
2. unveränderte Aufl., Heidelberg: F. H. Kerle, 1947,
695-734 (Die Apocalypse der deutschen Seele).

2508. Balthasar, Hans Urs von. "Kierkegaard et Nietzsche."
(Trad. par Meurice de Gandillac.) *Dieu Vivant* 1 (1945):
53-80.

2509. Bense, Max. "Die Idee des Naturerkenntnis bei
Nietzsche und Kierkegaard." *Unsere Welt* 29 (1937):33-36.

2510. Beyer, Harald. "Nietzsche og Kierkegaard." *Edda*
42 (1955):161-172.

2511. Bonifazi, Conrad. *Christendom Attacked. A Comparison of Kierkegaard and Nietzsche.* London: Rockliffe,
1953. 190p.

2512. Brock, Werner. *An Introduction to Contemporary
German Philosophy* [S. Kierkegaard and Nietzsche].
Cambridge: Cambridge Univ. Press, 1935, 46-87 and passim.

2513. Clair, André. "Enigme nietzschéenne et paradoxe
kierkegaardien." *Revue de Théologie et de Philosophie*
(1977):196-221.

2514. Earle, William A. "The paradox and death of God:
Kierkegaard and Nietzsche." In *Radical Theology: Phase
Two.* C. W. Christian and G. R. Wittig, eds. Lippincott,
1967, 27-42.

2515. Gottlieb, Roger S. "The Existing Individual and the
'Will-to-Power'. A Comparison of Kierkegaard's and
Nietzsche's Answers to the Question, What Is It to Make
a Transition from One Value System to Another?" Ph.D.,
Brandeis Univ., 1975, 365p. *Dissertation Abstracts* 36
(1975):2894A.

2516. Grau, Gerd Günther. "Nietzsche und Kierkegaard:
Wiederholung einer Unzeitgemässen Betrachtung." *Nietzsche-
Studien* 1 (1972):297-333.

2517. Griesemann, Otto A. "Nietzsche und Kierkegaard,
Seher unserer Zeit." *Der Convent.* Akadem. Monatsschrift
2 (Mannheim-Sandhofen) (1951):252-254.

2518. Hanna, Thomas L. "The Lyrical Existentialists: The
Common Voice of Kierkegaard, Nietzsche, and Camus." Ph.D.,
Univ. of Chicago, 1960.

2519. Hargreaves, H. J. "Nietzsche e Kierkegaard."
Kriterion (Bello Horizonte, Brasil) 7-8 (1949):193-201.

2520. Jaspers, Karl. "Kierkegaard und Nietzsche: Leiden
oder Lust als letztes." In Psychologie der Weltanschauungen. Berlin: Jul Springer, 1919 (xii-428p.), 225-226.
2. durchgeseh. Aufl., ibid., 1922 (xiii-486p.), 255-256.
4. univeränd. Aufl., ibid., 1954.

2521. Knodt, K. E. "Kierkegaard und Nietzsche." Monatsblätter für Deutsche Litteratur (Leipzig) (1897).

2522. Kraus, A. "Nietzsches und Kierkegaards Auffassung
vom Wesen der Musik." Nederlandsch Tijdschrift voor
Psychologie (Amsterdam) 8 (1940):265-274.

2523. Leendertz, J. W. "Kierkegaard, Schopenhauer,
Nietzsche en de existentie-philosophie." In Philosophia.
Onder redactie van Prof. Dr. H. van Oyen. Tweede deel:
Descartes-Hedendaagsche Wisjbegeerte. Utrecht: De Haan,
1949, 337-378.

2524. Löwith, Karl. Kierkegaard und Nietzsche, oder
philosophische und theologische Überwindung des Nihilismus.
Frankfurt am Main: Klostermann, 1933. 32p.

2525. Löwith, Karl. "Kierkegaard und Nietzsche." Deutsche
Vierteljahrsschrift für Literaturwissenschaft und Geistesgeschichte 11 (1933):43-66.

2526. Lubac, Henri de. "Nietzsche et Kierkegaard." In
Le Drame de l'Humanisme Athée. [1944]. 3d ed., revue et
augmentée. Paris: Éd. Spes, 1945, 71-113.

2527. Lund, Margaret. "The single ones [Kierkegaard et
Nietzsche]." The Personalist 41 (1960):15-24.

2528. Malantschuk, Gregor. "Kierkegaard og Nietzsche."
Det Danske Magasin 3 (1955):381-395.

2529. Marchesi, Angelo. "Due scelte di fronte a Cristo:
Kierkegaard et Nietzsche." In Il Cristo dei Filosofi.
Atti del XXX Convegno di Gallarate, 1975. Brescia:
Morcelliana, 1976, 149-166.

2530. Miéville, Henri-L. "Kierkegaard et Nietzsche:
Pères de l'existentialisme contemporain." Études de
Lettres (Lausanne) 8 (1965):79-90.

2531. Przywara, Erich. "Zwischen Nietzsche und Kierkegaard." In *Humanitas*. Der Mensch gestern und morgen.
Nürnberg: Glock and Lutz, 1952, 15-44.

2532. Rappoport, Angelo S. "Ibsen, Nietzsche, and Kierkegaard." *New Age* 3 (1908):21-22, 408-409, 426-429.

2533. Rohrmoser, Günter. *Nietzsche und das Ende der
Emanzipation*. Freiburg: Rombach, 1970. 156p.

2534. Rest, Walter. "Kierkegaard oder Nietzsche? Entscheidung an zwei geistigen Ecksteinen der Neuzeit."
Deutsche Universitätszeitung (Göttingen) 5 (1950):6-8.

2535. Schrey, H. H. "Die Ueberwindung des Nihilismus bei
Kierkegaard und Nietzsche." *Zeitschrift für Systematische
Theologie* 21 (1950):50-68.

2536. Sodeur, Gottlieb. *Kierkegaard und Nietzsche. Versuch einer vergleichender Würdigung*. Tübingen: Mohr and
Siebeck, 1914. 48p. (Religionsgeschichliche Volksbücher
für die deutsche christliche Gegenwart, 5. Reihe, 14. Heft.)

2537. Springer, J. L. "Kierkegaard en Nietzsche."
Het Drama der Wereldgeschiedenis. L. J. Rogier, ed.
Haarlem, 1951.

2538. Steffensen, Steffen. "Kierkegaard, Nietzsche und
der Nihilismus." *Ausblick* 26 (1976):38-40.

2539. Steffensen, Steffen. "Kierkegaard, Nietzsche og
nihilismen." In *Humanitet og Eksistens*. Bent Hahn et al.,
eds. Copenhagen: Gyldendal, 1976, 9-15.

2540. Struve, Wolfgang. "Die neuzeitliche Philosophie
als Metaphysik der Subjektivität. Interpretationen zu
Kierkegaard und Nietzsche." *Symposion* 1 (1948):207-335.

2541. Wenzel, Fritz. "Sören Kierkegaard und Friedrich
Nietzsche." *Zeitwende* (München) 14 (1937-38):526-536.

2542. Van Raemdonck, Ivon. "Kierkegaard en Nietzsche."
Dialoog 6 (1965-66):214-231.

Nieuwenhuis, Jacob

2543. Delfgaauw, B. "Jacob Nieuwenhuis en het Deense
denken ten tijde van Kierkegaard."

Norway

2544. Flottorp, Haakon. "Kierkegaard and Norway. A Study of 'Inwardness' in History with Illustrative Examples from Religion, Literature, and Philosophy." Ph.D. *Dissertation Abstracts* 15 (1955):890.

Ockham

2545. Klocker, Harry R. "From rationalism to faith: Ockham and Kierkegaard." *Modern Schoolman* 55 (1977):57-70.

Olsen, Regina

2546. Anonymous. "Sören Kierkegaards Verlöbnisbruch." *Der Bund* (Bern) 105, Sonntagsblatt no. 18.

2547. Fabro, Cornelio. "Why did Kierkegaard break up with Regina?" *Orbis Litterarum* 22 (1967):387-392.

2548. Heine, Anselm [Selma H.]. "Soeren Kierkegaard und Regine Olsen." *Die Nation* 22 (1904-05):557-559.

2549. Hejll, Richard. "Varfor brot Kierkegaard sin forlovning? [Why did Kierkegaard break off his engagement?]" *Den Enskilde* 12 (1956):25-31; 13 (1957):1-8.

2550. Jarlov, Genevieve. "Qui fut Kierkegaard? Les dramatiques fiançialles d. un philosophe." *Figaro Litteraire* (12.11.1955).

2551. Lukács, Georg von. "Das Zerschellen der Form am Leben: Sören Kierkegaard und Regine Olsen (dat. 1909)." In *Die Seele und die Formen*. Essays. Berlin: Fleischel, 1911 (373p.), 61-90.

2552. Lukács, Georg von. "The foundering of form against life. Sören Kierkegaard and Regine Olsen." In his *Soul and Form*. Trans. Anna Bostick. The MIT Press, 1971, 28-41.

2553. Sur, François. "Regine ou 'le precepte royal'." *La Table Ronde* (1963):15-29.

2554. Widmann, J. V. "Sören Kierkegaards Verlöbnisbruch." *Neue Freie Presse* (Wien) (1904):580.

2555. Wien, Alfred. "Sören Kierkegaard und Regine Olsen.
Zur 100. Wiederkehr von Kierkegaards Geburtstag am 5. Mai
1913." *Eckart* 7 (1912):445-456.

2556. Wien, Alfred. "Sören Kierkegaard und Regine Olsen."
Deutsche Zeitung, Unterh.-Beil. no. 472, 478 (1921).

Ortega y Gasset, José

2557. Weiss, Robert O. "The levelling process as a
function of the masses in the view of Kierkegaard and
Ortega y Gasset." *Kentucky Foreign Language Quarterly*
7 (1960):27-36.

Pascal, Blaise

2558. Allen, E. L. "Pascal and Kierkegaard." *London
Quarterly and Holborn Review* 162 (1937):150-164.

2559. Basave Fernandez del Valle, Agustin. "Pascal y
Kierkegaard." *Revista de Filosofía Mexicano* 6 (1973):
259-266.

2560. Bense, Max. "Pascal und Kierkegaard." *Europäische
Revue* 18 (1942):88-92.

2561. Bense, Max. "Pascal en Kierkegaard." *Nederlandsch
Tijdschrift voor Psychologie* 2 (1943-44):58-66.

2562. Brunschvieg, León. *Pascal: Oeuvres*. Paris, 1904-14,
XII, p. 100 ff., not. I.

2563. Dallago, Carl. "Augustinus, Pascal und Kierkegaard."
Der Brenner 6 (1921):642-734.

2564. Fabre, J. "Réflexions actuelles sur l'angoisse de
Pascal." *Revue Historique* 28/29 (1948-49):265-281.

2565. Fuglsang-Damgaard, H. "Pascal et Kierkegaard."
Revue d'Histoire et de Philosophie Religieuses 10 (1930):
242-263 (Conférence).

2566. Höffding, Harald. "Pascal et Kierkegaard." *Revue
de Métaphysique et de Morale* 30 (1923):221-246.

2567. Jolivet, Régis. "Pascal y Kierkegaard: Dos 'vidas
paralelas'." (Trad. José Oroz). *Augustinus* 7 (1962):
361-370.

2568. Lloyd Thomas, J. M. "Pascal und Kierkegaard."
Hibbert Journal 47 (1948):36-40.

2569. Molenaar, P. J. "Pascal en Kierkegaard." *Stemmen
des Tijds* 20 (1931):580-594.

2570. Müller, C. "Vom Gewissen bei Pascal und Kierkegaard." *Evangelische Theologie* 15 (1955):115-128.

2571. Patrick, Denzil G. M. *Pascal and Kierkegaard. A
Study in the Strategy of Evangelism*. I-II. London:
Lutterworth, 1947, xvi-234p., xvii-413p. (Lutterworth
Library, 23, 24).

2572. Pignagnoli, Sante. "Pascal e Kierkegaard. Alcuni
aspetti attraverso e citazioni pascaliane del *Diario*."
Convivium 30 (1962):542-554.

Penington, Isaac

2573. Hess, Mary W. "Kierkegaard and Isaac Penington."
Catholic World 162 (1946):434-437.

Percy, Walker

2574. Dewey, Bradley R. "Walker Percy talks about Kierkegaard: An annotated interview." *Journal of Religion*
54 (1974):273-298.

2575. Lawson, Lewis A. "Walker Percy's indirect communications." *Texas Studies in Literature and Language* 11
(1969):867-900.

2576. Maxwell, Robert. "Walker Percy's fancy." *Minnesota
Review* 7 (1967):3-4, 231-237.

2577. Taylor, L. J. "Walker Percy's knights of the
hidden inwardness." *Anglican Theological Review* 56 (1974):
125-151.

Picasso, Pablo

2578. Sedlmayr, Hans. "Kierkegaard über Picasso." *Wort
und Wahrheit* 5 (1950):356-370.

Plato

2579.   Cooper, R. M.   "Plato and Kierkegaard in dialogue."
Theology Today 31 (1974):187-198.

2580.   D'Agostino, Francesco.   "La fenomenologia dell'uomo
giusto: Un parallelo tra Kierkegaard e Platone." *Rivista
Internazionale di Filosofia del Diritto* 49 (1972):153-172.

2581.   Johansen, Karsten F.   "Platon og Kierkegaard."
Studenterkredsen (Copenhagen) 36 (1968):10-15.

Proudhon

2582.   Blum, Jean.   "Pierre-Joseph Proudhon et Sören
Kierkegaard."   *La Revue Scandinave* 2 (1910-11):276-287.

Proust, Marcel

2583.   Rof Carballo, Juan.   "El problema del seductor en
Kierkegaard, Prouse y Rilke."   *Cuadernos Hispanoamericanos*
35 (1958):5-30.

Ravaisson

2584.   Laruelle, François.   *Phénomène et Différence. Essai
sur l'Ontologie de Ravaisson.*   (Publications de l'Université
de Paris, X.   Lettres et Sciences Humaines.   Série A.
Thèses et Travaux, 11).   Paris: Klincksieck, 1971.   268p.

Renouvier, Charles

2585.   Hansen, Valdemar.   "L'idée de la liberté chez
Kierkegaard et Renouvier."   In *Proceedings of the Tenth
International Congress of Philosophy,* 1948.   Amsterdam:
North-Holland, 1949, 1191-1194.

Rilke, Rainer-Maria

2586.   Cardinal, Clive H.   "Rilke and Kierkegaard: Some relationships between poet and theologian." *Bulletin of the Rocky Mountain Modern Language Association* 23 (1969):34-49.

2587. Kohlschmidt, Werner. "Rilke und Kierkegaard." *Zeitschrift für Kirchengeschichte* 63 (1950-51):189-197. Reprinted in his *Die entzweite Welt. Studien zum Menschenbild in der neueren Dichtung.* Gladbeck: Frezeihen Verlag, 1953, 88-97.

2588.   Jancke, Rudolf. "Rilke-Kierkegaard." *Dichtung und Volkstum* N.F. des Euphorion 39 (1938):314-329.

2589.   Rof Carballo, Juan. "El problema del seductor en Kierkegaard, Prouse y Rilke." *Cuadernos Hispanoamericanos* 35 (1958):5-30.

Rolvaag

2590.   Simonson, Harold P.   "Rolvaag and Kierkegaard." *Scandinavian Studies* 49 (1977):67-80.

Rousseau, Jean-Jacques

2591.   Grimsley, Ronald.   "Rousseau and Kierkegaard." *Cambridge Journal* 7 (1954):615-626.

Rousselot, Pierre

2592.   Harper, Ralph.   "Two existential interpretations [S. Kierkegaard and Pierre Rousselot]." *Philosophy and Phenomenological Research* 5 (1945):392-400.

Rosenzweig, Franz

2593.   Oppenheim, Michael.   "Sören Kierkegaard and Franz Rosenzweig: The Movement from Philosophy to Religion." Ph.D., Univ. of California, Santa Barbara, 1976, 384p. *Dissertation Abstracts* 37 (1977):5898A.

Salinger

2594. Wiegand, William. "Salinger and Kierkegaard."
Minnesota Review 5 (1965):137-156.

Santayana, George

2595. Comstock, W. Richard. "Aspects of aesthetic existence: Kierkegaard and Santayana." *International Philosophical Quarterly* 6 (1966):189-213.

Sartre, Jean-Paul

2596. Bernstein, Richard J. "Consciousness, existence,
and action: Kierkegaard and Sartre." In *Praxis and Action:
Contemporary Philosophies of Human Activity*. Philadelphia:
Univ. of Pennsylvania Press, 1971, 84-164.

2597. Cortese, Alessandro. "Kierkegaard-Sartre: Appunti
di metodologia." *Filosofia e Vita* 6 (1965):31-49.

2598. Cumming, Robert. "Existence and communication."
Ethics 65 (1954-55):79-101.

2599. Curtis, J. L. "Heroic commitment, or the dialectics
of the leap in Kierkegaard, Sartre, and Camus." *Rice
University Studies* (Houston, Texas) 59 (1973):17-26.

2600. Flam, Leopold. "Sartre tussen Kierkegaard en Marx."
Tijdschrift van de Vrije Universiteit van Brussel 4
(1961-62):1-29.

2601. Flanner, Janet (Genet). "Letter from Paris."
New Yorker 17 April (1965):183-184. [Concerning Sartre's
reading of Kierkegaard.]

2602. Grooten, Johan. "Le soi chez Kierkegaard et Sartre."
Revue Philosophique de Louvain 50 (1952):64-89.

2603. Hohlenberg, Johannes. "Jean-Paul Sartre og has
forhold til Kierkegaard." *Samtiden* 56 (1947):310-322.

2604. Johnson, Howard A. "On Sartre and Kierkegaard."
American-Scandinavian Review 35 (1947):220-225.

2605. Johnson, Howard A. "Kierkegaard and Sartre."
Adam International Review 16 (1948):23-24.

2606. Larson, Curtis W. R. "Kierkegaard and Sartre."
The Personalist 35 (1954):128-136.

2607. Lögstrup, K. E. "Sartres og Kierkegaards skildring
af den daemoniske indesluttethed." *Vindrosen* 13 (1966):
28-42.

2608. Lowrie, Walter. "Existence as understood by Kierkegaard and/or Sartre." *Sewanee Review* 58 (1950):379-401.

2609. Prenter, R. "Sartre's conception of freedom considered in the light of Kierkegaard's thought." In
A *Kierkegaard Critique.* H. A. Johnson and N. Thulstrup,
eds. New York: Harper, 1962, 130-142.

2610. Prenter, R. "The concept of freedom in Sartre
against a Kierkegaardian background." Trans. by H. Kaasa.
Dialog 7 (1968):132-137.

2611. Roberts, D. E. "Faith and freedom in existentialism:
A study of Kierkegaard and Sartre." *Theology Today* 8
(1952):469-482.

2612. Soper, William Wayne. "The Self and Its World in
Ralph Barton Perry, Edgar Sheffield Brightman, Jean-Paul
Sartre, and Soeren Kierkegaard." Ph.D., Boston Univ.,
1962, 563p. *Dissertation Abstracts* 23 (1962):1042A.

Sastre, Alfonso

2613. Seator, Lynette. "Alfonso Sastre's 'Homenaje a
Kierkegaard', *La Sangre de Dios*." *Romance Notes* 15 (1974):
546-555.

Scheler, Max

2614. Rest, Walther. "Zwei formeln. Eine Interpretations-
studie zu Kierkegaard und Scheler." *Orbis Litterarum*
10 (1955):208-213. [Symposion Kierkegaardianum]

Schelling

2615. Dempf, Alois. "Kierkegaard hört Schelling."
Philosophisches Jahrbuch 65 (1956):147-161.

2616. Koktanek, Anton Mirko. *Schellings Seinslehre und Kierkegaard*. Mit Erstausgabe der Nachschriften zweier Schellingvorlesungen von G. M. Mittermair und Sören Kierkegaard. Vorwort von Alois Dempf. München: Oldenbourg, 1962. 179p.

2617. Majoli, Bruno. "La critica ad Hegel in Schelling e Kierkegaard." *Rivista di Filosofia Neo-Scolastica* 46 (1954):222-263.

2618. Oliver, Richard L. "Schelling and Kierkegaard. Experimentations in Moral Autonomy." Ph.D., Univ. of Oklahoma, 1977, 184p. *Dissertation Abstracts* 28 (1977): 2175A.

2619. Rinaldi, Francisco. "Della presenza schellinghiana nella critica di Kierkegaard a Hegel." *Studi Urbinati* 43 (1969):243-262.

2620. Spera, S. "L'influsso di Schelling nella formazione del giovane Kierkegaard." *Archivio di Filosofia* (1976): 73-108. [Issue devoted to Schelling.]

2621. Struve, Wolfgang. "Kierkegaard und Schelling." *Orbis Litterarum* 10 (1955):252-258. [Symposion Kierkegaardianum]

2622. Theunissen, Michael. "Die Dialektik der Offenbarung. Zur Auseinandersetzung Schellings und Kierkegaards mit Religionsphilosophie Hegels." *Philosophisches Jahrbuch* 72 (1964-65):134-160.

Schiller, Friedrich

2623. Svendsen, Paulus. "Schiller, Welhaven, Kierkegaard." *Nerthus* 3 (1972):7-18.

Schleiermacher

2624. Gerdes, Hayo. *Der geschichtliche biblische Jesus oder den Christus der Philosophen*. Erwägungen zur Christologie Kierkegaards, Hegels und Schleiermachers. (Radicale Mitte, 5). 2. Aufl. Berlin: Verlag Die Spur, 1974. 230p.

2625. O'Connor, D. T. "Schleiermacher and Kierkegaard: The odd couple of modern theology." *Religion in Life* 41 (1972):8-17.

Schopenhauer

2626. Holm, Sören. "Schopenhauer und Kierkegaard."
Schopenhauer-Jahrbuch 43 (1962):5-14.

Schottlaender

2627. Himmelstrup, J. "Einige Gegenbemerkungen zu Schoot-
laenders Kritik." *Philosophischer Anzeiger* 4 (1929-30):
42-50.

Schrempf, Christoph

2628. Herzog, Johannes. "Sören Kierkegaard und Christoph
Schrempf." *Die Christliche Welt* 43 (1929):438-448.

Schweitzer, Albert

2629. Dodd, E. M. "Kierkegaard and Schweitzer: An essay
in comparison and contrast." *London Quarterly and Holborn
Review* 170 (1945):148-153.

Scribe

2630. Grimsley, Ronald. "Kierkegaard and Scribe."
Revue de Littérature Comparée 38 (1964):512-530.

Shakespeare, William (See also Hamlet)

2631. Oppel, Horst. "Shakespeare und Kierkegaard. Ein
Beitrag zur Geschichte der Hamlet-Deutung." *Shakespeare-
Jahrbuch* 76 (N.F. 17) (1940):112-136.

2632. Ruoff, James E. "Kierkegaard and Shakespeare."
Comparative Literature 20 (1968):343-354.

2633. Sobosan, Jeffrey G. "One hand clapping. . .: A
study of the paradoxical in [Shakespeare's] *Lear* and
Kierkegaard." *Laval Théologique et Philosophique* 30
(1974):47-53.

Socrates

2634. Arnim, H. "Sokrates und das Ideal persönlichen
Vollkommenheit." Mitteilungen des *Vereins der Freunde des
humanistischen Gymnasiums* 21 (1922):32-46.

2635. Hess, Mary W. "Kierkegaard and Socrates."
Christian Century 82 (1965):736-738.

2636. Himmelstrup, J. *Sören Kierkegaards Sokratesauffassung.* Mit einem Vorwort von Gerh. v Mutius. Neumünster i.
Holst: K. Wachholz, 1927. 274p. [See no. 2642]

2637. Levi, Albert W. "The idea of Socrates: The philosophic hero in the Nineteenth Century." *Journal of the
History of Ideas* 17 (1956):89-108.

2638. Mesnard, P. "La vérité transcendantale du Socrate
d'Aristophane [interprétation de Kierkegaard]." In
Mélanges de Philosophie Greique. Offerts a Mgr. Dies.
Paris: J. Vrin, 1956.

2639. Neumann, Frederick. *Über das Lachen und Studien über
den planonischen Sokrates.* The Hague: Martinus Nijhoff,
1971. 169p.

2640. Neumann, Harry. "Kierkegaard and Socrates on the
dignity of man." *The Personalist* 48 (1967):453-460.

2641. Rilliet, Jean. "Kierkegaard et Socrate." *Revue de
Théologie et de Philosophie* 31 (1943):114-120.

2642. Schottlaender, Rud. "Sören Kierkegaards Sokratesauffassung. Bemerkungen zu dem gleichbetitelten Buche von
J. Himmelstrup." *Philosophischer Anzeiger* 4 (1929-30):
27-41. [See no. 2636]

2643. Weiss, Raymond L. "Kierkegaard's 'return' to
Socrates." *New Scholasticism* 45 (1971):573-583.

Solger

2644. Alleman, Beda. "Solger und Kierkegaard." *Ironie
und Dichtung* (1957):83-98.

Sörensen, Villy

2645. Vergote, H. B. "Un lecteur danois de Kierkegaard: Villy Sörensen [suivi de] Villy Sörensen: *Introduction au Concept d'Angoisse de Kierkegaard*. Trad. par H. B. Vergote. *Études Philosophiques* (1971):461-476.

Spinoza, Benedict

2646. Congleton, Ann. "Spinoza, Kierkegaard, and the Eternal Particular." Ph.D., Yale Univ., 1962.

2647. Muska, Rudolph Charles. "Antithetical Religious Conceptions in Kierkegaard and Spinoza." Ph.D., Michigan State Univ., 1960, 173p. *Dissertation Abstracts* 21 (1961):3489.

Steffens

2648. Hultberg, Helge. "Steffens and Kierkegaard." In *Kierkegaardiana*. Niels Thulstrup, ed. 10 (1977):190-197.

Stendhal

2649. Anonymous. "Gefahrliche Kompromisse [S. Kierkegaard and Stendhal]." *Germania* (6.1.1910). Also in *Hochland* December (1909), Beilage. Also in *Frankfurter Zeitung* (21.1.1910).

2650. Barthelme, Brigit. "A view of Julien Sorel, the protagonist of *The Red and the Black* with reference to Sören Kierkegaard's *The Concept of Irony*." In *Kierkegaardiana*. Niels Thulstrup, ed. Copenhagen: C. A. Reitzels Boghandel, 10 (1977):246-252.

Stieglitz, Charlotte

2651. Westphahl, Ulrich. "Charlotte Stieglitz und Soren Kierkegaard." *Frankfurter Zeitung* 70 (1926):1-2.

Stirner

2652. Falkenfeld, Hellmuth. "Kierkegaard und Stirner."
Neue Badische Landeszeitung (Mannheim) Kunst. 25 (1922).

2653. Falkenfeld, Hellmuth. "Kierkegaard und Stirner."
Baden-Badener Bühnenblatt (Baden-Baden) 2 (1922):116.

Strindberg, August

2654. Bjarnason, Loftur L. "Categories of Sören Kierkegaard's Thought in the Life and Writings of August Strindberg." Ph.D., Stanford Univ. *Abstracts of Dissertations,
Stanford University* 26 (1950-51):144-146.

Styron, William

2655. Robb, Kenneth A. "William Styron's Don Juan."
Critique 8 (1965-66):34-46.

Swami Vivekananda

2656. Chari, C. T. K. "Sören Kierkegaard and Swami
Vivekananda. A study in religious dialectics."
I: *Vedanda Kesari* 39 (1952):67-71; II: *ibid.*, 107-110.

2657. Chari, C. T. K. "On the dialectic of Swami
Vivekenanda and Sören Kierkegaard." *Revue Internationale
de Philosophie* 10 (1956):315-331.

Tennyson, Alfred

2658. Collins, Joseph J. "Tennyson and Kierkegaard."
Victorian Poetry 11 (1973):345-350.

Thomas Aquinas

2659. Brien, Abbé. "De l'univers de S. Thomas à l'univers
de Kierkegaard." *Travaux et Documents* (Paris) 6 (1946):
47-48.

2660. Castellani, L. De Kierkegaard a Tomás de Aquino.
Buenos Aires: Éditorial Guadalupe, 1974. 264p.

2661. Charlesworth, Max. "Sir Thomas Aquinas and the
decline of the Kantian-Kierkegaardian philosophy of
religion." In Tommaso d'Aquino nel sur VII Centenario.
Congresso Internazionale, Roma-Napoli, 17-24 Aprile 1974.
Roma, 1974. 530p.

2662. Fabro, Cornelio. "Kierkegaard e S. Tommaso."
Sapienza 9 (1956):4-5, 292-308.

2663. Goulet, Denis A. "Kierkegaard, Aquinas, and the
dilemma of Abraham." Thought 32 (1957):165-188.
[Interpretation of Genesit, Chapter 22.]

2664. McInerny, Ralph. "Connection seen in ethics of
Kierkegaard and Aquinas." Christian Messenger 82 (1964):4.

2665. Milano, Andrea. "Il divenire de Dio [Hegel, Kierkegaard e S. Tommaso d'Aquino]." In San Tommaso e il
Pensiero Moderno. Saggi. Roma: Pontificia Accademicia
di San Tommaso d'Aquino; Citta: Nuova Editrice, 1974,
284-294.

2666. Sen, Krishna. "A comparative study of the concept
of faith of Stace, Dewey, Kierkegaard, and St. Thomas
Aquinas." Philosophical Quarterly 29 (1956-57):69-74.

2667. Stengren, G. L. "Connatural knowledge in Aquinas
and Kierkegaardian subjectivity." In Kierkegaardiana.
Niels Thulstrup, ed. Copenhagen: C. A. Reitzels Boghandel,
10 (1977):182-189.

Tielsch, E.

2668. Schäfer, Klaus. "Kierkegaard--Kirchenvater der
Wertlehre: Bemerkungen zu E. Tielschs Untersuchung
'Kierkegaards Glaube'." In Kierkegaardiana. Niels
Thulstrup, ed. Copenhagen: Munksgaard, 6 (1966):152-180.

Unamuno, Miguel de

2669. Erro, Carlos Alberto. "Unamuno y Kierkegaard."
Sur (Buenos Aires) (1938):7-21.

2670. Estelrich y Artigues, Joan. "Kierkegaard i Unamuno."
Revista (Barcelona) 16. marzo (1919).

2671. Farré, Luis. "Unamuno, William James y Kierkegaard."
Cuadernos Hispano-Americanos (1954):64-88; 279-299.

2672. Fasel, Oscar A. "Observations on Unamuno and Kierkegaard." *Hispania* 38 (1955):443-450.

2673. Krane Paucker, E. "Kierkegaardian dread and
despair in Unamuno's *El que se Enterró*." *Cuadernos de la
Cátedra Miguel de Unamuno* (Salamanaca) (1966-67):75-91.

2674. Mac Gregor, J. "Dos precursores del existencialismo:
Kierkegaard y Unamuno." *Filosofía y Letras* (México) 22
(1951):43-44, 203-219.

2675. Meyer, François. "Kierkegaard et Unamuno." *Revue de
Littérature Comparée* 29 (1955):478-492.

2676. Palmer, Donald D. "Unamuno's Don Quijote and
Kierkegaard's Abraham." *Revista de Estudios Hispánicos*
3 (1969):295-312.

2677. Tornos, Andrés M. "Sobre Unamuno y Kierkegaard."
Pensamiento 18 (1962):131-146.

2678. Unamuno, Miguel de. *Del Semtimento Trágico de la
Vida*. Madrid, 1912, p. 7; 111-113; 117-118; 124; 154;
176-177; 197; 253; 280; 318. English trans.: *The Tragic
Sense of Life in Men and Peoples*. Trans. by J. E. Craw-
ford Flitch. With an introductory essay by Salvador de
Madariaga. London: Macmillan, 1921.

2678a. Uscatescu, Jorge. "Unamuno y Kierkegaard o la
interioridad secreta." *Arbor* 103 (1979):25-40.

2679. Webber, Ruth House. "Kierkegaard and the elabora-
tion of Unamuno's *Niebla*." *Hispanic Review* 32 (1964):
118-134.

Updike, John

2680. Hunt, George W. "John Updike: The Dialectical
Vision. The Influence of Kierkegaard and Barth." Ph.D.,
Syracuse Univ., 1974.

2681. Hunt, George W., S. J. "Kierkegaardian sensations
into real fiction: John Updike's *The Astronomer*."
Christianity and Literature 26 (1977):3-17.

Valéry, Paul

2682. Francovich, G. "Valéry y Kierkegaard." *Filosofía y Letras* (México) 16 (1948):27-84.

Vigny, Alfred de

2683. Grimsley, Ronald. "Kierkegaard, Vigny, and 'the poet'." *Revue de Littérature Comparée* 34 (1960):52-80.

Voltaire

2684. Grimsley, Ronald. "Some implications of the use of irony in Voltaire and Kierkegaard." In *Proceedings of the IV Congress of the International Comparative Literature Association.* François Jost, ed. Fribourg, 1964, 2 vols. The Hague: Mouton, 1966, 1018-1024.

Wahl, Jean

2685. Koppang, Ole. "Quelques pensées kierkegaardiennes dans la philosophie de Jean Wahl." *Orbis Litterarum* 10 (1955):112-117. [Symposion Kierkegaardianum]

Whitehead, Alfred N.

2686. Rose, Mary C. "Three Hierarchies of Value: A Study in the Philosophies of Value of Henri Bergson, Alfred North Whitehead, and Soeren Kierkegaard." Ph.D., The Johns Hopkins Univ., 1949. 310p.

Wilder, Thornton

2687. Ericson, Edward, Jr. "Kierkegaard in Wilder's *The Eighth Day.*" *Renascence* 26 (1974):123-138.

Wilhelm (Judge)

2688.   Perkins, Robert L.   "The family: Hegel and Kierkegaard's Judge Wilhelm."   *Hegel-Jahrbuch* (Meisenheim/Glan)
(1967):89-100.

Wittgenstein, Ludwig

2689.   Bell, Richard H.   "Kierkegaard and Wittgenstein:
Two strategies for understanding theology."   *Iliff Review*
31 (1974):21-34.

2690.   Gallagher, Michael P.   "Wittgenstein's admiration for
Kierkegaard."   *Month* 39 (1968):43-49.

2691.   Hustwit, Ronald E.   "Understanding a suggestion of
Professor Cavell's: Kierkegaard's religious stage as a
Wittgensteinian 'form of life'."   *Philosophy Research
Archives* 4 (1978).

2692.   Quinn, Wylie S.   "Kierkegaard and Wittgenstein:
The 'Religious' as a 'Form of Life'."   Ph.D., Duke Univ.,
1976, 222p.   *Dissertation Abstracts* 37 (1977):7804A.

CHAPTER 6:
Entries Arranged
by Subject

Absolute Other

2693. Hay, Gerald C., Jr. "Kierkegaard and the absolute
other." *Philosophical Studies* 22:78-89.

Absolute Paradox

2694. Daise, Benjamin. "Kierkegaard and the absolute
paradox." *Journal of the History of Philosophy* 14 (1976):
63-68.

2695. Guardini, Romano. "Kierkegaards Idee des absoluten
Paradoxes." *Die Schildgenossen* (Augsburg) 9 (1919):
191-198.

2696. Larsen, Robert E. "Kierkegaard's absolute paradox."
Journal of Religion 42 (1962):34-43.

2697. Stack, George J. "Kierkegaard and acosmism."
Journal of Thought 10 (1975): 185-193.

Act - Action

2698. Rougemont, Denis de. "Forme et transformation ou
l'acte selon Kierkegaard." *Hermès* (Janvier 1936).

2699. Simons, Peter M. "Kierkegaard's theory of action."
Journal of the British Society for Phenomenology 7 (1976):
111-122.

Aesthetics

2700. Adorno, Theodor Wiesengrund. *Kierkegaard. Costruzione dell'Estetico*. Milano: Longanesi, 1962. 404p.

2701. Baas, Fritz. "Das Ästhetische bei Sören Kierkegaard
in seinem Grundbestimmungen." Phil. Diss. Heidelberg,
1923, xiv-125p. (Daktylogr.)

2702. Baraldi, Sonia. "Del estadio estético en Kierkegaard." *Alcalá* (1955):13.

2703. Bignone, Ettore. "I. Soeren Kierkegaard. II. La
filosofia dello stadio estetico." *Le Cronache Letterarie*
(Firenze) 1 (1910):1, 3.

2704. Cantoni, Remo. "Kierkegaard e la vita estetica.
Saggio. introduttivo." In Kierkegaard's *Don Giovanni.
La Musica di Mozart e l'Eros*. 2d ed. Milano, 1945, 7-40.

2704a. Comstock, W. Richard. "Aspects of aesthetic
existence: Kierkegaard and Santayana." *International
Philosophical Quarterly* 6 (1966):189-213.

2705. George, Arapura Ghevarghese. *The First Sphere. A
Study in Kierkegaardian Aesthetics*. Bombay: Asia Publishing
House, 1966. 80p.

2706. Glenn, John D., Jr. "Kierkegaard on the unity of
comedy and tragedy." *Tulane Studies in Philosophy* 19
(1970):41-53. [*Aesthetics*, 1]

2707. Kühner, Karl. "Sören Kierkegaard und die Kunst."
Christliches Kunstblatt für Kirche, Schule und Haus
(Stuttgart) (August 1911).

2708. Matura, Ottokar. *Die Aesthetik in der Existential-
philosophie Kierkegaards*. Wien: Verlag Verf., 1933. 55p.

2709. Obenauer, K. J. "Der ästhetische Mensch in der
neueren deutschen Literatur." *Zeitschrift für Deutschkunde* (Berlin) 44 (1930):369-379 (375-376).

2710. Perpeet, Willi. *Kierkegaard und die Frage nach
einer Aesthetik der Gegenwart*. Halle: N. Niemeyer, 1940.
284p. Phil. Diss. Bonn, 1940. (Philosophie und Geistes-
wissenschaften, hrsg. von Erich Rothacker, Buchreihe, 8).

2711. Petroccione, Alfredo. *La Vida Estética en el Pensamiento de Kierkegaard* (Symposium sobre Existencialismo, 4). Rosario: Universidad del Litoral, Istituto de Filosofía, 1955. 26p.

2712. Sciacca, Michele Federico. *L'estetismo. Kierkegaard. Pirandello.* Milano: Marzorati, 1974. 416p.

2713. Sgalambro, Manlio. "Estetica e materialismo in Kierkegaard." *Tempo Presente* 9 (1964):69-72.

2714. Slataper, Camusso Giulia. "Romanticismo come letterarietà: Approssimazione all'estetismo kierkegaardiano." Atti del *Congresso Internazionale di Filosofia*, Roma, 1946. Vol. 2. Milano: Castellani, 1948, 453-455.

2715. Stack, George J. "Kierkegaard and romantic aestheticism." *Philosophy Today* 14 (1970):57-74.

2716. Stanford, Derek. "The aesthetics of Kierkegaard." *Twentieth Century* 151 (1952):348-354.

2717. Taylor, Douglas R. "The Aesthetic Methodology of Sören Kierkegaard's Pseudonymous Works." Ph.D., Florida State Univ., 1977, 328p. *Dissertation Abstracts* 38 (1977): 2854A.

2718. Vecchi, Giovanni. "Il problema dell'arte nell'esistenzialismo di Kierkegaard." *Rivista di Filosofia Neo-Scolastica* (Milano) 38 (1946):61-69.

Alienation

2719. Gwaltney, Marilyn Ethel. "The Concept of Alienation in Kierkegaard." Ph.D., State Univ. of New York at Buffalo, 1976, 171p. *Dissertation Abstracts* 37 (1977): 5181A.

2720. Wolf, William J. "Alienation and Reconciliation in the Writings of Soeren Kierkegaard." Ph.D., Union Theological Seminary in the City of New York, 1945, 333p.

America

2721. Link, Mae M. "Kierkegaard's Way to America: A Study in the Dissemination of His Thought." Ph.D., The American Univ., 1951.

Analogy

2722. Grosche, Robert. "La notion d'analogie et le problème théologique d'aujourd'hui [Karl Barth, Soren Kierkegaard, Theodor Haecker]." (Traduction de Yves Simon). *Revue de Philosophie* (Paris) 55 (1935):302-312.

2723. Melchiorre, Virgilio. "Il principio di analogia come categoria metafisica nella filosofia di Kierkegaard." *Giornale Critico della Filosofia Italiana* (Firenze) 34 (1955):56-66.

Anthropology

2724. Johnson, William A. "The anthropology of Sören Kierkegaard." *Hartford Quarterly* 4 (1964):43-52.

2725. Johnson, William A. "The anthropology of Sören Kierkegaard." In *The Presence of Kierkegaard in Contemporary American Life*. Lewis Lawson, ed. Metuchen (New Jersey): The Scarecrow Press, 1971, 151-161.

2726. Slök, Johannes. *Die Anthropologie Kierkegaards*. Köbenhavn: Rosenkilde og Bagger, 1954. 144p.

Anthropomorphism

2727. Cortese, Alessandro." "Anthropomorfisme." In *Kierkegaardiana* 9 (1974):271-318.

Anti-Intellectualism

2728. Swenson, David F. "The anti-intellectualism of Sören Kierkegaard." *Philosophical Review* 25 (1916): 567-586.

2729. Swenson, David F. "The anti-intellectualism of Kierkegaard." In *The Presence of Kierkegaard in Contemporary American Life*. Lewis Lawson, ed. Metuchen (New Jersey): The Scarecrow Press, 1971, 23-42.

Anxiety (Angst)

2730. Adler-Vonessen, Hildegard. "Angst in der Sicht von
S. Kierkegaard, S. Freud und M. Heidegger." *Psyche*
(Heidelberg) 25 (1971):692-715. [Summary, 714.]

2731. Arendt, Magdalene. "Die gelebte Angst des 'Angst-
Philosophen' Kierkegaard. Ein existenzanalytischer Auf-
riss." *Salzburger Jahrbuch für Philosophie* 17-18 (1973-74):
231-263.

2732. Kainz, Howard P., Jr. "The relationship of dread
to spirit in man and woman according to Kierkegaard."
Modern Schoolman 47 (1969):1-13.

2733. Kawamura, Eiko. *Das Problem des Weltbezugs bei
Kierkegaard. Dargestellt am Begriff der Angst* (Schriften
der Stiftung Europa-Kolleg Hamburg, 24). Hamburg, Stiftung
Europa-Kolleg; Hamburg: Fundament-Verlag Sasse, 1973. 139p.

2734. Kloeden, Wolfdietrich von. "Sören Kierkegaards
Der Begriff Angst im Kursunterricht der gymnasialen Ober-
stufe." In *Kierkegaardiana*. Niels Thulstrup, ed.
Copenhagen: C. A. Reitzels Boghandel, 10 (1977):253-261.

2735. Kritzeck, James. "Philosophers of Anxiety."
Commonweal 63 (1956):572-574.

2736. Malmquist, C. P. "A comparison of orthodox and
existential psychoanalytic concepts of anxiety." *Journal
of the Nervous and Mental Diseases* 131 (1960):371-382.

2737. Marcuse, Ludwig. "Zwei Diagnosen der Angst.
Kierkegaard und Freud." *Der Monat* 8 (1955):28-38.

2738. Paci, Enzo. "Il significato dell'introduzione
kierkegaardiana al *Concetto dell'Angoscia*. *Rivista di
Filosofia* (Bologna-Torino) (1954):392-398.

2739. Paci, Enzo. "Angoscia e relazione in Kierkegaard."
Aut-Aut (Milano) (1954):363-376.

2740. Paci, Enzo. "Su due significati del concetto dell'
angoscia in Kierkegaard." *Orbis Litterarum* 10 (1955):
196-207. [Symposion Kierkegaardianum]

2741. Roberts, David Everett. "The concept of dread."
Review of Religion 11 (1947):272-284.

2742. Tweedie, Donald F., Jr. "The Significance of Dread
in the Thought of Kierkegaard and Heidegger." Ph.D.,
Boston Univ., 1954.

2743. Wünsche, Horst. "*Der Begriff der Angst* und seine Stellung im Kierkegaardischen Philosophieren." Phil. Diss. Univ. Mainz [1953], ix-183p.

Apologetics

2744. Diamond, Malcolm L. "Kierkegaard and apologetics." *Journal of Religion* 44 (1964):122-132.

Atonement

2745. Cole, J. P. "Kierkegaard's doctrine of the atonement." *Religion in Life* 33 (1964):592-601.

Authority

2746. Croxall, T. H. "Kierkegaard on 'authority'." *Hibbert Journal* 48 (1950):145-152.

Being-With-Others

2747. Cutting, Patricia M. "The Possibility of Being-With-Others for Kierkegaard's Individaul One (Der Enkelte)." Ph.D., Univ. of New Mexico, 1976, 240p. *Dissertation Abstracts* 37 (1976):2939A.

Belief

2748. Pojman, Louis P. "Kierkegaard on justification of belief." *International Journal for the Philosophy of Religion* 8 (1977):75-93.

2749. Thulstrup, Marie. "Forstanden contra troen? En bemaerkning til Kierkegaards problemstilling." [Reason versus belief? A note concerning Kierkegaard's formulation of the problem.] *Dansk Teologisk Tidskrift* 17 (1954):89-97.

2750. Wahl, Jean. "La théorie de la croyance chez Kierkegaard." *Foi et Vie* (Paris) 35 (1934):639-660.

Bible

2751. Breuil, Roger. "La génie littéraire de la bible."
[Soren Kierkegaard: Om Forskjellen mellem et Genie og en
Apostel.] Réforme (6.12.1947).

2752. Dewey, Bradley Rau. "Kierkegaard and the Blue
Testament." Harvard Theological Review 60 (1967):391-409.

2753. "Kierkegaard and the Bible." Theology Today 10
(1953):247-248.

2754. Kloeden, Wolfdietrich von. "Ausformung und Vertiefung von Begriffen bei S. Kierkegaard als Folge seines
Bibelstudiums." In Kierkegaardiana 9 (1974):75-83.

2755. Morimoto, Paul S., ed. Kierkegaard and the Bible.
New York, 1953.

2756. Schrempf, Christoph. "Soren Kierkegaards Stellung
zu Bibel und Dogma." Zeitschrift fur Theologie und Kirche
(Freiburg i. Br. und Tubingen) 1 (1891):179-229.

Bibliography (See also Appendix, I, no. 3816-3919)

2757. Castagnino, Franco. Gli Studi Italiani su Kierkegaard, 1906-1966. (Collava del dentro di ricerche di
storia della storiografia filosofica, 2). Roma: Edizioni
dell'Ateno, 1972. 307p.

2758. Colette, Jacques. "Bulletin d'histoire de la
philosophie: Kierkegaard." Revue des Sciences Philosophiques et Theologiques (Paris) 54 (1970):654-480.

     Surveys the literature of the period 1955-1970.

2759. Cortese, M. Alessandro. "Una nuova bibliografia
Kierkegaardiana." Rivista di Filosofia Neo-Scolastica
(Milano) 55 (1963):98-108.

     156 entries. No annotations. Covers works published
     in the late forties through 1961. Many in Italian.
     Attempts to complete the International Kierkegaard
     Bibliography.

2760. Delfgaauw, Bernard. "De Kierkegaard-Studie in
Scandinavie." Tijdschrift voor Filosofie (Leuven) 18
(1956):121-129.

2761. Delfgaauw, Bernard. "De Kierkegaard-Studie in Scandinavie." *Tijdschrift voor Filosofie* (Leuven) 33 (1971):737-778.

2762. Estelrich y Artigues, Joan. "Bibliografia de S. Kierkegaard." *Revista Quaderns de Publicació Quinzenal* (1. Mayo 1919).

2763. Fabro, Cornelio. "Note de bibliografia Kierke-gaardiana." In *Studi Kierkegaardiani*. Cronelio Fabro, ed. Brescia: Morcelliana Editrice, 1957, 415-433.

2764. Fairhurst, Stanley J. "Sören Kierkegaard [biblio-graphy]." In *Existentialism: A Bibliography. Modern Schoolman* 31 (1953-54):19-33.

2765. Himmelstrup, Jens. *Sören Kierkegaard; International Bibliographi. Under Medvirken af Kield Birket-Smith.* Copenhagen: Nyt Nordisk Forlag, Arnold Busck, 1962. 216p.

    Contains list of works and editions by Kierkegaard, and books, articles, and reviews about him. 6995 entries, but no annotations. Systematically covers up to 1955 with spotty coverage to 1965.

2766. Jolivet, Régis. *Kierkegaard* (Bibliographische Einführungen in das Studium der Philosophie, 4). Bern: A. Francke, 1948. 33p.

    About 220 entries with occasional annotations. Index and introduction.

2767. Jorgensen, Aage. *Sören Kierkegaard-Litteratur, 1961-1970: En Forelobig Bibliografi [Sören Kierkegaard Literature, 1961-1970: An Outline Bibliography* In Danish]]. Aarhus: Akademisk Boghandel, 1971. 99p.

2768. Lawson, Lewis A. "A bibliography of periodical articles in the English language about Sören Kierkegaard." In *The Presence of Sören Kierkegaard in Contemporary American Life.* Lewis Lawson, ed. Metuchen (New Jersey): The Scarecrow Press, 1971.

2769. Moore, W. G. "Recent studies of Kierkegaard." *The Journal of Theological Studies* (London) 40 (1939): 225-231.

2770. Nielson, Edith Ortman, and Thulstrup, Niels. *Sören Kierkegaard; Contributions Toward a Bibliography [Sören Kierkegaard; Bidrag til en Bibliografi].*

2771. Perkins, Robert L. "Always himself: A survey of recent Kierkegaard literature." *Southern Journal of Philosophy* 12 (1974):539-551.

A survey of seventeen recent books.

2772. Preiss, Th. "Apropos de Kierkegaard (études critiques)." *Revue d'Histoire de la Philosophie Religieuse* 16 (1946):46-64.

2773. Sales, Michel. "Dix ans de publications kierkegaardiennes en langue française." *Archives de Philosophie* (Paris) 35 (1972):649-672.

2774. Theunissen, Michael. "Das Kierkegaardbild in der neueren Forschung und Deutung <1945-1957>." *Deutsche Vierteljahrsschrift für Literaturwissenschaft und Geistesgeschichte* (Halle) 32 (1958):576-612.

2775. Thulstrup, Niels. "Theological and philosophical Kierkegaardian studies in Scandinavia, 1945-1953." *Theology Today* (Princeton) 12 (1955):297-311.

2776. Woodbridge, Hensley Charles. "A bibliography of dissertations concerning Kierkegaard written in the U.S., Canada, and Great Britain." *American Book Collector* 12 (1961):21-22.

2777. Woodbridge, Hensley Charles. "Sören Kierkegaard: A bibliography of his works in English translation." *American Book Collector* 12 (1961):17-20.

2778. Yanitelli, Victor. "Bibliographical introduction to existentialism." *Modern Schoolman* 26 (1949):(345-363), 355-357.

Buddhism (See also Zen, no. 3649)

2779. Amore, R., and Elrod, J. "From ignorance to knowledge; a study in the Kierkegaardian and Theravada Buddhist notions of freedom." *Union Seminary Quarterly Review* 26 (1970):59-79.

2780. Jacobson, Nolon Pliny. "The predicament of man in Zen Buddhism and Kierkegaard." *Philosophy East and West* 2 (1952):238-253.

2781. Teo, Wesley K. H. "Self-responsibility in existentialism and Buddhism." *International Journal for the Philosophy of Religion* 4 (1973):80-91.

Capitalism

2782. Stark, Werner. "Kierkegaard and Capitalism."
Sociological Review 42 (1950):1-28; 87-114; *ibid.*, 64
(1972):120-149. Reprinted in *The Presence of Sören Kierkegaard in Contemporary American Life*. Lewis Lawson, ed.
Metuchen (New Jersey): The Scarecrow Press, 1971.

Category

2783. Kainz, Howard P. "Ambiguities and paradoxes in
Kierkegaard's existential categories." *Philosophy Today*
13 (1969):138-145.

2784. Stack, George J. "Kierkegaard's existential categories." *The Personalist* 57 (1976):18-33.

2785. Stack, George J. "Aristóteles y las categorías
existenciales de Kierkegaard." *Folia Humanística* 9 (1971):
1029-1041.

Catholicism

2786. Fabro, Cornelio. "Kierkegaard e o catolicismo."
Trad. do Rev. Dr. Fernando dos Santos, S. D. B.
Filosofia (Lisboa) 2 (1956):210-249.

2787. Fabro, Cornelio. "Influssi cattolici sulla
spiritualità kierkegaardiana." *Humanitas* 17 (1962):501-507.

2788. Fabro, Cornelio. "Spunti cattolici nel pensiero
di Sören Kierkegaard." *Doctor Communis* 26 (1973):251-280.

2789. Jardim, E. L. "Kierkegaard e o Catolicismo."
Estudos (Porto Alegre) 18 (1958):27-36.

2790. Lopes, Costa. "Kierkegaard e o catolicismo."
Theologica (Braga) 2 (1958):197-200.

2791. Neumann, Johannes. "Kierkegaard zwischen Protestantismus und Katholizismus." *Deutsches Pfarrerblatt* (Essen)
50 (1950):227-230.

2792. Romain, Willy-Paul. "Kierkegaard et la pensée
catholique." *Les Lettres* (Paris) 4 (1950):36-40.

2793. Roos, Heinrich. *Sören Kierkegaard y el catolicismo*.
Trad. de l'all. par J. Oyarzun (Razón y Fe, 40). Madrid:
Razón y Fe, 1959. 106p.

2793a. Roos, Heinrich. *Sören Kierkegaard auf der Suche
nach dem wahren Christentum* (Institut f. Europäische
Geschichte, Mainz. Vorträge. Nr. 30). Wiesbaden:
Steiner, 1961. 32p.

2794. Thieme, Karl. "Sören Kierkegaard und die katholische Wahrheit." *Religiöse Besinnung* (Abschlussheft:
Ökumen. Erfüllung) 4 (1933):19-33.

2795. Winkler, Robert. "Kierkegaard, Katholizismus und
Protestantismus." *Christentum und Wissenschaft* (Leipzig)
1930.

Children

2796. Scudder, J. R., Jr. "Kierkegaard and the respon-
sible enjoyment of children." *Educational Forum* 30 (1966):
497-503. Reprinted in *The Presence of Sören Kierkegaard in
Contemporary American Life*. Lewis Lawson, ed. Metuchen
(New Jersey): The Scarecrow Press, 1971.

2797. Sorainen, Kalle. "Kierkegaard lasten kasvattajana
[Kierkegaard as a child educator]." *Kasvaties ja Kuolu*
2 (1949):67-72.

Choice

2798. Cole, J. Preston. "The function of choice in human
existence." *Journal of Religion* 45 (1965):196-210.

2799. Croxall, Thomas H. "Kierkegaard on the choice."
Meddelelser fra Sören Kierkegaard Selskabet 2 (1950):37-38.

2800. Pait, James A. "Kierkegaard and the problem of
choice." *Emory University Quarterly* 2 (1946):237-245.

2801. Stack, George J. "Kierkegaard's analysis of choice:
The aristotelian model." *The Personalist* 52 (1971):643-661.

2802. Stack, George J. "Dialéctica de la elección en
Kierkegaard." *Folia Humanística* 9 (1971):139-159.

2803. Stack, George J. "Aristotle and Kierkegaard's
concept of choice." *Modern Schoolman* 46 (1948):11-23.

Christianity

2804. Allison, Henry E. "Christianity and nonsense."
Review of Metaphysics 20 (1967):432-460.

2805. Armieri, Salvatore. *Sören Kierkegaard e il Cristian-esimo* (Quaderni del Cenobio, 12). Lugano: Cenobio, 1956.
72p.

2806. Barckett, Richard M., S. J. "Sören Kierkegaard:
Back to Christianity." *Downside Review* 73 (1955):241-255.

2807. Brand, W. "Christentumsverkündigung nach Sören
Kierkegaard." *Der Alte Glaube* 7 (1905-06).

2808. Brechtken, J. "Die Dominanz der Praxis in christlichen: dargestellt am Beispeil Sören Kierkegaards."
Tijdschrift voor Filosofie 36 (1974):61-77.

2809. Brunkhorst, F. "Kierkegaards Angriff auf die
Christenheit." *Monatsschrift für Pastoraltheologie*
(Göttingen) 21 (1925):132-141.

2810. Buss, Hinrich. *Kierkegaards Angriff auf die bestehende Christenheit*. (Theologische Forschung. Veröffentlichung 49). Hamburg-Bergstedt: Reich, 1970. 214p.

2811. Celestin, George. "Kierkegaard and Christian
Renewal." *Dominicana* 49 (1964):149-157.

2812. Chantepie de la Saussaye. "Over Christendom en
Cultuur (Augustinus, Rousseau, Schleiermacher, Vinet,
Kierkegaard)." *Onze Eeuw* 13 (1913):217ff.

2813. Collins, James. "The mind of Kierkegaard. IV:
Becoming a Christian in Christendom." *Modern Schoolman*
26 (1949):293-322.

2814. Collins, James D. "Kierkegaard and Christian
philosophy." *Thomist* 14 (1951):441-465.

2815. de Feo, Nicola Massimo. "L'uomo-Dio nel cristianesimo di Kierkegaard." *Giornale Critico della Filosofia
Italiana* 44 (1965):369-385.

2816. Dunne, Mary Rachel. "Kierkegaard and Socratic
Ignorance: A Study of the Task of a Philosopher in Relation
to Christianity." Ph.D., Univ. of Notre Dame, 1970, 356p.
Dissertation Abstracts 31 (1971):4835A.

2817. Edwards, Paul. "Kierkegaard and the 'truth' of
Christianity." *Philosophy* 46 (1971):89-108.

2818. Elert, Werner. *Der Kampf um das Christentum.*
Geschichte der Beziehungen zwischen dem evangelischen
Christentum in Deutschland und das allgemeine Denken seit
Schleiermacher Und Hegel. München, 1921 (vii-513p.),
431-434.

2819. "Kierkegaard and Christianity." *Foi et Vie* 69
(1970):2-60.

   CONTENTS:
   Brun, J. "Actualité de Kierkegaard;"
   Viallaneix, N. "Kierkegaard ou l'anti-théologie;"
   Clet, J. "Une histoire presque comme les autres."

2820. Forrester, D. B. "The attack on christendom in
Marx and Kierkegaard." *Scottish Journal of Theology*
(London) 25 (1972):181-196.

2821. Fritzsche, Helmut. *Kierkegaards Kritik an der
Christenheit.* (Arbeiten zur Theologie. Reihe 1, H. 27).
Stuttgart: Calwer Verlag, 1966. 84p. [Lizenz d. Evang.
Verl.-Anst., Berlin.]

2822. Garelick, Herbert M. *The Anti-Christianity of Kierkegaard. A Study of* Concluding Unscientific Postscript.
New York: Humanities Press, 1966. 73p.

2823. Graham, D. Aelred. "Introducing Christianity into
Christendom: An impression of Sören Kierkegaard."
Clergy Review 24 (1944):535-541.

2824. Graue, Paul. "Sören Kierkegaards Angriff auf die
Christenheit." *Die Christliche Welt* 12 (1898):147-150,
170-179, 195-202.

2825. Hansen, Knud. "Der andere Kierkegaard. Zu Sören
Kierkegaards Christentumsverständnis." *Evangelische
Theologie* (München) 11 (1951-52):209-224.

2826. Heinecken, Martin J. "Kierkegaard as Christian."
Journal of Religion 37 (1957):20-30.

2827. Hirsch, Emanuel. "Der Kirchensturm von Kopenhagen.
Sören Kierkegaards Angriff auf Christenheit, Kirche und
Ortodoxe." *Sonntagsblatt* (Hamburg) 6 (1953):7-9. [Hrsg.
von Hanns Lilje.]

2828. Jorgensen, Alfred Th. *Sören Kierkegaard und das
biblische Christentum.* Berlin: E. Runge, 1914. 31p.
p. 283-310 (Biblische Zeit- und Streitfragen zur Aufklärung der Gebildeten, 9. Ser., Heft 9).

2829. Kroner, Richard J. "Existentialism and Christianity." *Encounter* 17 (1956):219-244.

2829a. Löwith, Karl. "Die philosophische Kritik der
Christlichen Religion im 19. Jahrhundert." *Theologische
Rundschau* N.F. 5 (1933):131-172, 201-226 (p. 201-212).

2830. Magel, Charles R. "Kierkegaard's Logically contra-
dictory Christianity." *Graduate Review of Philosophy*
3 (1960).

2831. Martin, H. V. "Kierkegaard's attack upon Christendom." *Congregational Quarterly* 24 (1946):139-144.

2832. Masi, Giuseppe. "Storicità e cristianesimo in Kierkegaard." *Archivio di Filosofia* (Milano-Roma) (1953):
115-132.

2833. "Meant for mankind: Kierkegaard and Christianity as
the regulating weight." *Times Literary Supplement* 68
(March 20, 1969):281-283.

2834. Michalson, Grodon Elliott. "A dramatic approach to
Christianity." *Christendom* 9 (1944):462-475.

2835. Nardi, Lorenzo. *Kierkegaard e il Cristianesimo
Tragico.* Roma: Edizioni Cremonese, 1976. 128p.

2836. Nelson, C. A. "The dimension of inwardness in
Christianity." *Augustana Quarterly* 21 (1941):125-140.

2837. Nicholson, G. E. "A dramatic approach to Christianity." *Christendom* 9 (1944):462-475.

2838. Otani, Hidehito. "The concept of a Christian in
Kierkegaard." *Inquiry* 8 (1965):73-83.

2839. Reck, D. W. "Christianity of Sören Kierkegaard."
Canadian Journal of Theology 12 (1966):85-97.

2840. Rhodes, Donald W. "The Christianity of Sören
Kierkegaard." *Canadian Journal of Theology* 12 (1966):85-97.

2841. Sperna Weiland, J. *Philosophy of Existence and
Christianity. Kierkegaard's and Jaspers' Thoughts on
Christianity.* (Philosophia Religionis, 3). Assen: Van
Gorcum, 1951. 144p.

2842. Sponheim, P. R. "Kierkegaard and the suffering of
the Christian man." *Dialectica* 3 (1964):199-206.

2843. Stewart, R. W. "Existential Christianity."
Expository Times 63 (1952):118-120.

2844. Stucki, P.-A. *Le Christianisme et l'Histoire d'Après
Kierkegaard.* (Coll. *Studia Philosophica.* Suppl. 11).
Bâle: Verlag Recht und Gesellschaft; Paris: Interdoc, 1964,
xvi-277p.

2845. Tavard, George H. "Christianity and the philosophy
of eixstence." *Theological Studies* 18 (1957):1-16.

2846. Theunissen, Gert H. "Sören Kierkegaard. Das
Christentum unter vier Augen." *Rheinischer Merkur* (Koblenz) 10 (1955):7.

2847. Vorländer, Karl. "Sören Kierkegaard und sein
*Angriff auf die Christenheit. Zeitschrift für Philosophie
und Philosophische Kritik.* N.F 111 (1897):2.3-222.

2848. Wieman, Henry Nelson. "The interpretation of
Christianity." *Christian Century* 56 (1939):444-446.

Christology (See also Christ, no. 2062-2110)

2849. Croxall, Thomas H. "Facets of Kierkegaard's Christology." *Theology Today* 8 (1951):327-339.

2850. Thomas, J. Heywood. "The christology of Sören
Kierkegaard and Karl Barth." *Hibbert Journal* 53 (1954-55):
280-288.

2851. Valenziano, Crispino. "Limiti della cristologia
kierkegaardiana." *Giornale di Metafisica* 20 (1965):20-29.

2852. Widmer, Gabriel. "Kierkegaard et le Christ."
Revue de Théologie et de Philosophie 13 (1963):273-291.

Church

2853. Altherr, Alfred. "Kierkegaard, der Kirchenfeind.
I-IV." *Schweizerisches Protestantenblatt* (Basel) 27
(1904):59-63, 67-70, 73-77, 83-85.

2854. Anonymous. "Die dänische Staatskirche der Angriff
Sören Kierkegaards. I-VII." *Kopenhagener Zeitung* (Köbenhavn) 1 (24.1-14.2.1856).   Forts. m. Titlen: "Die
dänische Staatskirche. Sören Kierkegaard und die Staatskirche. VIII-XIII." Ibid., (18.2-6.3-17.3-31.3.1856).

2855. Anonymous. "Die Kirche und Kierkegaard." *Tübinger
Chronik* (13.2.1931).

2856. Diem, Hermann. "Die Kirche und Kierkegaard. Vortrag, gehalten vor der Theolog. Faschaft in Tübingen.
[1.-] 2. Tiel." *Zwischen den Zeiten* 9 (1931):297-319,
386-404. Also in *Tidehverv* (1932):38-40, 59-64; 69-74;
88-91.

2857. Fabro, Cornelio. "Le problème de l'église chez Newman et Kierkegaard." *Revue Thomiste* 77 (1977):30-90.

2858. Fitzpatrick, Mallary, Jr. "Kierkegaard and the Church." *Journal of Religion* 27 (1947):255-262.

2859. Humanus. "Die ware Kierkegaard in de Kerk." *Kultuurleven* 23 (1956):411-420.

2860. Johnson, Howard A. "Kierkegaard and the Church." *Kierkegaardiana* 8 (1971):64-79.

2861. Jörg, Jos Edmund. "Dr. Kierkegaard und seine Kritik des protestantischen Kirchentums." In *Geschichte der Protestantismus in seiner neuesten Entwicklung. 2. Die Schwärmerkirche und die Bedingungen.* Freiburg i Br., 1858, 33-50.

2862. Miegge, G. "Kierkegaard e la chiesa." *Gioventu Cristiana* no. 10 (1931).

2863. Minear, Paul S. "The Church: Militant or triumphant?" *Andover Newton Bulletin* 47 (1955):25-31.

2864. Schückler, Georg. "Kierkegaard und die protestantische Kirche." *Begegnung* (Koblenz) 8 (1953):104-107.

2865. Stewart, R. W. "Is church like a theatre?" *Expository Times* 62 (1950-51):27-28.

2866. Storck, M. "Kierkegaard und die Kirche." *Pastoralblätter* (Stuttgart) 95 (1955):604-606.

Communication

2867. Adams, E. M. "Elucidation of Sören Kierkegaard's Categories of Communication and Their Application to the Communication of Christian Existence in Japan." [Dissertation abstract]. *Drew Gateway* 41 (1970):17-18.

2868. Anderson, Raymond E. "Kierkegaard's theory of communication." *Speech Monographs* 30 (1963):1-14.

2869. Anderson, Raymond E. "Kierkegaard's theory of communication." In *The Presence of Sören Kierkegaard in Contemporary American Life.* Lewis Lawson, ed. Metuchen (New Jersey): The Scarecrow Press, 1971, 206-229.

2870. Broudy, Harry S. "Kierkegaard on indirect communication." *Journal of Philosophy* 58 (1961):225-233.

2871. Caron, Jacques. "Dialectique de la communication chez Kierkegaard." *Philosophiques* (1976):167-181.

2872. Christopherson, Myrvin Frederick. "Sören Kierkegaard's Dialectic of Communication: An Approach to the Communication of Existential Knowledge." Ph.D., Purdue Univ. *Dissertation Abstracts* 27 (1966):271A-272A.

2873. McCarty, Robert Eugene. "The Wonder-Wounded Hearer: The Problem of Communication in Kierkegaard's Authorship and Its Application to an Understanding of *Hamlet*." *Dissertation Abstracts* 38:2814A.

2874. Mourant, John A. "The limitations of religious existentialism: The problem of communication." *International Philosophical Quarterly* 1 (1961):437-452.

2875. Oppenheim, M. D. "Taking time seriously. An inquiry into the methods of communication of Sören Kierkegaard and Franz Rosenzweig." *Studies in Religion* (Toronto) 7 (1978):53-60.

2876. Taylor, Mark C. "Language, truth, and indirect communication." *Tijdschrift voor Filosofie* 37 (1975): 74-88.

2877. Villard, Jean. "Kierkegaard et la communication de l'existence." *Revue de Théologie et de Philosophie* (1973): 250-254.

Communism

2877a. Hügli, Anton. "Kierkegaard und der Kommunismus." In *Kierkegaardiana* 9 (1974):220-247.

Community

2878. Bellezza, Vito E. "Il singolo e la comunità nel pensiero di Kierkegaard." (In *Kierkegaard e Nietzsche*.) *Archivio di Filosifia* (Milano-Roma) no. 2 (1953):133-189.

2879. Matthis, Michael James. "Kierkegaard and the Problem of Community." Ph.D., Fordham Univ., 1977, 277p. *Dissertation Abstracts* 38 (1977):322A.

2880. Wagndal, Per. "Sören Kierkegaard och samhället [S. Kierkegaard and the community]." *Var Lösen* 44 (1953): 189-197.

Concern

2881. Stack, George J. "Conern in Kierkegaard and Heidegger." *Philosophy Today* 13 (1969):26-35.

2882. Stack, George J. "Kierkegaard and subjective concern." *Journal of Thought* 9 (1974):95-104.

2883. Jung, Hwa Yol. "Confucianism and existentialism: Intersubjectivity as the way of man." *Philosophy and Phenomenological Research* 30 (1969):186-202.

2884. Müller, Christa. "Vom Gewissen bei Pascal und Kierkegaard." *Evangelische Theologie* (München) 15 (1955): 115-128.

2885. Shmuëli, Adi. *Kierkegaard and Consciousness*. Trans. by Naomi Handelman. Princeton (New Jersey): Princeton Univ. Press, 1971. 202p.

Conversion

2886. Chervin, Ronda de Sola. "The Process of Conversion in the Philosophy of Religion of Soeren Kierkegaard." Ph.D., Fordham Univ., 1967, 209p. *Dissertation Abstracts* 28 (1968):4207A.

Death

2887. Croxall, Thomas H. "The death of Kierkegaard." *Church Quarterly Review* 157 (1956):271-286.

2888. Hess, Mary W. "The death of Sören Kierkegaard." *Catholic World* 182 (1955):92-98.

2889. Jensen, Povl Johs. "S. Kierkegaard og demokratiet: En skitse." In *Kierkegaardiana* 10 (1977):70-84.

Demonic

2890. Clair, André. "Le mythe de Faust et le concept kierkegaardien de démoniaque." *Revue Philosophique de Louvain* 77 (1979):24-50.

2891. Drolet, Bruno. *Le Démoniaque chez S. A. Kierkegaard.*
Joliette (Québec): Centre de Diffusion Lanaudière, 1971.
98p.

2892. Grimsley, Ronald. "Modern conceptions of the
demonic." *Church Quarterly Review* 185 (1957):185-194.

2893. Mitrani, Nora. "La beauté du diable." In *Vues sur
Kierkegaard.* Henein & Wahba, eds. 1955, 50-57.

Decision

2894. Bloth, P. C. "Die theologische Kategorie
'Entscheidung' in ihrer Bedeutung für die Religionspägogik."
Kerygma und Dogma 9 (1963):18-40.

Despair

2895. Janke, Wolfgang. "Verzweiflung; Kierkegaards
Phänomenologie des subjektiven Geistes." In *Sein und
Geschichtlichkeit.* Ingeborg Schüssler and Wolfgang Janke,
eds. Frankfurt am Main: Klostermann, 1974, 103-113.

2896. Meerpohl, Bernhard. *Die Verzweiflung als metaphysisches Phänomen in der Philosophie Sören Kierkegaards.*
Wurzburg: C. I. Becker, 1934, xi-131p. (Abhandlungen zur
Philos. u. Psychol. der Religion, 30). Phil. Diss. Münster,
1934.

2897. Sack, Max. *Die Verzweiflung. Eine Untersuchung
ihres Wesens und ihrer Entstehung.* Mit einem Anhang
(p. 107-135): Sören Kierkegaards *Krankheit zum Tode.*
Kallmünz: Lassleben, 1930, vi-136p. Phil. Diss. München,
1931.

2898. Walther, Gerda. "Sören Kierkegaards Psychologie
der Verzweiflung." *Zeitschrift für Menschenkunde* (Heidelberg) 4 (1928):208-219.

Dialectic

2899. Dollinger, Robert. "Dialektisches bei Sören Kierkegaard." *Die Furche* 17 (1931):419-427.

2900.   Sannwald, Adolf.   "Kierkegaard und Feuerbach in der
Abhängigkeit von und im Kampf mit der idealistischen
Dialektik."   In *Der Begriff der 'Dialektik' und die
Anthropologie. Eine Untersuchung über das Ich-Verständnis
in der Philosophie des deutschen Idealismus und seiner
Antipoden.*   München, 1931, 215-270.   (Forschungen zur Gesch.
u. Lehre des Protestantismus.   R. 3., Bd. 4.)

2901.   Swenson, David F.   "The 'existential dialectic' of
Kierkegaard."   *Journal of Philosophy* 35 (1938):684-685.

2902.   Swenson, David F.   "The existential dialectic of
Sören Kierkegaard."   *Ethics* 49 (1939):309-328.

2903.   Stack, George J.   "On the notion of dialectics."
Philosophy Today 15 (1971):276-290.

2904.   Traub, Friedrich.   "Zum Begriff des Dialektischen."
Zeitschrift für Theologie un Kirche (Tübingen) 37 (N.F. 10)
(1929):380-388.   (Om Kierkegaard, p. 384f.).

Discourse

2905.   Holmer, Paul.   "Kierkegaard and kinds of discourse."
Meddelelser fra Sören Kierkegaard Selskabet 4 (1954):1-5.

Double

2906.   Čiževskyi, Dmitrij.   "Zum Doppelgangerproblem bei
Dostojevskij.   Versuch einer philosophischen interpretation."   In *O Dostojevskom.*   (Über Dostojevskij.   Eine
Sammelschrift, hrsg. von A. L. Bema).   Praha, 1929 (162p.),
9-38.   (Om S. Kierkegaard, passim).

2907.   Čiževskyi, Dmitrij.   "Zum Doppelgangerproblem bei
Dostojevskij.   Versuch einer philosophischen Interpretation."   In *Dostojevskij-Studien.*   Gesammelt und herausgegeben von D. Čiževskyi.   Reichenberg: Stiepel, 1931
(116p.), 19-50.   (Om S. Kierkegaard, p. 45, 48-50).
Veröffentlichungen der Slavistischen Arbeitsgemeinschaft an
der Deutschen Universität in Prag. I. Reihe: Untersuchungen,
Heft 8.

Doxology

2908. McLelland, J. C. "Doxology as suspension of the
tragic." *Theology Today* 31 (1974):114-120.

Dread (See Anxiety, no. 2730-2743)

Duty

2909. Schrader, George. "Kant and Kierkegaard on duty
and inclination (Symposium: Kierkegaard)." *Journal of
Philosophy* 65 (1968):688-701.

Dying

2910. Slote, Michael A. "Existentialism and the fear of
dying." *American Philosophical Quarterly* 12 (1975):17-28.

Education

2911. Calogero, G. "Frammenti pedagogici di Soeren
Kierkegaard." *I Problemi della Pedagogia* (Roma) 17 (1971):
10-23.

2912. Davis, Clifford. "The Philosophy of Sören Kierkegaard and Its Implications for Education." Ph.D., Univ.
of Southern California, 1977. *Dissertation Abstracts*
38 (1978):5984A.

2913. Hill, Brian V. "Sören Kierkegaard and educational
theory." *Educational Theory* 16 (1966):344-353. Reprinted
in *The Presence of Sören Kierkegaard in Contemporary
American Life*. Lewis Lawson, ed. Metuchen (New Jersey):
The Scarecrow Press, 1971, 191-205.

2914. Hill, Brian V. *Education and the Endangered
Individual. A Critique of Ten Modern Thinkers*. New York:
Teachers College Press, 1974. 322p.

2915. Hirsch, Emanuel. "Kierkegaard als Erzähler." In his
Wege zu Kierkegaard. Berlin: Die Spur, 1968, 20-33.

2916. Kleinman, Jaquline Agnew. "Public/Private--The Education of Sören Kierkegaard." Ph.D., The Ohio State Univ., 1971, 174p. *Dissertation Abstracts* 32 (1972):4046A.

2917. Kristensen, Juhl-Bagge. "The Relevance of Sören Kierkegaard's Existentialism to a Philosophy of Education." Ph.D., State Univ. of New York at Buffalo, 1971.

2918. Liotta, R. "L'educazione della possibilità in S. Kierkegaard." *Prospettive Pedagogiche* 5 (1968):204-213.

2919. Naess, Arne. "Kierkegaard and the values of education." *Journal of Value Inquiry* 2 (1968):196-200.

2920. Naess, Arne. "Kierkegaard and educational crisis." In *Danish Yearbook of Philosophy* 8 (1971):65-70. [Discussions, 70-93]

2921. Pojman, Louis P. "Kierkegaard's theory of subjectivity and education." In *Phenomenology and Education*, 1-27.

2922. Schaal, Helmut. *Erziehung bei Kierkegaard. Das 'Aufmerksammachen auf das Religiöse' als Pädagogische Kategorie.* (Pädagogische Forschungen, 8). Heidelberg: Quelle & Meyer, 1958. 128p.

2923. Serra, Antonio. "Istanze pedagogiche nel pensiero di Soeren Kierkegaard." *Rivista Rosminiana* 71 (1977): 133-149.

Eighteenth Century

2924. Fabro, Cornelio. "La critica de Kierkegaard al ochocientos." *Sapientia* 5 (1950):9-18.

2925. Fabro, Cornelio. "La critica de Kierkegaard al octocientos." *Sapientia* (La Plata) 5 (1950):9-18.

2926. Fabro, Cornelio. "Critica di Kierkegaard all' ottocento." *Atti del XV Congresso Nazionale di Filosofia,* 375-385.

Eros

2927. Crumbine, Nancy Jay. "The Same River Twice: A Critique of the Place of Eros in the Philosophy of Kierkegaard." Ph.D., The Pennsylvania State Univ., 1972, 191p. *Dissertation Abstracts* 33 (1973):6962A.

Ethics

2928. Bauer, Wilhelm. *Die Ethik Sören Kierkegaards*.
Kahla, 1913, iv-63p. Phil. Diss. Jena.

2929. Beach, Waldo, and Niebuhr, Richard. "Sören Kierkegaard." In *Christian Ethics. Sources of the Living
Tradition*. W. Beach and R. Niebuhr, eds. With introductions. New York: Ronald, 1955, 414-443 et passim.

2930. Bogen, James. "Kierkegaard and the 'teleological
suspension of the ethical'." *Inquiry* 5 (1962):305-317.

2931. Buber, Martin. "Von einer Suspension des Ethischen."
In *Gottesfinsternis. Betrachtungen zur Beziehung zwischen
Religion und Philosophie*. Zürich: Manesse, 1953, 138-144.

2932. Buber, Martin. "Suspension of ethics." In *Moral
Principles of Action: Man's Tehical Imperative*. Ruth N.
Anshen. New York: Harper, 1952, 223-227.

2933. Bukdahl, Jörgen K. "Etik og epoke: Om lighedstanden
hos Sören Kierkegaard." *Studenterkredsen* 35 (1967):9-16.

2934. Cantoni, Remo. "Kierkegaard e la vita etica.
Saggio introduttivo." In S. Kierkegaard: *Aut-Aut. Este-
tica ed Etica nella Formazione della Personalità*. 3. ed.
Milano, 1946, 7-35.

2935. Clive, Geoffrey. "Teleological suspension of the
ethical in Nineteenth-Century literature." *Journal of
Religion* 34 (1954):75-87.

2936. Colette, Jacques. "La dialectique kierkegaardienne
de l'existence et la sphère éthico-religieuse." *Revue de
Théologie et de Philosophie* 13 (1963):317-333.

2937. Diddi, R. "Il momento etico nel pensiero di Kierkegaard." *Pagine Nuove* (Roma) no. 6 (1948).

2938. Donnelly, John Joseph Patrick. "Sören Kierkegaard's
'Teleological Suspension of the Ethical': A Reinterpreta-
tion." Ph.D., Brown Univ., 1970, 168p. *Dissertation
Abstracts* 32 (1971):483A.

2939. Duncan, Elmer H. "Kierkegaard's teleological
suspension of the ethical: A study of exception-cases."
Southern Journal of Philosophy 1 (1963):9-18.

2940. Fahrenbach, Helmut. *Kierkegaards existenz-dialektische Ethik*. (Philosophische Abhandlungen, 29).
Frankfurt am Main: Klostermann, 1968. 194p.

2941. Friedrich, Paul. "Sören Kierkegaard als ethischer
Erzicher. Eine Studie." *Pädagogisches Archiv* (Braunschweig) 48 (1906):650-662.

2942. Friedrich, Paul. "Sören Kierkegaard als ethischer
Erzieher." *Das Literarische Echo* 9 (1906-07):1028.

2943. Friedrich, Paul. "Sören Kierkegaard als ethischer
Erzieher." In *Deutsche Renaissance. Gesammelte Aufsätze*.
Bd. 1-2. Leipzig: Xenion-Verlag, 1911 und 1913.

2944. Geismar, Eduard. "Das ethische Stadium bei Sören
Kierkegaard. Aus dem Dänischen übers. und für deutsche
Leser in den Anmerkungen ergänzt von Emanuel Hirsch."
Zeitschrift für Systematische Theologie (Gütersloh) 1
(1923-24):227-300.

2945. Glenn, John D., Jr. "Kierkegaard's ethical philosophy." *Southwestern Journal of Philosophy* 5 (1974):
121-128.

2946. Gordis, R. "The faith of Abraham. A note on Kierkegaard's 'teleological suspension of the ethical'."
Judaism (New York, N.Y.) 25 (1976):414-419.

2947. Halevi, Jacob L. "Kierkegaard's teleological
suspension of the ethical: Is it Jewish?" *Judaism* 8
(1959):291-302.

2948. Hanssens, Patrick. "Éthique et foi. Quelques
réflexions inspirées par S. Kierkegaard." *Nouvelle Revue
Théologique* 109 (1977):360-380.

2949. Holmer, Paul L. "Kierkegaard and ethical theory."
Ethics 63 (1953):157-170.

2950. Hughes, Roderick P., III. "The Notion of the Ethical
in Kierkegaard." Ph.D., Univ. of Notre Dame, 1973, 307p.
Dissertation Abstracts 33 (1973):6398A.

2951. Joergensen, Carl. "The ethics of Soeren Kierkegaard." In *Atti XII Congr. Internationale Filosofia*.
Firenze: Sansoni, 1961, 243-250.

2952. King, James. "Kierkegaard's critique of ethics."
*Proceedings of the American Catholic Philosophical Associa-
tion* 46 (1972):189-198.

2953. Klemke, E. D. "Some insights for ethical theory
from Kierkegaard." *Philosophical Quarterly* 10 (1960):
322-330.

2954. Klemke, E. D. "Some insights for ethical theory
from Kierkegaard." In *The Presence of Sören Kierkegaard
in Contemporary American Life*. Lewis Lawson, ed. Metuchen
(New Jersey): The Scarecrow Press, 1971, 79-91.

2955. Lal, Basant Kumar. "Kierkegaard's approach to ethics." *Philosophical Quarterly* 38 (1965):181-190.

2956. Mackey, Louis H. "The Nature and the End of the Ethical Life According to Kierkegaard." Ph.D., Yale Univ., 1954.

2957. Mackey, Louis. "The loss of the world in Kierkegaard's ethics. *Review of Metaphysics* 15 (1961-62): 602-620.

2958. Mackey, Louis H. "The loss of the world in Kierkegaard's ethics [Abstract]." *Journal of Philosophy* 58 (1961):701.

2959. Martensen, H. *Christian Ethics*. [Sören Kierkegaard.] Trans. from the Danish with the sanction of the author by C. Spence. Edinburgh: Clark, 1873, 217-236. (Clark's Foreign Theological Library, Series 3, vol. 39.)

2960. Martensen, Hans L. "Kierkegaard und die Situationsethik." *Scholastik* 26 (1951):556-564.

2961. McInerny, Ralph. "The teleological suspension of the ethical." *Thomist* 20 (1957):295-310.

2962. McInerny, Ralph. "Ethics and persuasion: Kierkegaard's existential dialectic." *Modern Schoolman* 33 (1956):219-239.

2963. Morra, Gianfranco. "La sospensione della morale secondo S. A. Kierkegaard." *Ethica* 1 (1962):121-137.

2964. Mourant, John A. "The ethics of Kierkegaard." *Giornale Metafisica* 7 (1952):202-226.

2965. Niebuhr, H. Richard, ed. *Christian Ethics. Sources of the Living Tradition*. Waldo Beach and Richard H. Niebuhr, eds. With introductions. New York: Ronald, 1955, 414-443 et passim.

2966. Ohara, Shin. "Kierkegaard's Authorship Considered as an Ethical Argument." Ph.D., Yale Univ., 1966, 387p. *Dissertation Abstracts* 27 (1967):3401A.

2967. Pareyson, Luigi. *L'etica di Kierkegaard nella Prima Fase del suo Pensiero*. Corso di Filosofia Morale dell'anno Accademico 1964-65 (Corsi Universitari). Torino: G. Giappichelli, 1965. 226p.

2968. Perkins, Robert L. "Persistent criticisms--Misinterpretations of Sören Kierkegaard's ethical thought." In *Mem. XIII Congr. Internationale Filosofia*. 7:377-388.

2969. Riezu, Jorge. "Kierkegaard y la 'ética de situación'." *Estudios Filosóficos* 13 (1964):219-252.

2970. Russell, Bruce. "What is the ethical in *Fear and Trembling*?" *Inquiry* 18 (1975):337-343.

2971. Schäfer, Klaus. "Kierkegaard--Kirchenvater der Wertlehre: Bemerkungen zu E. Tielschs Untersuchung 'Kierkegaards Glaube'." In *Kierkegaardiana*. Niels Thulstrup, ed. Copenhagen: Munksgaard, 7 (1966):152-180.

2972. Schamp, Adele. *Die Ethik Sören Kierkegaards*. Wien, 1949. 81p. Phil. Diss. Wien, 1949.

2973. Sciacca, M. F. "L'esperienza etico-religiosa di Sören Kierkegaard." *Logos* (Napoli) 20 (1937):121-128.

2974. Schmitt, Richard. "Kierkegaard's ethics and its teleological suspension." *Journal of Philosophy* 58 (1961):701-702.

2975. Schrag, Calvin D. "A note on Kierkegaard's teleological suspension of the ethical." *Ethics* 70 (1959): 66-68.

2976. Schrag, Oswald O. "Existential ethics and axiology." *Southern Journal of Philosophy* 1 (1962):35-47.

2977. Stack, George J. "Ethica de la subjectividad en Kierkegaard." *Folia Humanistica* 99 (1971):193-220.

2978. Stack, George J. "Kierkegaard. The self and ethical existence." *Ethics* 83 (1972-73):108-125.

2979. Stack, George J. "Kierkegaard. The self as ethical possibility." *The Southwestern Journal of Philosophy* (Norman, Oklahoma) 3 (1972):35-61.

2980. Stack, George J. "Aristotle and Kierkegaard's existential ethics." *Journal of the History of Philosophy* 12 (1974):1-19.

2981. Thompson, Warren K. A. "A brief evaluation of Kierkegaard as ethical critic." *Journal of the British Society of Phenomenology* 5 (1974):219-232.

2982. Tielsch, E. "Kierkegaards Ethik im Verhältnis zur 'klassischen' Ethik, insbesondere der Kants." In *Festschrift H. J. de Vleeschauwer*. (Communications of the University of South Africa). Pretoria: Publications Committee of the Univ. of South Africa, 1960 (232p.), 131-149.

2983. Ukkola, Helge. "Die ethische Existenz des Menschen im Denken Sören Kierkegaards." *Neue Zeitschrift für Systematische Theologie* 10 (1968):31-37.

2984. van Munster, Donulus O. F. M. "Das Prinzip der
Ethik. Eine Kierkegaardsche Annäherung." *Wissenschaft
und Weisheit* 26 (1963):197-205.

2985. Walker, Jeremy. "The idea of reward in morality
[Kierkegaard]. In *Kierkegaardiana* 8 (1971):30-52.

2986. Warnock, Mary. "Existentialist ethics." *New
Studies in Ethics* 2 (1975):361-420.

Evil

2987. Khan, Abrahim H. "Kierkegaard's conception of evil."
Journal of Religion and Health 14 (1975):63-66.

2988. Ricoeur, Paul. "Kierkegaard et le mal." *Revue de
Théologie et de Philosophie* 13 (1963):292-302.

Existence

2989. Anonymous. "That blessed word 'existential' [Kier-
kegaard]." *Christian Century* 72 (1955):1390-1392.

2990. Beck, Maximillian. "Von der Existenz der Philosophen." *Philosophische Hefte* (Berlin) 1 (1928):3-4.
(Sonderheft über Heidegger: *Sein und Zeit*.)

2991. Broudy, Harry S. "Kierkegaard's levels of existence." *Philosophy and Phenomenological Research* 1 (1941):
294-312.

2992. Collins, James D. "Three Kierkegaardian problems:
The meaning of existence." *New Scholasticism* 22 (1948):
371-416.

2993. Collins, James. "The mind of Kierkegaard: The
spheres of existence and the romantic outlook." *Modern
Schoolman* 26 (1949):121-147.

2994. Diem H. "Dogmatik und Existenzdialektik bei Sören
Kierkegaard." *Orbis Litterarum* Copenhague) 10 (1955):50-65.

2995. Diem, H. "Dogmatik und Existenzdialiktik bei Sören
Kierkegaard." *Evangelische Theologie* 15 (1955):492-506.

2996. Dollinger, Robert. "Das 'Existentielle' bei Kierkegaard." *Die Furche* (Berlin) 15 (1929):33-42.

2998. Garcia Vieyra, A. "Ontologia de la existencia."
Sapientia (Buenos Aires) 2 (1947).

2999. Gerken, Alexander O. F. M. "Theologie und Existenz bei Kierkegaard." *Wissenschaft und Weisheit* 32 (1969): 19-38.

3000. Hubscher, Alfred. "Der Existenzbegriff bei Heidegger, Sartre und Kierkegaard." *Kirchenblatt für die Reformierte Schweiz* (Basel) 105 (1949):194-199.

3001. Johnson, Ralph Henry. *The Concept of Existence in the* Concluding Unscientific Postscript. The Hague: Martinus Nijhoff, 1972, xvii-226p.

3002. Kean, Charles Duell. *The Meaning of Existence.* New York: Harper, 1947; London: Latimer, 1947.

3003. Leendertz, Willem. "Existentie bij Kierkegaard." In his *Dogma en Existentie.* Amsterdam, 1933, 21-27.

3004. Lögstrup, K. E. "Le concept de l'existence chez Kierkegaard." *Studia Theologica* 19 (1965):260-268.

3005. Lowrie, W. "'Existence' as understood by Kierkegaard and for Sartre." *Sewanee Review* (U.S.A.) 58 (1950): 379-401.

3006. MacCallum, Henry Reid. "Kierkegaard and levels of existence." *Univ. Toronto* (Ontario) 13 (1944):258-275.

3007. Maurhofer, Hugo. "Analytik der Existenz." *Neue Schweizer Rundschau* (Zürich) 24 (1931):726-735.

3008. Pfisler, Rudolf. "Zur Existenzdialektik Sören Kierkegaards." *Neue Schweizer Rundschau* (Zürich) N.F. 20 (1952):112-117.

3009. Peiper, Annemarie. "Die Bedeutung des Begriffs 'Existenzkategorie' im Denken Kierkegaards." *Zeitschrift für Philosophische Forschung* 25 (1971):187-201.

3010. Ramsey, Paul. "*Existenz* and the existence of God: A study of Kierkegaard and Hegel." *Journal of Religion* 28 (1948):157-176.

3011. Rohden, Valério. "A existência autêntica segundo Kierkegaard." *Revista Brasileira de Filosofia* 18 (1968): 298-304.

3012. Schulz, Walter. "Existenz und System bei Kierkegaard." In *Wesen und Wirklichkeit des Menschen.* Göttingen: Vandenhoeck und Ruprecht, 1957.

3013. Smith, John E. "The revolt of existence." *Yale Review* 43 (1964):364-371.

3014. Smith, Vincent E. "Existentialism and existence." *Thomist* 11 (1948):297-329.

3015. Smith, Vincent E. "Existentialism and existence."
Thomist 11 (1948):141-196.

3016. Stevens, Eldon Lloyd. "Kierkegaard's Categories of
Existence." Ph.D., Univ. of Colorado, 1964, 283p.
Dissertation Abstracts 26 (1965):5487.

3017. Weymann-Weyhe, W. "Sören Kierkegaard und die
christliche Existenz." *Die Kirche in der Welt* (Münster)
2 (1949):223-226.

3018. Wilde, Frank-Eberhard. *Kierkegaards Verständnis
der Existenz*. (Pubs. of the Kierkegaard Soc., Copenhagen,
3). Copenhagen: Rosenkilde & Bagger, 1969.

3019. Winkler, Robert. "Die Eigenart des theologischen
Erkennens. Ein Beitrag zum Problem der Existenz."
Zeitschrift für Systematische Theologie 9 (1931-32):277-318.
(Om S. Kierkegaard, p. 287-290.)

Existential

3020. Anonymous. "That blessed word 'existential'."
Christian Century 72 (1955):1390-1392.

3021. Dollinger, Robert. "'Existentielle' bei Kierkegaard." *Die Furche* (Berlin) 15 (1929):33-42.

3022. Emmet, Dorothy M. "Kierkegaard and the 'existential'
philosophy." *Philosophy* 16 (1941):257-271.

3023. Walen, Georg J. M. "Kierkegaard's existential
system." *Journal of Liberal Religion* 2 (1941):187-196.

Existentialism

3024. Abbagnano, N. "Kierkegaard e as origens do existencialismo." *Revista da Universidade de São Paulo* fascic. 1
(1950).

3025. Aiken, H. D., ed. "Advent of existentialism: Sören
Kierkegaard." In *Age of Ideology*. Boston: Houghton
Mifflin, 1956, 225-244.

3026. Alexander, Jan W. "La philosophie existentialiste
en France. Ses sources et ses problèmes fondamentaux."
French Studies (Oxford) 1 (1947):95-104.

3027.   Aliotta, Antonio. *Critica dell Esistenzialismo.*
[Scritti su Kierkegaard, Dostoievski, Berdiaev, Carlo Barth,
Heidegger, Jaspers, Marcel, Camus, Abbagnano, etc.].
Roma: Perrella, 1951. 184p.

3028.   Arendt, Hannah. "La philosophie de l'existence
(Trad. par Cathrine Mendelssohn). *Deucalion* (Paris) 2
(1947):217-245.

3029.   Armellini, Rina Anna. "Genesi ed evoluzione dell'
angoscia esistenzialista (profili di Kierkegaard, Dostojewski, Kaffka, Sartre e Camus)." *Centro di Cultura* Aldo,
Masieri, Rovigo. Numero Speciale della *Revista La Sorgente*
1950. 47p.

3030.   Arnou, R. "L'existentialisme a la manière de Kierkegaard et J.-P. Sartre." *Gregorianum* (Roma) 27 (1946):
63-88.

3031.   Beck, Maximillian. "Existentialism, rationalism,
and Christian faith." *Journal of Religion* 26 (1946):
283-295.

3032.   Beck, Maximillian. "Existentialism versus naturalism
and idealism." *South Atlantic Quarterly* 47 (1948):153-163.

3033.   Belmond, S. "A propos de 'Philosophie existentielle." *Études Franciscaines* (Paris) 34 (1939):676-681.

3034.   Benzow, Kristofer. "Sören Kierkegaard och existentialismen [S. Kierkegaard and existentialism]." *Svensk
Tidskrift* (Suède) 38 (1951):223-228.

3035.   Bixler, Julius Seelye. "The contribution of Exis-
tenz-Philosophie." *Harvard Theological Review* 33 (1940):
35-63.

3036.   Blackham, H. J. "Sören Kierkegaard (1813-1855)."
In *Six Existentialist Thinkers*. (Kierkegaard, Nietzsche,
Jaspers, Marcel, Heidegger, Sartre). London: Routledge &
Kegan Paul, 1952, 1-22.

3037.   Buri, Fritz. "Kierkegaard und die heutige Existenzphilosophie. Vortrag im Radio Basel 19.12.1950 im Rahmen
eines Zyklus über Existenzphilosophie." *Theologische
Zeitschrift* (Basel) 7 (1951):55-65.

3039.   Campbell, Robert. *L'esistenzialismo. S. Kierkegaard, K. Jaspers, G. Marcel, M. Heidegger, J.-P. Sartre.*
[Trad. dal francese]. Napoli: Ed. Rocco, 1955. 160p.

3040.   Carrasco de la Vega, Rubén. "Origen del existencialismo: Alma y doctrina de Kierkegaard." *Kollasuyo*
(La Paz) 10 (1951):50-61.

3041. Charlesworth, Max. "The meaning of existentialism."
Thomist 16 (1953):472-496.

3042. Chestov, Léon (Sjestov, Lev). "Job ou Hegel?
Apropos de la philosophie existentielle de Kierkegaard."
[Trad. par B. de Schloezer]. *La Nouvelle Revue Française*
23 (1935):755-762.

3043. Chestov. Léon. *Kierkegaard y la Filosofía Existen-
cial (Vox Clamantis in Deserto)*. Trad. de José Ferrater
Mora. Buenos Aires: Ed. Sudamericana, 1947, 332p. 2d ed.
Ibid., 1952, 327p.

3044. Chiesa, Mario. "Cinque esistenzialisti." *Rivista
Rosminiana* 44 (1950):67-75.

3045. Collins, James. *The Existentialists. A Critical
Study.* [S. Kierkegaard]. Chicago: Regnery, 1952.

3046. Conde, R. "Kierkegaard y el existencialismo."
Convivium 2 (1957):195-204.

3047. Dallen, James. "Existentialism and the Catholic
thinker." *Catholic World* 200 (1965):294-299.

3048. D'Athayde, Tristán. *El Existencialismo, Filosofía
de Nuestro Tiempo.* Trad. de Edgar Ruffo. Buenos Aires:
Emecé, 1949. 70p.

3049. Delfgaauw, Bernard. *Wat is Existentialisme? Kierkegaard, Marcel, Jaspers, Heidegger, Sartre.* 7de, herziene
druk. Baarn: Het Wereldvenster, 1969. 130p.

3050. de Almeida, Viera. "Filosofia existencial (Origem)."
Ocidente (Lisboa) 31 (1947):16-19.

3051. de Coster, Sylvain. "La crise de l'existentialisme."
Revue Internationale de Philosophie (Bruxelles) 1 (1939):
398-402.

3052. de Mondonca, A. "The origin of existentialism
[Kierkegaard]." *Journal of the University of Bombay*
21 (1952):107-119.

3053. Dollinger, Robert. "War Sören Kierkegaard Existen-
zialist?" *Evangelsich-lutherische Kirchenzeitung* (Berlin)
N.F. 9 (1955):332-336; 351-354.

3054. Earle, William. "Phenomenology and existentialism."
Journal of Philosophy 57 (1960):75-84.

3055. Eiler, Vernard. "Existentialism and the Brethren."
Brethren Life and Thought 5 (1960):31-38.

3056. Emmet, Dorothy M. "Kierkegaard and the 'existential'
philosophy." *Philosophy* (London) (1941):257-271.

3057.   Evans, Oliver.   "The rise of existentialism."
South Atlantic Quarterly 47 (1948):152-156.

3058.   Fabro, Cornelio.   "Kierkegaard und die Existentialisten."   *Sonntagsblatt*, hrsg. von Hanns Lilje (Hannover)
2 (1949):15.

3059.   Fondane, Benjamen.   "Le lundi existentiel et le
dimanche de l'histoire."   *L'existence*.   Essais par Albert
Camus, Benjamin Fondane [etc].   Paris: Gallimard, 1945,
25-53.   (Collection Métaphysique 1).   [Om S. Kierkegaard.]

3060.   Fondane, Benjamin.   "Kierkegaard et la philosophie
existentielle."   *Revue de Philosophie* 37:381-414.

3061.   Ford, Richard S.   "Existentialism: Philosophy or
theology?"   *Religion in Life* 28 (1956):433-442.

3062.   Fragata, Júlio.   "O existencialismo teológico de
Kierkegaard."   *Filosofia* (Losboa) 2 (1956):250-255.

3063.   Freehof, Solomon B.   "Aspects of existentialism."
Carnegie Magazine 22 (1949):292-294.

3064.   Garcia Vieyra, A.   "Ontologia de la existencia."
Sapientia (Buenos Aires) 2 (1947).

3065.   Gibson, A. Boyce.   "Existential religion and
existential philosophy [Kierkegaard]."   In *Danish Yearbook
of Philosophy* 8 (1971):94-98.   [Discussions, 99-114]

3065a.   Gigante, M.   "Il messaggio esistenziale di Kierkegaard e la filosofia hegeliana."   *Asprenas* (Napoli)
17 (1970):392-412.

3066.   Gignoux, Victor.   *La Philosophie Existentielle*.
[S. Kierkegaard, K. Jaspers, Heidegger, J.-P. Sartre,
G. Marcel, R. le Senne].   [1950].   2. ed.   Paris: Lefébvre,
1955.   92p.

3067.   Gonzalez Alvarez, Angel.   "Kierkegaard y el existencialismo."   *Cisneros* 11 (1946):29-38.

3068.   Grene, Marjorie.   "Sören Kierkegaard: The self
against the system."   In *Dreadful Freedom.   A Critique of
Existentialism*.   Chicago: Univ. of Chicago Press, 1948,
15-40 et passim.

3069.   Griffin, J. T.   "Fathers of existentialism."
Philosophical Studies 6 (1958):155-164.

3070.   Grimsley, Ronald.   *Existentialist Thought*.   [2d. ed.]
Mystic (Connecticut): L. Verry, 1964.   223p.

3071.   Gumbiner, Joseph Henry.   "Existentialism and father
Abraham."   *Commentary* 5 (1948):143-148.

3072. Harper, Ralph. "The dialectics: Kierkegaard." In
Existentialism. A Theory of Man. Cambridge (Massachusetts):
Harvard Univ. Press, 1948, 44-66, 159-160 et passim.

3073. Heinemann, F. H. *Existentialism and Modern Predicament.* New York and Toronto: Harper, 1953; London: Adam &
Charles Black, 1953, 30-46.

3074. Huber, G. "Comment les philosophies de l'existence
se sont-elles approprié la pensée kierkegaardienne." In
Danish Yearbook of Philosophy 9 (1971):37-42. [Discussions,
42-64]

3075. Irving, John A. "Thoughts on existentialism."
Queen's Quarterly 57 (1950):298-303.

3076. Ivanka, Endre von. "Was bleibt von der Existenzphilosophie? Zu dem Buch von L. Gabriel, *Existenzphilosophie von Kierkegaard bis Sartre.*" *Scholastik* 27 (1952):
400-408.

3077. Jolivet, Régis. "Les sources de l'existentialisme."
In *Les Doctrines Existentialistes de Kierkegaard à J.-P.
Sartre.* Paris, 1948, 33-59.

3078. Jolivet, Régis, en la Facultad [de Humanidades y
Ciencias de la Educación. Universidad Nacional de la
Ciudad Eva Perón] [résumé de deux conférences intitulées:
*Sartre: Le Monde de la Nausée et de la Liberté, L'exis-
tentialisme de Kierkegaard,* 30 et 31 juillet 1952].
Revista de Filosofia. La Plata (1952):74-77.

3079. Kean, Charles Duell. *The Meaning of Existence.*
[S. Kierkegaard]. New York: Harper, 1947; London: Latimer,
1947.

3080. King, Joe M. "Kierkegaard as an existentialist."
Furman Studies 15 (1967):35-44.

3081. Kranzlin, Gerhard. "Sören Kierkegaard." In
Existenzphilosophie und Panhumanismus. Scheldorf am
Kochelsee: Brunnen, 1950, 7-37. (Monographien zur
philosophischen Forschung, 11).

3082. Kraft, Juliun. "The philosophy of existence."
Philosophy and Phenomenological Research 1 (1941):339-358.

3083. Kreyche, G. "A glance at existentialism." *Ave*
102 (1965):10-13.

3084. Kuhn, Helmut. "Existentialism and metaphysics."
Review of Metaphysics 1 (1947):37-60.

3085. Kuhn, Helmut. "Existentialism, Christian and anti-
Christian." *Theology Today* 6 (1947):37-60.

3086.   Kuhn, Helmut. *Encounter with Nothingness. An Essay on Existentialism.* Hinsdale (Illinois): Regnery, 1949, 13-20, 29-30, 67-68, 124-129 et passim. (Humanist Library, 2).

3087.   Kurtz, Paul W.   "Kierkegaard, existentialism, and the contemporary scene." *Antioch Review* 21 (1961-62): 471-487.

3088.   Langan, T.   "The original existentialist revolt." In *Recent Philosophy, Hegel to the Present.* E. H. Gilson, ed. New York: Random House, 1966, 67-92.

3089.   Leendertz, J. W.   "Kierkegaard, Schopenhauer, Nietzsche en de existentiephilosophie." *Philosophia* redig. van H. van Oyen 2: Utrecht: De Haan, 1949, 337-378.

3090.   Léger, G.   "Kierkegaard et la philosophie de l'existence." *Revue des Sciences Philosophiques et Théologiques* (1961).

3091.   Licciardello, P. Nello.   "Itinerari dell'esistenzialismo romantico. S. Kierkegaard." *Teoresi* 15 (1960): 25-42.

3092.   Lombardi, R.   "Sören Kierkegaard, precursore dell' esistenzialismo." *La Civiltà Cattolica* (Roma) no. 2256 (1944).

3093.   Lunding, Erik. *Adalbert Stifter; mit einem Anhang über Kierkegaard und die existentielle Literaturwissenschaft.* Köbenhavn: Nyt Nordisk Forlag, 1946, 131-150. (Studien zur Kunst und Existenz).

3094.   Mac Gregor, J.   "Dos precursores del existencialismo: Kierkegaard y Unamuno." *Filosofía y Letras* (México) 22 (1951):43-44, 203-219.

3095.   MacIntyre, Alasdair.   "Existentialism." In *A Critical History of Philosophy.* D. J. O'Connor, ed. London: The Free Press of Glencoe-Collier, Macmillan Co., 1964, 509-529. [Spec. 509-516]

3096.   Mackey, Louis H.   "Kierkegaard and the problem of existential philosophy." *Review of Metaphysics* 9 (1956): 404-419.

3097.   Mackey, Louis.   "Kierkegaard and the problem of existential philosophy." *Review of Metaphysics* 9 (1956): 569-588.

3098.   Marcel, Gabriel.   "Some reflections on existentialism." *Philosophy Today* 8 (1964):248-257.

3099. Maritain, Jacques. "From existential existentialism to academic existentialism." *Sewanee Review* 56 (1948): 210-229.

3100. Martin, Vincent O. P. *Existentialism: Kierkegaard, Sartre and Camus*. (Compact Studies). Washington: Thomist Press, 1962. 48p.

3101. Mondoca, A. de. "The origin of existentialism." *Journal of the University of Bombay* 21 (1952):107-119.

3102. Montier, Jacques. "L'existentialisme aura cent ans le 11 novembre. Son inspirateur fut le philosophe danois S[o]ren Kierkegaard dont on va commémorer la disparition prématurée." *Le Progrès Égyptien* (3.11.1955).

3103. Morando, D. "Kierkegaard padre dell'esistenzialismo." *Rivista Rosminiana* no 2 (1942).

3104. Morando, Dante. "Kierkegaard padre dell'esistenzialismo." In *Saggi su L'Esistenzialismo Teologico*. Drescia: Morcelliana, 1949, 17-41. (Problemi e Opinioni).

3105. Mounier, Emmanuel. *Introduction aux Existentialismes*. [S. Kierkegaard]. Paris, 1947, 9-13.

3106. Mourant, John A. "The limitations of religious existentialism [Kierkegaard]." *International Philosophical Quarterly* 1 (1961):437-452.

3107. Murchland, Bernard. "The teaching of existentialism." *Philosophy Today* 21 (1977):227-240.

3108. Oppel, Horst. "Kierkegaard und die existentielle Literaturwissenschaft." *Dichtung und Volkstum* (N.F. des Euphorion, Zeitschrift für Literaturgeschichte) 38 (1937): 18-29.

3109. Pareyson, L. "Nota Kierkegaardiana." *Annali della Scuola Normale di Pisa* (Bologna) 8 (1939):53-68. Reprinted as "Sören Kierkegaard e l'esistenzialismo," in *Studi Sull'esistenzialismo*. Firenze: Sansoni, 1943. 2. ed. ibid. 1950, 412p. (Studi Filosofice già diretti da G. Gentile. Terza ser. 8).

3110. Paul, William W. "Faith and reason in Kierkegaard and modern existentialism." *Review of Religion* 20 (1956): 149-163.

3111. Paulsen, Anna. "Die Auswirkung Sören Kierkegaards in der Existenzphilosophie heute." *Die Stimme der Gemeinde*. Monatsschrift der Bekennenden Kirche (Stuttgart) 2 (1950): 13-14.

3112. Perry, Edmund. "Was Kierkegaard a biblical existentialist?" *Journal of Religion* 36 (1956):17-23.

3113. Prini, Pietro. *Storia del Esistenzialismo.* Roma:
Ed. Studium, 1971. 209p.

3114. Pruche, Benito. " Es ateo el Existencialismo?"
Trad. del Francés por Secundino Garcia. *Sapientia* 6
(1951):109-116.

3115. Rhoades, D. H. "Essential varieties of existentialism." *The Personalist* 35 (1954):32-40.

3116. Roubiczek, P. *Existentialism For and Against.*
Cambridge: University Press, 1964. 197p.

3117. San Miguel, José R. "En torno a Kierkegaard:
Posibilidad y sentido de una teología en el existencialismo." *Crisis* 4 (1957):433-445.

3118. Schrag, Oswald O. "The main types of existentialism."
Religion in Life 23 (1953-54):103-113.

3119. Schulz, Walter. "Existenz und System bei Sören
Kierkegaard." *Wesen und Wirklichkeit des Menschen.*
Göttingen: Vandenhoeck und Ruprecht, 1957, 107-128.

3120. Schuon, F. "Letter on existentialism." *Studies
in Comparative Religions* 9 (1975):66-69.

3121. Sciacca, G. M. *La Filosofia dell'Esistenza e Sören
Kierkegaard.* Palermo: Lilia, 1949.

3122. Sciacca, Michele Federico. "Interpretación crítica
del existencialismo." Trad. de Celia María del Degan.
Humanitas. Anuario del Centro de Estudios Humanísticos
(Univ. de Nuevo León) 4 (1963):67-79.

3123. Searles, Herbert L. "Kierkegaard's philosophy as a
source of existentialism." *The Personalist* 29 (1948):
173-186.

3124. Settimana di studio sull'esistenzialismo all'Università di Napoli (30 Aprile-5 Maggio 1956). *Centro Italiano
Studi Scientifici Filosofici e Teologici* (Ottobre 1956):
16-22.

3125. Shearson, William A. "The common assumptions of
existentialist philosophy." *International Philosophical
Quarterly* 15 (1975):131-147.

3126. Siebers, Bernardo. "Sören Kierkegaard y el existencialismo." *Archivos de la Sociedad Peruana de Filosofía* 3 (1950):9-20.

3127. Slök, Johs. "Das existenzphilosophische Motiv im Denken von Kierkegaard." *Studia Theologica* 9 (1955): 116-130.

3128. Slök, Johannes. "Das existenzphilosophische Motiv im Denken Sören Kierkegaards." *Orbis Litterarum* 12 (1957): 67-78.

3129. Smith, Vincent Edward. "Existentialism and existence. Parts 1-2." *Thomist* 11 (1949):141-196, 277-329; 146-160.

3130. Sörensen, Villy. "Kierkegaard og det eksistentielle." *Ord och Bild* 72 (1963):466-468.

3131. Stefanini, Luigi. *Esistenzialismo ateo ed Esistenzialismo teistico. Esposizione e Critica Costruttiva.* In appendice: *L'estetica dell' Esistenzialismo.* Padova: Casa ed. dott. Antonio Milani, 1952. 370p.

3132. Strenström, Thure. *Existentialismen. Studier i dess Idetradition och Litterara Yttringar.* Stockholm: Natur o Kultur, 1966. [Tradition of ideas and its literary manifestations.]

3133. Thomas, John Heywood. "Kierkegaard and existentialism." *Scottish Journal of Theology* 6 (1953):379-395.

3134. Thomas, G. F. "Christian existentialism: Kierkegaard." In his *Religious Philosophies of the West.* New York: Scribners, 1965, 290-336.

3135. Tillich, Paul. "Kierkegaard as an existential thinker." *Union Review* 4 (1942):5-7.

3136. Tillich, Paul. "Existential philosophy." *Journal of the History of Ideas* 5 (1944):44-70.

3137. Torii, Masao. "Jitsuzon Tetsugaku Kenkyu-Kirukegoru kara Haidegga e [Existential philosophy from Kierkegaard to Heidegger]." *Gozen* 1-5 September 1948-March 1949, 56p.

3138. Traub, Friedrich. "Existentielles Denken." *Zeitschrift für Theologie und Kirche* N.F. 12 (1931):261-285. (Om Kierkegaard, p. 261-272, 284.)

3139. Vallejos, M. A. R. "Sobre Kierkegaard y el existencialismo." *Universidad* (Santa Fe) (1975):13-22.

3140. Vidiella, J. *De Kierkegaard a Sartre. El Existencialismo.* (Marabú Zas., 83). Barcelona: Bruguera, 1963. 147p.

3141. Waelhens, A. de. "Kierkegaard en de hedendaagsche existentialisten." *Tijdschrift voor Philosophie* (leuven) 1 (1939):827-851.

3142. Wahl, Jean. "Existentialism: A preface." *New Republic* 113 (1945):442-444.

3143. Wahl, Jean. *Les Philosophies de l'Existence.* [S. Kierkegaard]. Paris: Armand Colin, 1954, 15; 22-39 et passim.

3144. Wahl, Jean. *Vom Nichts, vom Sein und von unserer Existenz. Versuch einer kleinen Geschichte des Existentialismus.* In die deutsche Sprache übertr. von Dominique Bernard. Augsburg & Basel: Die Brigg, 1954.

3145. Walen, Georg J. "Kierkegaard's existential system." *Journal of Liberal Religion* 2 (1941):187-196.

3146. Werner, Charles. "Kierkegaard et la Philosophie Existentielle." In *La Philosophie Moderne.* Paris: Payot, 1954, 282-307.

3147. Wilburn, Ralph G. "The philosophy of existence and the faith-relation." *Religion in Life* 30 (1961):597-517.

3148. Wild, John. "Kierkegaard and contemporary existential philosophy." *Anglican Theological Review* 38 (1956): 15-32.

3149. Wild, John. "Existentialism: A new view of man." *University of Toronto Quarterly* 27 (1957):79-95.

3150. Yanitelli, Victor. "Types of existentialism." *Thought* 24 (1954):495-508.

3151. Zander, Lev A. "Aux sources de l'existentialisme (Une méditation)." In *Vues sur Kierkegaard.* Henein & Wahba, eds. 1955, 38-44.

3152. Zeegers, V. "L'existentialisme de Kierkegaard à J.-P. Sartre." *Revue Générale Belge* (1951):1-18.

3153. Zuidema, S. U. "Het existentialisme bij Kierkegaard." *Philosophia Reformata* 15 (1950):40-45; 49-65.

Faith

3154. Anz, W. "Philosophie und Glaube bei S. Kierkegaard. Ueber die Bedeutung der Existenzdialektik für die Theologie." *Zeitschrift für Theologie und Kirche* 51 (1954):50-105.

3155. Bianchi, Cirillo. "Cristo scandalo della ragione e oggetto della fede secondo Kierkegaard." *Rivista Rosminiana* 68 (1974):316-321.

3156. Blanchet, Charles. "Kierkegaard ou la foi sauvage."
Esprit 39 (1971):916-928.

3157. Blanshard, Brand. "Kierkegaard on faith." *The
Personalist* 49 (1968):5-23. [See also M. Capek, no. 3161
and 3173]

3158. Brouillard, Henri. "La foi d'après Kierkegaard."
Bulletin de Littérature Ecclésiastique (Toulouse) 48
(1947):19-30.

3159. Burgess, Andrew John. "The Concept of Passionate
Faith; Kierkegaard and Analytical Philosophy of Mind."
Ph.D., Yale Univ., 1969, 250p. *Dissertation Abstracts*
31 (1970):1319A.

3160. Cain, David William. "Reckoning with Kierkegaard:
Christian Faith and Dramatic Literature." Ph.D., Princeton
Univ., 1976, 325p. *Dissertation Abstracts* 37 (1976):
2240A.

3161. Capek, Milic. "Professor Blanshard on Kierkegaard."
Modern Schoolman 48 (1970-71):44-53. [See also *Kierkegaard on Faith*, no. 3157 and 3173]

3162. Collins, J. "Faith and reflection in Kierkegaard."
Journal of Religion 37 (1957):10-19.

3163. Collins, James. "Fede e riflessione in Kierkegaard."
In *Studi Kierkegaardiani*. A cura di Cornelio Fabro.
Brescia: Morcelliana, 1958, 105-123.

3164. Diamond, Malcolm L. "Faith and its tensions:
A criticism of religious existentialism." *Judaism* 13
(1964):317-327.

3165. Donohue, Keven E. "Reflection and Faith in Sören
Kierkegaard." Ph.D., The Catholic Univ. of America,
1973, 264p. *Dissertation Abstracts* 33 (1973):6963A.

3166. Dupré, Louis. "La dialectique de l'acte de foi
chez Sören Kierkegaard." *Revue Philosophique de Louvain*
54 (1956):418-455.

3167. Fabro, Cornelio. "La fenomenologia della fede--
Ambiguità della fede in Soeren Kierkegaard." *Archivio di
Filosofia* (1957):187-197. [Il compito della fenomeno-
logia.]

3168. Fabro, Cornelio. "Foi et raison dans l'oeuvre de
Kierkegaard." *Revue des Sciences Philosophiques et
Théologiques* (Le Saulchoir) 32 (1948):169-206.

3169. Fruchon, Pierre. "Kierkegaard et l'historicité de
la foi. Autopsie de la foi et temporalité." *Recherches
de Sciences Religieuses* 61 (1973):321-351. [Summary, 352]

3170.   Gerber, R. J.   "Kierkegaard.   Reason and faith."
Thought 44 (1969):29-52.

3171.   Grönbech, Bo.   "Kritiske betragtninger over Sören
Kierkegaards kristendom [Critical reflections on the
Christian faith of Sören Kierkegaard]."   *Perspektiv*
1 (1953):3-8.

3171a.   Guterman, Norbert.   "Kierkegaard and his faith."
Partisan Review 10 (1943):134-142.

3172.   Keyserling, Hermann.   "Ein Beitrag zur Kritik des
Glaubens."   *Archiv für Systematische Philosophie* (Berlin)
N.F. 12 (1906):437-449.

3173.   Kleinman, Jackie.   "Capek on Blanshard on Kierkegaard."   *Modern Schoolman* 50 (1973):209-219.   [See no. 3157
and 3161]

3174.   Lakebrink, Bernhard.   "Kierkegaard und der christliche Glaube."   *Neues Abendland*.   Zeitschrift für Politik,
Geschichte, Kultur (Augsburg) 4 (1949):67-69.

3175.   Manzia, C.   "Il problema della fede in Kierkegaard."
Problemi scelti de teologia contemporanea.   Realazioni
lette nella sezione di teologia del *Congresso Interna-
zionale per il IV Centenario della Pontificia Università
Gregoriana*, 13.-17. ottobre 1953.   *Analecta Gregoriana*
vol. 68.   Series facultatis Theologicae, Sectio A, no. 11.
Romae: Apud aedes Univ. Gregorianae, 1954, viii-468p.
(S. Kierkegaard in p. 123-132.)

3176.   Martin, H. V.   *The Wings of Faith.   A Consideration
of the Nature and Meaning of Christian Faith in the Light
of the Work of Sören Kierkegaard*.   New York: The Philosophical Library, 1951.   132p.

3177.   Michalson, Carl.   "Kierkegaard's theology of faith."
Religion in Life 32 (1963):225-237.

3178.   Murphy, J. L.   "Faith and reason in the teaching of
Kierkegaard."   *American Ecclesiastical Review* 145 (1961):
233-265.

3179.   Niebuhr, Reinhold.   "Coherence, incoherence, and
Christian faith."   *Journal of Religion* 31 (1951):155-168.

3180.   Oyen, H. van.   "Der philosophische Glaube."
Theologische Zeitschrift 14 (1958):14-37.

3181.   Paci, Enzo.   "Kierkegaard e la dialettica della
fede."   (In *Kierkegaard e Nietzsche. . .*).   *Archivio di
Filosofia* (Milano-Roma) no. 2 (1953):9-44.

3182. Paresce, E. "Hume, Hamann, Kierkegaard e la filosofia della credenza." *Rivista Internazionale de Filosofia del Diritto* no. 4 (1949).

3183. Paul, William W. "Faith and reason in Kierkegaard
and modern existentialism." *Review of Religion* 20 (1956):
149-163.

3184. Roberts, Robert. "Faith and modern humanity: Two
approaches." *Christian Century* 95 (1978):329-333.

3185. Ruttenbeck, W. "Glaube und Schrift. Eine Betrachtung im Anschluss an S. Kierkegaard." *Der Geisteskampf
der Gegenwort* (Gütersloh) 65 (1929):254-263.

3186. Sen, Krishna. "A comparative study of the concept
of faith of Stace, Dewey, Kierkegaard, and St. Thomas
Aquinas." *Philosophical Quarterly Amalner* (India)
29 (1956-57):69-74.

3187. Stack, George J. "La comprensión de la fe en
Kierkegaard." *Folia Humanística* 12 (1974):219-233.

3188. Tracy, David. "Kierkegaard's concept of the act of
faith: Its structure and significance." *Dunwoodie Review*
3 (1963):194-215; ibid., 4 (1964):133-176.

Fate

3189. McKinnon, Alastair. "The conquest of fate in Kierkegaard." *Cirpho* 1 (1973):47-58.

Fear

3190. Shein, L. J. "El concepto Kierkegaardiano de temor
en relación con el yo." *Folia Humanística* 15 (1977):
297-306.

Fideism

3191. King, J. T. "Fideism and rationality." *New Scholasticism* 49 (1975):431-450.

3192. Melchiore, Virgilio. "Kierkegaard e il fideismo."
Rivista di Filosofia Neo-Scolastica (Milano) 45 (1953):
143-176.

Freedom

3193. Amore, R., and Elrod, J. "From ignorance to knowledge; a study in the Kierkegaardian and Theravada Buddhist
notions of freedom." *Union Seminary Quarterly Review*
26 (1970):59-79.

3194. Blass, Josef Leonhard. *Die Krise der Freiheit im
Denken Sören Kierkegaards. Untersuchungen zur Konstitution
der Subjektivität*. Ratingen b. Düsseldorf: Henn, 1968.
246p.

3195. Giesz, L. "Schwindel der Freiheit [Kierkegaard,
Nietzsche, Jaspers]." *Studium Generale* 14 (1961):509-520.

3196. Hansen, Valdemar. "L'idée de la liberté chez
Kierkegaard et Renouvier." Proceedings of *The Tenth
International Congress of Philosophy*. 1948. Amsterdam:
North Holland, 1949, 1191-1194.

3197. Hartt, Julian N. "Christian freedom reconsidered:
The case of Kierkegaard." *Harvard Theological Review*
60 (1967):133-144.

3198. Jolivet, Régis. "La liberté selon Kierkegaard."
Témoignages, St. Léger, Vauban (Yonne) (1955):359-369.

3199. Jolivet, Régis. "Kierkegaard et la liberté de
choix." *Orbis Litterarum* 10 (1955):107-111. [Symposion
Kierkegaardianum]

3200. Jolivet, Régis. "La libertà e l'onnipotenza
secondo Kierkegaard." In *Studi Kierkegaardiani*. A cura
di Cornelio Fabro. Brescia: Morcelliana Editrice, 1957,
165-179.

3201. Killinger, John. "Existentialism and human freedom."
English Journal 50 (1961):303-313.

3202. Lombardi, F. "Reflexiones sobre el concepto de
libertad en Kierkegaard." *Ciencia Fe* 14 (1958):499-518.

3203. Malantschuk, Gregor. "La dialectique de la liberté
selon Sören Kierkegaard [Paru sous le titre "Fridehens
dialektik hos S. Kierkegaard," dans le *Dansk Teologisk
Tidsskrift* 12 (1949):193-207]. (Trad. du danois par
J. Colette). *Revue des Sciences Philosophiques et Théologiques* 42 (1958):711-725.

(The) Friends

3204. Hubben, William. "Kierkegaard and the Friends."
Friends Intelligencer (1953):230-234.

God

3205. Bellezza, Vito A. "La lotta al teocentrismo nell'
esistenzialismo kierkegaardiano." *Archivio di Filosofia*
(Roma) 18 (1949):49-59.

3206. Cochrane, Arthur C. *The Existentialists and God.
Being and the Being of God in the Thought of Sören Kierke-
gaard, Karl Jaspers, Martin Heidegger, Jean-Paul Sartre,
Paul Tillich, Etienne Gilson, Karl Barth.* Philadelphia:
Westminster Press, 1956. 174p.

3207. Cole, J. Preston. "The existential reality of God:
A Kierkegaardian study." *Christian Scholar* 48 (1965):
224-235. Reprinted in *The Presence of Sören Kierkegaard
in Contemporary American Life.*Lewis Lawson, ed. Metuchen
(New Jersey): The Scarecrow Press, 1971, 92-106.

3208. Cortese, Alessandro. "Del nome di Dio come
l''edificante' in Soren Kierkegaard." In *L'analisi del
Linguaggio Teologico. Il Nome di Dio. Archivio di
Filosofia* (1969):539-550.

3209. de Feo, Nicola Massimo. "L'uomo-Dio nel cristianesimo di Kierkegaard." *Giornale Critico della Filosofia
Italiana* 44 (1965):369-385.

3210. Dumas, A. "La critique de l'objectivité de Dieu
dans la théologie protestante." *Revue des Sciences
Philosophiques et Théologiques* 52 (1968):408-426.

3211. Erro, Carlos Alberto. "Kierkegaard hablando sobre
Dios." In *Dialogo Existencial.* Buenos Aires, 1937.

3212. Evans, C. Stephen. "Kierkegaard on subjective
truth: Is God an ethical fiction?" *International Journal
for the Philosophy of Religion* 7 (1976):288-299.

3213. Evans, C. Stephen. "Mis-using religious language:
Something about Kierkegaard and 'the myth of God incarnate'."
Religious Studies 15 (1979):139-157.

3214. Fabro, Cornelio. "Le prove dell'esistenza di Dio
in Kierkegaard." *Humanitas* (Paris) 17 (1962):97-110.

3215. Fabro, Cornelio. "L'existence de Dieu dans l'oeuvre de Kierkegaard." In *L'Existence de Dieu*. Paris: Casterman, 1961, 37-47.

3216. Fruscione, S. "Kierkegaard di fronte all' esistenza di Dio." *Civiltà Cattolica* 102 (1951):618-631.

3217. Gillet, Lev. "Dieu est lumiere." In *Vues sur Kierkegaard*. Henein & Wahba, eds. 1955, 91-97.

3218. Hill, William J. "The God of the other dimension." *Thomist* 42 (1978):14-27.

3219. Kelly, Charles J. "Essential thinking in Kierkegaard's critique of proofs for the existence of God." *Journal of Religion* 59 (1971):133-153.

3220. Kuntz, Paul G. "The God we find: The God of Abraham, the God of Anselm, and the God of Weiss." *Modern Schoolman* 47 (1970):433-453.

3221. Martins, Diamantino. "O problema da demonstração de Deus em Kierkegaard." *Revista Portuguesa de Filosofia* 24 (1968):429-439.

3222. Milano, A. "Il 'divenire di Dio' in Hegel, Kierkegaard e San Tommaso d'Aquino." In *San Tommaso e il Pensiero Moderno*. Saggi. Roma: Pont. Accad. Romana di San Tommaso d'Aquino. Città Nuova, 1974, 284-294.

3223. Mourant, John A. "The place of God in the philosophy of Kierkegaard." *Giornale Metafisica* 8 (1953):207-221.

3224. Nielsen, Kai. "Rationality, intelligibility, and Alasdair MacIntyre's talk of God." *Religious Studies* 14 (1978):193-204.

3225. Slök, Johannes. "Kierkegaards Bestimmung des Begriffes 'Gottes Wort'." *Orbis Litterarum* 10 (1955): 236-244. [Symposion Kierkegaardianum]

3226. Smit, Gabriel. "Kierkegaard, den enkeling voor Gods anschijn." In *Hedendaagse Visres op den Mens*. Herleen: Winants, 1950, 20-38.

3227. Thomas, John H. "Kierkegaard on the existence of God." *Review of Religion* 18 (1953):18-30.

3228. Whittaker, John H. "Kierkegaard on names, concepts, and proofs for God's existence." *International Journal for the Philosophy of Religion* 10 (1979):117-130.

Gospel

3229. Hendry, George S. "The Gospel in an age of anxiety." *Theology Today* 12 (1955):283-289.

Greece

3230. Scopetéa, Sophia. "Sören Kierkegaard i Graekenland: Nogle spredte iagttagelser sögt optegnet." In *Kierke-gaardiana* 10 (1977):262-273.

Guilt

3231. Carr, C. "Kierkegaard: On guilt." *Journal of Psychology and Theology* 1 (1973):15-21.

3232. Edwards, C. N. "Guilt in the thought of Sören Kierkegaard." *Encounter* 27 (1966):141-157.

3233. Johnson, William A. "Guilt according to Freud and Kierkegaard." *Hartford Quarterly*, 14-54.

3234. Strunz, F. "Schuld." *Religion und Geisteskultur* (1914):253-260.

Herraic

3235. Hyman, Freida Clark. "Kierkegaard and the Hebraic mind." *Journal of Ecumenical Studies* 4 (1967):554-556.

History

3236. Armetta, Francesco. *Storia e Idealità in Kierke-gaard.* S. 1. , Dialogo. Palermo: Fiamma Serafica, 1972. 180p.

3237. Buske, Thomas. "Die Dialektik der Geschichte. Zur Theologie Sören Kierkegaards." *Neue Zeitschrift für Systematische Theologie* 5 (1963):235-247.

3238. Casalis, Matthieu. "L' 'histoire' selon Kierke-gaard." *Revue de Histoire et de Philosophie Religieuses* 48 (1968):1-31.

3239. Christiansen, Lars. "Die Kategorie der Geschichte bei Hegel und bei Kierkegaard." *Nerthus* 3 (1972):57-71.

3240. Colette, Jacques. *Histoire et Absolu. Essai sur Kierkegaard.* (L'athéisme interroge). Paris, Tournai: Desclée et Cie, 1972. 284p.

3241. Colette, Jacques. "Kierkegaard et la catégorie d'histoire." In *Kierkegaardiana.* Niels Thulstrup, ed. Copenhagen: Munksgaard, 5 (1964):85-93.

3242. Fruchon, Pierre. "Kierkegaard et l'historicité de la foi. La vision de l'historique: Illusion et vérité." *Recherches de Sciences Religieuses* 60 (1972):329-363. [Resume, 329]

3243. Holm, Sören. *Sören Kierkegaards Geschichtsphiloso- phie.* Einzig berechtigte Übers. aus dem Dänischen von Günther Jungbluth). Stuttgart: Kohlhammer, 1956. 120p.

3244. Löwith, Karl. "On the historical understanding of Kierkegaard." *Review of Religion* 7 (1943):277-241. (M. bibliography)

3245. Masi, Giuseppe. "Storicità e cristianesimo in Kierkegaard." In *Kierkegaard e Nietzsche. Archivio di Filosofia* no. 2 (1953):115-132.

3246. Melchiorre, Virgilio. "Metafisica e storia in Sören Kierkegaard." *Sapienza* (Bologna) 8 (1955):203-221.

3247. Onasch, K. "Gleichzeitigkeit und Geschichte; Fandbemerkungen zum Vergleich Dostojevskijs mit Kierke- gaard." *Zeitschrift für Religions- und Geistesgeschichte* 25 (1973):46-57.

3248. Paci, Enzo. "Storia ed apocalisse in Kierkegaard." In *Apocalisse e Insecuritas. Archivio di Filosofia* no. 2, (1954):141-162.

3249. Pieper, Annemarie. *Geschichte und Ewigkeit in den pseudonymen Schriften Sören Kierkegaards.* Meisenheim: Anton Hain, 1968, viii-240p. (Monographien zur Philosophis- chen Forschung, begr. v. G. Schischkoff, Bd. 55).

3250. Richter, Liselotte. "Existenz und Geschichte bei Sören Kierkegaard." *Theologische Literaturzeitung* 83 (1958):95-104.

3251. Schrag, Calvin O. "Existence and history." *Review of Metaphysics* 13 (1959):28-44.

3252. Troeltsch, Ernst. *Der Historismus und seine Pro- bleme. I. Buch: Das logische Problem der Geschichts- philosophie.* Tübingen: Mohr & Siebeck, 1922, xi-777p. (Ges. Schriften 3.) (Om S. Kierkegaard, p. 53-178, 307-312.)

3253. van Oyen, Hendrik. "Kierkegaards 'Meldung an die Geschichte'." *Theologische Zeitung* 19 (1963):426-445.

3254. Whittemore, Robert C. "On history, time, and Kierkegaard." *Journal of Religious Thought* 9 (1954): 134-155.

Hope

3255. Taylor, M. C. "Kierkegaard as a theologian of hope." *Union Seminary Quarterly Review* 28 (1973):225-233.

Humor

3256. Braun, Günther. *Der Begriff des Humors in Sören Kierkegaards Werk und die Bedeutung des Humors für dieses.* Bad Neuenahr, 1952, xii-95p. Phil. Diss. Univ. Mainz.

3257. Parrill, Lloyd Ellison. "The Concept of Humor in the Pseudonymous Works of Soeren Kierkegaard." Ph.D., Drew Univ., 1975, 296p. *Dissertation Abstracts* 36 (1975): 3772A.

3258. Sandok, Theresa H. O. S. M. "Kierkegaard on Irony and Humor." *Dissertation Abstracts* 36 (1976):1586A.

Idealism

3259. Anz, W. *Kierkegaard und der deutsche Idealismus.* Tübingen: J. C. B. Mohr (Paul Siebeck), 1956. 78p.

3260. Thulstrup, Maria Mikulová. "Kierkegaards möde med mystik gennem den spekulative idealisme." In *Kierkegaardiana* 10 (1977):7-69.

3261. Malantschuk, Gregor. "Die Begriffe Immanenz und Transzendenz bei Sören Kierkegaard." *Neue Zeitschrift für Systematische Theologie* 19 (1977):225-246.

Indian Philosophy

3262. Malhotra, M. K. "Kierkegaard und die indische Philosophie." *Wissenschaft und Weltbild* 9 (1956):202-205.

Individual

3263. Christensen, Arild. "Sören Kierkegaards individua-
tionsprincip." *Dansk Teologisk Tidsskrift* 16 (1953):
216-236.

3264. Collins, James D. "Three Kierkegaardian problems:
The nature of the human individual." *New Scholasticism*
23 (1949):147-185.

3265. Jacobsen, O. Thune. "Den enkelte i. Kierkegaardsk
Forstand [The individual in Kierkegaard's sense]."
Gads Danske Magasin 45 (1951).371-379.

3266. Roberts, Robert. "Kierkegaard on becoming an
'individual'." *Scottish Journal of Theology* 31 (1978):
133-152.

3267. Strickland, Ben. "Kierkegaard and counseling for
individuality." In *The Presence of Sören Kierkegaard in
Contemporary American Life*. Lewis Lawson, ed. Metuchen
(New Jersey): The Scarecrow Press, 1971, 230-239.

3268. Zillesen, Alfred. "Vom Umindividualisieren der
Individualität." *Christliche Freiheit* (Tübingen) 13
(1913):434-437.

Instant

3269. Ciarlo, H. O. "La noción de instante y presencia
en Kierkegaard." *Philosophia* (Mendoza) (1961):34-43.

3270. Hersch, Jeanne. "L'instant." In *Kierkegaard Vivant*.
Paris: Gallimard, 1966, 94-110.

Intersubjectivity

3271. Jung, Hwa Yol. "Confucianism and existentialism:
Intersubjectivity as the way of man." *Philosophy and
Phenomenological Research* 30 (1969):186-202.

Irony

3272. Kragh, Thyge V. "Er jysk ironi en nögle til Sören
Kierkegaards forfatterskab?" In *Kierkegaardiana* 9 (1974):
7-22.

3273. Piper, Otto. "Kierkegaards Ironie." *Die Christliche Welt* 44 (1930):767-728.

3274. Poole, Roger C. "Kierkegaard on irony." *New Blackfriars* 48 (1967):245-249.

3275. Rougemont, Denis de. "Kierkegaard revealed in his irony." *Arizona Quarterly* 1 (1945):4-6.

3276. Sandok, Theresa H. O. S. M. "Kierkegaard on Irony and Humor." *Dissertation Abstracts* 36 (1976):1586A. [Dissertation, see no. 3258]

3277. Stack, George J. "Kierkegaard's ironic stage of existence." *Laval Theologique et Philosophique* 25 (1969): 192-207.

Irrational

3278. Eisenhuth, Heinz Erich. *Der Begriff des Irrationalen als philosophisches Problem. Ein Beitrag zur existenzialen Religionsbegründung.* Göttingen: Vandenhoeck & Ruprecht, 1931, ix-274p. (Studien zur systematischen Theologie, Heft 8).

3279. Glässer, G. "L'irrazionalismo religioso di S. Kierkegaard. La dottrina del 'salto qualitativo'." *Bilychnis* (Roma) 28 (1926):99-112.

3280. McKinnon, Alastair. "Kierkegaard: 'Paradox' and irrationalism." *Journal of Existentialism* 7 (1966-67): 401-416.

3281. McKinnon, Alastair. "Kierkegaard's irrationalism revisited." *International Philosophical Quarterly* 9 (1969):165-176.

3282. Sciacca, Maria Giuseppe. "Significato dell'irrazionalismo di Kierkegaard." Atti del *XV Congresso Nazionale di Filosofia.* . .1948. Messina-Firenze: D-Anna, 1949, 643-652.

Journalism

3283. Swenson, David F. "A Danish thinker's estimate of journalism." *Ethics* 38 (1927-28):70-87.

Jews - Judaism

3284. Benedikt, Ernst. "Sören Kierkegaard och judendomen [S. Kierkegaard and the Jews]." *Judisk Tidskrift* 30 (1957): 318-319.

3285. Chalier, C. "Kierkegaard et le judaisme." *Les Nouveaux Cahiers* (Paris) 12 (1976):56-64.

3286. Fox, Marvin. "Kierkegaard and rabbinic judaism." *Judaism* 2 (1953):169-169. [See no. 3288]

3287. Fox, Marvin. "Kierkegaard and rabbinic judaism." *Judaism* 2 (April 1953):160-169.

3288. Halevi, Jacob L. "Kierkegaard and the midrash." *Judaism* 4 (1955):13-28. [See no. 3286]

3289. Halevi, J. L. "Kierkegaard's teleological suspension of the ethical: Is it Jewish?" *Judaism* 8 (1959):291-302.

3290. Steinberg, Milton. "Kierkegaard and judaism." *Menorah Journal* 37 (1949):163-180.

Kenosis

3291. Roos, H. "Sören Kierkegaard und die Kenosis-Lehre." In *Kierkegaardiana* 2 (1957):54-60.

Knowledge

3292. Hügli, Anton. *Die Erkenntnis der Subjektivität und die Objektivität des Erkennens bei Sören Kierkegaard.* (Basler Beiträge zur Philosophie und ihrer Geschichte, 7). Zürich: Thoelogischer Verlag, Editio Academica, 1973. 354p.

3293. Perkins, Robert L. "Kierkegaard's epistemological preferences." *International Journal for the Philosophy of Religion* 4 (1973):197-217.

3294. Stengren, George J. "Connatural knowledge in Aquinas and Kierkegaardian subjectivity." In *Kierke-gaardiana* 10 (1977):182-189.

3295. Wilshire, Bruce W. "Kierkegaard's theory of knowledge and new directions in psychology and psychoanalysis."
Review of Existential Psychology and Psychiatry 3 (1963):
249-261. Reprinted in *The Presence of Soren Kierkegaard
in Contemporary American Life*. Lewis Lawson, ed. Metuchen
(New Jersey): The Scarecrow Press, 1971, 43-59.

Language

3296. Hirsch, Emanuel. "Kierkegaards Sprache und Stil."
Sören Kierkegaard 1855-1955. Zum Kierkegaard-Gedenkjahr
vorgelegt. Düsseldorf & Köln: Diederichs, 1955, 12-17.
Reprinted in his *Wege zu Kierkegaard*. Berlin: Die Spur,
1968, 55-59.

3297. Sorainen, Kalle. "Kierkegaardin kuvakielesta
(Du langage imagé de Kierkegaard)." In *Kirjallisuudentut-
kijain Seuran Vuosikirja 22. Annuaire des Histoires de la
Litterature*. Helsinki, 1967, 85-107.

3298. Widenman, Robert. "Kierkegaard's terminology--and
English." In *Kierkegaardiana* 6 (1968):113-130.

3299. Zuurdeeg, Willem F. "Some aspects of Kierkegaard's
language philosophy." In *Atti XII Congr. Internationale
Filosofia*, Venezia, 12-18 settembre 1958. Vol. XII:
Storia della Filosofia Moderna e Contemporanea. Firenze:
Sansoni, 1961, 493-499.

Law

3300. Migliorini, Giulio. "Diritto e società in Kierkegaard e in Dostojevskij." *Rivista di Filosofia del Diritto*
38 (1961):474-490.

3300a. Mouty, Friedrich. *Zum Rechtsgedanken bei Kierkegaard*. Münich: Dissertationsdruk Schön, 1969. 332p.

3300b. Romano, Bruno. *Il Senso Esistenziale del Diritto
Nella Prospettiva di Kierkegaard*. (Pubblicazioni dell'Isti-
tuto di Filosofia del Diritto dell'Università di Roma. S.
III, 9). Milano: Giuffrè, 1973, xviii-321p.

Leap

3301. Glässer, G. "L'irrazionalismo religioso di S. Kierkegaard. La dottrina del 'salto qualitativo'." *Bilychnis* (Roma) 15 (1926):99-112.

3302. Kühnhold, Christa. *Der Begriff des Sprunges und der Weg des Sprachdenkens. Eine Einfluss in Kierkegaard.* Berlin, New York: de Gruyter, 1975, xi-183p.

Levels of Existence

3303. MacCallum, Henry Reid. "Kierkegaard and the levels of existence." *University of Toronto Quarterly* 13 (1944): 258-275.

Levelling

3304. Weiss, Robert O. "The leveling process as a function of the masses in the view of Kierkegaard and Ortega y Gasset." *Kentucky Foreign Language Quarterly* 7 (1960): 27-36.

Liberation

3305. Nageley, Winfield E. "Kierkegaard on liberation." *Ethics* 70 (1959):47-58.

Library (Kierkegaard's)

3306. Perkins, Robert L. "Soren Kierkegaard's library." *American Book Collector* 12 (1961):9-16.

3307. Rohde, H. P., ed. *The Auctioneer's Sales Record of the Library of Sören Kierkegaard.* Copenhagen: Royal Library [Also with Danish title]. 1967.

3308. Smith, Ronald G. "Kierkegaard's library." *Hibbert Journal* 50 (1951):18-21.

Literature

3309. Billeskov Jansen, F. J. "S. Kierkegaard et la
littérature française." In *Kierkegaardiana* 7 (1967):
188-192.

3310. Farber, Marjorie. "Subjectivity in modern fiction."
Kenyon Review 7 (1945):645-652.

3311. Lawson, Lewis A. "Kierkegaard and the modern
American novel." In *Essays in Memory of Christine Burleson
in Language and Literature by Former Colleagues and Students*.
Thomas G. Burton, ed. Johnson City: Res. Advisory Council,
East Tennessee State Univ., 1969, 113-125.

3312. Said, Edward W. "Molestation and authority in
narrative fiction." In *Aspects of Narration. Selected
Papers from the English Institute*. J. Hillis Miller, ed.
New York: Columbia Univ. Press, 1971, 47-68. [Incl. disc.
of Kierkegaard, Marx, and Vico in relation to requisite
conditions for fiction.]

Logic

3313. Holmer, Paul L. "Kierkegaard and logic." In
Kierkegaardiana 2 (1957):25-42. Reprinted in *The Presence
of Sören Kierkegaard in Contemporary American Life*. Lewis
Lawson, ed. Metuchen (New Jersey): The Scarecrow Press,
1971, 60-77.

Love

3314. Adorno, Theodor W. "Kierkegaard's Lehre von der
Liebe." *Zeitschrift für Religions- und Geistesgeschichte*
3 (1951):23-38.

3315. Adorno, Theodor W. "On Kierkegaard's doctrine of
love." *Studies in Philosophy and Social Science* 8 (1940):
413-429.

3316. Bonifaci, C. F. *Kierkegaard y el Amor*. Prólogo de
Joaquín Carreras Artau. Barcelona: Herder, 1963. 293p.

3317. De Rosa, Peter. "Some reflexions on Kierkegaard and
Christian love." *Clergy Review* 44 (1959):616-622.

3318. Friemond, Hans. *Existenz in Liebe nach Sören
Kierkegaard*. (Slazburger Studien zur Philosophie, 6).
Salzburg, München: Anton Pustet, 1965. 152p.

3319. Masi, Giuseppe. "Il significato cristiano dell'amore in Kierkegaard." In *Studi Kierkegaardiani*. A cura di Cornelio Fabro. Brescia: Morcelliana Editrice, 1957, 203-242.

3320. Müller, Johannes. "Die christliche Liebe nach Sören Kierkegaard." *Zeitschrift für Theologie und Kirche* (Tübingen) 18 (1908):47-59.

3321. Niebuhr, Reinhold. "Kierkegaard and love." *New York Times Book Review* 51 (1946):8.

3322. Outka, Gene H. *Agape: An Ethical Analysis*. New Haven: Yale Univ. Press, 1972. 321p.

3323. Schrempf, Chr. "Die christliche Liebe nach Sören Kierkegaard." *Die Christliche Welt* (Leipzig) 5 (1891): 611-615, 635-637, 663-665, 684-687.

3324. Sobosan, J. G. "Reflections on Kierkegaard and the dynamics of love." *The American Ecclesiastical Review* (Washington, D.C.) 167 (1973):226-235.

3325. Tisseau, Paul. "Kierkegaard et l'amour." *Foi et Vie* (Paris) 35 (1934):661-677.

3326. Zenker, E. V. "Sören Kierkegaard--Philosophie und Liebe." *Freie Welt* (Berlin) 4 (1925):15-23, 12-18, 19-24, 14-20.

Man

3327. Brandell, Georg. "Människouppfattningen hos Sören Kierkegaard och i Goethes Faust [The concept of man in Sören Kierkegaard and in Geothe's Faust]." *Religion och Kultur* 25 (1954):100-103.

3328. Heiss, Robert. "Sören Kierkegaards Bild vom Menschen." *Blätter für Deutsche Philosophie* (Berlin) 10 (1936): 225-239.

3329. Jacobson, Nolan Pliny. "The predicament of man in Zen Buddhism and Kierkegaard." *Philosophy East and West* 2 (1952):238-253.

3330. Lindström, Valter. "Kierkegaards inlägg in debatten om människan [Kierkegaard's contribution to the debate concerning man]." *Finsk Tidskrift* 151 (1952):210-220.

3331. Prenter, Regin. "L'homme, synthèse du temps et de l'éternité d'après Soeren Kierkegaard." *Studia Theologica* (Lund, tr. Kobenhavn, 1948) 2 (1949-50):5-20.

3332. Price, George. *The Narrow Pass. A Study of Kierkegaard's Concept of Man*. London: Hutchinson, 1963. 224p.

3333. Ramsey, Robert Paul. "Natural law and the nature of man." *Christendom* 9 (1944):369-381.

3334. Rudolph, Arthur W. "The concept of man in Hegel and Kierkegaard." *ITA Humanidades* (São José dos Campos) 8 (1972):55-71.

3335. Saraiva, Maria Manuela Simões. "Kierkegaard e o problema filosófico do homen." *Filosofia* (Lisboa) 2 (1956): 256-266.

3336. Schoeps, Hans-Joachim. "Was ist der Mensch? Die Antwort Sören Kierkegaards." *Universitas* 15 (1960):185-192.

3337. Standley, N. V. "Kierkegaard and man's vocation." *The Vocation Guidance Quarterly* (Washington) 20 (1971): 119-122.

Marriage

3338. Bourgeois, Patrick. "Kierkegaard. Ethical marriage or aesthetic pleasure." *The Personalist* 57 (1976):370-375.

3339. Tielsch, E. "Kierkegaard und die Phänomenologie der Ehe." *Zeitschrift für Philosophische Forschung* 11 (1957):161-187.

Mask

3340. Starobinski, Jean. "Kierkegaard et les masques." *Nouvelle Revue Française* 13 (1965):607-622; 809-825.

Medicine

3341. Soulès, Alberte Noéli. *La Médecine et les Médecins dans L'Oeuvre de Kierkegaard*. Paris: Foulon, 1949. 50p. (Thèse pour le Doctorat de Médecine.)

Melancholy

3342. Anonymous. "Nero und die Schwermut. Sören Kierkegaard." *Psyche* (Heidelberg) 2 (1948-49):321-326.

3343. Guardini, Romano. *Vom Sinn der Schwermut* [1928].
Neuausg. Zürich: Der Arche [1949]. 63p. (Die kleinen
Bücher der Arche, 86-87: Graz, Wien & München: Stiasny
[1950]. 63p. (Dichtung der Gegenwart, 11).

3344. Guardini, Romano. *Ritratto della Malinconia*.
(Vom *Sinn der Schwermut*) [Contiene passi scelti da opere di
S. A. Kierkegaard]. Versione dal tedesco [e dal danese]
di Romana Guarnieri [1952]. 2a ed. Brescia: Morcelliana,
1954. 67p. (Fuochi III. serie).

3345. Mayr, R. "Von der Schwermut. Gedanken zu einem
Thema Kierkegaards." *Die Besinnung* (Nürnberg) 3 (1948):
255-260.

3346. McCarthy, Vincent A. "'Melancholy' and 'religious
melancholy' in Kierkegaard." In *Kierkegaardiana*.
Niels Thulstrup, ed. Copenhagen: C. A. Reitzels Boghandel,
10 (1977):152-165.

3347. Rehm, Walter. "[I. P.] Jacobsen, [S. K.] und die
Schwermut." In *Experimentum Medietztis*. *Studien zur
Geistes- und Literaturgeschichte des 19. Jahrhunderts*.
München: Rinn, 1947, 184-239.

Metaphysics

3348. Versfeld, Martin. "Kierkegaard and metaphysics."
In *The Mirror of Philosophers*. New York-London: Sheed &
Ward, 1960, 44-70.

Midrash

3349. Halevi, Jacob L. "Kierkegaard and the Midrash."
Judaism 4 (1955):13-28.

Monarchism

3350. Poswick, Ferdinand. "La place du monachisme pour
Kierkegaard dans les rapports catholiques-protestants."
Coll. Cist. 32 (1970):75-82.

Moment

3351. Croxall, T. H. "The Christian doctrine of hope and
the Kierkegaardian doctrine of 'the moment'." *Expository
Times* 56 (1944-45):292-295.

3352. Daane, James. "Kierkegaard's Conception of the
Moment. An Investigation into the Time-Eternity Concept of
Sören Kierkegaard." Ph.D., Princeton Theological Seminary,
1947, 187p. *Dissertation Abstracts* 35 (1974):2379A.

Mood

3353. McCarthy, Vincent A. "The Meaning and Dialectic
of Moods in Kierkegaard." Ph.D., Stanford Univ., 1974,
339p. *Dissertation Abstracts* 35 (1974):3871A.

Music

3354. Croxall, Thomas H. "Kierkegaard on music."
Publications of the Royal Music Association 73 (1946-47):
1-11. (A paper based on Kierkegaard's essay: *De Umiddle-
bare Erotiske Stadier.*)

3355. Croxall, Thomas H. "A strange but stimulating essay
on music." *Musical Times* 90 (1949):46-48.

3356. Lenoir, Raymond. "Kierkegaard et la musique."
Revue d'Esthétique 2 (1949):416-421.

Mysterious

3357. Kemp, Robert. "Kierkegaard et le mystérieux."
Les Nouvelles Littéraires, Artistiques et Scientifiques
(Paris) (5.1.1956).

Mysticism

3358. Wahl, Jean. "Le mysticisme de Kierkegaard."
Hermès no. 1 (1930).

Nature

3359. Sorainen, Kalle. "Kierkegaard luonnonkuvaajana
[The description of nature by Kierkegaard]." *Valvoja*
(1956):173-177.

Negation

3360. King, Winston L. "Negation as a Religious Category."
Journal of Religion 37 (1957):105-118.

Nihilism

3361. Arendt, Dieter. "Der Nihilismus-Ursprung und
Geschichte im Spiegel der Forschungsliteratur Seit 1945."
*Deutsche Vierteljahresschrift für Literaturwissenschaft
und Geistesgeschichte* 43 (1969):544-566.

3362. Dauenhauer, Bernard P. "On Kierkegaard's alleged
nihilism." *Southern Journal of Philosophy* 12 (1974):
153-163.

3363. Schrey, H. H. "Die Ueberwindung des Nihilismus bei
Kierkegaard und Nietzsche." *Zeitschrift für Systematische
Theologie* (Berlin) 21 (1950):50-68.

3364. Stack, George J. "Kierkegaard and nihilism."
Philosophy Today 14 (1970):274-292.

3365. Steffensen, Steffen. "Kierkegaard, Nietzsche og
nihilismen." In *Humanitet og Eksistens*. Bent Hahn et al.,
eds. Copenhagen: Gyldendal, 1976, 9-15.

3366. Steffensen, Steffen. "Kierkegaard, Nietzsche und
der Nihilismus." *Ausblick* 26 (1976):38-40.

Objectivity

3367. Gandillac, Maurice de. "Kierkegaard et l'objectif."
La Nef (Paris) 2 (1945):117-121.

Offense

3368. Clive, Geoffrey. "Seven types of offense."
Lutheran Quarterly 10 (1958):11-25.

Ontological Argument - Ontology

3369. Capone Braga, Gaetano. "Il valore dell' argomento
ontologico secondo il Kierkegaard." *Sophia* 22 (1954):
148-151.

3370. Rohatyn, Dennis A. "Kierkegaard sobre el argumento
ontológico." Trad. del ingles J. Igal. *Pensamiento*
33 (1977):205-211.

3371. Schäfer, Klaus. *Hermeneutische Ontologie in den
Climacus-Schriften Sören Kierkegaards.* München: Kösel,
1968. 333p.

Other

3372. Gomes, F. Soares. "Revolução do pensamento:
Redescoberta da 'categoria afectiva' do outro." *Revista
Portuguesa de Filosofia* 31 (1975):3-27.

Paradox

3373. Cristaldi, Mariano. "Struttura del paradosso
Kierkegaardiano." *Teoresi* 12 (1957):115-133.

3374. Daise, Benjamin. "Kierkegaard and the absolute
paradox." *Journal of the History of Philosophy* 14 (1976):
63-68.

3375. Duncan, Elmer H. "Kierkegaard's uses of 'paradox'--
Yet once more." *Journal of Existentialism* 8 (1967):319-328.

3376. Garelick, Herbert. "The irrationality and supra-
rationality of Kierkegaard's paradox." *Southern Journal
of Philosophy* 2 (1964):75-86.

3377. Herbert, Robert. "Two of Kierkegaard's uses of
'paradox'." *Philosophical Review* 70 (1961):41-55.

3378. Larsen, K. Olesen. "Zur Frage des Paradoxiebegriffs in *Philosophische Brocken* und *Abschliessende Unwissenschaftliche Nachschrift*." *Orbis Litterarum* 10 (1955):130-147. [Symposion Kierkegaardianum]

3379. Larsen, Robert E. "Kierkegaard's absolute paradox." *Journal of Religion* 62 (1962):34-43.

3380. Lin, Timothy Tian-Min. "Various interpretations of Kierkegaard's paradox: An appraisal and suggestion." *Southern Journal of Philosophy* 9 (1971):287-291.

3381. Lin, Timothy Tian-Min. "Is Kierkegaard's paradox paradoxical?" *Journal of Religious Thought* 28 (1971):21-26.

3382. Lönning, Per. "Kierkegaard's 'paradox'." *Orbis Litterarum* 10 (1955):156-165. [Symposion Kierkegaardianum]

3383. McKinnon, Alastair. "Kierkegaard: 'paradox' and irrationalism." *Journal of Existentialism* 7 (1966-67): 401-416.

3384. McKinnon, Alastair. "Believing the paradoks: A contradiction in Kierkegaard?" *Harvard Theological Review* 61 (1968):633-636.

3385. Steilen, Josef. *Der Begriff 'Paradox': Eine Begriffsanalyse im Anschluss am Sören Kierkegaard*. Trier: Theologische Fakultät, 1974, xix-295p. (Diss., Univ. Trier)

3386. Steilen, J. "*Paradox* als theologischer Grundbegriff bei Sören Kierkegaard." *Trierer Theologische Zeitschrift* (Trier) 84 (1975):193-199.

3387. Wahl, Jean. "S. Kierkegaard: Le paradoxe." *Revue des Sciences Philosophiques et Théologiques* (Paris) 24 (1935):218-231.

Personality

3388. Friedman, Rudolph. "Kierkegaard: The analysis of the psychological personality." *Horizon* 8 (1943):252-273.

3389. Hansen, Valdemar. "Le principe de personalité chez trois penseurs danois: Hoffding, Kierkegaard, Poul Moller." In *Atti XII Congr. Internationale di Filosofia*, Venezia 12-18 settembre 1958. Vol. XII: *Storia della Filosofia Moderna e Contemporanea*. Firenze: Sansoni, 1961.

3390. Kronfeld, Arthur. "Die Bedeutung Kierkegaards für die Psychologie der Person." *Zeitschrift für Angevandte Psychologie* 44 (1933):294-295.

3391. Zeigler, L. "Personal existence: A study of Buber
and Kierkegaard." *Journal of Religion* 40 (1960):80-94.

Phenomenology

3392. Robert, Jean-Dominique. "Approche rétrospective de
la phénoménologie husserlienne." *Archives de Philosophie*
(1972):320-334.

Philosophy

3393. Dunne, Mary Rachel. "Kierkegaard and Socratic
Ignorance: A Study of the Task of a Philosopher in Relation
to Christianity." Ph.D., Univ. of Notre Dame, 1970, 356p.
Dissertation Abstracts 31 (1971):4835A.

3394. Johnson, Ralph H. "Kierkegaard on philosophy."
Dialogue 17 (1978):442-455.

3395. Mackey, Louis H. "Notes toward a definition of
Philosophy." *Franciscan Studies* 33 (1973):262-272.

3396. McKinnon, Alastair. "Kierkegaard's remarks on
philosophy." *Journal of the History of Philosophy* 11
(1973):513-522.

3397. Wild, John. "Kierkegaard and classical philosophy."
Philosophical Review 49 (1940):536-551.

3398. Wild, John. "Kierkegaard and classical philosophy."
Journal of Philosophy 35 (1938):685-686.

Pietism

3399. Bochi, Giulia. *Peccato e Fede. Motivi Pietistici
nel Pensiero di Kierkegaard.* Faenza: Tip. F. Lega, 1957.
150p.

3399a. Thulstrup, Marie M. *Kierkegaard og Pietismen.*
(Sören Kierkegaards Selskabets populaere skrifter 13).
Copenhagen: Munksgaard, 1967.

Poetry

3400. Pareyson, Luigi. "Kierkegaard e la poesia d'occasione." *Rivista di Estetica* 10 (1965):248-255.

Polemic

3401. Hansen, Holger. "Sören Kierkegaard som polemiker
[Sören Kierkegaard as a polemic]." *Nordisk Tidskrift*
(Suède) 28 (1952):36-52.

Politics

3402. Johnson, Howard. "Kierkegaard and politics."
American-Scandinavian Review 43 (1955):246-254. Reprinted
in *Anglican Theological Review* 38 (1956):32-41. Also
reprinted in *The Presence of Soren Kierkegaard in Contemporary American Life*. Lewis Lawson, ed. Metuchen (New
Jersey): The Scarecrow Press, 1971, 107-119.

3403. Kirmmse, Bruce H. "Kierkegaard's Politics. The
Social Thought of Soren Kierkegaard in Its Historical
Context." Ph.D., Univ. of California at Berkeley, 1977,
1030p. *Dissertation Abstracts* 39 (1978):1047A.

3404. Möller, A. Egelund. *Sören Kierkegaard om Politik*.
Copenhagen: Frolaget "Strand," 1975. 191p.

3405. Moore, S. R. "Kierkegaard's politics." *Perspectives* 10 (1969):235-251.

3406. Wäsche, H. "Die politische Bedeutung Sören Kierkegaards." *Lübeckische Blätter* 80 (1938):336-340.

Possibility

3407. King, James. "Further remarks on Kierkegaard and
possibility [G. J. Stack, "The basis of Kierkegaard's concept. . .]." [See Stack, no. 3408] *New Scholasticism*
47 (1973):375-380.

3408. Stack, George J. "The basis of Kierkegaard's concept of existential possibility." *New Scholasticism* 46
(1972):139-172. [See J. King, no. 3407]

3409. Stack, George J. "The language of possibility and existential possibility." *Southwestern Journal of Philosophy* 4 (1973):77-90.

Posterity

3410. Diem, Hermann. "Kierkegaard et la postérité." *Revue d. Histoire et de Philosophie Religieuses* 46 (1966): 1-16.

Primitive

3411. Henry, J. "The term 'primitive' in Kierkegaard and Heidegger." In *The Concept of the Primitive*. Ashley Montagu, ed. New York: Free Press, 1968, 212-228.

Protestantism

3412. Bosc, Jean. "La pensée protestante. Kierkegaard." *Foi et Vie* (Paris) 37 (1936):484-487.

3413. Dollinger, R. "Sören Kierkegaard und der Protestant-ismus." *Luther-Jahrbuch* 32 (1965):74-130.

3414. Marchal, Georges. "Kierkegaard et le protestantisme." *La Table Ronde* (Paris) (1955):66-72.

3415. Peterson, Erik. "Kierkegaard und die protestantische Theologie." *Wort und Wahrheit* (Wien) 3 (1947).

3416. Peterson, Erik. "Kierkegaard und der Protestantismus." *Wort und Wahrheit* (Wien) 3 (1948):579-584.

Pseudonym - Pseudonymous Works

3417. Grossart, Friedrich. "Grundmotiv und Aufbau der pseudonyme Schriften Kierkegaards." *Deutsche Viertel-jahrsschrift für Literaturwissenschaft und Geistesgeschicht* (Halle) 19 (1941):139-182.

3418. McKinnon, Alastair. "Kierkegaard and his pseudonyms: A preliminary report [Abstract]." *Journal of Philosophy* 65 (1968):720.

3419. McKinnon, Alastair. "Kierkegaard and his pseudonyms:
A preliminary report." In *Kierkegaardiana* 7 (1968):64-76.

3420. McKinnon, Alastair. "Kierkegaard's pseudonyms: A
new hierarchy." *American Philosophical Quarterly* 6 (1969):
116-126.

3421. Morra, Gianfranco. "Chi sono gli pseudonimi di
Kierkegaard." *Ethica* 11 (1972):41-50.

3422. Taylor, Douglas R. "The Aestheitc Methodology of
Soren Kierkegaard's Pseudonymous Works." Ph.D., Florida
State Univ., 1977, 328p. *Dissertation Abstracts* 38 (1977):
2854A.

Psychoanalysis

3423. Taylor, Mark C. "Psychoanalytic dimensions of
Kierkegaard's view of selfhood." *Philosophy Today*
19 (1975):198-212.

Psychology

3424. Esser, P. H. "Kierkegaard en de 'existentielle
Psychologie'." *Nederlandsch Tijdschrift voor Psychologie
en Grenzgebiete* 5 (1937):335-362.

3425. Friedmann, Rudolph. "Kierkegaard. An analysis of
the psychological personality." *Horizon* 46 (1943):252-273.

3426. Höffding, Harald. *Outlines in Psychology*. Trans.
by Mary E. Lowndes. London: Macmillan, 1891. Reg.
(Macmillan's Manuels for Students: Psychology).

3427. Kronfeld, Arthur. "Die Bedeutung Kierkegaards für
die Psychologie der Person." *Zeitschrift für Angevandte
Psychologie* 44 (1933):294-295.

3428. Kronfeld, Arthur. "De Bedeutung Kierkegaards für
die Psychologie. Vortrag am 10. Internationale Kongres
für Psychologie in Köbenhavn." *Acta Psychologica*
1 (1936):135-156. (G. Revész, ed.)

3429. Mullen, John D. "The German romantic background of
Kierkegaard's psychology." *Southern Journal of Philosophy*
16 (1978):649-660.

3430. Nordentoft, Kresten. *Kierkegaard's Psychology*.
Trans. by Bruce H. Kirmmse. Pittsburgh (Pennsylvania):
Duquesne Univ. Press, 1978. 408p.

3431. Ritter, Joachim. "Über ein neues Kierkegaard-Buch und über die Möglichkeit, Kierkegaard psychologisch zu deuten." Blätter für Deutschen Philosophie (Berlin) 8 (1934-35):431-437.

3432. Skinhöj, Erik, and Skinhöj, Kirsten. "Sören Kierkegaard in American psychology." Acta Psychiatrica et Neurologica Scandinavica 30 (1955):315-325.

3433. Strickland, Ben. "Kierkegaard and counseling for individuality." Personnel and Guidance Journal 44 (1966): 470-474. Reprinted in The Presence of Sören Kierkegaard in Contemporary American Life. Lewis Lawson, ed. Metuchen (New Jersey): The Scarecrow Press, 1971, 230-239.

3434. Valentiner, Theodor. X. Internationale Psychologen-kongress in Kopenhagen (22. bis 27. August 1932). Zeitschrift für Angevandte Psychologie 44 (1933):294-295.

3435. Wilshire, Bruce W. "Kierkegaard's theory of know-ledge and new directions in psychology and psychoanalysis." Review of Existential Psychology and Psychiatry 3 (1963): 249-261.

Purity of Heart

3436. Vergote, Henri-Bernard. "La pureté du coeur chez Sören Kierkegaard." Études Philosophiques (1972):503-524. [Résumé, Summary, 503]

Religion

3437. Adams, Robert Merrihew. "Kierkegaard's arguments against objective reasoning in religion." The Monist 60 (1977):228-243.

3438. Allison, Henry E. "Kierkegaard's dialectic of the religious consciousness." Union Seminary Quarterly Review 20 (1965):225-233.

3439. Anonymous. "Über die religiöse Entwicklung Sören Kierkegaards." Ergänzungsblätter zur Allgemeine Evangel-isch-Lutherisch Kirchenzeitung (Leipzig) 12 (1879):213-222.

3440. Brodeur, Claude. "La structure de la pensée religieuse suivant Kierkegaard." Interprétation (Montréal) 5 (1971):3-10.

3441.   Charlesworth, Max.   "St. Thomas Aquinas and the
decline of the Kantian-Kierkegaardian philosophy of
religion."   In *Tommaso d'Aquino nel suo VII Centenario*.
Roma, 1974.

3442.   Chervin, Ronda de Sola.   "The Process of Conversion
in the Philosophy of Religion of Soeren Kierkegaard."
Ph.D., Fordham Univ., 1967, 209p.   *Dissertation Abstracts*
28 (1968):4207A.

3443.   Copleston, Frederick C.   "Existence and religion."
Dublin Review 220 (1947):50-63.

3444.   Corsano, Antonio.   "Dimensioni del fatto religioso."
Giornale Critico della Filosofia Italiana 51 (1973):
516-524.

3445.   Diamond, M. L.   "Faith and its tensions: A criticism
of religious existentialism."   *Judaism* 13 (1964):317-327.

3446.   Dupre, Louis.   "Themes in contemporary philosophy
of religion."   *New Scholasticism* (1969):577-601.

3447.   Gabriel de Sotiello, O. F. M. Cap.   "Cristianismo
y mundanidad. Algunos aspectos del pensamiento religioso
de Kierkegaard."   *Naturaleza y Gracia* (Salamanca) 3 (1956):
93-118.

3448.   Gemmer, Anders.   "Religionsphilosophische Grundgedanken bei Kierkegaard."   *Geisteskultur (Comenius-Gesell-
schaft)* (Berlin) 34 (1925):19-27.

3449.   Gibson, A. Boyce.   "Existential religion and existential philosophy [Kierkegaard]."   In *Danish Yearbook of
Philosophy* 8 (1971):94-98.   [Discussions, 99-114]

3450.   Holmer, Paul L.   "Kierkegaard and religious proposi-
tions."   *Journal of Religion* 35 (1955):135-146.

3451.   Jensenius, Knud.   "Sören Kierkegaard og det
religiöse [S. Kierkegaard and religion]."   *Gads Danske
Magasin* (1950):137-142.

3452.   Jolivet, Régis.   "Le problème de la religion de
Kierkegaard."   *Revue Philosophique de Louvain* 47 (1949):
137-142.

3453.   Jones, Jere Jene.   "On the Distinction Between
Religiousness 'A' and Religiousness 'B' in the *Concluding
Unscientific Postscript* of Sören Kierkegaard."   Ph.D.,
The Univ. of Nebraska-Lincoln, 1971, 256p.   *Dissertation
Abstracts* 32 (1971):1017A.

3454.   Khan, A. H.   "Kierkegaard's religion A und religion
B: Same or different?"   *Studies in Religion* (Toronto)
6 (1976-77):169-176.

3455. Muska, Rudolph Charles. "Antithetical Religious
Conceptions in Kierkegaard and Spinoza." Ph.D., Michigan
State Univ., 1960, 173p. *Dissertation Abstracts* 21 (1961):
3489.

3456. Magnino, B. "Il problema religioso di Sören Kierkegaard." In *Studii Kierkegaardiani*. A cura di Cornelio
Fabro. Brescia: Morcelliana, 1957.

3457. Quinn, Wylie S. "Kierkegaard and Wittgenstein: The
'Religious' as a 'Form of Life'." Ph.D., Duke Univ., 1976,
222p. *Dissertation Abstracts* 37 (1977):7804A.

3458. Reuter, Hans. *S. Kierkegaards religionsphilosophische
Gedanken im Verhältnis zu Hegels religionsphilosophischen
System*. Erfurt: G. Richter, 1913, vi-68p. Phil. Diss.
Berlin, 1913.

3459. Salomon, Gottfried. *Beitrag zur Problematik von
Mystik und Glauben*. Strassburg & Leipzig: J. Singer, 1916,
vi-99p. (Om S. Kierkegaard, p. 61-70: Von der Sünde und der
Nachfolge). Phil. Diss. Strassburg, 1916.

3460. Sefler, George F. "Kierkegaard's religious truth:
The three dimensions of subjectivity." *International
Journal for the Philosophy of Religion* 2 (1971):43-52.

3461. Smith, J. Weldon. "Religion A/religion B."
Scottish Journal of Theology 15 (1962):245-265.

3462. Schmitt, Richard A. "The paradox in Kierkegaard's
religiousness." *Inquiry* 8 (1965):118-135.

3463. Thrändorff, Ernst. "Sören Kierkegaard in der Schul-
Kirchengeschichte." *Monatsblätter für den Evangelische
Religionsunterricht* 14 (1921):24-38.

3464. Troeltsch, Ernst. "Religionsphilosophie und princi-
pielle Theologie." *Theologische Jahresbericht* (Berlin)
18 (1899):532-533. (Lit. 1898).

Repetition

3465. Chaning-Pearce, M. "*Repetition*. A Kierkegaard study."
Hibbert Journal 41 (1942-43):361-364.

3466. Grau, Gerd-Günther. "Nietzsche und Kierkegaard:
Wiederholung einer Unzeitgemässen Betrachtung."
Nietzsche-Studien 1 (1972):297-333.

3467. Guirguis, Renée. "Notes sur *La Répétition*."
Vues sur Kierkegaard. Henein & Wahba, eds. 1955, 22-25.

3468. Heinemann, F. H. "Origin and repetition." *Review of Metaphysics* 4 (1950-51):201-214.

3469. Kraus, A. "Kierkegaards Begriff der Wiederholung auf Grund einer Interpretation seiner pseudonymen Schrift *Wiederholung* von Constantin Constantius." *Nederlandsch Tijdschrift voor Psychologie* (Amsterdam) 7 (1939):311-328.

3470. Martin, H. V. "Kierkegaard's category of repetition." *Expository Times* 44 (1943):265-268.

3471. McLane, Henry Earl, Jr. "Kierkegaard's Use of the Category of Repetition. An Attempt to Discern the Structure and Unity of His Thought." Ph.D., Yale Univ., 1961.

3472. Mikhail, Faiza. "La répétition. Fragment de lettre imaginaire écrite par Constantin Constantius à son ami anonyme." In *Vues sur Kierkegaard*. Henein & Wahba, eds. 19-5, 33-37.

3473. Nusser, Gudrun. "Der Begriff *Wiederholung* bei Kierkegaard." *Theologische Zeitung* 20 (1964):423-439.

3474. Reimer, Louis. "Die Wiederholung als Problem der Erlösung bei Kierkegaard." In *Kierkegaardiana* 7 (1968): 19-63.

3475. Schuckler, Georg. *Die Existenzkategorie der Wiederholung dargestellt am Werk Sören Kierkegaards*. Bonn, 1952. 333p. (Maschinenschr.). Phil. Diss. Bonn, 1952.

3476. Stack, George J. "Kierkegaard and the phenomenology of repetition." *Journal of Existentialism* 7 (1966-67): 111-128.

3477. Stack, George J. "Repetition in Kierkegaard and Freud." *The Personalist* 58 (1977):249-260.

3478. Stack, George J. "Kierkegaard: Repetición existencial." *Folia Humanística* 14 (1976):523-536.

Reward

3479. Walker, Jeremy. "The idea of reward in morality [Kierkegaard]." In *Kierkegaardiana* 8 (1971):30-52.

Romanticism

3480. Slataper, Camusso Giulia. "Romanticismo come lette-
rarieta: Approssimazione all'estetismo kierkegaardiano."
In Atti del *Congresso Internazionale di Filosofia*, Roma,
1946. Vol. 2. Milano: Castellani, 1948, 453-455.

3481. Wahl, Jean. "Kierkegaard et le romantisme." In
Vues sur Kierkegaard. Henein & Wahba, eds. 1955, 5-12.

3482. Wahl, Jean. "Kierkegaard et le romantisme."
Orbis Litterarum 10 (1955):297-302. [Symposion Kierke-
gaardianum]

Sacred

3483. Malantschuk, Gregor. "Il concetto di 'sacro' in
Sören Kierkegaard." Trad. dal danese di Salvatore Spera.
In *Prospettive sul Sacro*. A cura di Enrico Castello.
Roma: Istituto di Studi Filosofici, 1974, 225-234.

3484. Malantschuk, G. "Begrebet det hellige hos Sören
Kierkegaard." In *Kierkegaardiana* 10 (1977):85-94.

Sacrifice

3485. Crocker, Sylvia Fleming. "Sacrifice in Kierkegaard's *Fear and Trembling*." *Harvard Theological Review*
68 (1976):125-139.

Scepticism

3486. Popkin, Richard H. "Kierkegaard and scepticism."
*Algemene Nederlands Tijdschrift voor Wijsbegeerte en
Psychologie* 51 (1958-59):123-141.

Secret

3487. Fondane, Benjamin. "Soeren Kierkegaard et la catégorie du secret." In *La Conscience Malheureuse*. Paris,
1936, 199-227.

Seducer (See also Don Juan)

3488. Elsen, Claude. "Le mythe du séducteur." *La Table Ronde* (Paris) (1955):79-81.

3489. Nostiz, Osw. von. "Kierkegaard und der Verführer." *Begegnung* (Koblenz) 5 (1950):132-134.

Self

3490. Cole, J. Preston. *The Problematic Self in Kierkegaard and Freud.* New Haven/London: Yale Univ. Press, 1971. 244p.

3491. Dietrichson, Paul. "Kierkegaard's concept of self." *Inquiry* 8 (1965):1-32.

3492. Dupré, Louis K. "The constitution of the self in Kierkegaard's philosophy." *International Philosophical Quarterly* 3 (1963):506-526.

3493. Elrod, John W. "An Interpretation of Sören Kierkegaard's Concept of the Self in the Pseudonymous Corpus." Ph.D., Princeton Univ., 1972, 412p. *Dissertation Abstracts* 37 (1976):404A.

3494. Elrod, John W. "The self in Kierkegaard's pseudonyms." *International Journal for the Philosophy of Religion* 4 (1973):218-240.

3495. Elrod, John W. "Feuerbach and Kierkegaard on the self." *Journal of Religion* 56 (1976):348-365.

3496. Gozzini, M. "La tragedia dell'io in Sören Kierkegaard." *L'Ultima* (Firenze) no. 34-35 (1948).

3497. Grooten, Johan. "Le soi chez Kierkegaard et Sartre." *Revue Philosophique de Louvain* 50 (1952):64-89.

3498. Hartman, Robert S. "The self in Kierkegaard." *Journal of Existential Psychiatry* 2 (1962):409-436.

3499. Holl, Jann. *Kierkegaards Konzeption des Selbst. Eine Untersuchung über d. Voraussetzungen und Formen seines Denkens.* (Monographien zur philosophischen Forschung, 81). Meisenheim a. Glan: Hain, 1972. 280p.

3500. Pleines, Jürgen-Eckardt. "Zum Begriff des Selbstverständnisses im Werke Sören Kierkegaards." *Salzburger Jahrbuch für Philosophie* 10/11 (1966-67):105-149.

3501. Smith, Joel R. "The Dialectic of Selfhood in the
Works of Sören Kierkegaard." Ph.D., Vanderbilt Univ.,
1977, 198p. *Dissertation Abstracts* 38 (1977):1456A.

3502. Sontag, Frederick. "Kierkegaard and the search
for a self." *Journal of Existentialism* 7 (1966-67):443-457.

3503. Stack, George J. "Kierkegaard. The self as ethical
possibility." *The Southwestern Journal of Philosophy*
(Norman, Oklahoma) 3 (1972):35-61.

3504. Sugerman, S. "Sin and madness; a study of the self
in Sören Kierkegaard and Ronald Laing." *Drew Gateway*
41 (1970):48-49.

3505. Taylor, Mark C. "Psychoanalytic dimensions of
Kierkegaard's view of selfhood." *Philosophy Today* 19
(1975):198-212.

3506. Taylor, Mark C. "Kierkegaard on the structure of
selfhood." In *The Presence of Sören Kierkegaard in Contemporary American Life*. Lewis Lawson, ed. Metuchen (New
Jersey): The Scarecrow Press, 1971, 84-103.

3507. Vogt, Annemarie. *Das Problem des Selbsteins bei
Heidegger und Kierkegaard*. Giessen: H. & J. Lechte, 1936,
vi-61p. Phil. Diss. Giessen, 1936.

Self-Acceptance

3508. Madden, M. C. "Kierkegaard on self-acceptance."
Review and Expositor 48 (1951):302-309.

Seriousness (Ernst)

3509. Castilla del Pino, C. "El concepto de 'gravedad'
in Kierkegaard." *Actas Luso-españolas de Neurología y
Psiquiatría* 10 (1950):33-37.

3510. Theunissen, Michael. *Der Begriff Ernst bei Sören
Kierkegaard*. (Symposion, 1). Freiburg: Alber, 1958. 186p.

Sermon

3511. Holmer, Paul L. "Kierkegaard and the sermon."
Journal of Religion 38 (1957):1-9.

Silence

3512. Crumbine, Nancy J. "On silence." *Humanitas* 11
(1975):147-165.

Sin

3513. Bohlin, Torsten. "Angst, Verzweiflung und Glaube.
Ein Beitrag zum Verständnis der Sündenauffassung bei Kier-
kegaard." *Glaube und Ethos*. Festschrift für Georg Wehrung.
Stuttgart, 1940, 141-151.

3514. Fischer, Hermann. *Subjektivität und Sünde. Kierkegaards Begriff d. Sünde mit ständiger Rücks. auf Schleiermachers Lehre von d. Sünde.* Itzehoe: Verlag Die Spur,
1963. 155p.

3515. Hamilton, Kenneth M. "Kierkegaard on Sin."
Scottish Journal of Theology 17 (1964):289-302.

3516. Künneth, Walter. *Die Lehre von der Sünde, darges-
tellt an der Lehre Sören Kierkegaards in ihrem Verhältnis
zur Lehre der neuesten Theologie.* [Teildr.] Gütersloh:
Bertelsmann, 1927. 59p. Theol. Diss. Erlangen, 1927.
Also: *Die Lehre von der Sünde dargestellt an dem Verhältnis
der Lehre Sören Kierkegaards zur neuesten Theologie.*
(Ein Auszug des Buches erschien als Inaug.-Diss.).
Gütersloh: Bertelsmann, 1927, vii-274p.

Social - Sociology

3518. Demson, David. "Kierkegaard's sociology, with notes
on its relevance to the Church." *Religion in Life*
27 (1958):257-265.

3519. Kirmmse, Bruce H. "Kierkegaard's Politics. The
Social Thought of Sören Kierkegaard in Its Historical
Context." Ph.D., Univ. of California at Berkeley, 1977,
1030p. *Dissertation Abstracts* 39 (1978):1047A.

3520. Matthis, Michael J. "The social in Kierkegaard's
concept of the individual." *Philosophy Today* 23 (1979):
74-83.

3521. Moore, S. "Religion as the true humanism--Reflec-
tions on Kierkegaard's social philosophy." *Journal of the
American Academy of Religion* (March 1969):15.

3522. Schweickert, Alfred. *Sören Kierkegaards Soziologie.* Heidelberg, 1924, v-83p. (Maschinenschrift). Phil. Diss. Heidelberg, 1924.

3523. Salmona, Bruno. "La socialità nel *Diario* di Kierkegaard." *Sapienza* 11 (1958):409-423.

3524. Bonaventura, Vobis. "Hegel, Marx und Kierkegaard in ihrem Beitrag zum Thema 'Der Einzelne und die Gemeinschaft'." *Franziskanische Studien* (Münster i. Westf.) 35 (1953): 87-90.

Soul-Sickness

3525. Gilmartin, Thomas V. "Soul-Sickness: A Comparison of William James and Soeren Kierkegaard." Th.D., Graduate Theological Union, 1974, 321p. *Dissertation Abstracts* 36 (1976):6763A.

Speculative Thought

3526. McInerny, Ralph M. "Kierkegaard and speculative thought." *New Scholasticism* 40 (1966):23-35.

Stages (See also Existence, Levels)

3527. Kainz, Howard P. "Kierkegaard's 'three stages' and the levels of spiritual maturity." *Modern Schoolman* 52 (1974-75):359-380.

3528. Mensi von Klarbach, Alfred v. "Sören Kierkegaards Stadien." *Allgemeine Zeitung.* International Wochenschr. für Wissenschaft, Kunst und Technik (München) 114 (1911): 630.

3529. Paci, Enzo. "Il cammino della vita [Kierkegaard]." *Aut-Aut* (1954):111-126.

3530. Stack, George J. "Kierkegaard's ironic stage of existence." *Laval Théologique et Philosophique* 25 (1969): 192-207.

Subjectivity

3531. Barth, Peter. "Die Subjektivität bei Kierkegaard."
Zeitschrift für Theologie und Kirche (Tübingen) 29 (1921):
(N.F. 2) 72-87.

3532. Ferreira da Silva, V. "Kierkegaard e o problema da
subjectividade." *Revista Brasileira de Filosofia* 6 (1956):
70-76.

3533. Hendel, Charles W. "The subjective as a problem."
Philosophical Review 62 (1953):327-354.

3534. Keane, Ellen Marie. "The Equation of Subjectivity
and Truth in Kierkegaard's *Postscript*." Ph.D., Univ. of
Notre Dame, 1965, 188p. *Dissertation Abstracts* 26 (1965):
5485.

3535. Malevez, Léopold. "Subjectivité et vérité chez
Kierkegaard et dans la théologie chrétienne." In *Mélanges
J. Maréchal*, t. II. Bruxelles: Éd. Universelle; Paris:
Desclée de Brouwer, 1950, 408-423.

3536. McLane, Earl. "Kierkegaard and subjectivity."
International Journal for the Philosophy of Religion
8 (1977):211-232.

3537. Richter, Liselotte. *Der Begriff der Subjektivität
bei Kierkegaard. Ein Beitrag zur christlichen Existenzdarstellung.* Würzburg: K. Triltsch, 1934, iv-110p. Phil.
Diss. Marburg, 1934. 2. Aufl. ibid. eod., 110p.

3538. Roberts, James Deotis. "Kierkegaard on truth and
subjectivity." *Journal of Religious Thought* 18 (1961):
41-56.

3539. Robinson, William. "The objectivity of the subjective in Kierkegaard." *Shane Quarterly* 16 (1955):144-150.

3540. Rohrmoser, Günter. "Kierkegaard und das Problem
der Subjektivität." *Neue Zeitschrift für Systematische
Theologie* 8 (1966):289-310.

3541. Sefler, George F. "Kierkegaard's religious truth:
The three dimensions of subjectivity." *International
Journal for the Philosophy of Religion* 2 (1971):43-52.

3542. Solomon, Robert C. "Kierkegaard and 'subjective
truth'." *Philosophy Today* 21 (1977):202-215.

3543. Stack, George J. "The meaning of 'subjectivity is
truth'." *Midwest Journal of Philosophy* (1975):26-40.

3544. Stein, Waltraut J.   "Truth as subjectivity: The
thought of Sören Kierkegaard." *Religious Humanism* 4 (1970):
78-82.

3545. Wahl, Jean. "Subjectivité et transcendance."
Bulletin de la Société Française de Philosophie (Paris)
37 (1937):161-163.

3546. Wiseman, William J. J. "Subjectivity in the Existential Method of Sören Kierkegaard." Ph.D., Temple Univ.,
1948.

Suffering

3547. Ansbro, John J. "Kierkegaard's gospel of suffering."
Philosophical Studies 16 (1967):182-192.

3548. Dewey, Bradley R. "Kierkegaard on suffering: Promise
and lack of fulfillment in life's stages." *Humanitas J.I.M.*
9 (1973):21-45.

3549. Khan, Abrahim Habibulla. "The Treatment of the Theme
of Suffering in Kierkegaard's Works." Ph.D., McGill Univ.
(Canada), 1973. *Dissertation Abstracts* 34:7823A.

3550. Koutsouvilis, A. "Is suffering necessary for the
good man?" *The Heythrop Journal* 13 (1972):44-53.

3551. Miri, Sujata. *Suffering*. Simla: Indian Institute
of Advanced Study, 1976. 107p.

3552. Tisseau, Pierre-Henri. "Kierkegaard et la souffrance."
Études Philosophiques 18 (1963):315-322.

Technocracy

3553. Richter, Liselotte. "Kierkegaard und das Zeitalter
der Technokratie." *Zeichen der Zeit* (Berlin) (1955):
402-406.

Terminology

3554. Widenman, Robert. "Kierkegaard's terminology--and
English." In *Kierkegaardiana* 7 (1967):113-130.

Testament

3554a. Dewey, B. R. "Kierkegaard and the blue Testament."
Harvard Theological Review 60 (1967):391-409.

3555. Dollinger, Robert. "Sören Kierkegaard und das Alte
Testament." *Die Junge Kirche* 9 (1941):188-197.

3556. Sorainen, Kalle. "Einige Beobachtungen im Bezug auf
die lateinischen Übersetzungen Sören Kierkegaards aus dem
griechischen Neuen Testament." In *Kierkegaardiana* 9 (1974):
56-74.

Theology

3557. Anz, Wilhelm. "Philosophie und Glaube bei Sören
Kierkegaard. Über die Bedeutung der Existenzdialektik für
die Theologie." *Zeitschrift für Theologie und Kirche*
(Tübingen) 51 (1954):50-105.

3558. Aubry, Edwin Ewart. "Kierkegaard, father of dialectical theology." In *Present Theological Tendencies*.
New York and London: Harper, 1936, 60-73.

3559. Barth, Karl. *Die Protestantische Theologie im 19.
Jahrhundert*. Ihre Vorgeschichte und ihre Geschichte.
Zürich: Evangelische Verlag, 1947.

3560. Barth, Karl. "Kierkegaard and the theologians."
[Reprint] trans. by H. M. Rumscheidt. *Canadian Journal
of Theology* 13 (1967):64-65.

3561. Bärthold, A. *Zur Theologischen Bedeutung Sören
Kierkegaards*. Halle: J. Fricke, 1880. 80p.

3562. Beck, A. Fr. "Übersichtliche Darstellung des jetzigen Zustandes der Theologie in Dänemark." *Theologische
Jahrbücher* (Tübingen) 3 (1844):497-536.

3563. Bell, Richard H. "Kierkegaard and Wittgenstein:
Two strategies for understanding theology." *Iliff Review*
31 (1974):21-34.

3564. Bridel, Philippe. "Théologie de Vinet et Barthisme."
Revue de Théologie et de Philosophie (Lausanne) 24 (1936):
87-91.

3565. Brown, James. *Kierkegaard, Heidegger, Buber and
Barth. Subject and Object in Modern Theology*. (Croall
Lectures, 1953). [Originally appeared with title:
Subject and Object in Modern Theology]. New York: P. F.
Collier, 1962. 192p.

3566. Buske, Thomas. "Die Dialektik der Geschichte. Zur
Theologie Sören Kierkegaards." *Neue Zeitschrift für
Systematische Theologie* 5 (1963):235-247.

3567. Cruickshank, A. "Theology and Kierkegaard's *Postscript.*" *Church Quarterly* 1 (1969):206-211.

3568. Diem, H. "Kierkegaards Hinterlassenschaft an die
Theologie." In *Antwort. Karl Barth zum 70. Geburtstag.*
Zollikon-Zürich: Evangelische Verlag, 1956, 472-489.

3569. Dumas, A. "La critique de l'objectivite de dieu dans
la theologie protestante." *Revue des Sciences Philosophiques et Théologiques* 52 (1968):408-426.

3570. Dupré, L. *Kierkegaards Theologie of de Dialectiek
van het Christen-Worden.* Utrecht: Het Spectrum; Antwerpen:
N. V. Standaard-Beokhandel, 1958. 230p.

3571. Dupré, Louis K. *Kierkegaard as Theologian. The
Dialectic of Christian Existence.* New York: Sheed & Ward,
1963, xx-229p.

3572. Ferm, Deane W. "Two conflicting trends in Protestant
theological thinking." *Religion in Life* 25 (1956):582-594.

3573. Ferre, Nels F. S. "Rise and role of neo-orthodoxy."
Morav. Th. S. Bul. (1959):35-48.

3574. Grosche, Robert. "La notion d'analogie et le
problème théologique d'aujourd'hui." [K. Barth, S. Kierkegaard, Th. Haecker]. (Trad. d. Yves Simon). *Revue de
Philosophie* (Paris) 55 (1935):302-312.

3575. Hirsch, Emanuel. "Sören Kierkegaard." *Der Weg der
Theologie.* Stuttgart: W. Kohlhammer, 1937 (128p. Sammlung
von Aufsätze), 108-124.

3576. Holmer, Paul L. "Kierkegaard and theology."
Union Seminary Quarterly Review 12 (1957):23-31.

3577. Kraege, Jean-Denis. "Théologie analytique et
théologie dialectique." *Revue de Théologie et de Philosophie* 3 (1979):13-33.

3578. Lönning, Per. *The Dilemma of Contemporary Theology:
Prefigured in Luther, Pascal, Kierkegaard, Nietzsche.*
Oslo: Norwegian Universities Press, 1962, 140p.; New York:
Humanities Press, 1964, 139p.

3579. Mackintosh, Hugh R. "The theology of Kierkegaard."
Congregational Quarterly 7 (1929):282-296.

3580. Makintosh, Hugh Ross. "Kierkegaard: The theology of
paradox." In *Types of Modern Theology. Schleiermacher to
Barth*. A. B. Macaulay, ed. London: Nisbet, 1937, 218-262;
New York: Scribner, 1939.

3581. Niebergal, Friedrich. "Predigttypen und Predigtaufgaben der Gegenwart 5: Kierkegaard, Barth und Thurneysen,
Dehn, Ehrhard." *Die Christliche Welt* (Gotha) 39 (1925):
738-743.

3582. Owen, H. P. "Existentialism and ascetical theology."
Church Quarterly Review 160 (1959):226-231.

3583. Pelikan, Jaroslav. *From Luther to Kierkegaard. A
Study of the History of Theology*. St. Louis: Concordia,
1950, vi-171p.

3584. Peterson, Erik. "Kierkegaard und die protestantische
Theologie." *Wort und Wahrheit* (Wien) 3 (1947).

3585. Peterson, Erik. "L'influsso di Kierkegaard sulla
teologia protestante contemporanea." *Humanitas* no. 7 (1947).

3586. *Problemi Scelti di Teologia Contemporanea*. Relazioni lette nella Sezione di teologia del Congresso Internazionale per il IV Centenario della Pontificia Universita
Gregoriana, 13-17 Ottobre 1953. (*Analecta Gregoriana*,
vol. 68. Series Facultatis Theologicae, Sectio A., no. 11).
Romae: Apud aedes Univ. Gregoriannae, 1954, viii-468p.

3587. Riconda, Giuseppe. "L'eredita ci Kierkegaard e la
teologia dialettica nel suo significatio speculativo."
Filosofia 25 (1974):215-232.

3588. Schaeder, Erich. *Theozentrische Theologie. Eine
Untersuchung zur Dogmatischen Prinzipienlehre I-II*.
Leipzig: A. Dichert, 1909 and 1914 (vii-211p. and
viii-324p.), I: p. 2, 215ff.; II: p. 141, 166.

3589. Schröer, Henning. *Die Denkform der Paradoxalität
als Theologisches Problem*. Eine Untersuchung zu Kierke-
gaard und d. neueren Theologie als Beitrag zur theolog.
Logik (Forschungen zur systematischen Theologie und
Religionsphilosophie, 5). Göttingen: Vandenhoeck &
Ruprecht, 1960. 207p.

3590. Smith, Elwyn Allen. "Kierkegaard and dogmatic
theology: An epistemological impasse." *Evangelical
Quarterly* (1945):106-123.

3591. Spinka, M. "Soren Kierkegaard and the existential
theology." In *Christian Thought from Erasmus to Berdyaev*.
Prentice-Hall, 1962, 146-155.

3592. Thomas, John H. "The relevance of Kierkegaard to the demythologizing controversy." *Scottish Journal of Theology* 10 (1957):239-252.

3593. Thust, Martin. "Sören Kierkegaard und die wissenschaftliche Theologie." *Zeitwende* (München & Berlin) (1927):173ff.

Therapy

3594. West, George K. "Kierkegaard and Adler: A Comparison of the Categories in Living As Seen by Both Authors, and the Consequent Implications for Therapy." Ph.D., Florida State Univ., 1975, 274p. *Dissertation Abstracts* 37 (1976): 138.

Time

3595. Bedell, G. C. "Kierkegaard's conception of time." *Journal of the American Academy of Religion* 37 (1969): 266-269.

3596. Daane, James. "Kierkegaard's Concept of the Moment. An Investigation into the Time-Eternity Concept of Sören Kierkegaard." Ph.D., Princeton Theological Seminary. *Dissertation Abstracts* 35 (1974):2379A.

3597. Gunder-Hansen, Edwin. "Gedanken über Sören Kierkegaards Zeitkritik." *Kantstudien* (Leipzig) N.F. 42 (1942-42):210-216.

3598. Hamilton, Wayne Bruce. "Sören Kierkegaard's Conception of Temporality." Ph.D., McGill Univ. (Canada), 1972. *Dissertation Abstracts* 33:2977A.

3599. Hamilton, Wayne B. "Existential tiem: A re-examination." *Southern Journal of Philosophy* 13 (1975):297-307.

3600. Masterson, Patrick. "Kierkegaard's view of time. A reply to J. Heywood Thomas." *Journal of the British Society for Phenomenology* 4 (1973):41-44. [See no. 3605]

3601. Nizet, Jean. "La temporalité chez Sören Kierkegaard." *Revue Philosophique de Louvain* 71 (1973):225-245. [Résumé, Abstract, 245-246]

3602. Ottonello, Pier Paolo. *Kierkegaard e il Problema del Tempo.* Genova: Tilgher, 1972. 126p. [Incl. "Studi Kierkegaardiani in Italia," 93-108.]

3603. Schrag, Calvin O. "Kierkegaard's existential reflections on time." *The Personalist* 42 (1961):149-164.

3604. Taylor, Mark C. "Time's struggle with space. Kierkegaard's understanding of temporality." *Harvard Theological Review* 66 (1973):311-329.

3605. Thomas, J. Heywood. "Kierkegaard's view of time."
Journal of the British Society for Phenomenology 4 (1973):
33-40. [Klaus Hartmann, comments on J. Heywood Thomas'
paper, 45.][P. Masterson, reply to Thomas, see no. 3600.]

3606. Widenman, Robert. "Some aspects of time in Aristotle
and Kierkegaard." In *Kierkegaardiana* 8 (1971):7-22.

Tragic

3607. Johansen, Karsten Friis. "Kierkegaard on 'the
tragic'." In *Danish Yearbook of Philosophy* 13 (1976):
105-146.

3608. Mesnard, Pierre. "La catégorie du tragique est-elle
absente de l'oeuvre et de la pensée de Kierkegaard?"
Orbis Litterarum 10 (1955):178-190. [Symposion Kierke-
gaardianum]

Transcendence

3609. Gerry, Joseph. "Kierkegaard: The Problem of Transcendence: An Interpretation of the Stages." Ph.D.,
Fordham Univ., 1959.

3610. Malantschuk, Gregor. "Die Begriffe Immanenz und
Transzendenz bei Sören Kierkegaard." *Neue Zeitschrift
für Systematische Theologie* 19 (1977):225-246.

3611. Sperna Weiland, J. "Het begrip transcendentie in
de filosofie van Kierkegaard." *Vox Theologica* (Assen)
20 (1949):9-17.

3612. Teschner, George A. "The Relation of Man to Tran-
scendence in the Philosophy of Kierkegaard." Ph.D., New
School for Social Research, 1975, 251p. *Dissertation
Abstracts* 36 (1976):6152A.

3613. Teschner, George A. "Psychology of faith and the
meaning of transcendence in the philosophy of Kierkegaard." *Journal of Psychology and Theology* 5 (1977):
300-311.

Translations

3614. Cortese, Alessandro. "Récentes traductions ital-
iennes de Sören Kierkegaard." In *Kierkegaardiana* 5 (1964):
107-130.

Truth

3615. Borgia, S. *Sapere Assuloto e Verità Soggettiva*.
Presentazione di Bruno Widmar [Hegel, Kierkegaard].
Galatina: Editrice Salantina, 1971. 134p.

3616. Brechtken, J. "Wahrheit in Praxis." *Tijdschrift
voor Filosofie* 37 (1975):391-419.

3617. Edwards, Paul. "Kierkegaard and the 'truth' of
Christianity." *Philosophy* 46 (1971):89-108.

3618. Evans, C. Stephen. "Kierkegaard on subjective
truth. Is God an ethical fiction?" *International Journal
for the Philosophy of Religion* 7 (1976):288-299.

3619. Fabro, Cornelio. "La 'comunicazione della verità'
nel pensiero di Kierkegaard." In *Studi Kierkegaardiani*.
Con un inedito di S. Kierkegaard. A cura di Cornelio
Fabro. Brescia: Morcelliana Editrice, 1957, 125-163.

3620. Frutos, Eugenio. "La enseñanza de la verdad en
Kierkegaard." *Revista de Filosofía* 9 (1950):91-98.

3621. Haecker, Theodor. "Der Begriff der Wahrheit bei
Sören Kierkegaard. Ein Vortrag." *Hochland* 26 (1929):
476-493.

3622. Haecker, Theodor. *Der Begriff der Wahrheit bei
Sören Kierkegaard*. Innsbruck: Brenner-Verlag, 1932. 76p.

3623. Haecker, Theodor. "La notion de la vérité chez
Sören Kierkegaard." Trad. de l'allemand par Jean Chuzeville. In *Essais sur Kierkegaard, Petrarque, Geothe.
Religion et Philosophie, Musique et Poésie*. Paris, 1934,
9-83. (Collections des Iles, 4).

3624. Hare, Peter H. "Is there an existential theory of
truth?" *Journal of Existentialism* 7 (1967):417-424.

3625. Holmer, Paul L. "Kierkegaard and the Truth: An
Analysis of the Presuppositions Integral to His Definition
of the Truth." Ph.D., Yale Univ., 1946, 312p.
Dissertation Abstracts 26 (1966):4002.

3626.   Malantschuck, Gregor.   "Das Verhältnis zwischen
Wahrheit und Wirklichkeit in Sören Kierkegaards existentiellem Denken."   *Orbis Litterarum* 10 (1955):166-177.

3627.   Malevez, Leopold.   "Subjectivité et vérité chez
Kierkegaard et dans la théologie chrétienne."   In *Mélanges
Joseph Maréchal* II.   Bruxelles: Ed. Universelle, 1950;
Paris: Desclée de Brouwer, 1950, 408-423.

3628.   Murphy, Arthur E.   "On Kierkegaard's claim that
'truth is subjectivity'."   [Not previously publ.], in
*Reason and the Common Good.   Selected Essays of A. E.
Murphy*.   William H. Hay et al., eds.   Englewood Cliffs
(New Jersey): Prentice Hall, 1963, 173-179.

3629.   Pinto, J. da Costa.   "A verdade em Kierkegaard."
Revue Portuguesa de Filosofia 33 (1977):84-88.

3630.   Schacht, Richard.   "Kierkegaard on 'truth is subjectivity' and 'the leap of faith'."   *Canadian Journal of
Philosophy* 2 (1973):297-313.

3631.   Schultzky, Gerolf.   *Die Wahrnehmung des Menschen bei
Sören Kierkegaard.   Zur Wahrheitsproblematik d. theolog.
Anthropologie*.   (Studien zur Theologie und Geistesgeschichte
des neunzehnten Jahrhunderts, 28).   Göttingen: Vandenhoeck
und Ruprecht, 1977.   244p.

3632.   Solomon, Robert C.   "Kierkegaard and 'subjective
truth'."   *Philosophy Today* 21 (1977):202-215.

3633.   Stack, George J.   "La verdad como subjetividad.
Interpretación [Kierkegaard]."   *Folia Humanistica* 15
(1977):607-618.

3634.   Thiselton, Anthony C.   "Kierkegaard and the nature of
truth."   *The Churchman* (London) 89 (1975):85-107.

3635.   van den Nieuwenhuizen, M.   *Dialiktiek van de vrijheid.
Zonde en zondevergeving bij Sören Kierkegaard*.   Assen:
Van Gorcum, 1968, xiv-146p.

3636.   Vela, Raffaele, O. P.   "Kierkegaard e la verità
esistenziale."   *Vita Sociale* 23 (1966):231-239.

3637.   Walker, Jeremy.   "Kierkegaard's concept of truth-
fulness."   *Inquiry* 12 (1969):209-224.

3638.   Weisshaupt, Kurt.   *Die Zeitlichkeit der Wahrheit*.
Eine Untersuchung zur Wahrheitsbegriff Sören Kierkegaards
(Symposion, 41).   Freiburg i Br.: Alber, 1973.   160p.

Unhappiness

3639. Lessing, Arthur. "Hegel and existentialism, on unhappiness." *The Personalist* 49 (1968):61-77.

Value

3640. Duncan, Elmer Hubert. "Kierkegaard and Value Theory: A Study of the Three Spheres of Existence." Ph.D., Univ. of Cincinnati, 1962, 136p. *Dissertation Abstracts* 23 (1962):2171.

3641. McMinn, J. B. "Value and subjectivity in Kierkegaard." *Review of Existentialism* 53 (1956):477-488.

Verification

3642. Carnell, Edward J. "The Problem of Verification in Soeren Kierkegaard." Ph.D., Boston Univ., 1949, 270p.

Virtue

3643. Cutting, Pat. "Kierkegaard's answer to the questions: Can virtue be taught?" *Southwest Philosophical Studies* 2 (1977):102-107.

Waiting

3644. Shouery, Imad. "Phenomenological analysis of waiting." *Southwestern Journal of Philosophy* 3 (1972): 93-101.

Woman

3645. Garside, Christine. "Can a woman be good in the same way as a man?" *Dialogue* (Canada) 10 (1971):531-541.

3646. Kuhle, Sejer. "Sören Kierkegaard und die Frauen." *Orbis Litterarum* 10 (1955):118-129. [Symposion Kierkegaardianum]

3647.   Droop, Fritz.   "Kierkegaard und die Frauen."
Hamburger Fremdenblatt no. 204 (1913).

Wonder

3648.   Arendt, R. P.   "Der Begriff des Wunders, besonders
im Hinblick auf Bultmann und Kierkegaard." *Neue Zeitschrift
für Systematische Theologie* 12 (1970):146-164.

Zen Buddhism

3649.   Jacobson, Nolan Pliny.   "The predicament of man in
Zen buddhism and Kierkegaard." *Philosophy East and West*
2 (1952):238-253.

CHAPTER 7:
Memoirs, Portraits, Personal

3650. Anonymous. "Etats européens.--Le Danemark. Questions religieuses [S. Kierkegaards dod]." *Annuaire des deux Mondes*. Histoire génerale des divers états. VI. 1855-56. Paris (20.10.1856) (972p.), p. 489.

3651. Anonymous. "Über die religiöse Entwicklung Sören Kierkegaards." Ergänzungsblätter zur *Allgemeine Evangelische-Lutherisch Kirchenzeitung* (Leipzig) 12 (1879): 213-222.

3652. Anonymous. "Die letzten Tage Kierkegaards." *Der Brenner* (Innsbruck) 8 (1925):70-76.

3653. Anonymous. "Sören Kierkegaard. Das Geheimnis einer Lebensform." *Geisteskampf der Gegenwart* (Gütersloh) 69 (1933):153.

3654. Anonymous. "Kierkegaard, the Dane. A personal Christian protest." *News Week* 43 (1954):66.

3655. Andersen, Georges. "Le martyre de Kierkegaard, éclairé par les flambeaux de son jubilé." *Combat* (Paris) (10.11.1955).

3656. Bärthold, A. "Sören Kierkegaard und das Pfarrhaus." *Das Pfarrhaus* (Leipzig) 1 (1885):9.

3657. Bellisario, Vincenzo. "Il dramma di Kierkegaard." *Rivista di Filosofia Neo-Scolastica* (Milano) 34 (1942): 127-136.

3658. Billeskov Jansen, F. J. "L'héritage de Kierkegaard dans les pays nordiques." *Cahiers du Sud* 50 (1963):18-27.

3659.   Bohlin, Torsten.   "La piété de Kierkegaard."
Foi et Vie (Paris) 35 (1934):621-638.

3660.   Brophy, Liam.   "Kierkegaard; the Hamlet in search of
holiness." *Social Justice Review* 47 (1955):291-292.

3661.   Brandt, Frithiof.   "The great earthquake in Soren
Kierkegaard's life." *Theoria* 15 (1949):38-53.

3662.   Butler, C.   "Impressions of Kierkegaard." *Downside
Review* 55 (1937):363-369.

3663.   Campbell, Charles.   "Aesthetic language transformed:
The 'poetry' of Sören Kierkegaard." [Abst., article avail-
able from Scholars Press, Missoula MT.] *Journal of the
American Academy of Religion* 45 (1977):75.

3664.   Christensen, Arild.   "Kierkegaard's secret afflic-
tion: An explanation of his term 'the thorn in the flesh'."
Harvard Theological Review 42 (1949):255-271.

3665.   Collins, James.   "The fashionableness of Kierkegaard." *Thought* 22 (1947):211-215.

3666.   Cortese, Alessandro.   "L 'organico' culturale
(paragrafi kierkegaardiani)." *Ve P.* 48 (1965):132-144.

3667.   Cortese, Alessandro.   "Soeren Aabye Kierkegaard,
abbozzo sulla sua vita." *Ve P.* 48 (1965):38-54.

3668.   Cristaldi, Mariano. *Problemi di Storiografia
Kierkegaardiana.* (Istituto di Filosofia Teoretica).
Catania: N. Giannotta, 1973.   197p.

3669.   Croxall, T. H.   "Kierkegaard in the choice."
Meddelelser fra Sören Kierkegaard Selskabet 2 (1950):
37-38.

3670.   Croxall, T. H.   "Was Kierkegaard a cripple?"
Meddelelser fra Sören Kierkegaard Selskabet 2 (1950):58-60.

3671.   Croxall, T. H.   "The death of Kierkegaard."
Church Quarterly Review 157 (1956):271-286.

3672.   Deuser, Hermann. *Sören Kierkegaard, die Paradoxe Dialektik des politischen Christen: Voraussetzungen bei Hegel;
die Reden von 1847-48 im Verhältnis von Politik und Ästhetic.*
München: Kaiser; Mainz: Matthias Grunewald Verlag, 1974, 254p.

3673.   Diem, Hermann.   "Kierkegaard et la postérité."
Revue d.Histoire et de Philosophie Religieuses 46 (1966):
1-16.

3674.   Dupré, Louis K.   "Kierkegaard, the melancholy Dane."
America 94 (1955):689-690.

3675. Eller, V. "Four who remember; Kierkegaard, the Blumhardts, Ellul, and Muggeridge." *Katallagete* 3 (1971): 6-12.

3676. Esser, P. H. "Kierkegaards ontwikkeling en uitgroet als psychologisch problem." *Nederlandsch Tijdschrift voor Psychologie* (Amsterdam) 4 (1936):150-166.

3677. Fabro, Cornelio. "Critica di Kierkegaard all'Otto-cento." *Atti del XV Congresso Nazionale di Filosofia.* . . 1948. Messina-Firenze: D'Anna, 1949, 375-385.

3678. Ferrie, W. S. "Kierkegaard: Hamlet or Jeremiah?" *Evangelical Quarterly* 8 (1936):142-147.

3679. Formery, Bernard. "La passion de Sören Kierkegaard." *Le Monde* (Paris):(12.11.1955).

3680. Franken, J. Christiann. "Die psychologische Kritik Kierkegaards." In *Kritische Philosophie und dialektische Theologie*. Prolegomena zu einer phisolophischen Behandlung des Problems der christlichen Gemeinschaft. Amsterdam: H. J. Paris, 1932 (x-439p.), 71-80. Phil. Diss. Utrecht, 1932.

3681. Friedmann, Rudolph. "Kierkegaard. An analysis of the psychological personality." *Horizon* (1943):252-273.

3682. Garde, Annelise. "Grafologisk undersögelse af Sören Kierkegaards handskrift i arene 1831-1855." In *Kierkegaardiana* 10 (1977):200-233. [Summary in English, 234-238.]

3683. Geismar, Eduard. "La personnalité de Kierkegaard." (Conférences à l'Institut des Études scandinaves de la Faculté des lettres de Paris, 2. & 4.2.1933). *Revue de Métaphysique et de Morale* (Paris) 40 (1933):137-159.

3684. Groethuysen, B. *Mythes et Portraits*. [Sören Kier-kegaard]. *Les Essais* (Paris) 23 (1947):191-202.

3685. Guardini, Romano. "Der Ausgangspunkt der Denkbewegung Sören Kierkegaards." *Hochland* 24 (1927):12-33.

3686. Guterman, N. "Kierkegaard and his faith." *Partisan Review* 10 (1943).

3687. Hamburger, M. "A refusal to review Kierkegaard." In *Art as a Second Nature: Occasional Pieces 1950-1974*. New York: Carionet New Press, dist. by Dufour (New York), 1975. 156p. [The last years of Kierkegaard.]

3688. Harms, Ernst, and Kronfeld, Arthur. "Der 'Fall Kierkegaard'." *Psychotherapeutische Vierteljahrsschrift* (Bern & Wien) 3 (1936):40-42.

3689. Havelaar, Just. "Kierkegaard im Kampf mit sich selbst." De Stem (Arnhem) 3 (1923):177-181.

3690. Held, Matthew. "The historical Kierkegaard: Faith or Gnosis." Journal of Religion 37 (1957):260-266.

3691. Henriksen, Aage. "Kierkegaards reviews of literature." Orbis Litterarum (Copenhagen) 10 (1955):75-83.

3692. Hess, M. Whitcomb. "The death of Sören Kierkegaard." Catholic World 182 (1955):92-98.

3693. Hirsch, Emanuel. "Zum Verständnis von Kierkegaards Verlobungszeit (Kierkegaard-Studien, 1. Stück). Zeitschrift für Systematische Theologie (Gütersloh) 5 (1927):55-75.

3694. Höffding, Harald. "La personalidad de Sören Kierkegaard." Revista de Occidente (Madrid) 8 (1930):1-33.

3695. Hohlenberg, J. "Kierkegaard tel qu'il était." La Table Ronde (Paris) (1955):16-32.

3696. Hohlenberg, Johannes. "Kierkegaard tel qu'il était." (Trad. du danois par P.-H. Tisseau). La Table Ronde (Paris) (1955):18-32.

3697. Howitt, William. "The brothers Kierkegaard." In The Literature and Romance of Northern Europe. Vol. 2. London: Colburn, 1852, 239-240.

3698. Julzler, Konrad. "Sören Kierkegaard und zein Vater." Die Neue Furche (Tübingen) 6 (1952):599-606.

3699. Koch, F. W. "Leben unter einer Wolke der Schwermut. Sören Kierkegaard (gestorben am 11. November 1855) ahnte unser Zeitalter des Unbehagens und der Angst." Morgen (Berlin) (9.11.1955).

3700. Kofoed-Hansen, H. P. "Notice sur la vie et les oeuvres de S. A. Kierkegaard." In En quoi l'Homme de Génie Diffère-t-il de l'Apôtre? Copenhagen, 1886, 3-8.

3701. Kronfeld, Arthur, and Harms, Ernst. "Der 'Fall Kierkegaard'." Psychoterapeutische Vierteljahrsschrift (Bern & Wien) 3 (1936):40-42.

3702. Lindström, Valter. "La théologie de l'imitation de Jésus-Christ chez Sören Kierkegaard. Pour le centenaire de la mort de Kierkegaard." Trad. de l'allemand par Jean Carrère. Revue d'Histoire et de Philosophie Religieuses (Strasbourg) 35 (1955):379-392.

3703. Lowtzki, F. [Sören Kierkegaard.] Revue Française de Psychanalyse (Paris) 9 (1936):204-314.

3704. Lowtzki, F. "Die Wiederholung bei Sören Kierkegaard." *Alma ach der Psychoanalyse* (Wien) 11 (1936): 175-186.

3705. Lowrie, Walter. "Der Vater Sören Kierkegaards." *Die Zeit* (Hamburg) 10 (1955):6.

3706. Lowrie, Walter. "Die Eltern Sören Kierkegaards." *Sören Kierkegaard 1855-1955. Zum Kierkegaard-Dedenkjahr vorgelegt.* Düsseldorf-Köln: Diederichs, 1955, 18-24.

3707. Lund, Henriette. *S. Kierkegaards Familie und Privatleben.* Originalauszüge aus einer nur als Mskpt. gedr. und daher wenig bekannten dän. Schrift von Sören Kierkegaard's Nichte, Fraulein K. Lund. Übers. von Julie von Reincke. S. K.: Ausgewählte christliche Reden. Giessen: J. Ricker, 1901 (xv-158p.), 121-158. 2. Aufl. Giessen: A. Töpelmann, 1909, 140p. 3. Aufl. ibid., 1923, 128p.

3708. MacGillivray, Arthur, S. J. "Melancholy Dane: Sören Kierkegaard." *Catholic World* 163 (1946):338-342.

3709. Mackey, Louis H. "Loss of the world in Kierkegaard." *Review of Metaphysics* 15 (1962):602-620.

3710. MacRae, D. G. "The Danish malady." *LifeLetters* 47 (1945):85-90.

3711. Malantschuk, Gregory. "Kierkegaard and the Totalitarians." *American-Scandinavian Review* 31 (1946): 246-248.

3712. Maurois, André. "La vie de Kierkegaard, grand philosophe danois." *Les Nouvelles Littéraires* 18 (1960): 1, 4. [Rev. art.]

3713. McKinnon, Alastair, and Cappelörn, Niels Jörgen. "The period of composition of Kierkegaard's published works." *Kierkegaardiana* 9 (1974):133-146.

3714. Mensi von Klarbach, Alfred v. "Sören Kierkegaards Stadien." *Allgemeine Zeitung*, Internationale Wochenschrift für Wissenschaft, Kunst und Technik. (München) 114 (1911): 630.

3715. Muckermann, Friedrich. "Das Geheimnis von Kierkegaard." *Der Gral* (Ravensburg) 23 (1929):1060.

3716. Neumann, Johannes. "Kierkegaards Liebeskonflikt." *Psyche* (Heidelberg) 2 (1948-49):327-370.

3717. Neumann, Johannes. "Kierkegaards 'Pfahl im Fleisch'." *Internationale Zeitschrift für Individual-Psychologie* 18 (1949):7-14.

3718. Niedermeyer, Gerhard. "Zu dem Kierkegaardbilde." *Zeitwende* (München) 2 (1926):449-463, 542-543.

3719. Niedermeyer, Gerhard. "Ostern bis Pfingsten 1848 d. Wende in der religiösen Krise Kierkegaards, zugleich seine erste und entscheidende Berührung mit Luther." *Lutherisch Vierteljahrschrift der Luther Gesellschaft* (München) (1927):42-53.

3720. Nordau, Max. *Dégénerescence*. Trad. de l'allemand par Auguste Dietrich. I-II. Paris, 1894-95; II. p. 170ff. (p. 204, 205, 255).

3721. Nostiz, Osw von. "Kierkegaards Dämon." *Wirtschafts-Zeitung* (Stuttgart) 4 (1909):9.

3722. Nyman, Alf. "La vita di Sören Kierkegaard alla luce della moderna ricerca." *Scritti di Sociologia e Politica in Anore di Luigi Sturzo, II.* Bologna: Zanichelli, 1953.

3723. Oppel, Horst. "Die Nachwirkung Kierkegaards in der nordischen Dichtung." *Nordische Rundschau* 9 (1936-38): 145-157.

3724. Otani, Masaru. "Something about Kierkegaard's inner history." *Orbis Litterarum* 10 (1955):191-195. [Symposion Kierkegaardianum]

3725. Paci, Enzo. "Il cammino della vita [Kierkegaard]." *Aut-Aut* (Milano) (1943):111-126.

3726. Pape, W. "S. Aa. Kierkegaard. Skizze seines Lebens und Wirkens." *Der Beweis des Glaubens* (Gütersloh) 14 (1878):169-189.

3727. Perris, Carlo. "Psicopatologia ed esistenzialismo: Il problema della vita di Kierkegaard e la valutazione critica dei rapporti tra psicopatologia clinica e filosofia esistenziale." In *Studi Kierkegaardiani*. A cura di Cornelio Fabro. Brescia: Morcelliana, 1957, 283-322.

3728. Pfeiffer, Johannes. "Kierkegaards Kampf gegen den Dichter." *Das Innere Reich* (Berlin) 3 (1936):491-501.

3729. Plachte, K. "Das Vermächtnis Sören Kierkegaards." *Deutsches Pfarrerblatt* (Essen) 43 (1939):725.

3730. Plitt, G. "S. A. Kierkegaard. Skizzirt von J. C. Heuch." Nachtrag. Noch. ein Wort aus dem Norden über Kierkegaard. Mittgetheilt von G. Plitt." *Zeitschrift für die gesammte Lutherische Theologie und Kirche* (Leipzig) 25 (1864): 295-309, 309-310.

3731. Rasmussen, Emil. *Jesus. Eine vergleichende psycho-pathologische Studie.* Übertr. und hrsg. von Arthur Rothenburg. Leipzig, 1905, 115-126.

3732. Riconda, Giuseppe. "L'eredità di Kierkegaard e la teologia dialettica nel suo significato speculativo." *Filosofia* 25 (1974):215-232.

3733. Saggan, Carl. *Skyldig--ikke skyldig. Et par kapitler af Michael og Soren Kierkegaards ungdomsliv.* Copenhagen: Gad, 1967.

3734. Sechi, V. "The poet." In *Kierkegaardiana.* Niels Thulstrup, ed. Copenhagen: C. A. Reitzels Boghandel, 10 (1977):166-181.

3735. Smith, Elwyn Allen. "Psychological aspects of Kierkegaard." *Character and Personality* 12 (1944):195-206.

3736. Smith, Elwyn Allen. "Psychological aspects of Kierkegaard." *Character and Personality* 12 (March 1944): 195-206.

3737. Stewart, H. L. "Sören Kierkegaard as major prophet of the XIXth century." *Expository Times* 61 (1949-50): 271-273.

3738. Swenson, David F. "A Danish thinker's estimate of journalism." *Ethics* 38 (1927-28):70-87.

3739. Thibon, G. "Le drame de Kierkegaard." *Études Carmélitaines* (Paris) 23 (1938):140-150.

3740. Thomsen, Eric H. "That tremendous dane." *Religious Life* 2 (1933):247-260.

3741. Thust, Martin. "Der ästhetische Mensch. Erste Einführung in den Geist Sören Kierkegaards." *Preussische Jahrbücher* (Berlin) 190 (1922):49-63.

3742. Thust, Martin. "Das Marionettentheater Sören Kierkegaards." *Zeitwende* (München) 1 (1925):18-38.

3743. Tillich, Paul. "Kierkegaard as existential thinker." *Union Review* 4 (1942).

3744. Tisseau, P.-H. "Vie de Sören Kierkegaard." *La Table Ronde* (Paris) (1955):9-17.

3745. van der Leeuw, G. "De psychologie van Sören Kierkegaard." *Tijdschrift voor Wijsbegeerte* (Assen) 27 (1934): 21-25.

3746. Wahl, Jean. "Le mysticisme de Kierkegaard." *Hermès* no. 1.

3747. Weigert, Edith. "Sören Kierkegaards Gemutsschwank-
ungen." *Psyche* (Heidelberg) 14 (1960-61):608-616.

3748. Willey, Basil. "Kierkegaard: The melancholy Dane."
Cambridge Review 72 (1951):468-469.

CHAPTER 8:
Anniversary
and Commemoration

3749. Adorno, Theodor W. "Kierkegaard noch einmal: Zum hundertundfünfzigsten Geburtstag." *Neue Deutsche Hefte* 95 (1963):5-25.

3750. Andersen, Georges. "Le martyre de Kierkegaard, éclairé par les flambeaux de son jubilé." *Combat* (Paris) (19.11.1955).

3751. Anonymous. "Kierkegaard. Zu seinem 50 jahrigen Todestage. I-V. *Allgemeine Evangelisch-Lutherisch Kirchenzeitung* (Leipzig) 39 (1905):1068-1069, 1095-1097, 1117-1121, 1141-1146, 1163-1167.

3752. Anonymous. "Kierkegaard centennial." *Theology Today* 12 (1955):244-246.

3753. Anonymous. "Semana Kierkegaardiana." *Agazeta* (Sao Paulo) (24.10.1955).

3754. Anonymous. "Centenário de Kierkegaard." *Correio da Manha.* (Rio de Janeiro) (12.11.1955).

3755. Antunes, M. "No centenário de Kierkegaard." *Brotéria* (Lisboa) 62 (1956):56-63.

3756. A V V. "Centenários dêste ano [Montesquieu-S.K.]." *Kriterion* (Bello Horizonte) 8 (1955):391-393.

3757. Christine Berger-Gerster. "Zum 100. Todestag Sören Kierkegaards." *Das Goetheanum.* Wochenschr. für Anthroposophie (Basel) 34 (1955):358-359.

3758. Bochler, A. "Soeren Aabye Kierkegaard 1813-1855." *Neue Wege.* Blätter für den Kampf der Zeit (Zürich) 49 (1955):512-515.

3759. Bordier, Roger. "Une existence efficace." *Combat* (Paris) (10.11.1955).

3760. Brack, J. Paul. "Kierkegaard als Aufgabe. Zu seinem 100. Todestag am 11. November." *National Zeitung* (Basel) Sonntagsbeilage (6.11.1955).

3761. Brandt, Frithiof. "Le centenaire de Sören Kierkegaard." *La Métropole* (Antwerpen) (29.&30.10.1955).

3762. Branczik, Leo. "Sören Kierkegaard, der asketische Don Juan. Zu seinem 100. Geburtstage am 5. Mai 1913." *Der Merkur* 4 (1913):334-337.

3763. Bruhn, S. "Kierkegaard zum Gedächtnis an seinem Tod vor 50 Jahren." *Glauben und Wissen* (Stuttgart) 3 (1905):367-375.

3764. Buch, Jörgen. "Kierkegaard anniversary." *Hibbert Journal* 62 (1963):24-26.

3765. Cochrane, A. C. "On the anniversaries of Mozart, Kierkegaard and Barth." *Scottish Journal of Theology* 9 (1956):251-263.

3766. Colette, Jacques. "Un anniversaire philosophique au Danemark: Kierkegaard." *Revue Nouvelle* 38 (1963): 324-335.

3767. de Urmeneta, F. "Glosas al centenario de Kierkegaard." *Las Ciencias* (Madrid) 21 (1956):273-278.

3768. Diem, H. "Sokrates in Dänemark. Zum 100. Todestag von Sören Kierkegaard am 11. November 1955." *Schweiz Monatshefte* 35 (1955):422-431.

3769. Dirks, Walter. "Kierkegaard und der Beginn der Lebensangst. Zum 100. Geburtstag des grossen dänischen Philosophen." *Deutsche Zeitung Historische Zeitung für Weltgeschicht* (Stuttgart-Frankfurt am Main) 10 (1955):4.

3770. Dollinger, Robert. "Zum 125. Geburtstag Sören Kierkegaards." *Deutsches Pfarrerblatt* (Essen) 42 (1938): 313.

3771. Eloesser, Arthur. "Sören Kierkegaard. Zu seinem 100. Geburtstage." Sonntagsbeilage no. 17 zur *Vossischen Zeitung* (27.4.1913):129-131.

3772. Eremita, Victor [Pseud.]. "Commémoration du centenaire de Kierkegaard." *Études Philosophiques* (Marseille) 10 (1955):722-724.

3774. Feldkeller, Paul. "Sören Kierkegaard. Zu seinem 120. Geburtstag." *Stuttgarter Neues Tageblatt* (5.5.1933).

3775. Flam, L. "Kierkegaard (geboren op 5 Mei 1813)."
TVUB 5 (1963):204-216.

3776. Flatow, Ernst. "Zum 100. Geburtstag Sören Kierkegaards, 5. Mai 1913." *Logos* (Tübingen) 4 (1913):242-246.

3777. Forgey, Wallace. "A pastor looks at Kierkegaard."
Andover Newton Bulletin 47 (1955):32-39 (Kierkegaard centennial issue).

3778. Formery, Bernard. "La passion de Sören Kierkegaard."
Le Monde (Paris) (12.11.1955).

3779. Gabriel, Leo. "Sören Kierkegaard. Zu seinem 100.
Todestag." *Oesterreichische Neue Tageszeitung* (Wien)
(10.11.1955).

3780. Gabriel, Leo. "Der religiöse Skandal. Sören Kier-
kegaard-Gedanken zum 100. Todestag des 'prognostischen
Genies' Europas." *Salzburger Nachrichten* (11.11.1955).

3781. "Gloomy Dane: The Sesquicentennial of Kierkegaard's
Birth." *Tablet* 217 (1963):482.

3782. Gross, G. "Sören Kierkegaard. Zu dessen 100.
Geburtstag am 5. Mai." *Monatschrift für Pastoraltheologie*
(Berlin) 9 (1912-13):293-307.

3783. Guerra, Luis B. "A cien años de la desaparición de
S. Kierkegaard." *Noticias Graficas* (La Plata) (10.11.1955).

3784. Henein, Georges. "Vues sur Kierkegaard, 1813-1855."
L'Égypte Nouvelle 3. Série, no. 576 (28.10.1955).

3785. Höffding, Harald. "Sören Kierkegaard. 5. Mai
1813-5. May 1913." (Discours prononcé le 5. mai 1913 à
l'Université de Copenhague.) *Revue de Métaphysique et de
Morale* (Paris) 21 (1913):713-732. Ogs. s. Saertr.: Paris:
Libr. A. Colin, 1913. 14p.

3786. Hohlenberg, Johannes. "Sören Kierkegaard. Tale
holdt ved Chicagos universitet i anledning af hundrears-
dagen for Kierkegaards död." *Manedsrevyen Horisont*
2 (1956):8-15.

3787. Hohoff, K. "Zum 125. Geburtstag Kierkegaards."
Propyläen 35 (1938).

3788. Hohoff, C. "Zum 100. Geburtstag [Todestag] Soren
Kierkegaards. Der Sprung zu Gott." *Christ und Welt*
(Stuttgart) 8 (1955):6.

3789. Humanus [Pseud.]. "Bij het centenarium van Kierkegaards' dood." *Kultuurleven* (Antwerpen) 22 (1955):
667-676.

3790. Junghans, H. M. "Sören Kierkegaard. 1813-1855."
Deutsche Sängerschaft. Zeitschrift d. deutschen Sängerschaft. Rothenburg ob der Tauber (1955):304-306.

3791. Kerr, Hugh T. "A Kierkegaardian centenary."
Theology Today 12 (1955):291-294.

3792. Koch, F. W. "Leben unter einer Wolke der Schwermut.
Sören Kierkegaard (gestorben am 11. November 1855) ahnte
unser Zeitalter des Unbehagens und der Angst." *Morgen*
(Berlin) (9.11.1955).

3793. Lehmann, Eduard. "Einleitung. Sören Kierkegaard
5. Maj 1813-11. Nov. 1855." In *Sören Kierkegaard*. Berlin,
1913, 7-24 (Klassiker der Religion, 8. & 9. Bd.).

3794. Lehmann, Eduard. "Sören Kierkegaard. 5. Mai 1813-
5. Mai 1913." *Onze Eeuw* (Haarlem) 13 (1913):54-66.

3795. Madsen, Victor. "Kopenhagener Brief: Der hundert-
jahrige Geburtstag Sören Kierkegaards." *Zeitschrift für
Bücherfreunde* (Leipzig) N.F. 5 (1913):148-149.

3796. Marcel, Gabriel. "Points d'interrogation."
La Table Ronde (Paris) (1955):76-78.

3797. Mesnard, Pierre. "Kierkegaard. No. 150 aniversario
do seu nascimento 1813-1963." Trad. condensada de A.
Martins. *Revue Portuguesa de Filosofia* 19 (1963):403-405.

3798. Meuer, Adolf. "Zum 75. Todestag Sören Kierkegaards."
Germania (Berlin) (12.11.1930).

3799. Michel, W. "Zu Kierkegaards 75. Todestag am 11."
Der Tag (Berlin) (11.11.1930).

3800. Miller, Samuel H. "Kierkegaard: Then and now."
Andover Newton Bulletin 47 (1955):5-11 (Kierkegaard centennial issue).

3801. Minear, Paul S. "Kierkegaard centennial."
Theology Today 12 (1955):244-246.

3802. Montier, Jacques. "L'existentialisme aura cent ans
le 11 novembre. Son inspirateur fut le philosophie danois
S[o]ren Kierkegaard dont on va commémorer la disparition
prématurée." *Le Progrès Égyptien* (3.11.1955).

3803. Olinto, Antonio. "A influencia de Kierkegaard."
O Globo (Rio de Janeiro) (12.12.1949).

3804. Polh, Franz Heinrich. "Der christliche Sokrates.
Zu Sören Kierkegaards 100. Todestag am 11. November 1955."
Die Neue Schau (Kassel) 16 (1955):298-299.

3805. Prévost, Alain. "Le centenaire de la mort de Soeren Kierkegaard, philosophe existentialiste." *Le Matin* (Antwerpen) (11.11.1955).

3806. Rau, P. "Sören Kierkegaard. Ein protestantischer 'Heiliger' des Nordens. Zu seinem 100. Geburtstage." *Die Reichsbote* (Berlin) (6.5.1913).

3807. Reuter, Hans. "Zum Gedächtnis Kierkegaards. I-II." *Protestantenblatt* (Berlin-Bremen) 46 (1913):611-614; 670-673.

3808. Savin, Maurice. "En lisant Kierkegaard 1951-1955." *La Table Ronde* (Paris) (1955):33-42.

3809. Sawatzki, Günther. "Der junge Kierkegaard. Zur 125. Wiederkehr seines Geburtstages (5. Mai 1813)." *Deutsche Rundschau* 64 (1938):116-121.

3810. Sawatzki, Günther. "Promenade in Kopenhagen." *Sonntagsblatt*, hrsg. von Hanns Lilje. Hamburg, (1955): 9-10.

3811. *Sören Kierkegaard 1855-1955. Zum Kierkegaard-Gedenkjahr vorgelegt.* Düsseldorf-Köln: Diederichs, 1955. 30p.

3812. Stübe, Rudolf. "Sören Kierkegaard. Ein Gedenkwort zu seinem 199. Geburtstag." *Deutsch-Evangelisch* (Leipzig) 4 (1913):264-268.

3813. Theunissen, Gert H. "Sören Kierkegaard--und wir heute." *Sören Kierkegaard 1855-1955. Zum Kierkegaard-Gedenkjahr vorgelegt.* Düsseldorf-Köln: Diederichs, 1955, 3-11.

3814. Weidmann, H. "Kierkegaard heute! Zu seinem hundertsten Todestag." *Kirchenblatt für die Reformierte Schweiz* (Basel) 111 (1955):338-340.

3815. Wien, Alfred. "Sören Kierkegaard. Zur 100. Wiederkehr von Kierkegaards Geburtstag am 5. Mai 1913. Ein Lebensbild." *Westermanns Ill. Deutsche Monatshefte* (Braunschweig) 57 (1913):428-434.

Appendix:
Kierkegaard Bibliographies

(See also no. 2757-2778)

3816. Abbagano, Nicola. "Kierkegaard in Italy." *Meddelelser fra Sören Kierkegaard Selskabet* 2 (1950):49-53.

3817. Alker, E. "Neue Bücher über Kierkegaard." *Literarische Handweiser* (Freiburg i Br.) 66 (1930):415-424.

3818. Anderson, James Maitland. "Sören Kierkegaard and the English-speaking world." *Hovedstaden* 4 (1913):7-8.

3819. Anonymous. "Sören Kierkegaard in Deutschland." *Theologisches Literaturblatt* 3 (1882):177-178.

3820. Anonymous. "Indications bibliographiques [pour la France]." *Foi et Vie* (Paris) (1934):718-720.

3821. Anonymous. "Kierkegaard in France." *Times Literary Supplement* 34 (1935):324.

3822. Anonymous. "Sören Kierkegaard in Frankreich." *Kölnische Zeitung* (29.10.1936).

3823. Bacca, Juan David García. "Kierkegaard y la filosofía contemporánea española." *Quadernos Americanos* 151 (1967):94-105.

3824. Bach, Giovanni. "Note sulla Cultura scandinava." *Archivio di Sotria della Filosofia* (Roma) 1 (1932):61-72.

3825. Baumann, Peter Christian. "Das Genie auf der Schulbank. Kann Kierkegaard ins Deutsche übersetzt werden?" *Die Zeit* (Hamburg) 4 (1949):4.

3826. Bellezza, Vito A. "Traduzioni di Kierkegaard."
Italia che Scrive (Roma) 32 (1949):1-2.

3827. Benz, Ernst. "Neueste Kierkegaard-Studien in den
romanischen und ibero-amerikanischen Landern." *Zeitschrift
fur Religions- und Geistesgeschichte* 9 (1957):65-66.

3828. Boer, R. C. "Kierkegaard in Noorwegen." *Onze Eeuw*
(Haarlem) 24 (1924):152-169.

3829. Brachfeld, Oliver. "Kierkegaard en Allemagne."
Revue d' Allemagne 6 (1932):596-603.

3830. Brock, Erich. "Neue Tagebucher Kierkegaards."
Neue Zuricher Zeitung no. 650 (1931).

3831. Colette, Jacques. "Chronique kierkegaardienne."
Revue Nouvelle 37 (1963):181-188.

3832. Colette, Jacques. "Bulletin d'histoire de la philosophie: Kierkegaard." *Revue des Sciences Philosophiques et
Theologiques* 54 (1970):654-680.

3833. Colette, Jacques. "Etudes kierkegaardiennes
recentes." *Revue Philosophique de Louvain* 70 (1972):
116-130.

3834. Cortese, Alessandro. "Una nuova bibliografia
Kierkegaardiana [Complète la *Sören Kierkegaard International
Bibliografi* par une *Integrazione alle Edizioni Italiane
e Agli Scritti in Lingua Italiana* et un *Supplemento* pour
1956 - août 1962]. *Rivisti Filosofia Neo-Scolastica*
55 (1963):98-108.

3835. Cortese, Alessandro. "Récentes traductions ital-
iennes de Soren Kierkegaard." In *Kierkegaardiana*. Niels
Thulstrup, ed. Copenhagen: Munksgaard, 5 (1964):107-130.

3836. Crites, S. D. "The author and the authorship.
Recent Kierkegaard literature." *Journal of the American
Academy of Religion* 38 (1970):37-54.

3837. Dayton, D. W. "Reconsidering Kierkegaard [review
article]." *Christianity Today* 16 (1972):32-33.

3838. Delfgaauw, Bernard. "De Kierkegaard-studie in
Scandinavië." [Literatuuroverzicht]. *Tijdschrift voor
Philosophie* 17 (1955):523-530.

3839. Delfgaauw, Bernard. "De Kierkegaard-studie in
Scandinavië, II." [Literatuuroverzicht]. *Tijdschrift voor
Philosophie* 18 (1955):699-710.

3840. Delfgaauw, Bernard. "De Kierkegaard-studie in
Scandinavië, III." [Literatuuroverzicht]. *Tijdschrift
voor Philosophie* 18 (1956):121-129.

3841. Delfgaauw, Bernard. "De Kierkegaard-studie in
Scandinavië." [Literatuuroverzicht]. *Tijdschrift voor
Philosophie* 21 (1959):317-343.

3842. Delfgaauw, Bernard. "De Kierkegaard-studie in
Scandinavië." *Tijdschrift voor Philosophie* 33 (1971):
737-778.

3843. Delfgaauw, Bernard. "De Kierkegaard-studie in
Scandinavië." *Tijdschrift voor Philosophie* 38 (1976):
136-158.

3844. Derycke, Gaston. "Du nouveau sur Kierkegaard."
Cassandre (Bruxelles) (9.5.1943).

3845. Diem, Hermann. "Methode der Kierkegaardforschung."
Orbis Litterarum 10 (1955):50-65.

3846. Drudis, Raimundo. "Las traducciones alemanas de
Kierkegaard." *Arbor* 33 (1956):266-268.

3847. Dupré, L. "Nieuwe duitse Kierkegaardliteratuur."
Bijdragen 18 (1957):290-298.

3848. Durfee, Harold A. "The second stage of Kierkegaardian scholarship in America." *International Philosophical Quarterly* 3 (1963):121-139.

3849. Fabro, Cornelio. "Kierkegaard in inglese [Biblio-
graphica]." *Euntes Docete, Roma* 1 (1948):163-166.

3850. Fabro, Cornelio. "Recenti studi danesi su Kierkegaard." *Rassegna di Filosofia* (Roma) 1 (1952):347-354.

3851. Fabro, Cornelio. "Un nuovo Kierkegaard tedesco
[Sotto la dir. di E. Hirsch, presso la Casa ed. Diederichs;
seconda trad. tedesca integrale presso l'Ed. Jacob Hegner].
Giornale Critico della Filosofia Italiana 41 (1962):120-122.

3852. Fairhurst, Stanley J. "Sören Kierkegaard [a bib-
liography]." *Modern Schoolman* 21 (1953):19-22.

3853. Fitzpatrick, Mallery, Jr. "Current Kierkegaard
Study: Whence--Whither." *Journal of Religion* 50 (1970):
79-90.

3854. Garin, Eugenio. "Kierkegaard in Italia." *Rivista
Critica della Storia Filosofia* 28 (1973):452-456.

3855. Handa, Ichiro. "Japan and Kierkegaard." *Meddelelser
fra Sören Kierkegaard Selskabet* 2 (1950):38-41.

3856. Hannay, Alastair. "A kind of philosopher: Comments
in connection with some recent books on Kierkegaard."
Inquiry 18 (1975):354-365.

3857. Hansen, Valdemar. "Quelques publications récentes
sur Kierkegaard en Amériques et en France." *Theoria*
(Göteborg) 6 (1940):83-87.

3858. Hansen, Valdemar. "Nyere dansk Kierkegaardslittera-
tur [New Danish literature on Kierkegaard]." *Nordisk
Tidskrift* (Suède) 27 (1951):152-155.

3859. Hansen-Löve, F. "Der deutsche Sören Kierkegaard."
Wort und Wahrheit (Wien) 7 (1952):624-626.

3860. Hermann, Ulrich. "Deutsche Bücher zu Kierkegaard."
Eckart (Berlin) N.F. 2 (1926):145.

3861. Holmer, Paul L. "Theological and philosophical
Kierkegaardian studies in Scandinavia, 1945-1953."
Trans. by Paul Holmer. *Theology Today* 12 (1955):297-311.
[Niels Thulstrup, author.]

3862. Kampmann, Th. "Kierkegaards Werke deutsch."
Theologie und Glaube (Paderborn) 42 (1952):358-362.

3863. Kampmann, Theoderich. "Kierkegaardiana." *München
Theologische Zeitschrift* 9 (1958):215-217.

3864. "Kierkegaard in France." *Times Literary Supplement*
34 (1935):324.

3865. Köberle, A. "Neue Kierkegaard-Deutung." *Evangelische Welt* (Bethel) 7 (1953):212-213.

3866. Kraushaar, Otto Frederick. "Kierkegaard in English."
Journal of Philosophy 39 (1942):561-583.

3867. Kraushaar, Otto Frederick. "Kierkegaard in English."
Journal of Philosophy 39 (1942):589-607.

3868. Landsberger, Fritz. "Mensch, Leben, Existenz. Eine
Buchchronik." *Die Neue Rundschau* (der freien Bühne) 39
(1928):312-319.

3869. Leemans, Victor. "Kierkegaardiana." *Kultuurleven*
(Antwerpen) 21 (1954):376-378.

3870. Lowrie, Walter. "How Kierkegaard got into English."
In Sören Kierkegaard's *Repetition*. Princeton, 1941,
175-212.

3871. Lowrie, Walter. "Translators and interpretators
of Sören Kierkegaard." *Theology Today* 12 (1955):312-327.

3872. Mackey, L. "Philosophy and poetry in Kierkegaard
[review article]." *Review of Metaphysics* 23 (1969):
316-332.

3873. Massuh, Victor. "Dos libros sobre Kierkegaard."
Notas y Estudios de Filosofía 4 (1953):255-259.

3874. Maude, Mother Mary. "A Kierkegaard bibliography."
Theology 41 (1941):297-300.

3875. McKinnon, Alastair, and Cappelörn, Niels Jörgen.
"The period of composition of Kierkegaard's published
works." In *Kierkegaardiana* 9 (1974):133-146.

3876. Mesnard, P. "Kierkegaard aux prises avec la conscience française." *Revue de Littérature Comparée* 29
(1955):453-477.

3877. Moore, W. G. "Recent studies of Kierkegaard."
Journal of Theological Studies 40 (1939):225-231.

3878. Mürr, G. "Neue Kierkegaard-Bücher." *Hamburger
Correspondent* (2.8.1913).

3879. Mustard, Helen M. "Sören Kierkegaard in German
literary periodicals, 1860-1930." *Germanic Review* (U.S.A.)
26 (1951):83-101.

3881. Ontani, Masaru. "The past and present state of
Kierkegaard studies in Japan." *Orbis Litterarum* 18
(1963):54-59.

3882. Oppel, Horst. "Die Nachwirkung Kierkegaards in
der nordischen Dichtung." *Nordische Rundschau* 9 (1936-38):
145-157.

3883. Perkins, Robert L. "Always himself: A survey of
recent Kierkegaard literature." *Southern Journal of
Philosophy* 12 (1974):539-551.

3884. Rest, Walter. "Ausländische Werke über Kierkegaard."
Catholica (Münster) 9 (1952-53):150-151.

3885. Reichmann, Ernani. "Kierkegaard in Brazil."
Kierkegaardiana 5 (1964):78-79.

3886. Richter, Liselotte. "Konstruktives und Destruktives
in der neuesten Kierkegaard-Forschung." *Theologisches
Literaturzeitung* 77 (1952):141-148.

3887. Rohatyn, Dennis A. "Kierkegaard: North American
Dissertations 1934-1973 in the fields of Philosophy,
Religion, and General Literature." *Kierkegaardiana* 9
(1974):390-393.

3888. Rougemont, Denis de. "Kierkegaard en France."
La Nouvelle Revue Française 24 (1936):971-976.

3889. Ruttenbeck, Walter. "Zur neuesten Kierkegaard-Literatur." *Zeitschrift für Kirchengeschichte* 53 (1934): 695-701.

3890. Saathoff, Albrecht. "Neue Kierkegaard-Bücher." *Monatsschrift für Pastoraltheologie* (Göttingen) 20 (1924): 42-44.

3891. Sales, Michel. "Dix ans de publications kierkegaar-diennes en langue française (1960-1971)." *Archives de Philosophie* 35 (1972):649-672.

3892. Schoeps, Hans Joachim. "Über das Frühecho Sören Kierkegaards in Deutschland." *Zeitschrift für Religions- und Geistesgeschichte* (Leiden-Heidelberg) 3 (1951):160-165. Also in *Meddelelser fra Sören Kierkegaard Selskabet* (Copenhagen) 3 (1951):93-100.

3893. Schückler, Georg. "Deutsche Kierkegaard-Ausgabe." *Begegnung* (Koblenz) 7 (1952):71-72.

3894. Sechi, Vanina. "Perspectives in contemporary Kier-kegaard research." *Meddelelser fra Sören Kierkegaard Selskabet* 4 (1953):10-12.

3895. Soe, N. H. "Neuere dänische Kierkegaard-Forschung." *Theologische Literaturzeitung* 96 (1971):2-18.

3896. Steere, Douglas V. "Kierkegaard in English." *Journal of Religion* 24 (1944):271-278.

3897. Struve, Wolfgang. "Das deutsche Kierkegaard-Studium." *Meddelelser fra Sören Kierkegaard Selskabet* (Copenhagen) 3 (1951):79-84.

3898. Stybe, Svend Erik. "Trends in Danish philosophy." *Journal of the British Society for Phenomenology* 4 (1973): 153-170.

3899. Tillich, Paul. "Kierkegaard in English." *American-Scandinavian Review* 30 (1942):254-257.

3900. Theunissen, Michael. "Das Kierkegaardbild in der neueren Forschung und Deutung (1945-1957)." *Deutsch Vierteljahrsschrift für Literaturwissenschaft und Geistes-geschichte* 32 (1958):576-612.

3901. Thomte, Reidar. "Kierkegaard im amerikanischen religiösen Denken." *Lutherische Rundschau* (Zürich) 5 (1955):147-157.

3902. Trillhaas, Wolfgang. "Neuausgabe der Werke Kierke-gaards." *Die Sammlung* (Göttingen) 6 (1951):430-431.

3904. Thulstrup, Niels, ed. *Kierkegaardiana*. Vols. I-X, 1955-1977, Copenhagen.

3905. Thulstrup, Niels. "Studiet af Kierkegaard udenfor Skandinavien. En kritisk skitse. 1945-1952. [The study of Kierkegaard outside Scandinavia. A critical sketch. 1945-1952]." *Dansk Teologisk Tidsskrift* 16 (1953):65-80.

3906. Thulstrup, Niels. "Kierkegaard-studiet i Skandinavien 1945-1952, en kritisk oversigt." *Edda* (1954):79-96; 97-122.

3907. Thulstrup, Niels. "Die historische Methode in der Kierkegaard-Froschung durch ein Beispiel beleuchtet." *Orbis Litterarum* 10 (1955):280-296. [Symposion Kierkegaardianum]

3908. Thulstrup, Niels. "Ziele und Methoden der neuesten Kierkegaard-Forschung mit besonderer Berücksichtigung der skandinavischen." *Orbis Litterarum* 10 (1955):303-318. [Symposion Kierkegaardianum]

3909. Thulstrup, Niels. "Theological and philosophical Kierkegaardian studies in Scandinavia, 1945-1953." *Theology Today* 12 (1955):297-312.

3911. Thulstrup, Niels. "America discovers a new 'classic'." *Danish Foreign Office Journal* (Special number for the United States)(1955):19-20.

3912. Ulrich, Hermann. "Deutsche Bücher zu Kierkegaard." *Eckart* (Berlin) 20 (1926):145ff.

3913. van Tieghem, Paul, ed. *Répertoire Chronologique des Littératures Modernes*. Paris, 1935.

3914. Wendland, Walter. "Kierkegaard-Literatur." *Theologischer Jahresbericht* (Leipzig) 29 (1911)(Lit. 1909): 917.

3915. Widenman, Robert. "Kierkegaard's terminology--and English." In *Kierkegaardiana* 6 (1968):113-130.

3916. Wolf, Werner. "Zur Übersetzung Kierkegaards." *Theologische Literaturzeitung* (Berlin) 78 (1953):443-446.

3917. Woodbridge, Hensley C. "Sören Kierkegaard: A bibliography of his works in English translation." *American Book Collector* 12 (1961):17-20.

3918. Woodbridge, Hensley Charles. "A bibliography of dissertations concerning Kierkegaard written in the United States, Canada, and Great Britain." *American Book Collector* 12 (1961):21-22.

3919. Yanitelli, Victor. "A bibliographical introduction to Kierkegaard." *Modern Schoolman* 26 (1949):345-363.

Addendum

Barfoed, Niels. *Don Juan: En Studie i Dansk Literatur.* Copenhagen: Gyldendal, 1978. 359p. [English summary, 345-353; incl. sections on Tirso de Molina, Molière, Mozart, Carsten Hauch, Frederik Paludan-Müller, and Sören Kierkegaard.]

Buhler, Pierre. "Individu: Quelques réflexions à propos d'une catégorie oubliée." *Revue d'Histoire et de Philosophie Religieuses* 58 (1978):193-215.

Bukdahl, Jörgen K. "Kierkegaard mellem ideologi og utopi II: Problemer og perspkitver i de senere ars Marxistisk inspirerede Kierkegaard-loesning." *Dansk Teologisk Tidsskrift* 40 (1977):31-56.

Bukdahl, Jörgen K. "Kierkegaard brugt i en marxistisk tid." *Kritik* 47 (1978):121-139.

Campbell, Charles. "Aesthetic language transformed: The 'poetry' of Sören Kierkegaard [Abstract, article available from Scholars Press, Missoula MT]." *Journal of the American Academy of Religion* 45 (1977):75.

Campredon, Alain. "Nouvelles lectures de Kierkegaard."
Revue de Théologie et de Philosophie 3 (1979):63-72.

Cantoni, Remo. *La Coscienza Inquieta: Sören Kierkegaard.*
Milan: Saggiatore, 1976. 403p.

Colette, Jacques. "Expérience, subjectivité et langage."
Revue des Sciences Philosophiques et Theologiques 60 (1976):
625-637.

Colette, Jacques. "Review of Christa Kuhnhold. *Der Begriff
des Sprunges* und der *Weg des Sprachdenkens.* Eine Einführung
in Kierkegaard. Berlin-New York: Walter de Gruyter, 1975."
Revue de Métaphysique et de Morale, 84e annee, no. 3
(1979):421-426.

Comstock, W. Richard. "Hegel, Kierkegaard, Marx on 'the
unhappy consciousness'." *International Jahr W. R.*
11 (1978):91-119.

Crowley, Sue M. "John Updike: *The Rubble of Footnotes Bound
into Kierkegaard.*" [Abstract, article available from
Scholar's Press, Missoula, MT.] *Journal of the American
Academy of Religion* 45 (1977):359.

Delfgaauw, Bernard. "Kierkegaard en Marx over democratie."
Gids 141 (1978):466-480.

Evans, C. Stephen. "Kierkegaard on subjective truth: Is
God an ethical fiction?" *International Journal for the
Philosophy of Religion* 7 (1976):288-299.

Fabro, Cornelio. "La fondazione metafisica della libertà
di scelta in S. Kierkegaard." In *Studi di Filosofia in
o. di Gustavo Bontadini*, Vol. II. Milan: Vita e Pensiero,
1975, 86-116.

Fox, Marvin. "Kierkegaard and rabbinic Judaism." In
Faith and Reason: Essays in Judaism. Robert Gordis and
Ruth B. Waxman, eds. New York: KTAV, 1973, 115-124.
[Orig. pub. *Judaism* 2 (1953):160-169.]

Gottlieb, Roger S. "A critique of Kierkegaard's doctrine
of subjectivity." *Philosophical Forum* (Boston) 9 (1978):
475-496.

Grant, M. Colin. "Power of the unrecognized 'blick':
Adam and humanity according to Sören Kierkegaard and Emil
Brunner." *Studies in Religion* 7 (1978):47-52.

Halevi, Jacob. "Kierkegaard and the Midrash." In
Faith and Reason: Essays in Judaism. Robert Gordis and
Ruth B. Waxman, eds. New York: KTAV, 1973, 125-140.
[Orig. pub. *Judaism* 4 (1955):160-169.]

Hanssens, Patrick. "Die Dialektik von der Vertiefung der
Begierde als Dynamik des Glaubens." *Neue Zeitschrift für
Systematische Theologie* 20 (1978):91-112.

Hashimoto, Jun. *Seren Kierukegoru Nenpyo*. Tokyo:
Maraisha, 1976. 53p.

Henningsen, Bernd. *Die Politik des Einzelnen: Studien zur
Genese der skandinavischen Ziviltheologie: Ludvig Holberg,
Sören Kierkegaard, N. F. S. Grundtvig*. (Studien zur
Theologie & Geistesgeschichte des neunzehnten Jahrhunderts,
26). Göttingen: Vandenhoeck & Ruprecht, 1977. 200p.

Hirsch, Emanuel. *Kierkegaard-Studien, 1-11*. Unveränd.
Neudr. d. Ausg. Gütersloh, 1930 u. 1933. Vaduz/Liechten-
stein, Topos-Verlag, 1978, xii-446p., ixp.-p. 452-961.
[Ursprüngl. als: Studien des Apologetischen Seminars in
Wernigerode, H. 29 u H. 31, H. 32 u. H. 36.]

Hohlenberg, Johannes Edouard. *Sören Kierkegaard*. Trans.
by T. H. Croxall [Copyright 1954] (Octagon Books). New York:
Farrar, Straus & Grioux, 1978. 321p.

Jensen, Povl Johs. "S. Kierkegaard og demokratiet: En
skitse." In *Kierkegaardiana* 10 (1977):70-84.

Jones, Joe R. "Some remarks on authority and revelation
in Kierkegaard." *Journal of Religion* 57 (1977):232-251.

Jörgensen, Merete. *Kierkegaard som Kritiker: En undersögelse
af forholdet Mellem det Aestetiske og det Etiske i Kierkegaards Litteraere Kritik*. Copenhagen: Gyldendal, 1978.
302p.

Klein, Alessandro. *Antirazionalismo di Kierkegaard*.
(Studi di Filosofia, 17). Milano: Mursia, 1979. 188p.

Kudo, Yasuo. *Kiruke-go-ru*. Tokyo: Shimizu, 1976. 216p.

Kvist, Jens. *Menneske--og sa? En Kritisk redegörelse for
Antropologien hos Henholdsvis Sören Kierkegaard og N. F. S.
Grundtvig*. Arhus: Teol, 1977. 89p.

Lindahl, Elder M. "My Father's world?" *Covenant Quarterly*
35 (1977):27-33.

Malantschuk, Gregor. "Die Begriffe Immanenz und Transzendenz bei Sören Kierkegaard." *Neue Zeitschrift für Systematische Theologie* 19 (1977):225-246.

Malantschuk, Gregor. *Fra Individ til den Enkelte*.
Copenhagen: C. A. Reitzel, 1978. 277p.

Manolescu, Nicolae. "Conspect filosofic." *Steaua* 29
 (1978):12.

McLane, Earl. "Kierkegaard and subjectivity." *International Journal for the Philosophy of Religion* 8 (1977):
211-232.

Oppenheim, Michael D. "Taking time seriously: An inquiry
into the methods of communication of Sören Kierkegaard and
Franz Rosenzweig." *Studies in Religion* 1 (1978):53-60.

Ostenfeld, Ib. *Sören Kierkegaard's Psychology*. Trans. and
ed. by Alastair McKinnon. Waterloo (Ontario): Wilfrid
Laurier Univ. Prews, 1979, xiv-68p.

Padilla C., Euclides. "Libertad estética de don Juan.
El seductor en Kierkegaard (1813-1855)." *Revista de
Filosofia de la Universidad de Costa Rica* 16 (1978):
193-202.

Parrill, Lloyd. "Concept of Humor in the Pseudonymous
Works of Sören Kierkegaard." [Diss. Abst.] *Drew Gateway*
46 (1975-76):116-117.

Paulsen, Anna. *Menschsein Heute. Analysen aus Reden
Sören Kierkegaards*. Hamburg: Wittig, 1973. 203p.

Philonenko, Alexis A. "Review" of Kierkegaard's *OEuvres
Complètes*. Paris: De L'Orante. *Revue de Métaphysique
et de Morale* 83 année, no. 3 (1978):422-427.

Pojman, Louis P. "Kierkegaard on justification of belief."
International Journal for the Philosophy of Religion
8 (1977):75-93.

Pojman, Louis P. *Kierkegaard as Philosopher*. Swindon
(England): The Waterleaf Press, 1978. 34p.

Robert, André de. "Ironie, Humor et Foi." *Études Théologiques et Religieuses* 53 (1978):295-308.

Roberts, Robert. "Kierkegaard on becoming an 'individual'."
Scottish Journal of Theology 31 (1978):133-152.

Roberts, Robert. "Faith and modern humanity: Two
approaches." *Christian Century* 95 (1978):329-333.

Santurri, Edmund N. "Kierkegaard's *Fear and Trembling* in
logical perspective." *Journal of Religious Ethics* 5
(1977):225-247.

Schär, Hans Rudolf. *Christliche Sokratik: Kierkegaard über
den Gebrauch der Reflecion in der Christenheit.* (Basler
& Berner Studien zur hist. & systematischen Theologie, 34).
Frankfort: Lang, 1977. 214p.

Scopetéa, Sophia. "Sören Kierkegaard i Graekenland: Nogle
spredte iagttagelser sögt optegnet." In *Kierkegaardiana*
10 (1977):262-273.

Skoldager, Emanuel. *Hvorfor blev Sören Kierkegaard ikke
Grundtvigianer?* (Sören Kierkegaard Selskabets populaere
skrifter 16). Copenhagen: C. A. Reitzel, 1977. 121p.

Slök, Johs. "Afmytologisering af Kierkegaard." *Dansk
Teologisk Tidsskrift* 40 (1977):120-127.

Spera, Salvatore. *Il Pensiero del giovane Kierkegaard.*
Indagini critiche sulla filosofia della religione e studi
sugli aspetti inediti del pensiero kierkegaardiano (Studi
filosofici e religiosi, 11). Padova: Cedam, 1977. 217p.

Steiger, Lothar. "Det er jo Meine Zuthat (SV IV 210).
Kierkegaards Erfahrung über Hegel oder etwas über des
Johannes Climacus Philosophische Bissen." *Evangelische
Theologie* 38 (1978):372-386.

Stemmler, Wolfgang. *Max Frisch, Heinrich Böll und Sören Kierkegaard.* Münich: Philos. Fakultät der Ludwig-Maximilians-Univ., 1972. 267p.

Teschner, George. "Psychology of faith and the meaning of transcendence in the philosophy of Kierkegaard." *Journal of Psychology and Theology* 5 (1977):300-311.

Utterback, Sylvia W. "Kierkegaard's inverse dialectic." *American Academy of Religion. Philosophy of Religion and Theology. Proceedings* (1976):4-16.

Viallaneix, Nelly. "Kierkegaard retrouvé." *Études Théologiques et Religieuses* 52 (1977):197-204.

Westphal, Merold. "Kierkegaard as prophetic philosopher." *Christian Scholar's Review* 7 (1977):109-118.

Zimmerman, R. L. "Kierkegaard's immanent critique of Hegel." *Philosophical Forum* (Boston) 9 (1978):459-474.

Index of Authors
and Editors

(Numbers followed by r refer to book reviews)

ABOUT THE COMPILER

FRANÇOIS H. LAPOINTE is Professor of Psychology at Alabama's Tus-
kegee Institute. He is the author of *Ludwig Wittgenstein: A Comprehensive
Bibliography* (Greenwood Press, 1980), *Jean-Paul Sarte and His Critics*, as
well as articles in *American Psychologist*, *Philosophy Today*, *Man and
World*, and many other journals.